THE WORD

"Quid igitur? Damnamus veteres? Minime; sed post priorum studia en domo Domini quod possumus laboramus."

"So what—are we condemning the ancients? Not at all; instead, following their earlier studies in the house of God, we work to the best of our ability."

—Jerome, Prologue to his Latin translation of the Pentateuch

THE WORD

A READER'S TRANSLATION OF THE NEW TESTAMENT

TRANSLATED BY
JOSH JAMES

CROSS CITY
CREATIONS

Text, cover, and illustrations copyright © 2021 by Josh James.

All rights reserved. No part of this book may be reproduced, transmitted, or stored in an information retrieval system in any form or by any means without prior written permission from the publisher.

ISBN 978-1-7357296-6-4 (Paperback with Thumb Index Edition 2021)

The Library of Congress has catalogued the hardcover edition as follows:
Library of Congress Catalog Number: 2021903001
James, Josh
    The Word: A Reader's Translation of the New Testament.
    ISBN 978-1-7357296-5-7 (Hardcover)

Cross City Creations
Walnut, Mississippi 38683
www.crosscitycreations.com

TABLE OF CONTENTS

PREFACE	1
THE GOOD MESSAGE	4
ACCORDING TO MATTHEW	*5*
ACCORDING TO MARK	*45*
ACCORDING TO LUKE	*71*
ACCORDING TO JOHN	*113*
THE APOSTLES' ACTS	146
THE APOSTLES' ACTS	*147*
PAUL'S LETTERS	188
TO THE ROMANS	*189*
TO THE CORINTHIANS (I)	*205*
TO THE CORINTHIANS (II)	*221*
TO THE GALATIANS	*231*
TO THE EPHESIANS	*237*
TO THE PHILIPPIANS	*243*
TO THE COLOSSIANS	*247*
TO THE THESSALONIANS (I)	*251*
TO THE THESSALONIANS (II)	*255*
TO TIMOTHY (I)	*257*
TO TIMOTHY (II)	*263*
TO TITUS	*267*
TO PHILEMON	*269*

THE GENERAL LETTERS   270

TO THE HEBREWS   271
FROM JAMES   283
FROM PETER (I)   287
FROM PETER (II)   293
FROM JOHN (I)   297
FROM JOHN (II)   301
FROM JOHN (III)   302
FROM JUDE   303

JOHN'S REVELATION   306

JOHN'S REVELATION   307

PREFACE

FIVE HUNDRED YEARS AGO, IT WAS A CRIME PUNISHABLE BY death to translate the Bible into the English language. William Tyndale, credited with translating the first Modern English Bible, was burned at the stake for it in 1536. Within seventy-five years of Tyndale's death, a half dozen English Bibles were being used in worship and home Bible study. None of the editions available at that time are still in circulation (the KJV used today is often the 1769 edition). But the influence of these men continues to permeate both our religious and secular worlds. They gave their lives and suffered persecution and exile for the words we hold dear even now.

A significant part of this translation project took place in 2011, the 400th anniversary of the publication of the King James Bible. With that in mind, I have been honored to continue in the work of those translators by translating it again into the language we use today. This is a process that is never completed or perfected since language continues to evolve. Jerome, the translator of the Latin Vulgate, stated in defense of his work, "So what—are we condemning the ancients? Not at all; instead, following their earlier studies in the house of God, we work to the best of our ability." The KJV translators echoed this sentiment in their "Translators to the Reader" in the first edition of the King James Bible in 1611. So it became my motto for this project. Am I saying that our plethora of translations is not enough? Not at all! I am working in God's house to the best of my ability, following their example, so that I may present this holy Message to God's people as they did. Following them has been my cherished honor.

THE GOAL OF THIS TRANSLATION

Considering those words from Jerome, the goal of this translation is to reacquaint us with the early format of these Holy Writings. This is not a translation designed for use in the pulpit or deep theological study. It is for reading. In our search to simplify the process of Bible study, we have long depended on chapters and verses for finding proof for what we believe in the Bible.

But the Bible was not intended to be a law code. The New Testament in particular was described as different from the law code of the Old Testament. This is discussed at length in the letters to the Romans, Galatians, and Hebrews. At first, it was read out loud. The shorter books, as letters, were read in the worship assembly in their entirety (as the Colossian letter demonstrates).

But the study of the Scriptures in our day is typically done on a verse-by-verse basis. While there is a need for that kind of study of verses and short passages, it has an inherent problem. We often neglect the simple reading of Scripture for these other methods of study. Furthermore, when we do read, we are constantly reminded of how much we are reading. "Matthew chapter one, verse one; verse two," etc.

Without the distractions of these verse and chapter divisions, reading longer passages of the Bible is easy and enjoyable. It is like reading a favorite novel with a bonus: it is spiritual milk for our nourishment. You will be able to notice elements of each author's style. From book to book, the vocabulary changes. The length of sentences and the use of transition words between sentences change. You will get to know each of the New Testament authors as they give their eyewitness accounts of the gospel. This is my favorite part of reading the text in its original language. I want you to get to enjoy it yourself through this translation.

GETTING THE MOST FROM THIS TRANSLATION

There are several ways that this translation is different from the ones we most often use for study. I have already discussed the removal of chapter and verse divisions. These will be the major distinction from most Bibles you have used, though it is not the only one to do this.

Additionally, I have limited the use of specialized language. This decision was not taken lightly, so please let me explain. When we use a word only in one context, it tends to lose its larger meaning. Some words, like church, parable, and baptism, have different meanings for different people. In other cases, such as Christ, a title can be misunderstood for a name.

Third, I have employed the use of gender-neutral pronouns where the context allows for it. I am aware that this has become a matter of debate among users of English translations in recent years. But readers in the first century understood the masculine pronouns in generic passages like we do gender-neutral ones. Those of us who have studied the English Bible for years have heard these passages explained. We know they apply to all people, so this is not a hurdle for us as we interpret the Bible. But those with very little Christian background may misunderstand that such verses apply only to some people. For example, when Jesus says, "Let him take up his cross and follow me," is he speaking only to men? In passages where the context indicates that the pronoun's referent is male, I have retained the masculine pronouns. This is true for the qualifications of elders and deacons, as well as the worship leaders in 1 Corinthians 14. It is also true in passages mentioning marriage or circumcision. I was careful and made this decision based on each pronoun's context to preserve the accuracy of its interpretation.

Finally, the 27th edition of Nestle-Aland's Novum Testamentum Graece was the primary Greek text used for this translation. I consulted other texts (and at times preferred them), but this one was the base text.

INTRODUCTION

Thank you for reading this translation. I hope it renews your love and appreciation for God's Word. I hope it helps you to get more from the translation you use for your deeper study and worship.

In the Name and for the glory of Jesus,

Josh James

THE
WORD

THE GOOD
MESSAGE

According to
MATTHEW

THE GENEALOGICAL RECORD OF JESUS THE MESSIAH, THE SON OF David and son of Abraham:

Abraham fathered Isaac.
Isaac fathered Jacob.
Jacob fathered Judah and his brothers.
Judah fathered Perez and Zerah by Tamar.
Perez fathered Hezron.
Hezron fathered Aram.
Aram fathered Amminadab.
Amminadab fathered Nahshon.
Nahshon fathered Salmon.
Salmon fathered Boaz by Rahab.
Boaz fathered Obed by Ruth.
Obed fathered Jesse.
Jesse fathered King David.
David fathered Solomon by Uriah's wife.

Solomon fathered Rehoboam.
Rehoboam fathered Abijah.
Abijah fathered Asa.
Asa fathered Jehoshaphat.
Jehoshaphat fathered Joram.
Joram fathered Uzziah.
Uzziah fathered Jotham.
Jotham fathered Ahaz.
Ahaz fathered Hezekiah.
Hezekiah fathered Manasseh.
Manasseh fathered Amon.
Amon fathered Josiah.
Josiah fathered Jeconiah and his brothers around the time of the Babyonian exile.

After the Babylonian exile, Jeconiah fathered Shealtiel.
Shealtiel fathered Zerubbabel.
Zerubbabel fathered Abihud.
Abihud fathered Eliakim.
Eliakim fathered Azor.
Azor fathered Zadok.
Zadok fathered Achim.
Achim fathered Eliud.
Eliud fathered Eleazar.
Eleazar fathered Matthan.
Matthan fathered Jacob.
Jacob fathered Joseph (Mary's husband).
To her was born Jesus (who is called Messiah).

So the total number of generations from Abraham to David was fourteen generations. There were fourteen generations from David to the Babylonian exile. There were fourteen generations from the Babylonian exile to the Messiah.

Now this is how the birth of Jesus the Messiah happened. When Mary was engaged to Joseph (before they had slept together), it was discovered that she was pregnant by the Holy Spirit. Now her husband Joseph was a fair man and did not want to make a public example of her. He wanted to divorce her secretly. Get this—while he was thinking about that, an angel from the Master appeared to him in a dream. He said, "Joseph, son of David: do not be afraid to take Mary to be your wife. You see, the child in her has been conceived by the Holy Spirit. She will give birth to a son, and you must name him Jesus because he will save his people from their sins. This all has happened so that the message proclaimed by the Master through the prophet might be fulfilled:

> 'Look! The virgin will become pregnant and give birth to a son,
> and they will name him Immanuel.'"

(The translation of Immanuel is "God with us.")

So when Joseph woke up from his dream, he did as the angel from the Master commanded him: he took her to be his wife but did not have sex with her until she had given birth to a son. Then he named him "Jesus."

Now Jesus was born in Bethlehem, Judea, during the reign of King Herod the Great. Look: astrologers from the East came to Jerusalem and said, "Where is the newborn king of the Jews? You see, we have seen his star in the East and have come to worship him."

However, when King Herod heard this, he became upset (and all of Jerusalem was upset too!). Then he gathered all the chief priests and scribes from among the people. He inquired of them where the Messiah was to be born.

They said to him, "He is to be born in Bethlehem, Judea, because this is what was spoken by the prophet:

> 'And you, Bethlehem, in the land of Judah:
> In no way are you the least significant among the rulers of Judah.

You see, a ruler will come from you,
Who will shepherd Israel my nation.'"

Then Herod secretly called the astrologers and asked them specifically how long ago the star had appeared. He sent them to Bethlehem and said, "Go; search carefully for the child and report back to me when you find him so that I may also go and worship him."

So when they had listened to the king, they went. Get this—the star that they had seen in the East went in front of them until it came to a stop over the place where the child was. When they saw the star do that, they celebrated very joyfully. Then they went into the house and saw the child with Mary his mother. They bowed down and worshiped him, and then opened their storage boxes and brought gifts to him: gold, incense, and ointment. Then, since they were warned in a dream not to return to Herod, they left for their country by another road.

Get this—after they left, an angel from the Master appeared to Joseph in a dream and said, "Get up! Take the child and his mother and flee to Egypt. Stay there until I tell you otherwise. You see, Herod is about to search for this child and kill him." So he got up, took the child and his mother during the night, and left for Egypt. He was there until the death of Herod so that the message that was spoken by the Master through the prophet might be fulfilled:

"I have called my son out of Egypt."

When Herod saw that he had been tricked by the astrologers, he became extremely angry and had all the children in Bethlehem and its area killed—all those who were two years old and under, based on the amount of time that he had discovered from the astrologers. Then the statement made by Jeremiah the prophet was fulfilled:

"A noise was heard in Ramah—
Weeping and a lot of mourning.
Rachel is weeping for her children,
And she does not want to be comforted,
Because they are no more."

So after Herod died, the angel from the Master appeared in a dream to Joseph in Egypt and said, "Get up! Take the child and his mother, and go to the land of Israel. You see, those who have been searching to take the child's life have died."

Then he got up, took the child and his mother, and went back to the land of Israel. But once he heard that Archelaus reigned over Judea in place of his father Herod, he was afraid to go back there. After being warned in a dream, he left for the region of Galilee. When he got there, he settled in a city called Nazareth. So the statement made by the prophets was fulfilled:

"He will be called a Nazarene."

IN THOSE DAYS, JOHN THE IMMERSER MADE HIS APPEARANCE, preaching in the Judean desert, "Repent because the kingdom of heaven has arrived!"
You see, this is what was spoken by Isaiah the prophet:

"The voice of someone crying in the desert:

'Prepare the Master's road!
Make his pathways even!'"

As for John, his clothing was made from camel's hair, and he wore a leather belt around his waist. His diet consisted of locusts and wild honey. At that time, the inhabitants of Jerusalem went out to him (as well as the inhabitants of Judea and all the area around the Jordan River). They were being immersed by him in the Jordan River and confessing their sins.

Now when he saw many of the Pharisees and Sadducees coming to take part in his immersion, he said to them, "Spawns of snakes! Who warned you to flee from the wrath that is about to come? From now on, produce fruit consistent with repentance! Furthermore, do not even think about saying among yourselves, 'We have Father Abraham.' You see, I am telling you that God can raise up children to Abraham from these stones! The ax is already lying at the root of the trees, so every tree that does not bear good fruit will be cut down and thrown into the fire!

"Yes, I am immersing you in water, but someone stronger than I is coming after me. I am not good enough to carry his shoes! He will immerse you in the Holy Spirit and fire. His winnowing fork is in his hand, and he will thoroughly cleanse his threshing floor. He will gather his wheat into the barn, but he will burn the chaff with unquenchable fire!"

Then Jesus came from Galilee to John at the Jordan River to be immersed by him. However, John tried to prevent him by saying, "I need to be immersed by you—and you are coming to me?"

But Jesus answered him, "Let it happen now because this is the right way for us to fulfill all righteousness."

Then John allowed him to be immersed. Now when Jesus had been immersed, he immediately came up out of the water. Then the heavens were opened up for him, and he saw God's Spirit descend like a dove and come upon him! Get this—a voice spoke from heaven, "This is my dear Son; I am very happy with him!"

Then Jesus was carried into the desert by the Spirit to be tempted by the devil. Then he fasted for forty days and forty nights and was hungry afterward.

Then the tempter came and said to him, "If you are God's Son, tell these stones to become bread."

But Jesus answered, "It is written: 'Man must not live by bread only, but by every word that comes from God's mouth.'"

Then the devil took him into the holy city, stood him up on the ledge of the temple, and said to him, "If you are God's Son, throw yourself down, because it is written:

He will give his angels orders for you,
And they will lift you up in their hands,
So that you do not bump your foot against a stone."

Jesus said to him, "It's also written: 'You must not put your Master God to the test.'"

The devil took him again, this time to a very high mountain. He showed him all the kingdoms of the world, along with their splendor. Then he said to him, "I will give you all these if you will bow down and worship me."

Then Jesus said to him, "Go away, Satan! It is written, 'You must worship your Master and

God, and you must perform religious rituals only to him.'"

Then the devil left him, and—get this—angels came and took care of him.

When he heard that John had been arrested, he left for Galilee. Then he moved away from Nazareth and went to settle in Capernaum, which is beside the sea near the regions of Zebulun and Naphtali. This happened to fulfill the message that was spoken by Isaiah the prophet:

> Land of Zebulun and land of Naphtali—
> The way to the sea, the Jordan Valley, Galilee belonging to the gentiles—
> The nation who lived in darkness has seen a great light,
> And light has risen on those who live in the region and shadow of death.

From then onward, Jesus began to preach and say, "Repent because the kingdom of heaven has arrived!"

As he was walking along the Sea of Galilee, he saw two brothers: Simon (who is called Peter) and his brother Andrew. They were casting their nets into the sea because they were fishermen.

He said to them, "Follow after me, and I will cause you to fish for people." They immediately left their nets and followed him.

As he went on from there, he saw two other brothers: James (the son of Zebedee) and his brother John. They were in the boat with their father Zebedee, mending their nets. He called them, and they immediately left the boat and their father and followed him.

HE TRAVELED THROUGHOUT GALILEE—TEACHING IN THEIR synagogues, preaching the good news about the kingdom, and healing every disease and disability among the people.

So his fame spread throughout Syria. They brought him everyone who was in poor health: those who were tormented with various diseases and pains, those possessed by demons, epileptics, and those who were paralyzed. Then he healed them. Large crowds followed him from Galilee, Decapolis, Jerusalem, Judea, and the Jordan Valley. When he saw the crowds, he went up to a mountain. When he had sat down, his disciples came to him. Then he opened his mouth and began to teach them.

> Blessed are those who are poor in spirit because the kingdom of heaven belongs to them.
> Blessed are those who mourn because they will be comforted.
> Blessed are those who are considerate because they will inherit the earth.
> Blessed are those who hunger and thirst for what is right because they will be satisfied.
> Blessed are those who are merciful because they will be shown mercy.
> Blessed are those who are pure in heart because they will see God.
> Blessed are those who make peace because they will be called God's children.
> Blessed are those who are persecuted for doing what is right because the kingdom of heaven belongs to them.
> Blessed are you when they insult and persecute you—when they falsely say every

evil thing about you because of me. Celebrate and be very excited because your reward in heaven is great! You see, this is how they persecuted the prophets who came before you.

"You are the salt of the earth. But if the salt becomes tasteless, how can it become salty again? It is not good for anything except being thrown outside to be trampled by people.

"You are the light of the world. A city cannot be hidden when it is built on a hill. No one lights a lamp and then puts it under a measuring basket. No, they put it on a lampstand so that it might give light to the whole household. In the same way, your light must shine in front of people so that they might see your good actions and give glory to your Father who is in heaven.

"Do not think that I have come to destroy the Law or the Prophets. I have not come to destroy them—on the contrary, I came to fulfill them! I am truly telling you: not a single letter or pen-stroke will ever pass away from the Law until the sky and the earth pass away—until everything is fulfilled! So whoever nullifies a single one of these commands—even the least significant—and teaches others to do the same, will be called the least significant in the kingdom of heaven. On the other hand, whoever does and teaches these commands will be called great in the kingdom of heaven. You see, I am telling you: unless your righteousness surpasses the righteousness of the scribes and Pharisees, you will never enter the kingdom of heaven!

"You have heard that it was said to those who lived a long time ago: 'You must not murder. Whoever murders someone will be subject to condemnation.' But I am telling you that whoever stays angry with their brother will be subject to condemnation. Whoever calls their brother an idiot will be subject to the council. Whoever calls someone a moron will be subject to the fiery hell. So if you bring your gift to the altar and there you remember that your brother has something against you, leave your gift there before the altar. Leave and reconcile with your brother first, and then go offer your gift. Quickly make friends with your enemy while you are with him on the road so that your enemy does not deliver you to the judge. Then the judge will deliver you to the deputy, and he will throw you into prison. I am truly telling you: you will never leave there until you have paid the last penny!

"You have heard that it was said: 'You must not commit adultery.' But I am telling you that whoever looks at a woman with a strong desire for her has already committed adultery with her in his heart. Now if your right eye causes you to sin, remove it and throw it away. You see, you would be better off for one part of your body to be lost than for your whole body to be thrown into hell! If your right hand causes you to sin, cut it off and throw it away. You see, you would be better off for one part of your body to be lost than for your whole body to go to hell!

"It was said: 'Whoever divorces his wife must give her a notice of divorce.' But I am telling you that whoever divorces his wife—unless the reason is sexual infidelity—causes her to commit adultery. Furthermore, whoever marries the woman who has been divorced commits adultery.

"You have also heard that it was said to those who lived a long time ago: 'You must not swear false oaths; you must fulfill your oaths to the Master.' But I am telling you not to swear an oath at all. Do not swear an oath by heaven (because that is God's throne), by earth (because it is his footrest), or by Jerusalem (because it is the city of the Great King). Do not even swear an oath by your head because you are not able to make a single hair white or black. The yes you say must mean 'yes,' and no must mean 'no.' Anything beyond this is from the evil one!

"You have heard that it was said, 'An eye for an eye, and a tooth for a tooth.' But I am telling you not to set yourself against an evil person. On the contrary, if someone slaps you on your right cheek, turn the other to them too. If someone wants to sue you for your shirt, give them your robe too. If someone forces you to go one mile, go two with them. Give to the person who asks something from you, and do not turn away a person who wants to borrow something from you.

"You have heard that it was said, 'You must love your neighbor and hate your enemy.' But I am telling you to love your enemies and pray for those who persecute you so that you might be the children of your Father who is in heaven. You see, he causes his sun to rise over the evil and the good, and he sends rain to fall over the righteous and unrighteous. You see, if you love only those who love you, what reward do you have? Do the tax collectors not do the same thing? If you greet only your brothers, what are you doing better than anyone else? Do the gentiles not do the same thing? So you must be perfect just as your heavenly Father is perfect.

"Be careful not to do your righteous acts in front of people to be seen by them. Otherwise, you do not have a reward from your Father who is in heaven. So when you give assistance, do not sound a trumpet in front of you as the hypocrites do in the synagogues and crowded streets. They do this so that they will be praised by people. I am truly telling you: they are already receiving their full reward! But when you give assistance, do not let your left hand know what your right hand is doing. That way, the assistance you give will be secret, and your Father, who sees what is done in secret, will repay you.

"Do not be like the hypocrites when you pray, because they love to pray while standing in the synagogues and on the street corners. They do this so that they will be seen by other people. I am truly telling you: they are already receiving their full reward! But when you pray, go into your personal room and close the door so that you can pray to your Father who is in secret. Then your Father, who sees what is done in secret, will repay you.

"When you pray, do not use mindless repetition as the gentiles do. You see, they think that they will be heard because of their many words. So you should not be like them because your Father knows what you need before you ask him! So this is how you should pray:

> Our Father who is in heaven:
> May your name be set apart!
> May your kingdom come!
> May your will be done on earth as it is in heaven!
> Give us the bread that we need for today.
> Forgive us of our debts
> in the way we have also forgiven those who have debts toward us.
> Do not lead us into temptation, but rescue us from the evil one.

"You see, if you forgive people of the wrongs they have done, your heavenly Father will also forgive you of your wrongs. But if you do not forgive people, your Father will not forgive you of your wrongdoing, either!

"Furthermore, do not be sad like the hypocrites when you fast. You see, they manipulate their faces so that it will be apparent to people that they are fasting. I am truly telling you: they are already receiving their full reward! But when you fast, anoint your head and wash your face so it will not be apparent to people that you are fasting. On the contrary, it will be apparent to your Father who is in heaven. Then your Father who sees what is done in secret will repay you!

"Do not store up treasure on the earth (where moths and rust destroy and where thieves break in and steal). On the contrary, store up treasure in heaven (where neither moths nor rust destroy and where thieves do not break in or steal). You see, wherever your treasure is, your heart will be there too.

"The lamp of the body is the eye. So if your eye is clear, your whole body will have light. But if your eye is evil, your whole body will be dark. So if the light that is in you is dark, how great a darkness that is!

"No one can serve two masters. You see, either they will hate one and love the other, or they will be devoted to one and treat the other with contempt. You cannot serve both God and money!

"Because of this, I am telling you: do not be worried about your life (what you will eat or drink) or your body (what you will wear). Is there not more to your life than food? Is there not more to your body than clothing? Look at the birds of the sky. You see, they do not sow, reap, or gather into barns, but your heavenly Father feeds them! Are you not worth more than they? Which one of you can add an hour to your age by worrying? Furthermore, why would you worry about clothing? Learn from the lilies of the field and how they grow! They do not labor or spin fabric. Yet I am telling you that not even Solomon with all his majesty was clothed like one of these! So if God clothes the grass of the field like this (which is alive today but is thrown into the furnace tomorrow), will he not clothe you much better? You have such small faith! So do not be worried and say, 'What will we eat? What will we drink? What will we wear?' You see, the gentiles chase after these things; but your heavenly Father knows that you need all these things. On the contrary, seek God's kingdom and his righteousness first, and all these things will be provided for you. Do not worry about tomorrow because tomorrow will worry about itself. One day's trouble is enough for one day!

"Do not criticize, so that you are not criticized. You see, you will be criticized with the very criticism that you show, and the standard by which you measure others will be measured against you. So why do you see the splinter in your brother's eye but not notice the beam in your own eye? How can you tell your brother, 'Let me get that splinter out of your eye?' Look! That beam is in your eye! You hypocrite! Get the beam out of your eye first; then you will see clearly enough to get the splinter out of your brother's eye.

"Do not give dogs what is holy, and do not toss your pearls down in front of pigs. Otherwise, they will trample them down with their feet and turn around to tear you into pieces.

"Ask and it will be given to you. Seek and you will find. Knock and the door will be opened for you. You see, whoever asks receives, whoever seeks finds, and the door will be opened for whoever knocks. What kind of person among you would give their son a stone if he asked them for bread? Who would give him a snake if he asked for a fish? So if you (who have the capacity to be evil) know to give good presents to your children, certainly your Father in heaven will give good things to those who ask him for them.

"So what you want people to do for you is precisely what you must do for them. You see, this is the Law and the Prophets.

"Enter through the narrow gate because the gate that leads to destruction is wide and its road is spacious (and there are many who are entering through it). How narrow is the gate—and how difficult is the road—that leads to life (and there are few who are finding it)!

"Beware of false prophets—those who come to you clothed like sheep, although secretly they are insatiable wolves. You will recognize them by their fruits. They do not gather grapes from thorn-bushes or figs from thistles, do they? In the same way, each good tree produces good fruit, and the rotten tree produces rotten fruit. A good tree cannot produce rotten fruit, and a rotten tree cannot produce good fruit, right? Each tree that does not produce good fruit is cut down and thrown into the fire. Thus you will recognize them by their fruit.

"Not everyone who says to me, 'Master! Master!' will enter into the kingdom of heaven. Rather, whoever does the will of my Father who is in heaven will enter the kingdom. Many people will say to me on that day, 'Master! Master! Did we not prophesy in your name, cast out demons in your name, and do many miracles in your name?' Then I will tell them plainly, 'I never knew you. Get away from me, you who practice wickedness!'

"So whoever hears these words of mine and does them will be compared to a wise man: he built his house upon the bedrock. Then the rain fell, the surging water came, and the winds blew. These beat against that house, but it did not fall because it was founded on the bedrock. Furthermore, whoever hears these words of mine and does not do them will be compared to a foolish man: he built his house upon the sand. Then the rain fell, the surging waters came, and the winds blew. These beat against that house, and it fell (and its fall was intense)."

Now once Jesus had finished saying these words, the crowds were amazed at his teaching. You see, he was teaching them as though he had authority—not like their scribes. So large crowds followed him when he came down from that mountain.

Get this—a leper came, bowed in front of him, and said, "Master, if you want to do so, you are able to cleanse me!"

Then he reached out his hand, took hold of him, and said, "I want to do this; be cleansed!" Immediately he was cleansed of his leprosy. Then Jesus said to him, "Make sure that you tell no one. No, go show yourself to the priest and offer the gift that Moses commanded as a testimony to them."

Now when he entered Capernaum, a captain came to him begging and saying, "Master, my child is lying paralyzed at my house, and he is being tortured terribly!"

Then he said to him, "When I come I will heal him."

Then the captain answered, "Master, I do not deserve for you to come under my roof. No, just say the word and my child will be healed. You see, I am a man under authority myself, and I have soldiers under me. I say to one, 'Go,' and he goes; I say to another, 'Come here,' and he comes. I tell my servant, 'Do this,' and he does it."

When Jesus heard this, he was amazed. He said to those who followed him, "I am truly telling you: I have not found such faith with anyone in Israel. So I am telling you: many will come from the east and west and sit down to eat with Abraham, Isaac, and Jacob in the kingdom of heaven. But the sons of the kingdom will be thrown out into the outer darkness. Weeping and gnashing of teeth will be there!" Then Jesus told the captain, "Go—may it happen for you because you believed!" Then his child was healed at that very hour.

When Jesus came to Peter's house, he saw that Peter's mother-in-law was lying in bed with a fever. He took hold of her hand and her fever left her, so she got up and served them a meal.

Now when it had become late, many demon-possessed people were brought to him. He cast out those spirits with a word and healed all who were in poor health so that what was said by Isaiah the prophet would be fulfilled:

"He has taken our weaknesses and carried our sicknesses."

So when Jesus saw the crowd around him, he commanded them to go to the shore. Then one scribe approached him and said to him, "Teacher, I will follow you wherever you go."

Jesus said to him, "The foxes have dens and the birds of the sky have nests, but the Son of Man has nowhere to lay his head."

Another of his disciples said to him, "Master, allow me first to go bury my father."

Jesus said to him, "Follow me; let the dead bury their own dead."

Then he got on the boat, and his disciples followed him. Get this—a violent storm came up on the sea so that the boat was being covered by the waves. But Jesus was asleep. They came to him, woke him, and said, "Save us, Master! We are about to die!"

Then he said to them, "Why are you afraid? You have such little faith!" Then he got up, chastised the winds and the sea, and the weather became very calm.

The men were amazed and said, "What kind of person is this? Even the winds and sea obey him!"

Then he arrived on the shore in the village of the Gadarenes. Two demon-possessed men came from among the tombs and met him. They were very violent—so much so that no one could travel through that road. Get this—they cried out, "What business do you have with us, Son of God? Have you come here to torture us before the appointed time?" Now a herd of many pigs was feeding a good distance away from them. The demon-possessed men begged him, "If you are going to cast us out, send us into that herd of pigs."

So he told them, "Go!"

Then they came out and went into the pigs, and get this—the whole herd rushed down the steep bank into the sea and drowned in the water! Then the herdsmen fled. They went into the city and told them everything—even about the demon-possessed men. Get this—the whole city came out to meet Jesus. When they saw him, they begged him to leave their region. So he got on a boat, crossed the sea, and came to his hometown.

Get this: they brought him a paralyzed man who had been laid on a stretcher. When Jesus saw their faith, he told the paralyzed man, "Cheer up, child, your sins are forgiven."

Get this—some of the scribes said among themselves, "He is blaspheming!"

Since Jesus knew what they were thinking he asked them, "Why are you thinking evil things in your hearts? You see, which is easier: to say, 'Your sins are forgiven,' or 'Get up and walk'? Well, just so you know that the Son of Man has the right to forgive sins," then he told the paralyzed man, "Get up, carry your stretcher, and go to your house." Then the man got up and went to his house! When the crowd saw that, they became afraid and praised God, who had given this right to people.

Then Jesus went on from there and saw a man sitting at the tax office. (His name was Matthew.) He told him, "Follow me," so the man got up and followed him.

Look at what happened while he was reclining to eat in that man's house: many tax collectors and sinners came to sit and eat with Jesus and his disciples. When the Pharisees saw that, they said to his disciples, "Why does your teacher eat with tax collectors and sinners?"

But Jesus heard them and said, "Those who are healthy do not need a doctor, but those who are sick do. You need to go learn what this means: 'I want compassion—not sacrifice.' You see, I have come to call sinners, not righteous people."

Then the disciples of John came to him and said, "Why do we and the Pharisees fast often, and yet your disciples do not fast?"

So Jesus told them, "Can the wedding guests fast while the groom is still with them? The days will come when the groom is taken from them. Then they will fast. No one sews a piece of non-shrunken cloth into an old robe. You see, its patch pulls away from the robe and a worse tear is made. Also, no one puts fresh wine into old wineskins. Otherwise, the skins will burst, the wine will pour out, and the skins will be ruined. No, they put fresh wine into new wineskins, and both are preserved."

Get this—while he was saying this, a certain ruler came and knelt before him. He said, "My daughter just now died, but if you come lay your hand on her, she will live again." So Jesus and his disciples got up and followed him.

Now get this—a woman who had had a bleeding disease for twelve years came up behind him and touched the hem of his robe. You see, she thought to herself, "If I could only touch the hem of his robe, I will be rescued from this disease."

So Jesus turned, and when he saw her he said, "Cheer up, daughter; your faith has rescued you." So the woman was rescued at that very time.

Then Jesus went into the ruler's house and saw the flute players and the grieving crowd. He said, "Go away, because the girl is not dead—she's only sleeping." Then they laughed at him; but after the crowd had been put outside, he went in and took her hand, and the girl was raised from the dead! This news spread throughout the entire land.

When Jesus went on from there, two blind men followed him and cried out, "Show us compassion, Son of David!" When he went into the house, the blind men followed him.

Jesus said to them, "Do you believe that I can do this?"

They said to him, "Yes, Master!"

Then he touched their eyes and said, "May it happen for you based on your faith." Then their eyes were opened, but Jesus warned them, "See to it that no one knows." But they went out and talked about him throughout that entire land.

While they were leaving, get this—other people brought him a man who was mute because of demon-possession. After Jesus cast out the demon, the mute man spoke. Then the crowds were amazed and said, "Nothing like this has ever happened in Israel!"

But the Pharisees said, "He casts out demons by the power of the ruler of demons!"

Then Jesus passed through all the cities and villages, teaching in their synagogues and proclaiming the Good Message of the kingdom. He healed every illness and every disease. When he saw the crowds he felt compassion for them because they were troubled and neglected, like sheep that did not have a shepherd. Then he said to his disciples, "There is a lot to harvest, but there are only a few workers. So pray to the Master of the harvest, so that he will send out workers into his harvest."

THEN HE CALLED HIS TWELVE DISCIPLES AND GAVE THEM POWER over unclean spirits so that they would be able to cast them out and heal every illness and sickness. Here are the names of the twelve apostles:

First was Simon (who was called Peter). Then there was his brother Andrew. There were James (the son of Zebedee) and his brother John. There were Philip and Bartholomew, Thomas, Matthew (that tax collector), James (the son of Alpheus), Thaddeus, Simon (the Canaanite), and Judas Iscariot (who also betrayed him).

Jesus sent out these twelve men and commanded them, "Do not go down the roads to other nations or enter the Samaritans' cities. Instead, go to the lost sheep from the house of Israel. As you go, preach this: 'The kingdom of heaven has come near!' Heal those who are sick, raise the dead, cleanse those who have leprosy, and cast out demons. You received this for free, so give it for free. Do not take gold, silver, or copper coins in your belt. Do not carry a bag for the journey or extra undershirts, sandals, or a staff. You see, workers earn their food. In whatever city or village you enter, inquire who is there who is worthy and stay there until you leave the city. When you enter the house, greet it. Then, if the house is worthy, your peace needs to stay upon it. But if it is unworthy, your peace needs to return to you. If anyone does not welcome you or listen to what you say, when you leave that house or city, shake the dust from your feet. I am truly telling you—on Judgment Day, it will be more bearable for the land of Sodom and Gomorrah than for that city.

"Look—I am sending you out like sheep among wolves, so you need to be as wise as snakes and as innocent as doves. Be careful about people. You see, they will deliver you over to the court and flog you in their synagogues. You will be brought before both rulers and kings because of me so that you will testify to them and to the nations. When they deliver you over, do not be concerned about what you will say. You see, what you are to say will be given to you at that time. You see, you will not be the ones speaking—rather, your Father's Spirit will be speaking through you. A brother will deliver his own brother over to death, and a father will deliver his son. Children will rebel against their parents and put them to death. Furthermore, you will be hated by everyone because of my name. But the one who is persistent to the end—he will be saved. So when they persecute you in one city, flee to another one. You see, I am truly telling you: you will not run out of cities in Israel to work in before the Son of Man comes.

"A disciple is not in charge of their teacher, and a slave is not in charge of their master. It is enough for the disciple to become like their teacher and for the slave to become like their master. If they have labeled the Master of the house Beelzebub, certainly they will also label his household that way!

"So do not be afraid of them. You see, nothing is hidden that will not be revealed, and there is no secret that will not be understood. Whatever I tell you in the dark, you are to say in the light.

What you hear me whisper into your ear, you are to proclaim from the housetops. Furthermore, do not be afraid of those who kill the body but are unable to kill your soul. Instead, you should fear the one who is able to destroy both the soul and body in hell. Are two sparrows not sold for a penny? Yet, not one of them falls to the ground without your Father knowing. No, even the hairs on your head—they have been counted by him. So do not be afraid—you are worth more than many sparrows. So about everyone who acknowledges me in front of people: I will also acknowledge them before my Father who is in heaven. On the other hand, about everyone who refuses to acknowledge me before people: I also will refuse to acknowledge them before my Father who is in heaven.

"Do not think that I have come to bring peace to the world. I have come to bring a sword, not peace. You see, I have come to turn

> A man against his father,
> A daughter against her mother,
> And a bride against her mother-in-law.
> So a man's enemies will be his own household.

"Whoever loves their father or mother more than me is not worthy of me, and whoever loves their son or daughter more than me is not worthy of me. Whoever does not take their cross and follow behind me is not worthy of me. Whoever finds their life will lose it, and whoever loses their life because of me will find it.

"Whoever welcomes you welcomes me. Whoever welcomes me welcomes the one who sent me. Whoever welcomes a prophet just for being a prophet will receive a prophet's reward. Whoever welcomes a righteous man just for being a righteous man will receive a righteous man's reward. Whoever gives one of the least significant of these people a cup of cold water just for being a disciple—I am truly telling you—will never lose their reward."

When Jesus finished giving these commands to the twelve disciples, he went on from there to teach and preach in their cities.

NOW WHEN JOHN HEARD IN PRISON ABOUT WHAT THE MESSIAH was doing, he sent to him (by his disciples) and asked him, "Are you the one who was coming or should we wait for someone else?"

Jesus answered them, "Go tell John what you hear and see. The blind receive their sight, the crippled people walk, those with leprosy are cleansed, the deaf people hear, the dead are raised, and the poor receive good news. Whoever is not offended by me is blessed!"

As those men were leaving, Jesus began to talk to the crowd about John. "What did you go out to see in the desert? Was it a reed shaken by the wind? No! What did you go out to see? Was it a man clothed in fine clothing? Look—those who wear fine clothing live in kings' houses. So what did you go out to see? Was it a prophet? Yes, I am telling you—more than a prophet. This is the one about whom this was written: 'Look! I am sending my messenger into your presence. He will prepare your road in front of you.'

"I am truly telling you—no one born from women has ever come up who is better than John the Immerser. But the person who is least significant in the kingdom of heaven is greater than he. From the days of John the Immerser to this day, the kingdom of heaven has suffered violence, and violent people seek to lay siege to it. You see, all the prophets (and the Law) prophesied until John came. If you are willing to accept this, he is Elijah, the one who was to come. Whoever has an ear needs to listen!

"To what will I compare this generation? It is like little children sitting in the marketplace—they call out to one another: 'We played the flute for you, but you did not dance! We sang a funeral song, and you did not mourn!' You see, John appeared and neither ate nor drank, so they say, 'He has a demon.' The Son of Man came and both ate and drank, so they say, 'Look! He is a gluttonous man and a drunk—a friend to tax collectors and sinners.' Yet, wisdom is vindicated by its actions."

Then he began to ridicule the cities in which his greatest miracles had been performed because they did not repent. "You are in trouble, Chorazin! You are in trouble, Bethsaida, because if these miracles that were performed among you had instead been performed in Tyre and Sidon, they would have repented a long time ago with sackcloth and ashes! Yet, I am telling you—it will be better for Tyre and Sidon on Judgment Day than for you! As for you, Capernaum, have you been as exalted as the heavens? You will go down to the grave! You see, if the miracles that were performed among you had been performed in Sodom, it would have remained to this day. Yet I am telling you—Judgment Day will be more bearable for the land of Sodom than for you!"

At that time Jesus responded, "I praise you, Father, Master of heaven and earth, because you have hidden these things from the wise and intelligent people but have revealed them to children. Yes, Father—I praise you because that is how blessing comes to you. Everything has been given to me by my Father. No one recognizes the Son except for the Father, and no one recognizes the Father except for the Son and anyone to whom the Son wishes to reveal him. Everyone who is tired and burdened: come to me, and I will give you rest. Take my yoke upon you. Learn from me because I am considerate and humble-hearted. You will find rest for your lives. You see, my yoke is easy, and my burden is light."

At that time, Jesus passed through the fields on the Sabbath. Now his disciples were hungry and began to pull up heads of grain and eat.

When the Pharisees saw that, they said to him, "Look! Your disciples are doing something they have no right to do on the Sabbath!"

Then he said to them, "Have you not read what David and those who were with him did when they were hungry—how that they went into God's house and ate the Bread of the Presence, which neither he nor they had any right to eat? It was only for the priests! Have you not also read in the Law that the priests in the temple on Sabbath days profane the Sabbath, and they are not guilty of anything? No, I am telling you: someone here is more significant than the temple, and if you knew what 'I want compassion, not sacrifice' meant, you would not have condemned innocent people. You see, the Son of Man is Master over the Sabbath."

When he moved on from there, he came to their synagogue. Now get this—a man was there who had a paralyzed hand.

They asked him, "Is it right to heal on the Sabbath?" (They asked this so that they would be able to accuse him of something.)

Then he said to them, "If one of you had just one sheep, and it were to fall into a ditch on a

Sabbath, who among you would not take hold of it and lift it up out of the ditch? So certainly a man is more valuable than a sheep! So it is right to do good things on a Sabbath." Then he told the man, "Reach out your hand."

So he reached out, and it became healthy like the other one. Then the Pharisees went out and took council against him so that they might kill him. But Jesus knew this and left from there.

Large crowds followed him, and he healed them all. He also warned them not to point him out publicly, so that what was said through Isaiah the prophet would be fulfilled:

> Look: my son whom I have chosen—
> My loved one who has made my soul happy!
> I will put my Spirit upon him,
> And he will proclaim justice to the nations.
> He will not argue or shout,
> And no one will hear his voice in the streets.
> He will not break a bruised reed,
> And he will not snuff out a smoldering wick,
> Until he sends out justice with victory.
> Then the nations will put their hope in his name.

Then a blind and mute demon-possessed man was brought to him, so he healed him. Then the mute man could speak and see. The whole crowd was amazed and said, "Could this really be the Son of David?"

But the Pharisees who heard them said, "He only casts out demons by the power of Beelzebul!" ("the ruler of demons.")

Since Jesus knew this, he became angry with them and told them, "Every kingdom that is divided against itself will become deserted, and every city or house divided against itself will not last. If Satan is casting out Satan, he is divided against himself, so how can his kingdom last? Furthermore, if I am casting out demons by the power of Beelzebul, by whose power do your sons cast them out? Because of this, they will be your judges! On the other hand, if I am casting out these demons by the power of God's Spirit, then God's kingdom has come upon you. Also, how can anyone enter a strong man's house and take his possessions unless they first tie up the strong man? Then they rob his house! Whoever is not with me is against me, and whoever does not gather with me scatters!

"Because of this, I am telling you: every sin and blasphemy can be forgiven for people, but blasphemy against the Spirit cannot be forgiven! Whoever says something against the Son of Man—he can be forgiven—but whoever speaks against the Holy Spirit—he will not be forgiven, neither in this age nor the one that is to come!

"Either call the tree good and its fruit good or call the tree rotten and its fruit rotten. You see, you recognize the tree by its fruit. You spawn of snakes! How can you say anything good if you are so evil? You see, the mouth speaks out of the overflow of the heart. A good man brings out good things from his good treasury, but an evil man brings out evil things from his treasury. I am telling you: on Judgment Day people will pay for their speech—for every useless word they say. You see, you will be made righteous because of your words, and you will be condemned because of your words."

Then some of the scribes and Pharisees responded to him. "Teacher, we want to see a sign from you."

Then he answered them, "An evil and faithless generation is seeking a sign, and no sign will be given to it except for the sign of Jonah the prophet. You see, just as Jonah was in the belly of the fish for three days and three nights, the Son of Man will also be in the heart of the earth for three days and three nights. Men from Nineveh will rise up in the Judgment with this generation and will condemn it because they repented in obedience to Jonah's preaching. Look! Here is someone greater than Jonah! The queen of the south will rise up in the Judgment with this generation and will condemn it, because she came from the ends of the earth to hear Solomon's wisdom, and look! Here is someone greater than Solomon!

"When an unclean spirit comes out of a man, it travels through arid places looking for rest, but he does not find it. Then it says, 'I will return to the house I came from.' When it goes back, it finds it empty, swept, and cleaned up, so it goes out and brings seven spirits with it that are more evil than it is. Then they enter the man and live there. So the resulting condition of the man is worse than it was at first. That is how this evil generation will be."

While he was speaking, get this—his mother and his brothers stood outside because they wanted to talk to him. Then someone said, "Look! Your mother and your brothers are standing outside—they want to talk to you."

Then he responded to the one who told him that, "Who is my mother, and who are my brothers?" Then he reached out his hand toward his disciples and said, "Look—my mother and my brothers! You see, whoever does the will of my Father who is in heaven—that person is my brother, my sister, and my mother."

O N THAT DAY, JESUS LEFT THE HOUSE AND SAT DOWN BESIDE THE sea. A large crowd flocked to him, so he got into a boat and sat down. Then the whole crowd remained standing on the shore, and he told them many things with allegories.

"Look! A sower went out to sow. So when he was sowing, some of the seeds fell along the side of the road, and the birds came and devoured them. Others fell upon rocky ground where the soil was not deep. Immediately they sprang up because the soil was not deep, but they were scorched when the sun rose and dried up because they were not rooted. Still others fell on thorny ground, and the thorns grew up and choked them. Even more others fell on good ground and bore fruit—some bore one hundred times as much fruit as was sown, others sixty times as much, and others thirty times as much. Whoever has ears needs to listen!"

Then his disciples came and said to him, "Why are you speaking to them with allegories?"

Then he answered them, "You have been granted the right to understand the secrets of the kingdom of heaven, but they have not been given that right. You see, more will be given to anyone who has something, and they will have more than enough! But as for the one who has nothing, even what they do have will be taken away from them. This is why I am talking to them with allegories because even though they see, they do not see. Even though they hear, they do not hear or understand. So Isaiah's prophecy has been fulfilled with them. The prophecy said:

> Even though you hear, you will hear but never understand.
> Even though you see, you will see but never see the real picture.
> You see, this nation's heart has become fat;
> They hear with impaired ears, and they have shut their eyes.
> They will never see with their eyes;
> They will never hear with their ears;
> They will never understand with their heart or turn around,
> Or else I would heal them.

"On the contrary, how blessed your eyes are because they see! How blessed your ears are because they hear! I am truly telling you that many prophets and righteous people wanted to see what you see but did not see it. They wanted to hear what you hear but did not hear it.

"So you need to listen to the allegory about the sower. Whenever someone hears the message about the kingdom and does not understand, the evil one comes and takes what was sown in their heart. This is what was sown beside the road. Now as for what was sown on rocky ground: this is the one who hears the message and immediately celebrates that they have received it, but it never takes root within them except temporarily. Then when difficulty or persecution comes because of the word, they immediately abandon it. Now as for the seed sown among thorns: this is the one who hears the word, but worldly concerns and deceptive riches choke the word, and it becomes fruitless. As for the seed sown on good ground: this is the one who hears the word and understands it—the one who bears fruit, some producing one hundred times, others sixty times, and others thirty times what was sown."

Then he put another allegory before them. "The kingdom of heaven has been compared to a man who sowed good seed in his field. But while his men slept, his enemy came, sowed weeds among the wheat, and then left. When the field sprouted and produced fruit, then the weeds became visible too. Now the house master's servants approached him and said, 'Sir, did you not sow good seed in your field? So where are the weeds coming from?'

"He said to them, 'An enemy has done this.'

"Then his servants said to him, 'So do you want us to go out and pull the weeds?'

"But he said, 'No, or else when you are pulling the weeds, you might also uproot the wheat with them. Let them grow together until the harvest; on harvest day I will tell the reapers, "First pull the weeds and bind them into bundles to be burned. Then gather the wheat into my barn."'"

He set another allegory in front of them. "The kingdom of heaven is like a mustard seed that a man took and sowed in his field. Even though it is the smallest of all his seeds, when it has grown it is the biggest plant of them all—it becomes a tree, so the birds of the sky come and build nests in its branches."

He spoke another allegory to them. "The kingdom of heaven is like yeast that a woman took and hid in thirty-five liters of flour until the whole batch was leavened."

Jesus said all of this to the crowds in allegories—he did not say anything to them without allegories. So what was said by the prophet was fulfilled:

> I will open my mouth with allegories.
> I will say things that have been hidden since the creation of the world.

Then he left the crowd and went into his house. His disciples came to him and said, "Explain to us that allegory of the weeds in the field."

Then he answered them, "The one who sowed the good seed is the Son of Man. The field is the world. As for the seeds: they are the sons of the kingdom, and the weeds are the sons of the evil one. The enemy who sowed them is the devil. The harvest is at the end of time, and the harvesters are angels. Just as the weeds are pulled and burned in the fire, that is how the end of time will be. The Son of Man will send his angels, and they will pull out of his kingdom all who offend and break the law. Then they will throw them into the blazing oven. That is where there will be weeping and clenched teeth. Then those who are righteous will shine like the sun in their Father's kingdom. Whoever has ears needs to listen!

"The kingdom of heaven is like treasure buried in a field. When a man found it, he covered it back up. Because of his excitement, he went and sold everything he had and bought that field.

"Also the kingdom of heaven is like a merchant who was seeking fine pearls. When he found a very expensive pearl, he went out, sold everything he had, and bought it.

"Also the kingdom of heaven is like a net thrown into the sea. It gathers in from every nation. When it is full, they hoist it up onto the shore, sit down, and separate it—the good ones are put into containers, and the bad ones are thrown out. This is what the end of time will be like: The angels will come and pick out the evil people from among the good, and they will throw them into the blazing oven. That is where there will be weeping and clenched teeth.

"Do you understand all these allegories?"

They said to him, "Yes."

Then he told them, "Because of this, every scribe who learns about the kingdom will be like the ruler of an estate—he brings new and old things out of his treasury."

So when Jesus finished saying these allegories, he went away from there. When he arrived in his hometown, he taught them in their synagogues to the extent that they were amazed at him and said, "Where did this wisdom and these miracles come from? Is he not the carpenter's son? Is his mother not named Mary? Are not James, Joseph, Simon, and Jude his brothers? Are not all his sisters with us? So where did all this come from?" Thus they were offended by him.

But Jesus told them, "A prophet is not without honor except in his hometown and his household." So he did not perform many miracles there because of lack of faith.

DURING THAT TIME, HEROD THE TETRARCH HEARD THE RUMORS about Jesus and said to his servants, "He is John the Immerser. He has risen from the dead—that is why these miracles are performed by him."

Now Herod had seized John, chained him up, and put him in prison because of Herodias (his brother Philip's wife). You see, John had told him, "You have no right to have her as your wife." So he wanted to kill him, but he was afraid of the crowd because they considered John to be a prophet.

At Herod's birthday celebration, the daughter of Herodias danced in the middle of the room and pleased Herod. Because of this, he promised her with an oath that he would give her whatever she asked. Since she previously had been instructed by her mother, she said, "Give me the head of John the Immerser—right here on a platter."

Then the king was sorry, but because of his oaths and his party guests, he commanded for it to be given to her. He sent word and had John beheaded in the prison. Then he brought John's head on a platter and gave it to the girl, and she gave it to her mother.

Then John's disciples came and took the body. They buried him and went to tell Jesus. When Jesus heard that, he left there by ship and went by himself to a deserted place. When the crowds heard about it, they followed him by land from the cities. Then he came out and saw a large crowd. He felt compassion for them and healed them of their sicknesses.

When it had become late, his disciples went out to him and said, "This place is uninhabited, and the day is over already. Send the crowd away so that they can go into the villages and buy food for themselves."

Then Jesus said to them, "They do not have to go away. You give them something to eat."

So they told him, "We have nothing here except five pieces of bread and two pieces of fish!"

Then he said, "Bring them here to me."

So he commanded the crowd to sit down on the grass, and he took the five pieces of bread and the two pieces of fish. He looked up toward the sky, said a blessing, broke up the bread, and gave it to his disciples. Then they gave it to the crowd. They all ate until they were full, and then they took up the extra scraps—twelve baskets full! (There were around five thousand men who ate, not counting women and children!)

Then he commanded his disciples to get on the ship and leave ahead of him for the other shore while he dismissed the crowd. After the crowd had been dismissed, he went up to the mountain alone to pray. It had already become late, and he was alone there.

Now the ship was already over a mile away from the shore, and it was being beaten with the waves because the wind was against them. Just before sunrise, he came toward them—walking on the sea!

When his disciples saw him walking on the sea, they became upset. You see, they said, "It is a ghost!" Then they cried out in fear.

Just then, Jesus spoke to them, "Cheer up! It is I! Do not be afraid."

Then Peter responded, "Master: if it is you, tell me to come to you upon the water."

Then he said, "Come!"

So Peter got down from the ship, walked on the sea, and went to Jesus! But when he saw the strong winds, he became afraid and began to sink, so he cried out, "Master! Save me!"

So Jesus immediately reached out his hand, took hold of him, and said to him, "You have such small faith—why did you doubt?"

Then when they got back up into the ship, the wind ceased. So those who were in the ship worshiped him and said, "You really are the Son of God!"

WHEN THEY WENT ASHORE, THEY CAME TO THE LAND CALLED Gennesaret. The men of that place recognized him and sent word to the whole surrounding region. Then they brought him all the people who had health problems, and they begged him only that they could touch the hem of his robe. So all who touched it were rescued from their health problems.

Then some Pharisees and scribes came to Jesus from Jerusalem and said, "Why do your disciples disregard the elders' tradition? You see, they are not washing their hands in a ritual when they eat bread."

So Jesus answered them, "Well, why do you sidestep God's command and favor your tradition? You see, God said, 'Honor your father and mother,' and, 'Whoever badmouths their father or mother must be put to death.' But you say that whoever tells their father or mother, 'What you were supposed to receive from me is instead a gift to God,' is not dishonoring their father at all. So you have made God's statement useless because of your tradition. You hypocrites! Isaiah spoke correctly about you:

> This nation honors me with their lips,
> But their heart is far away from me.
> They worship me pointlessly
> Because they teach the commands of people
> As if they were my teachings."

Then he summoned the crowd and spoke to them. "Listen and understand! What enters the mouth does not defile a person. No, it is what comes out of a person's mouth—that defiles them!"

Then his disciples came to him and said, "Do you realize that the Pharisees were offended when they heard what you said?"

So Jesus answered, "Every plant that my heavenly Father has not planted will be uprooted. Leave them alone! They are blind guides for blind people, and if blind people are guiding blind people, both of them will fall into a ditch."

Then Peter answered him, "Explain that allegory to us!"

Then he said, "Do you still not understand? Are you not aware that everything that enters the mouth goes into the belly and is passed out of the body into the toilet? But what comes out of the mouth comes from the heart—that is what defiles a person. You see, these all come from the heart: arguments, evil, murder, adultery, prohibited sexual practices, stealing, false promises, and gossip. These things are what defile a person. On the contrary, eating with unwashed hands does not defile a person."

Then Jesus left that place and traveled to the regions of Tyre and Sidon. Get this—a Canaanite woman from that area came and cried out, "Show compassion to me, Son of David! My daughter is terribly possessed by a demon!" But he would not answer her with a single word.

Then his disciples came to him and asked him, "Send her away because she is following us and crying out!"

Then Jesus answered her, "I have been sent only to the lost sheep of the house of Israel."

Then she approached him, bowed down before him, and said, "Master! Help me!"

Jesus answered, "It is not right to take bread from the children and give it to the dogs."

Then she said, "Yes, Master, but you see, even the dogs eat the crumbs that fall from their master's table!"

Then Jesus answered her, "Ma'am, you have a lot of faith! May your request be as you wish." So her daughter was healed at that very time.

When Jesus left there, he went to the Sea of Galilee. He walked up to the top of a mountain and sat there. Then a large crowd came to him, bringing with them crippled, blind, deformed, and mute people (and many other people). They set these people down at his feet, and he healed them. So the people in the crowd were amazed when they saw the mute people speaking, the deformed people healthy, the crippled people walking, and the blind people seeing, so they praised the God of Israel.

Then Jesus summoned his disciples and said, "I feel sorry for the crowd because they have stayed with me for three days already and do not have anything to eat. Plus, I do not want to dismiss them without food or else they might pass out on their way back."

Then his disciples said to him, "Where will we find enough bread in this wilderness to satisfy this large of a crowd?"

So Jesus said to them, "How much bread do you have?"

They said, "We have seven pieces and a few fish."

Then he instructed the crowd to sit down on the ground. He took the seven pieces of bread and the fish, gave thanks for them, and broke it up into pieces. He distributed it to his disciples, and they distributed it to the crowd. They all ate and were full. Then they took up the leftover scraps—seven baskets full! Now the number of those who ate was four thousand men (not counting women and children)! Then he dismissed the crowds, went up onto a ship, and went to the district of Magadan.

THEN THE PHARISEES AND SADDUCEES CAME AND TESTED HIM by asking him to show them a sign from heaven. But he said to them, "When it is late you say, 'It is good weather because the sky is bright red.' When it is early you say, 'There will be a storm today because the sky is darkening to a red.' You know how to interpret the appearance of the sky—can you not interpret the signs of the times? An evil and adulterous generation is looking for a sign, but no sign will be given to it except the sign of Jonah." Then he left them and went away.

As his disciples were coming to the shore, they had forgotten to bring bread. Then Jesus said to them, "Watch out. Beware of the yeast from the Pharisees and Sadducees."

Then they began discussing among themselves, "We did not bring any bread."

But since Jesus knew this he said, "Why are you discussing among yourselves that you do not have any bread? You have such little faith! Do you not yet realize? Do you not remember, either, the five pieces of bread for the five thousand people and how many baskets of scraps you picked up? Do you not also remember the seven pieces of bread for the four thousand people and how many baskets of scraps you picked up? How do you not realize that I am not talking to you about actual bread? Beware of the yeast of the Pharisees and Sadducees!" Then they understood that he was not telling them to beware of the yeast that is in bread, but that they were to beware of the teaching of the Pharisees and Sadducees.

Then Jesus went to the area of Caesarea Philippi. He asked his disciples, "Who do people say the Son of Man is?"

They said, "Some say John the Immerser, and some say Elijah, while others say Jeremiah or one of the other prophets."

He said to them, "What about you? Who do you say I am?"

Then Simon Peter answered, "You are the Messiah, the Son of the Living God."

Jesus answered him, "You are blessed, Simon the son of Jonah! You see, flesh and blood have not revealed this to you. On the contrary, my Father who is in heaven has revealed it. I am telling you that you are Peter, but I will build my congregation on that bedrock, and the gates of the grave will not withstand it. I will give you the keys to the kingdom. Whatever you bind on earth will have been bound in heaven, and whatever you allow on earth will have been allowed in heaven." Then he commanded his disciples to tell no one that he was the Messiah.

From then on, Jesus began to show his disciples that he would need to go to Jerusalem and suffer a lot because of the elders, chief priests, and scribes. He also began to show them that he would be killed, and that he would be raised up on the third day.

Then Peter took him aside and began to reprimand him. "God forbid it, Master! This will never happen to you!"

Then he turned around and said to Peter, "Get out of my way, Satan! You are a trap for me because you are thinking about man's ways and not God's ways!"

Then Jesus said to his disciples, "Anyone who wants to follow behind me must renounce themselves, pick up their cross, and follow me because whoever wants to spare their own life will lose it. But whoever loses their life because of me will regain it. You see, what good would it be for someone to win the whole world, only to lose their life? Or what would someone trade to spare their life? You see, the Son of Man is going to come in his Father's glory with his angels, and then he will repay each person as their actions deserve. I am truly telling you: there are some people standing here who will not experience death before they see the Son of Man coming in his kingdom."

THEN AFTER SIX DAYS, JESUS TOOK PETER, JAMES, AND HIS brother, John, and led them up a high mountain by themselves. Then he was transformed in front of them: his face shone like the sun, and his clothes became as white as its light! Then get this—Moses and Elijah appeared with them and carried on a conversation with Jesus!

Then Peter said to Jesus, "Master, it is a good thing that we are here! If you want, I will set up three tents here—one for you, one for Moses, and one for Elijah!"

While he was still talking, get this—a bright cloud overshadowed them, and a voice spoke from the cloud. "This is my dear Son. I have chosen him—listen to him!"

When his disciples heard this, they fell on their faces and became terribly afraid. Then Jesus came, touched them, and said, "Get up; do not be afraid." They raised their eyes and saw no one except for Jesus himself.

Then, as they went down from the mountain, Jesus commanded them, "Tell no one what you saw until the Son of Man has been raised from the dead."

His disciples asked him, "So why do the scribes say that Elijah must come first?"

He replied to them, "Elijah does come first, and he will set everything right, but I am telling you: Elijah has already come, and they did not recognize him. No, they did whatever they wanted with him. In the same way, the Son of Man is going to suffer a lot because of them." Then the disciples put it together that he was talking to them about John the Immerser.

Then, as they approached a crowd of people, a man came to him, fell on his knees, and said,

"Master, show compassion to my son because he experiences seizures and suffers terribly. You see, numerous times he has fallen into fire or into water. So I brought him to your disciples, but they were not able to heal him."

Then Jesus answered, "What a faithless and twisted generation this is! How long will I be with you? How long must I put up with you? Bring him here to me." Then Jesus reprimanded the demon, and it came out of the child—he was healed at that very instant.

Then Jesus' disciples came to him privately and said, "Why were we unable to cast it out?"

He told them, "It is because of the smallness of your faith. You see, I am truly telling you: if you have faith the size of a mustard seed, you will be able to tell this mountain, 'Move from there to there,' and it will move. Then nothing will be impossible for you."

Now when they met up in Galilee, Jesus said to them, "The Son of Man is going to be betrayed into the hands of men; they will kill him, but he will be raised from the dead on the third day." Then they all became very sad.

WHEN THEY ARRIVED AT CAPERNAUM, THE MEN WHO collected the temple tax approached Peter and said, "Is your teacher not going to pay the temple tax?"

He said, "He is."

Then he went to the house, and before he opened his mouth, Jesus said, "Simon, what do you think about the kings of earth? From whom do they collect taxes and tolls—from their children or from other people?"

So Peter said, "From other people."

Jesus told him, "Well then—the children are exempt. But so that we do not offend them, go to the sea, cast a fishhook, and bring up the first fish that you catch. Open its mouth and you will find a coin. Then take it and give it to them to pay for both my tax and yours.

At that time, two of Jesus' disciples came to him and said, "So who will be the most important in the kingdom of heaven?"

Then he called a little child to his side and stood him between them. He said, "I am truly telling you: unless you change and become like little children, you will never enter the kingdom of heaven. So whoever humbles himself like this little child—that person is the greatest in the kingdom of heaven. Also, whoever receives such a child as this one in my name receives me.

"But as for whoever causes one of these little ones who believe in me to sin: they would be better off if a large millstone were hung around their neck and they were thrown into the open sea. The world is in trouble because of these temptations to sin! You see, it is necessary that temptations to sin should come, but the person who brings this temptation is in trouble!

"So if your hand or foot tempts you to sin, cut it off and throw it away from you. You would be better off to enter life deformed or crippled than to have two hands and feet and be thrown into the eternal fire. Also, if your eye tempts you to sin, remove it and throw it away from you. You would be better off to enter life with one eye than to have two eyes and be thrown into that fiery hell.

"Be careful that you do not mistreat one of these little ones. You see, I am telling you: their angels in heaven always see the face of my Father who is in heaven. What do you think? If a hundred sheep were to belong to one man, and just one of them were to become lost, would he not leave the other ninety-nine on the mountain and go look for the lost sheep? Furthermore, I am telling you: if he were to find it, he would rejoice over it more than he would over the ninety-nine that were never lost. In the same way, it is not your Father's will that any of these little ones should be lost.

"So if your brother sins against you, go correct him—keeping it between you and him alone. If he listens to you, you have won back your brother. Yet if he does not listen to you, take another person or two with you so that 'every fact would be confirmed on the basis of two or three witnesses.' Then if he does not listen to them, tell it to the congregation. But if he does not listen to the congregation, he must become like a gentile or tax collector to you. I am truly telling you: whatever you bind on the earth will have been bound in heaven, and whatever you allow on the earth will have been allowed in heaven. Again, I am telling you: if two of you on the earth agree about anything you pray about, it will happen for them because of my Father who is in heaven. You see, wherever two or three are gathered in my name, I am there in the middle of them."

Then Peter went and said to him, "Master, how many times can my brother sin against me and I still forgive him—seven times?"

Jesus said to him, "I would not say seven times—more like seven times seventy. Because of this, the kingdom of heaven has been compared to a man—a king who wanted to settle accounts with his servants. So he began to settle accounts, and one man was brought to him who owed him two hundred thousand years' wages. Since he had no way to pay it, the master commanded that he be sold (as well as his wife, his children, and all that he owned) so that it could be repaid.

"Then the slave bowed before him and said, 'Be patient with me, and I will repay everything.'

"Since the master of that slave felt compassion for him, he let him go and forgave him of the loan.

"Then that slave went out and found one of his fellow slaves who owed him three months' wages. He grabbed him, began to choke him, and said, 'Repay what you owe.'

"Then his fellow slave bowed down and begged him, 'Be patient with me, and I will repay you.'

"But he did not want to be patient, so he went and threw him into prison until he could pay the debt. So when his fellow slaves saw what happened, they were very hurt. They went and explained to their master everything that happened.

"Then his master summoned him and told him, 'You evil slave! I forgave you of all that debt because you begged me to do it. Should you not also have shown compassion to your fellow slave, just as I showed compassion to you?' Then his master became enraged and handed him over to the torturers until he could pay everything he owed. My heavenly Father will also do this to you unless each of you whole-heartedly forgives your brother."

When Jesus had finished saying these things, he left Galilee and went to the region of Judea, to the shore of the Jordan River. A large crowd followed him, and he healed them there.

THEN SOME PHARISEES CAME TO HIM AND TESTED HIM, "IS IT right for a man to divorce his wife for any reason?"

So he answered, "Have you not read that from the beginning the Creator 'created them male and female?' He also said, 'Because of this, a man will leave his father and mother and be united with his wife. The two of them will become one body.' So the two of them no longer exist—they are one body. So man must not separate what God has joined together."

They asked him, "So why did Moses command us to give her a document of release and divorce her?"

He said to them, "Because of your hardened hearts, Moses allowed you to divorce your wives, but it has not been that way since the beginning. No, I am telling you—whoever divorces his wife and marries another woman commits adultery, unless the divorce is because of prohibited sexual activity."

His disciples said to him, "If this is really what the relationship of a man with his wife is, it would be better not to marry!"

Then he said to them, "Not everyone accepts this statement—only those to whom that has been granted. You see, there are some men who are born abstinent—from their mother's womb. Some men are forced into abstinence by people, and others cause themselves to be abstinent because of the kingdom of heaven. May those who are able accept this!

Then some people brought children to him so that he would lay his hands on them and pray, but his disciples scolded them. So Jesus said, "Leave the children alone and do not prevent them from coming to me because the kingdom of heaven belongs to children like these." Then he laid his hands on them and departed from there.

Now get this—one man came to him and said, "Teacher! What good thing must I do so that I can have eternal life?"

Then Jesus asked him, "Why do you ask me 'what good thing'? There is only one who is good. Now if you want to enter into life, keep the commands."

He asked him, "Which ones?"

Jesus said, "Do not murder, do not commit adultery, do not steal, do not lie, honor your father and mother, and love your neighbor as you love yourself."

The young man said to him, "I have kept all these—what else am I lacking?"

Jesus said to him, "If you want to be perfect, go sell your possessions and give your money to the poor. Then you will have treasure in heaven. Come! Follow me."

But when the young man heard what he said, he went away sad because he had many possessions.

Then Jesus said to his disciples, "I am truly telling you: how difficult it is for rich people to enter the kingdom of heaven! Again, I am telling you: it is easier for a camel to pass through the eye of a needle than for a rich person to enter God's kingdom."

When his disciples heard that, they were shocked! They said, "So who can be saved?"

Jesus looked at them and told them, "This is impossible for people, but everything is possible for God."

Then Peter answered him, "Look! We have left everything and have followed you. So what will happen for us?"

Then Jesus said to them, "I am truly telling you: when the Son of Man sits on his glorious throne in the new age, those of you who have followed me will sit on twelve thrones too—

judging the twelve tribes of Israel. Furthermore, whoever has left houses, brothers, sisters, fathers, mothers, children, or fields because of my name will receive a hundred times as much, and they will inherit eternal life. So many who will be first are last, and many who will be last are first.

"You see, the kingdom of heaven is like a man—a landowner who went out while it was still early to hire workers for his vineyard. So when he agreed with the workers to pay a day's wages that day, he sent them into his vineyard. He also went out around nine in the morning and saw other men standing in the marketplace doing nothing. He said to them, 'You also should go into my field, and I will pay you whatever is right.' So they went to his vineyard.

"He went out again around noon and around 3:00 p.m. and did the same thing for them. Then he went out around 5:00 p.m. and found other men standing there. He said, 'Why have you stood here doing nothing all day?'

"They told him, 'No one has hired us.'

"He told them, 'You also should go to my vineyard.'

"Now when it had become late, the master of the vineyard said to his foreman, 'Summon the workers and pay them their wages, starting with the last ones to be hired and ending with the first ones.'

"Well, when those who were hired at around 5:00 p.m. came, each of them received a day's wages. When those who were hired first came, they thought that they would receive more, but each of them also received a day's wages. When they received it, they complained against the landowner and said, 'These last ones worked only one hour, and you have made them equal to us—the ones who have put up with the day-long work and the heat!'

"Then he answered one of them, 'Friend, I have not wronged you. Did you not agree with me for a day's wages? Do I not have the right to do what I want with what is mine? Are you jealous because I am a generous man?'

"Just like that, the last will be first, and the first will be last."

THEN JESUS WENT UP TO JERUSALEM AND TOOK ALONG ONLY HIS twelve disciples. On the way there he said to them, "Look: we are going up to Jerusalem, and the Son of Man will be betrayed to the high priests and scribes. They will condemn him to death and deliver him over to the gentiles so that they can make fun of him, flog him, and crucify him. Then he will be raised from the dead on the third day."

Then the mother of Zebedee's sons came to him with her sons. She bowed down and asked him for something.

Then he said to her, "What do you want?"

She said to him, "Say that these two sons of mine can have thrones in your kingdom—one on your right side and one on your left side."

Then Jesus answered, "You do not know what you are asking. Can you drink the cup that I am going to drink?"

They told him, "We can do it."

He said to them, "You will drink my cup, but it is not my privilege to grant anyone to sit on my right and left sides—that is for those who are set up that way by my Father."

When the other ten heard this, they became angry at the two brothers. Then Jesus summoned them and said, "You know that the rulers of the nations gain dominion over the nations, and those who are influential exercise authority over them. That is not how it will be with you. On the contrary, whoever wants to be influential among you will become your servant, and whoever wants to be the chief will be your slave. The same is true for the Son of Man—he did not come to be served, but rather to serve and give his life as a ransom for many people."

Then as they went away from Jericho, a large crowd followed him. Get this—two blind men who were sitting by the road heard that Jesus was passing by, and they cried out, "Show compassion to us, Master! Son of David!"

Then the crowd scolded them, trying to keep them quiet, but they cried out all the more, "Show compassion to us, Master! Son of David!"

Jesus stopped, summoned them, and asked, "What do you want me to do for you?"

They told him, "Master, we want our eyes to be opened!"

Since Jesus felt sorry for them, he touched their eyes, and immediately they received their sight and followed him.

WHEN HE CAME CLOSE TO JERUSALEM, HE ENTERED BETHPHAGE and went to the Mount of Olives. Then Jesus sent two disciples, telling them, "Go into the village that is in front of you. As soon as you have entered it, you will find a donkey tied to a post—and a colt with it. Untie it and bring it to me, and if someone says anything to you, say, 'The Master needs them.'" Then he sent them.

Now this happened to fulfill what was said through the prophet:

> Tell the daughter of Zion: 'Look! Your king is coming to you.
> He is modest, riding on a donkey—
> on a colt, the offspring of a pack animal.'

The disciples went and did just as Jesus had commanded them: they led the donkey and colt to him, laid their outer robes on them, and seated him on top of them. Most of the crowd spread their own robes out in the road, while others cut down tree branches and spread them out in the road. Furthermore, the crowd who went before him and behind him cried out, "Save us, Son of David! Blessed is the one who comes in the Master's name! Save us in the highest heaven!"

So as he was entering Jerusalem, the whole city was shaken up! They said, "Who is this?"

The crowd said, "He is Jesus, the prophet from Nazareth, Galilee!"

Then Jesus entered the temple and threw out all the ones who were buying and selling in the temple. He also overturned the cashiers' tables and the chairs for those who sold doves. He said to them, "It is written: 'My house will be called a house of prayer.' Yet, you have made this very house a den of robbers!"

Then the blind and crippled people came to him in the temple, so he healed them. The chief priests and scribes saw the miracles that he was performing—as well as the children who were crying out in the temple, "Save us, Son of David!" Then they were enraged and said to him, "Do you hear what they are saying?"

Jesus told them, "Yes. Have you never read this? 'You have prepared praise to come from the mouths of infants and nursing babies!'" Then he left them, went out of the city to Bethany, and spent the night there.

Now he was hungry when he was going up to the city early in the morning. He saw a single fig tree beside the road and went up to it, but he did not find anything on it except for leaves. Then he said to it, "May fruit never appear on you anymore—forever!" Then the fig tree withered immediately!

His disciples saw this and were amazed. They said, "Look at how the fig tree withered immediately!"

So Jesus answered them, "I am truly telling you—if you would have faith and not doubt, you would not just do this to the fig tree! No, you would also tell this mountain, 'Be lifted up and thrown into the sea,' and it would happen! Yes, whatever you ask in prayer you will receive when you believe."

WHILE HE WAS TEACHING IN THE TEMPLE, THE CHIEF PRIESTS and elders of the people came to him and said, "With what authority are you doing these things, and who gave you that authority?"

Then Jesus said to them, "I am going to ask you one thing, too, and if you tell me the answer, then I will tell you the authority with which I am doing these things. John's immersion: where did it come from? Was it from heaven or from people?"

Then they debated among themselves. They said, "If we say, 'from heaven,' he will say: 'So why did you not believe in him?' But if we say, 'from people,' we are afraid of the crowd. You see, they all consider John to be a prophet!" So they answered Jesus, "We do not know."

Jesus himself then spoke, "So I also will not tell you the authority with which I do these things. What do you think? A man had two children. He approached the first one and said, 'Child, go work in the vineyard today.' Yet the child said, 'I do not want to.' Later, he changed his mind and went out to the vineyard. The father approached his other child in the same way. Then the child said, 'I am going, sir.' But he did not go. Which of the two did their father's will?"

They told Jesus, "The first one."

Jesus told them, "I am truly telling you—the tax collectors and prostitutes are going in front of you into God's kingdom! You see, John came to you with the way of righteousness, and you did not believe in him. But the tax collectors and prostitutes did believe in him, and when you saw this, you did not change your minds afterward so as to believe in him.

"Listen to another allegory: a man who oversaw a household planted a vineyard, set up a fence around it, dug a wine-press in it, and built a lookout tower. He hired it out to farmers and went away on a journey. When the time came to harvest the fruit, he sent his servants to the farmers to collect his fruit. So the farmers took the servants—they beat one, killed one, and stoned another to death. Another time he sent other servants—even more than the first time—and they did the same things to them. Afterward, he sent his son to them because he said, 'They will respect my son.' But when the farmers saw his son, they said amongst themselves, 'This is the heir! Come on! Let's kill him, and we will have his inheritance!' So they took him, threw him out of the vineyard, and killed him. Because of this, what will the master of the vineyard do to those farmers when he comes?"

They told him, "Surely he will kill them torturously and hire out the vineyard to other farmers—ones who will return the fruit to him at their times of harvest!"

Jesus asked them, "Have you never read in this in the Scriptures?

> The stone that the builders rejected has become the main cornerstone;
> This has happened because of the Master, and it is wonderful in our opinion!

"Because of this, I am telling you—God's kingdom will be taken from you and will be given to the nations who produce its fruits! Furthermore, whoever falls on this stone will be smashed to pieces, and it will crush whomever it falls on!"

Now when the chief priests and Pharisees heard his allegories, they knew that he was talking about them. Even though they sought to seize him, they were afraid of the crowd because the crowd considered him to be a prophet.

Then Jesus responded again and spoke to them with allegories. "The kingdom of heaven has been compared to a man—a king who prepared a wedding feast for his son. So he sent his servants to summon those who had been invited to the feast, but they did not want to come. A second time he sent other servants and told them, 'Tell those who were invited, "Look—my meal has been prepared! My bulls and fattened cows have been slaughtered, and everything is ready. Come to the wedding feast!"' But they did not change their minds—they left (one went to his field, and another to his place of business). Some of the others seized his servants, insulted them, and killed them. Then the king was infuriated and sent his army. They killed those murderers and burned down their city. Then he said to his servants, 'The wedding feast is prepared, but those who were invited did not deserve to come. So go to the edges of town and invite whomever you find to come to the wedding feast. Then those servants went out to those roads and gathered up everyone they found—both evil and good people. Thus the wedding feast was filled with people reclining to eat. When the king came in to see those who were reclining to eat, he saw a man there who was not wearing a wedding garment. He said to him, 'Friend, how did you get in here without wearing a wedding garment?' The man had nothing to say. Then the king said to those who were serving, 'Tie him up hand-and-foot and throw him out into the darkness outside. That is where there will be weeping and clenched teeth.' You see, many are invited, but few are chosen."

Then the Pharisees went away and held a meeting on how they could entrap him with his words. So they sent their disciples to him with some of Herod's sympathizers and said, "Teacher: we know that you are genuine—that you teach God's way truthfully and are not concerned about anyone's opinions because you do not pay attention to the appearance of a man. So tell us what you think: is it right to pay taxes to Caesar or not?"

But Jesus knew their evil intent and asked them, "Why are you testing me, hypocrites? Show me the coin used to pay the tax." Then they brought him a day's-wage coin. Then he asked them, "Whose portrait and inscription are these?"

They told him, "Caesar's."

Then he told them, "Return to Caesar what is Caesar's, and return to God what is God's!" When they heard this, they were amazed, and they went away and left him.

On that day some Sadducees (who claim that there is no resurrection) approached him and asked him, "Teacher: Moses said, 'If a man dies without having children, his brother must marry the man's wife and raise descendants for his brother.' Now seven brothers lived among us. When the first one had married, he died; and since he did not have descendants, he left his wife to his brother. In the same way, the second and third—eventually all seven brothers—died. Last of all, the wife died. So in the 'resurrection,' out of the seven brothers, whose wife would she be? You see, they all had her!"

Then Jesus answered them, "You are wrong because you do not understand the Scriptures or God's power. You see, in the resurrection they do not marry and are not given in marriage. No, they are like the angels in heaven. As for the resurrection of the dead—have you not read what was told to you by God? 'I am the God of Abraham, the God of Isaac, and the God of Jacob.' He is not the God of the dead but of the living!" When the crowd heard this, they were amazed at his teaching.

When the Pharisees heard that he had silenced the Sadducees, they assembled together as a group. Then one of them—an expert in the Law of Moses—tested him by asking, "Teacher: what is the greatest command in the Law?"

Then he told him, "'You must love the Master your God with all your heart, with all your soul, and with all your understanding.' That is the greatest—and most important—command. The second-most important is like it: 'You must love your neighbor like yourself.' All the Law and Prophets depend on these two commands."

While the Pharisees were still assembled together, Jesus asked them, "What do you think about the Messiah? Whose son is he?"

They told him, "David's."

He said to them, "So how is it that David—by the Spirit—calls him 'Master'? He says:

> The Master said to my Master:
> 'Sit at my right side until I put your enemies under your feet.'

"So if David calls him 'Master,' how can he be his son?" Then no one could answer him with a single word. Furthermore, from that day on no one dared to ask him any more questions.

THEN JESUS SPOKE TO THE CROWDS AND HIS DISCIPLES, "THE scribes and Pharisees sit in Moses' judgment seat. So do and observe whatever they tell you, but do not do what they do. You see, they tell, but they do not do. They bundle up heavy and hard-to-carry burdens and put them on people's shoulders, but they themselves are unwilling to lift their finger to move them. No, they do all their actions to be seen by people. You see, they enlarge their prayer boxes and lengthen the tassels on their robes. Furthermore, they love the best seats at the dinner table, the best seats in the synagogues, greetings in the marketplaces, and being called 'Rabbi' by people. But you must not be called 'Rabbi.' You see, you have only one teacher, and you are all brothers. Also, do not call anyone your 'Father' on the earth because you have only one heavenly Father. Do not be called 'Teacher,' either, because you have only one Teacher—the Messiah. The greatest person among you will be your servant. So whoever applauds themselves will be humiliated, and whoever humbles themselves will be applauded.

"You are in trouble, scribes and Pharisees—you hypocrites! You see, you slam shut the kingdom of heaven in people's faces because you refuse to enter it yourselves, and when others try to get in, you refuse them from entering it.

"You are in trouble, scribes and Pharisees—you hypocrites! You see, you travel around both land and sea to make a single convert, and whenever they become a convert, you make them twice as much an heir of hell as yourselves!

"You are in trouble, blind guides who say, 'If anyone swears an oath by the sanctuary, it is nothing, but if anyone swears an oath by the sanctuary's gold, they are obligated to fulfill it.' You see, which is more important—the gold or the sanctuary that makes the gold holy? You also say, 'If anyone swears an oath by the altar, it is nothing, but if anyone swears an oath by the offering on the altar, they are obligated to fulfill it.' You blind people! Which is more important—the offering or the altar that makes the offering holy? So whoever has sworn an oath by the altar swears by it and by everything that is on it. Whoever swears by the sanctuary swears by it and by the one who lives in it. Furthermore, whoever swears by heaven swears by God's throne and by the One who is seated on it!

"You are in trouble, scribes and Pharisees—you hypocrites! You see, you offer ten percent of your mint, dill, and cumin, but you have abandoned the important aspects of the Law of Moses: justice, mercy, and faithfulness. You should have done these things without abandoning those! You blind guides! You filter out the gnat and then gulp down the camel!

"You are in trouble, scribes and Pharisees—you hypocrites! You see, you clean the outside of the cup and saucer, but inside they are full of greediness and self-indulgence! You blind Pharisee! First, you need to clean the inside of the cup so that the outside can be cleaned also!

"You are in trouble, scribes and Pharisees—you hypocrites! You see, you are like whitewashed tombs—outside they look beautiful, but inside they are filled with dead people's bones and absolute filthiness. In the same way, to people you appear to be righteous too, but inside you are filled with hypocrisy and rebellion.

"You are in trouble, scribes and Pharisees—you hypocrites! You see, you build up the tombs of the prophets and decorate the monuments of righteous people. You say, 'If we had lived in the days of our ancestors, we would not have taken part with them in shedding the prophets' blood.' So you testify against yourself that you are the descendants of those who killed the prophets. As for you—fulfill the reputation of your ancestors! You snakes—you vipers' nests! How will you ever escape hell's judgment? Because of this, I myself am sending you prophets, wise men, and scribes. You will kill and crucify some of them, you will flog some of them in your synagogues, and you will persecute them from one city to another. So all the righteous blood that has been shed on the earth—from the blood of Abel, the righteous man, to the blood of Zechariah, Berechiah's son whom you killed between the sanctuary and the altar! I am truly telling you—all these things will happen to this generation!

"Jerusalem! Jerusalem! The city that kills the prophets and stones the messengers sent to it! How often I have wanted to gather your children together as a hen gathers its chicks under her wing! Yet you did not want me to! Look—your house has been signed over to you empty. You see, I am telling you that you will not see me from now on—until you say, 'Blessed is the one who comes in the Master's name!'"

THEN JESUS EXITED THE TEMPLE AND LEFT, AND HIS DISCIPLES approached him to point out the temple's construction to him. Then he answered them, "Do you not see all these? I am truly telling you—not even a single stone here will be left upon another. None will escape being destroyed."

When he was sitting on the Mount of Olives, his disciples approached him privately and said, "Tell us—when will these things happen, and what will be the signal of your coming and of the conclusion of this age?"

So Jesus answered them, "See to it that no one deceives you. You see, many will come in my name and say, 'I am the Messiah,' and they will deceive many people. You are going to hear about wars, as well as rumors from wars. See to it that you do not become upset. You see, this must happen, but the end is not coming yet because one nation will rise up against another, and one kingdom against another, and there will be food shortages and earthquakes everywhere. No, all this is just the beginning of the birth pains.

"Then they will turn you in to be persecuted and kill you, and you will be hated by all nations because of my name. Then many will be caused to sin—they will turn one another in and will hate one another. Furthermore, many false prophets will rise up and deceive a lot of people. Then, because of the overflow of rebellion, many people's love will be extinguished. But those who persist to the end will be saved, and this Good Message about the kingdom will be proclaimed throughout the whole world as a testimony to all the nations. Then the end will come.

"So whenever you see the 'desecrating sacrilege' standing in the Holy Place—what was said by Daniel the prophet," (May the reader understand!) "then those who are in Judea need to flee to the mountains. Whoever is on a housetop must not come down to get anything from their house, and whoever is in the field must not turn around to get their outer garment. Those who are pregnant and nursing mothers will be in trouble in those days!

"Pray that your getaway will not take place during the winter or on a Sabbath because that will be a time of terrible misery, unlike anything that has happened from the beginning of the world to this day—even unlike any other will ever be! Now unless those days had been limited, no one would have been saved. But those days have been limited because of the chosen ones.

"At that time, if someone tells you, 'Look! Here is the Messiah!' or 'Here!' do not believe it. You see, false messiahs and false prophets will rise up and will provide great signs and miracles to deceive the chosen ones too—if that is possible. Look—I have told you in advance. So if they tell you, 'Look! He is in the desert!' do not go out. 'Look! He is in one of the inner rooms!' Do not believe it. You see, just as the lightning comes from the east and flashes all the way to the west—that is how the Son of Man's coming will be. Wherever the corpse is, that is where the vultures will assemble.

> Immediately after the misery of those days,
> The sun will be darkened, and the moon will not provide its light.
> The stars will also fall from the sky,
> and the powers of the skies will be dislocated.

"At that time, the sign of the Son of Man will appear in the sky. Then all the tribes of the earth will mourn, and they will see 'the Son of Man coming with the clouds of the sky,' with strength and a lot of glory. He will send his angels with a loud trumpet, and they will assemble his chosen ones from the four winds—from one end of the sky to the other. Learn from the allegory of the fig tree. When its branch has become tender and sprouts leaves, you know that the summer is near. Just like this, when you see these things, you also know that it is near—at the door! I am truly telling you: this generation will never pass away until all these things happen. The sky and the earth will pass away, but my words will never pass away! Now as far as that day and hour are concerned, no one knows—not even the angels of heaven or the Son—only the Father alone.

"You see, the Son of Man's coming will be just like the days of Noah—just as they lived in those days before the flood: eating, drinking, marrying, and giving in marriage. That is, until the day Noah entered the ark! They did not know until the flood came and took them all away—that is how the Son of Man's coming will be. Then two people will be in the field—one will be taken, and the other will be left. Two women will be grinding at the mill—one will be taken, and the other will be left. So watch out because you do not know what day your Master is coming. Understand this: if the head of the house knew what time of the night that the thief was coming, he would have watched and not left his house to be broken into. Because of this, you also must be ready because the Son of Man is coming at a time that you will not expect!

"So who is the faithful and sensible servant whom the master will appoint over his household—to hand out their food at the right time? Blessed is that servant whose master finds him working when he comes! I am truly telling you: he will put him in charge of all his possessions! So if the evil servant said to himself, 'My master is taking too long,' and then began to beat his fellow servants and eat and drink with the drunks, that servant's master will come on a day that he does not expect, at a time when he does not know. Then he will cut him in half and assign him to share in what the hypocrites get. That is where there will be weeping and clenched teeth!

"Then again, the kingdom of heaven will be like ten maidens who picked up their lanterns and went out to meet the groom. Now five of them were foolish and five were wise. You see, the foolish ones picked up their lamps but did not take any oil with them. The wise ones, on the other hand, took oil in some flasks along with their lamps. Since the groom was taking a long time, they all dozed off and fell asleep.

"Then, in the middle of the night, the cry came: 'Look! The groom! Come out to meet him!' Then all those maidens got up and trimmed the wicks in their lanterns.

"So the foolish ones told the wise ones: 'Give us some of your oil because our lamps are going out!'

"But the wise ones replied, 'No, because there will not be enough for us and you. Instead, go to the vendors and buy some for yourselves.'

"So while they were gone to buy it, the groom came, and those who were ready went in to the wedding feast with him. Then the door was shut. Later on, the rest of the maidens came and said, 'Master! Master! Open the door for us!'

"But he answered them, 'I am truly telling you—I do not know you.'

"So you need to be watchful; because you do not know what day or hour it will happen! You see, it will be like a man who was going on a journey. He called his personal servants and distributed his possessions to them. So he gave one hundred years' worth of wages to one, forty years' worth of wages to another, and twenty years' worth of wages to the other—he gave to each one based on his ability. Then he went on his journey. Right away, the one who had one hundred years' worth of money took it, worked with it, and earned an additional hundred years' worth of money. In the same way, the one who had forty years' worth of money earned an additional forty years' worth of money. But the one who received twenty years' worth of wages went out, dug into the ground, and buried his master's money. After a long time, those servants' master returned and settled accounts with them.

"The one who had received one hundred years' worth of wages approached him and also brought the additional hundred years' worth of money. He said, 'Master: you distributed one hundred years' worth of money to me. Look! I have earned another hundred years' worth of money.'

"His master told him, 'Well done, good and faithful servant! You have been trustworthy with a few things—I will put you in charge of many things! Enter into your master's joy.'

"Then the one who had received forty years' worth of money approached him and said, 'Master: you distributed forty years' worth of money to me. Look! I have earned an additional forty years' worth of money.'

"His master told him, 'Well done, good and faithful servant! You have been trustworthy with a few things—I will put you in charge of many things! Enter into your master's joy.'

"Then the one who had received twenty years' worth of wages approached him and said, 'Master, I knew that you were a rough man—you harvest where you have not sown, and you gather where you have not scattered seeds. So I was afraid, and I went out and hid your twenty years' worth of money in the ground. Look: you have what belongs to you.'

"Then his master answered him, 'Wicked and lazy servant! You knew that I harvest where I have not sown and gather where I have not scattered seeds. So you should have deposited my money with the bankers so that when I came, I would receive what belonged to me, plus interest! So take the twenty years' worth of money from him and give it to the one who has two hundred years' worth of money. You see, more will be given to the one who already has a lot, and as for the person who does not have much, whatever he has will be taken away from him. Then throw the worthless servant out into the darkness outside. That is where there will be weeping and clenched teeth!'

"So when the Son of Man comes with his glory—and all the angels come with him—he will sit on his glorious throne and will assemble all the nations in his presence. Then he will separate them from one another as a shepherd separates the sheep from the goats. He will set the sheep on his right side and the goats on his left side.

"Then the king will say to those on his right side, 'Come here, you who have been blessed by my Father! Inherit the kingdom that has been prepared for you since the beginning of the world. You see, I was hungry, so you gave me something to eat. I was thirsty, so you gave me something to drink. I was a guest, so you invited me in. I was naked, so you clothed me. I was sick, so you looked after me. I was in prison, so you came to visit me.'

"At that time, the righteous ones will answer him: 'Master: when did we see you hungry and feed you? When did we see you thirsty and give you something to drink? When did we see you as a guest and invite you in? When did we see you naked and clothe you? When did we see you sick or in prison and visit you?'

"Then the king will answer them: 'I am truly telling you—you have done this for me to the same extent that you have done this for the least significant of these brothers of mine.' Then he will tell those on his left side: 'Get away from me, you who have been cursed! Enter the eternal fire that has been prepared for the devil and his angels! You see, I was hungry, but you did not give me anything to eat. I was thirsty, but you did not give me anything to drink. I was a guest, but you did not invite me in. I was naked, and you did not clothe me. I was sick and in prison, and you did not look after me.'

"Then they will also reply to him: 'Master: when did we see you hungry, thirsty, as a guest, naked, sick, or in prison, and not take care of you?'

"Then he will answer them, 'I am truly telling you—you did not do this for me to the same extent that you did not do this to the least significant of these people.' Then these will go away into eternal punishment, but the righteous will go into eternal life."

So when Jesus had finished saying these words, he told his disciples, "Understand that after two days, the Passover will come, and the Son of Man will be arrested so that he may be crucified."

THEN THE CHIEF PRIESTS AND ELDERS OF THE PEOPLE CONVENED a court with the High Priest, who was named Caiaphas. They deliberated with one another so that they might seize Jesus secretly and kill him, but they said, "Not during the Passover festival or else a riot could arise among the people."

So while Jesus was staying in Bethany, in the house of Simon the leper, a woman who had a flask of expensive perfume approached him and poured it out upon his head as he was reclining to eat. When his disciples saw this, they became angry and said, "Why was this wasted? You see, this could have been sold for a lot of money and donated to the poor!"

But Jesus knew this and asked them, "Why are you giving this woman trouble? She has done a good thing for me because you will always have the poor with you, but you will not always have me. You see, since she has put this perfume on my body, she has prepared me for burial. I am truly telling you—wherever this Message is proclaimed throughout the world, what she has done will also be talked about in memory of her."

Then one of the twelve apostles, the one named Judas Iscariot, went to the chief priests and said, "What would you want to give me to hand him over to you?" So, they specified thirty pieces of silver for him, and from then on, he sought an opportunity to betray him.

On the First Day of Unleavened Bread, the disciples approached Jesus and said, "Where do you want to eat the Passover meal?"

So he said, "Go to so-and-so in the city and tell him that the Teacher says, 'My time is coming near, and I am observing the Passover with my disciples at your house.'" So his disciples did as Jesus instructed them to do and prepared the Passover meal.

When evening came, he reclined to eat with his disciples. While they were eating, he said, "I am truly telling you—one of you will betray me."

They became very upset, and each one began to ask him, "I am not the one, am I, Master?"

Then he answered, "The one who dipped his hand in the bowl with me—he will betray me.

The Son of Man will die just as it was written about him, but the one by whom the Son of Man is betrayed—he is in trouble! It would have been better for that man never to have been born."

Then Judas (the one who betrayed him) said, "I am not the one, am I, Rabbi?"

Jesus told him, "You have spoken correctly."

While they were eating, Jesus took some bread, asked a blessing for it, broke it, and gave it to his disciples. He said, "Take this and eat it. This is my body." Then he took a cup, gave thanks, and gave it to them. He said, "All of you—drink from this because it is my covenantal blood, which is shed for the forgiveness of many people's sins. Now I am telling you—I will never drink from this fruit from the vine, from now until that day when I drink it in a new way in my Father's kingdom."

Then they sang, and afterward went out to the Mount of Olives. Then Jesus said to them, "You will all be turned against me tonight. You see, it is written:

> I will strike the shepherd, and the sheep of the flock will be scattered.

"Then, after I have been raised, I will go in front of you to Galilee."

Peter answered him, "Even if everyone else is turned against you, I will never turn against you!"

Jesus told him, "I am truly telling you—on this very night, before a rooster crows, you will refuse to acknowledge me three times."

Peter said to him, "Even if I must die with you, I will never refuse to acknowledge you!" All the other disciples also said similar things.

THEN JESUS WENT WITH THEM TO THE FIELD CALLED "Gethsemane" and said to his disciples, "Sit here while I go over there and pray." So he took Peter and the two sons of Zebedee and began to grieve and be upset. Then he told them, "My soul is deeply grieved—to the point of death. Stay here and watch with me." He went a little farther and fell on his face, praying and saying, "My Father, if it is possible, may this cup pass by me! But may it not happen as I want, but as you want!"

Then he came to the disciples and found them sleeping; and he said to Peter, "So can you not watch with me for even one hour? Watch and pray that you will not enter into temptation. You see, the spirit is ready, but the body is weak."

Again—for the second time—he went farther and prayed, "My Father, if this cup cannot pass by me until I drink it, may your will be done!" Then he came back and found them sleeping again because their eyes were heavy. So he left them again and went on farther. He prayed for a third time, saying the same prayer again. Then he came to his disciples and told them, "You are still sleeping and resting! Look—the time has come, and the Son of Man is being betrayed into sinners' hands! Get up—let us go! Look! The one who is betraying me is near."

While he was still speaking, get this—Judas, one of the twelve, came. Along with him, a large crowd with swords and clubs came from the chief priests and elders of the people. The one who betrayed him gave them a signal and said, "He will be the one I kiss. Seize him." So he came right up to Jesus and said, "Hello, Rabbi!" Then he made a point to kiss him.

So Jesus asked him, "Friend, is this why you came?"

Then they came, violently laid hands on Jesus, and seized him. Now get this—one of those who were with Jesus reached out his hand, drew his sword, and attacked the servant of the high priest, cutting off his ear! Then Jesus said to him, "Return your sword to its place because everyone who draws a sword will be killed by a sword. Do you not think that I can call out to my Father, and he will provide me immediately with more than 72,000 angels? In that case, how would the Scriptures that say this must happen be fulfilled?" That very second, Jesus said to the crowd, "Have you come to arrest me with swords and clubs, as if you were going out against an insurgent? Every day I sat in the temple and taught, yet you did not seize me. But all this has happened so that the prophets' Scriptures would be fulfilled." Then all his disciples abandoned him and fled. So those who seized Jesus led him to Caiaphas, the high priest (to the place where the scribes and elders had assembled).

Now Peter followed him from a distance until he came to the high priest's courtyard. He went inside and sat down with the attendants to see what the outcome would be.

The chief priests and the whole council were looking for false testimony against Jesus so that they could put him to death. They did not find any testimony even though many false witnesses came forward, but two came forward later and said, "This man said, 'I can destroy God's sanctuary and rebuild it in three days.'"

Then the high priest stood up and said to him, "Are you not going to respond to anything these men are testifying against you?" But Jesus remained silent. Then the high priest said to him, "I put you under oath before the living God—tell us whether you are the Messiah, God's Son."

Jesus said to him, "You have spoken correctly; but I am telling you—from now on, you will see the Son of Man sitting at the right hand of Power and coming on the clouds of the sky."

Then the high priest tore his robe and said, "He has blasphemed! What do you think?"

They all responded by saying, "He deserves to die!"

Then they spit in his face and punched him, while some slapped him and said, "Prophesy to us, messiah! Who hit you?"

Now Peter was sitting outside in the courtyard, and a young girl approached him, saying, "You were with Jesus the Galilean, too!"

But he refused to acknowledge it before them all and said, "I do not know what you are talking about."

When he went out to the gateway, another woman saw him and said to those who were there, "This man was with Jesus of Nazareth."

Yet again, he refused to acknowledge it—with an oath, "I do not know that man!"

After a little while, those who were standing among the crowd approached Peter and said, "Surely you are one of them, too, because your accent gives you away."

Then he began to invoke a curse on himself and swear an oath, "I do not know that man!"

Immediately a rooster crowed, and Peter remembered Jesus' statement—when he said, "Before a rooster crows, you will refuse to acknowledge me three times." Then he went outside and wept inconsolably.

When early morning came, all the chief priests and elders of the people took council against Jesus so that they might put him to death. They tied him up, led him out, and turned him over to Pilate (the governor).

When Judas (the one who betrayed him) saw that he had been condemned, he regretted it and returned the thirty pieces of silver to the chief priests and elders. He said, "I have sinned by betraying innocent blood."

But they said, "What does that have to do with us? See to it for yourself."

So he threw the silver into the sanctuary and left, and then he went out and hanged himself. Then the chief priests picked up the silver and said, "It would not be right for us to put it into the treasury, because it is blood money." So after consulting with one another, some of them bought a ceramic worker's field as a burial place for travelers. Because of this, the field has been called "The Field of Blood" to this day. Then what was spoken by Jeremiah the prophet was fulfilled:

> So I took the thirty pieces of silver, the estimated price that was set by the sons of Israel, and they gave it for the ceramic worker's field just as the Master commanded me.

THEN JESUS WAS PRESENTED BEFORE THE GOVERNOR. THE governor questioned him, "Are you the king of the Jews?"

Jesus said, "You have spoken correctly." Yet he did not respond to the accusation that was made against him by the chief priests and elders.

Then Pilate said to him, "Do you not hear how much they are testifying against you?" But he did not respond to him—not even to one statement—so that the governor was incredibly amazed.

Now every Passover, the governor customarily would release one prisoner for the crowd—whomever they wanted. At that time, they were holding an infamous prisoner named Jesus Barabbas. So while they were assembled, Pilate said to them, "Whom do you want me to release for you—Jesus Barabbas or the Jesus who is called 'Messiah?'" You see, he thought that they had arrested him because of jealousy.

Also, while he was sitting on his judgment seat, his wife sent for him and said, "Do not have anything to do with that righteous man because I have suffered a lot today in a dream because of him."

Now the chief priests and elders convinced the crowd to request Barabbas and then put Jesus to death. So the governor spoke back to them, "Which of the two should I release for you?"

They said, "Barabbas!"

Pilate said to them, "So what should I do with the Jesus who is called 'Messiah?'"

They all replied, "He needs to be crucified!"

Then he said, "Why? What evil thing has he done?"

But they cried out even more, "He needs to be crucified!"

When Pilate saw that he was not getting anywhere—rather, a riot was beginning to break out—he took some water, washed his hands in front of the crowd, and said, "I am innocent of this man's blood. See to this for yourselves!"

Then all the people responded, "May his blood be blamed on us and our children!"

Then he released Barabbas for them, had Jesus scourged, and turned him over to be crucified. The governor's soldiers took Jesus into the headquarters and gathered the whole cohort of soldiers around him. Then they removed his clothes and wrapped a scarlet military cloak around him. They also wove a crown from thorns, put it on his head, and put a reed in his right hand. They fell down on their knees in front of him and mocked him, saying, "Hail! The king of the Jews!" Then they spit on him, took the reed from him, and hit him on the head. When they finished mocking him, they removed the military cloak, put his clothes back on him, and led him out to be crucified. As they came out, they found a man from Cyrene named Simon and forced him to carry Jesus' cross.

When they came to the place called Golgotha (which is called the Skull's Place), they gave him wine mixed with bitter herbs to drink. When he tasted it, he did not want to drink it. Once they crucified him, they distributed his clothes by casting lots for them and then sat there to keep watch over him. Now they had written his accusation and placed it above his head:

>This is Jesus, the King of the Jews.

Then they crucified two insurgents with him—one on his right side and the other on his left. All the people who passed by him said bad things about him and shook their heads. They said, "The one who would destroy the sanctuary and rebuild it in three days! Save yourself if you are God's son! Come down from that cross!"

The chief priests also made fun of him (along with the scribes and elders). They said, "He saved others but cannot save himself! Is he the king of Israel? If so, he must come down from the cross now, and then we will believe in him. He trusted in God—now God must rescue him if he wants him! You see, he said, 'I am God's Son!'"

The insurgents who were crucified with him also insulted him in the same way.

Now from noon until 3:00 p.m., the whole land became dark. At about 3:00 p.m., Jesus cried out with a loud voice, "Eli! Eli! Lema sebachthani?"

That means, "My God! My God! Why have you abandoned me?"

Now some of the people who were standing there heard this and said, "He is calling for Elijah!" Immediately one of them ran, took a sponge, filled it with sour wine, and stuck it on a reed to give him something to drink.

But the rest of them said, "Leave him alone; let's see if Elijah saves him!" Then Jesus cried out again with a loud voice and breathed his last breath.

Now get this—the inner curtain of the sanctuary was torn in two from the top to the bottom! The ground shook, the rocks were split, and the tombs were opened. Then the bodies of many saints who had been laid to rest were raised, and they went out of the tombs into the holy city after Jesus' resurrection and were seen by many people!

So when the centurion and those who were keeping watch over Jesus with him saw the earthquake and the other things that happened, they became very afraid. They said, "This man was truly God's Son!"

Now several women were there who were watching from far away. They had followed Jesus from Galilee so that they could take care of him. Among them were Mary (from Magdala), Mary (the mother of James and Joseph), and the mother of Zebedee's sons.

When it became evening, a wealthy man from Arimathea named Joseph came. He also had become a disciple of Jesus. He approached Pilate and requested the body of Jesus. Then Pilate gave the order to hand it over to him. So Joseph took the body, wrapped it in clean linen cloth, and put it in his new tomb, which he had cut into a large mass of rock. He rolled a large stone over to the door of the tomb and left. Now Mary (the one from Magdala) and the other Mary were also sitting there in front of the grave.

On the next morning (which was the day after preparation for the Sabbath), the chief priests and Pharisees assembled before Pilate and said, "Master, we have remembered—while that liar was still alive, he said, 'I will be raised after three days.' So command that the grave be secured until the third day or else his disciples might come, steal him away, and tell the people: 'He has been raised from the dead.' That final lie would be worse than the one he said!"

Pilate said to them, "Take a security team; go and make it as secure as you know how."

So they went and secured the grave by sealing the stone with the security team.

AFTER THE SABBATH, AT DAWN ON THE FIRST DAY OF THE WEEK, Mary (the one from Magdala) and the other Mary came to see the grave. Now get this—there was a strong earthquake! You see, an angel from the Master came down from the sky, approached the grave, and rolled away the stone. Then he sat on top of it. Now he looked like lightning, and his clothing was as white as snow. The men who were guarding the tomb trembled because they were afraid of him, and they fainted like dead men.

The angel spoke to the women, "You do not need to be afraid because I know that you are looking for Jesus, the one who was crucified. He is not here because he has been raised—just as he said. Come! Look at the place where he had been lying! Now go quickly and tell his disciples that he has been raised from the dead. Look! He is going ahead of you to Galilee. You will see him there. Look! I have told you!"

So they left the tomb quickly, with fear and great excitement, and ran to tell his disciples. Now get this—Jesus met them and said, "Hello!"

So they approached him, took hold of his feet, and worshiped him.

Then Jesus said to them, "Do not be afraid. Go and tell my brothers that I am going to Galilee, and they will see me there."

While they were going, get this—some of the security guards went into the city and told the chief priests everything that had happened. The chief priests assembled with the elders, and after reaching an agreement, they paid the soldiers a considerable amount of money and said, "Say: 'His disciples came during the night and stole him away while we were sleeping.' Then, if this news reaches the governor, we will plead with him and keep you out of trouble." So they took the money and did as they were instructed, and this rumor has been spread by the Jews to this very day.

Now the eleven disciples went to Galilee, to the mountain where Jesus had directed them to go. When they saw him, they bowed down, even though some were skeptical.

Then Jesus approached them and told them, "All power in heaven and on the earth has been given to me. So go and make disciples of all the nations by immersing them in the name of the Father, the Son, and the Holy Spirit and by teaching them to observe everything that I have commanded you. Look! I will be with you every day until the end of the age!"

ACCORDING TO
MARK

THE BEGINNING OF THE GOOD MESSAGE OF JESUS THE MESSIAH, God's Son, just as it was written by the prophet Isaiah:

> Look! I am sending my messenger in front of you.
> He will prepare your way.
> The voice of someone crying out in the desert:
> 'Prepare the Master's way! Straighten his paths!'

John the Immerser showed up in the desert, proclaiming an immersion characterized by repentance for the forgiveness of sins. Now all of Judea would come out to him, as well as everyone from Jerusalem, and they would be immersed by him in the Jordan River as they confessed their sins. John was clothed in camel's hair and wore a leather belt around his waist. He typically ate locusts and wild honey.

He would preach: "Someone who is stronger than me is coming after me. I myself am not worthy to untie the straps on his sandals. I have immersed you in water, but he will immerse you in the Holy Spirit!"

It just so happened in those days that Jesus came from Nazareth, Galilee, and he was immersed by John in the Jordan River. Now as soon as he came up out of the water, he saw the sky divided and the Spirit coming down to him like a dove. Then a voice came from the sky: "You are my dear Son. I am very proud of you!"

Then the Spirit carried him out into the desert, and he remained in the desert for forty days as he was being tested by Satan. He was with the wild animals, and the angels took care of him.

Now after John was arrested, Jesus came into Galilee proclaiming God's Good Message, saying: "The time has been completed, and God's kingdom has come near! Repent and have faith in the Good Message!"

Then he went along beside the Sea of Galilee and saw Simon and Andrew (Simon's brother) casting nets in the sea—they were fishermen, you see. Jesus said to them, "Come follow me, and I will cause you to fish for people." So they immediately left their nets and followed him.

Next, he went on a little farther and saw James (the son of Zebedee) and John (his brother), as they were preparing their nets in the boat. Then he called them, and they left Zebedee, their father, in the boat with the hired workers and followed behind him.

THEN HE WENT INTO CAPERNAUM AND WENT RIGHT INTO THE synagogue on the Sabbath Day to teach. They were all amazed at his teaching because he was teaching them like someone who had authority—not like the scribes.

Now there was a man with an unclean spirit in their synagogue at that time, and he cried out, "What do you have to do with us, Jesus of Nazareth? Have you come to destroy us? We know who you are: the Holy One from God!"

Jesus reprimanded him by saying, "Be quiet and come out of him!"

Then the unclean spirit shook the man back and forth, cried out with a loud voice, and went out of him. So they were all so amazed that they discussed among themselves, "Who is this? A new teaching given with authority! He even commands the unclean spirits, and they obey him!" Thus his fame spread everywhere right away, throughout the whole area surrounding Galilee.

Then he went out from the synagogue and came to the house of Simon and Andrew, along with James and John. Now Simon's mother-in-law was lying down with a fever, and they told him about her. So he came to her, picked her up by taking her hand, and the fever left her. Then she served them some food.

Now when it had become late and the sun had set, people brought him everyone who was in poor health or was possessed by demons. So the whole city was gathered around the door. Then he healed many who were suffering with various diseases. He also cast out many demons and would not allow them to speak because they knew who he was.

So very early (while it was still dark), he got up, went outside, and went to a deserted place, and there he prayed. Then Simon and the others who were with him went to search for him. They found him and told him: "Everyone is looking for you."

He said to them, "Let's go somewhere else, to the neighboring villages, so that I can preach there. You see, this is why I have come."

So he went and preached in their synagogues throughout all of Galilee and cast out demons. Then a man with leprosy approached him and begged him—falling on his knees. He said to him, "If you want, you are able to cleanse me!"

Then he showed compassion by reaching out his hand, touching him, and telling him, "I want to do this—be cleansed."

Then he sternly warned him and sent him out, telling him: "See to it that you do not tell anyone. No, go and show yourself to the high priest, and bring what Moses commanded you to bring for your purification as a testimony to them." But he went out and began to proclaim and advertise this story a lot, so that Jesus could no longer enter the city publicly. Instead, he stayed out in the deserted places, and people came to him from everywhere.

THEN HE WENT BACK INTO CAPERNAUM, AND WITHIN DAYS, IT was rumored that he was at home. So many people were assembled around that there was no longer even any room at the door, and he taught them the Message. Now some people arrived, bringing a paralyzed man who was being carried by four men. Since they could not bring him to Jesus (on account of the crowd), they removed part of the roof where Jesus was. Then they dug through it and lowered down the bed on which the paralyzed man was lying.

When Jesus saw their faith, he told the paralyzed man, "Child, your sins are forgiven."

But some of the scribes were sitting there and discussing amongst themselves: "Why is this man saying such things? He is blaspheming! Who can forgive sins except for God alone?"

Now since Jesus immediately knew in his spirit that they were discussing these things amongst themselves, he said to them, "Why are you discussing this in your hearts? Which is easier—to tell the paralyzed man, 'Your sins are forgiven,' or to tell him, 'Get up, pick up your bed, and walk'? Well, so that you may know that on the earth the Son of Man has the authority to forgive sins,"—he told the paralyzed man: "I command you—get up, pick up your bed, and go to your house."

Then he got up, immediately picked up his bed, and left—in front of everyone! So they were all amazed, and they gave praise to God: "We have never seen anything like this!"

Then he again went out beside the sea, and the entire crowd came to him, so he taught them. As he traveled farther, he saw Levi (the son of Alphaeus) sitting at the tax office, so he told him, "Follow me." Then he got up and followed him.

Now it just so happened that as he was reclining to eat in Levi's house, many tax collectors and sinners were reclining to eat with Jesus and his disciples. You see, there were many of them, and they followed him.

So when the scribes who were among the Pharisees saw that he was eating with the tax collectors and sinners, they asked his disciples, "Why does he eat with tax collectors and sinners?"

When Jesus heard this, he said to them, "Healthy people do not need a doctor, but those who are in poor health do! I have come to invite sinners, not righteous people."

Now John's disciples and the Pharisees made a practice of fasting. They came and asked him, "Why do John's disciples and the Pharisees' disciples fast, but your disciples do not?"

Then Jesus said to them, "Can the groomsmen fast as long as the groom is with them? They cannot fast as long as they have the groom with them. But the days are coming when the groom will be taken away from them; and then on that day they will fast. No one sews a patch made of new cloth onto an old piece of clothing, or else the new cloth that was added will pull away from the old piece of clothing—then the tear will be made worse. Also, no one puts fresh wine into old wineskins, or else the wine will tear the wineskins and both the wine and the skins will be wasted. No, fresh wine is put into new wineskins."

NOW IT JUST SO HAPPENED THAT HE WAS PASSING THROUGH THE fields on the Sabbath Day, and his disciples began to make their path by picking some heads of wheat. Now the Pharisees told him: "Look! Why are they doing what they have no right to do on the Sabbath?"

So he said to them, "Have you never read what David did when he and those who were with him were in need and hungry—how he went into the House of God while Abiathar was the high priest and ate the Bread of the Presence, which no one has the right to eat except for the priests? He also gave it to those who were with him!" Then he told them, "The Sabbath was made for mankind, not mankind for the Sabbath! So the Son of Man is even the Master over the Sabbath." Then he went back into the synagogue.

Now a man was there who had a paralyzed hand. So they carefully watched him to see if Jesus would heal him on the Sabbath so that they could be able to accuse him of something.

Then he said to the man who had the paralyzed hand, "Get up in front of everyone," and he asked them, "Is it right to do anything on the Sabbath, whether good or evil—to save life or to kill?"

But they kept silent, and he looked around at them with anger, upset at the callousness of their hearts. He said to the man, "Reach out your hand." Then he reached out his hand, and it was restored. Then the Pharisees immediately left with Herod's sympathizers and conspired against him so that they could kill him.

Then Jesus went back toward the sea with his disciples, and a very large crowd followed him from Galilee, Judea, Jerusalem, Idumea, and from across the Jordan—some were even from the area of Tyre and Sidon! When the large crowd heard what he had been doing, they came to him. So he told his disciples to have a boat standing by for him so that the crowd would not crush him. You see, he had healed many of them, and so everyone who had a tormenting illness fell on him so that they could touch him. Even when the unclean spirits saw him, they fell down before him and cried out, "You are God's Son!" He often rebuked them so that they would not expose him.

THEN HE WENT UP THE MOUNTAIN AND SUMMONED THE ONES he wanted, and they went out to him. He appointed twelve of them—the ones he called "apostles"—so that they would be with him and that he would send them to preach, to have power to cast out demons. He called these twelve: Simon (to whom he gave the name Peter), James (Zebedee's son), John (James's brother—he gave them the name Boanerges, which means "Thunderous Sons"), Andrew, Philip, Bartholomew, Matthew, Thomas, James (Alphaeus's son), Thaddeus, Simon (the extremist), and Judas Iscariot (who was also his betrayer).

Then he went into a house, and another crowd assembled so that they were unable even to eat a meal. Those who listened to him went out to seize him because, they said, "He is out of his mind!"

Even some scribes who had come down from Jerusalem said, "He is possessed by the devil! He casts out demons by the power of the prince of demons!"

Then he summoned them and spoke to them in allegories: "How can Satan cast out Satan? Also, if a kingdom is divided against itself, that kingdom cannot last, and if a house is divided against itself, that house cannot last. So if Satan has risen up against himself and is divided, he cannot stand—his end has come. But no one is able to enter a strong man's house and rob him of his possessions unless they first tie up the strong man. Then they rob his house. I am truly telling you: all the sins and blasphemies of mankind will be forgiven—as many times as they have blasphemed! But if anyone blasphemes the Holy Spirit, they will never have forgiveness. No, they are guilty of an eternal sin." (He said this because they said, "He has an unclean spirit.")

Then his mother and his brothers came and stood outside. They sent someone in to call for him. Now a crowd was sitting around him, and they told him, "Look! Your mother, your brothers, and your sisters are outside looking for you."

So he answered them, "Who are my mother and my brothers?" Then he looked at the people who were sitting around him and said, "Look! My mother and my brothers! You see, whoever does God's will—that person is my brother, sister, and mother."

Then he began to teach again by the sea, and such a large crowd was assembled around him that he got into a boat and sat down, on the sea, and the whole crowd was on the land. He taught them with many allegories and spoke to him with his teachings:

"Listen! Get this—a sower went out to sow. It just so happened that as he sowed, some of the seed fell by the road, and the birds came and devoured them. Then some fell on rocky soil, where it did not have much earth, and it sprang up immediately because it did not have much depth of soil. So when the sun rose, the plant was scorched and withered because it did not have a root system. Still, some fell on thorny soil, and the thorns came up and choked it, so it did not produce fruit. Then some fell on good soil, and it produced fruit, coming up and growing! One produced thirty times what was sown, another sixty times what was sown, and another a hundred times what was sown." Then he said, "Whoever has an ear to listen needs to listen!"

Then, when he happened to be alone, those who were with him (along with the twelve) asked him about the allegories. So he told them, "The secret of God's kingdom has been granted to you, but for those people—the ones who are outside—everything comes in allegories, so:

> Though they see, they will see and not recognize,
> And though they hear, they will hear and not understand,
> Or else they would return, and he would forgive them."

Then he asked them, "Do you not understand this allegory? Then how will you come to understand any of the allegories? The sower sows the Message. These are the ones beside the road: the Message is sown there, but whenever they hear it, immediately Satan comes and takes away the Message that was sown in them. These are the ones that are sown in rocky soil: whenever they hear the Message they joyfully and immediately accept it, but they do not have a root system within them. They are temporary, so whenever affliction or persecution comes because of the Message, they immediately fall into sin. Still others are those who have been sown in thorny soil. These are the ones who hear the Message, and their concern for the present, the deception of wealth, and their desire for other things come in and choke the Message so that they become fruitless. Then there are those who are sown on good ground, who hear the Message, accept it, and produce fruit—one producing thirty, another sixty, and another one hundred times what was sown."

Then he told them, "A lamp is not brought in to be put under a measuring basket or under a couch, is it? Is it not put on a lampstand? You see, nothing is hidden that will not be revealed, and nothing has been kept secret, except that it could come to be clearly visible. Whoever has an ear to listen needs to listen!" Then he told them, "Watch and listen: the standard of measuring that you use will be used to measure and add to you. You see, more will be given to the one who has something, and whatever a person who has nothing might possess—even that will be taken from them."

Then he said, "This is what God's kingdom is like: a man who sowed seed on the ground. He went to sleep and woke up, night and day, and the seed sprouted and grew—and he didn't know how! The ground produces fruit automatically—first the grass, then the ear, and then the total number of wheat on the head. So when the fruit has been produced, he immediately sends out his sickle because the harvest has come."

Next, he said: "How should we compare God's kingdom, or with what kind of allegory should we describe it? It is like a mustard seed—whenever it is sown in the ground, it is smaller than all of the other seeds that are in the ground, but when it has been sown, it grows and becomes larger than all the herbs. It produces large branches so that the birds of the sky are able to live under its shade."

So he spoke the Message to them with many allegories like these since they could not listen. He never spoke to them except with allegories, but he explained everything when he was alone with his disciples.

WHEN IT BECAME EVENING THAT DAY, HE TOLD THEM: "LET'S GO to the other side of the Sea of Galilee." So they left the crowd and took him there since he was already in the boat. There was also another boat with them. It just so happened that a fierce gust of wind and waves splashed up onto the boat so that the boat was filling with water already! Yet, he was in the stern of the ship on a cot, asleep.

They woke him and asked him, "Teacher! Don't you care that we are about to die?"

So he got up, scolded the wind, and told the sea: "Silence! Calm down!" Then the wind ceased, and the sea became extremely calm. He told them, "Why are you afraid? Do you not have faith yet?"

So they were very terrified and said to one another, "Just who is this? Even the wind and sea obey him!"

Then they arrived at the seashore in the district of the Gerasenes. Now right as he was getting out of the boat, a man with an unclean spirit ran from among the tombs to meet him. He had made his home among the tombs, and no one could even chain him up any longer. You see, he had often been bound with shackles and chains, but the chains were ripped in half by him, and the shackles were shattered. No one had the power to control him. So he was out among the tombs and on the mountains throughout every night and day, crying out and cutting himself with stones. Now when he saw Jesus at a distance, he ran and bowed down to him. He cried out with a loud voice, "What business do you have with me, Jesus the Son of the supreme God? I put you under oath before God—do not torture me!"

You see, Jesus had told him, "Unclean spirit: come out of that man!" He also asked him, "What is your name?"

He told Jesus, "My name is Legion because there are many of us!" Then he begged Jesus profusely not to send the demons out of the district. Now there was a large herd of pigs grazing on the mountainside. So he begged Jesus, "Send us into the pigs so that we may enter them." Then Jesus gave them permission, and the unclean spirits came out and entered the pigs. So the herd (about two thousand pigs) rushed down the steep bank into the sea, and they drowned in the sea.

Then the men who tended the pigs fled and announced this to the city and countryside, so they came out to see what had happened. They approached Jesus and saw the man who had been possessed by the Legion—he was sitting down, clothed, and in his right mind. So they became afraid. Those who saw what happened told them everything about what happened to the demon-possessed man and about the pigs. So they began to beg him to leave their district.

Now as he was getting into the boat, the man who had been possessed begged him to let him stay with Jesus. But he did not let him. Instead, he told him: "Go to your house—to your family—and tell them about everything that the Master has done for you, as well as the compassion he showed you."

So the man left and began to preach in the Decapolis about everything that Jesus had done for him, and everyone was amazed.

WHEN JESUS HAD CROSSED BACK OVER TO THE OTHER SIDE OF the sea by boat, a large crowd assembled around him as he was beside the sea. Then one of the leaders of the synagogue (named Jairus) came. When he saw Jesus, he fell down at his feet and begged him profusely: "My daughter is on her deathbed. Come lay your hands on her so that she would be rescued and live!" Then Jesus left with him, and a large crowd followed him and rushed up against him.

Now there was a woman who had been dealing with a bleeding problem for twelve years. She had suffered a lot at the hands of many doctors and had spent everything she owned, but she was no better. In fact, she became even worse! She had heard about Jesus, so she went behind him with the crowd and touched his robe. You see, she said: "If I can only touch his robe, I will be healed!" Then her discharge of blood dried up immediately, and she recognized in her body that she had been rescued from her suffering.

Then Jesus immediately realized that power had gone out from him, and he turned to the crowd and said, "Who touched my clothes?"

His disciples told him, "You see the crowd rushing against you, and yet you say, 'Who touched me?'"

So he looked around to see who had done this. Now the woman (who was afraid and shaking because she knew what had happened to her) came, fell down before him, and told him the whole truth.

Then he told her, "Daughter, your faith has rescued you. Go in peace, and be healed from your suffering."

While he was still speaking, some people came from the leader of the synagogue's house and said, "Your daughter has died. Why trouble the Teacher any longer?"

But Jesus overheard the message that was said, and he told the leader of the synagogue: "Do not be afraid—just have faith." Then he did not let anyone accompany him except for Peter, James, and John (James's brother). They came into the leader of the synagogue's house, and he saw the commotion—both with weeping and heavy crying—so he went in and told them: "Why are you causing a commotion and weeping? The child is not dead—only sleeping."

Then they made fun of him, but he sent them all out, took the child's father and mother and the disciples with him, and went in where the child was. He took the child's hand and said to her, "Talitha! Qumi." (That is translated as "Little girl! I command you to get up!") Then the little girl got up immediately and walked around. (You see, she was twelve years old.) So they were all immediately astounded, in complete shock. Then he told them plainly and extensively that no one was to know what happened, and he told them to give her something to eat.

Then he left from there and went to his hometown. His disciples followed him, and when the Sabbath was underway, he began to teach in the synagogue, so many people listened and were amazed. They said, "Where does he come from? What is this wisdom that has been given to him, and what about these miracles that are happening by his hands? Is this man not the carpenter—the son of Mary and brother of James, Joseph, Jude, and Simon? Furthermore, are his sisters not here with us also?" Thus, they were offended by him.

Then Jesus said to them, "A prophet is not disrespected except in his hometown, among his relatives, and in his household." So he was unable to perform even a single miracle there except that he laid his hands on a few sick people and healed them. He was surprised by their lack of faith, so he traveled around the surrounding villages to teach. Then he invited the twelve and began to send them two at a time. He gave them authority over the unclean spirits, and he commanded them not to take anything for the journey except a single staff—no bread, no pack, no money in their belts. "Taking only one pair of sandals on your feet, do not put on an extra shirt." Then he told them, "When you enter the house wherever you go, stay there until you leave that area. Then if that place will not welcome you or listen to you, go out from there and shake the dirt out from under your feet as a testimony to them." So they went out and preached for them to repent, and they cast out many demons and anointed many sick people with olive oil and healed them.

Then King Herod heard about Jesus. You see, his name had become famous, and people said, "John the Immerser has been raised from the dead—because of this, miraculous powers are at work within him!"

But others said, "He is Elijah."

Even others said, "He is a prophet like one of the prophets!"

Yet, when Herod heard about him, he said, "The one I beheaded—John—he has been raised!" You see, Herod himself had sent for John to be arrested. He chained him up in prison because of Herodias (the wife of his brother Philip)—because Herod had married her.

You see, John had been telling Herod, "It is not right for you to have your brother's wife." So Herodias held a grudge against him and wanted to kill him. But she could not do so because Herod was afraid of John, since he knew John was a righteous and holy man. So Herod protected him, and whenever he would listen to John, he was often confused, but he was glad to listen to him.

Well, a day of opportunity arose when Herod prepared a feast on his birthday for his important officials, the commanders of Roman cohorts, and the elite persons of Galilee. Then the daughter of Herodias herself entered the room and danced, and she pleased Herod and those who were eating with him.

Then the king said to the young girl, "Ask me for whatever you want, and I will give it to you!" Then he swore an oath to her: "I will give you whatever you ask of me—up to half of my kingdom!"

So she went out and asked her mother, "What should I request?"

Then she said, "Ask for the head of John the Immerser!"

So she ran into the room right away to the king, and she asked: "I want you to give me the head of John the Immerser on a platter right now!"

Then the king became very upset, but because of his oaths and his dinner guests, he did not want to reject her. So the king immediately sent for an executioner and commanded him to bring John's head. The executioner went, beheaded John in the prison, brought his head on a platter, and gave it to the young girl. Then she gave it to her mother. When John's disciples heard about it, they came, took his body, and buried him in a tomb.

THEN THE APOSTLES ASSEMBLED WITH JESUS AND BROUGHT HIM a report of everything that they had done and taught. Then he told them, "Come—just you—to a deserted place and rest for a little while." You see, there were many people who were coming and going, and they did not have an opportunity to eat. So they went by themselves on a boat to a deserted place. While they were traveling, many people saw them and recognized them, and they ran there together by land from all the cities and went up to them. When he got out of the boat, he saw a large crowd and felt compassion for them because they were like sheep without a shepherd. So he began to teach them many things.

Now several hours had already passed, and his disciples approached him and said, "This place is a desert, and several hours have passed already. Send them away so that they can go into the surrounding fields and villages to buy food for themselves and have something to eat."

But he answered them, "You give them something to eat."

They told him, "Should we go out and buy two hundred days' wages worth of bread and give it to them to eat?"

Then he said to them, "How much bread do you have? Go see."

When they knew how much they had, they said, "Five pieces—and two fish."

So he commanded all the people to sit down—group by group—on the green grass. They lied down in groups of hundreds—about five thousand in all. So he took the five pieces of bread and the two fish. He lifted his eyes toward the sky, said a blessing, broke the bread, and gave it to his disciples so that they could set it before them. Then he distributed the two fish to everyone. So everyone ate and was full. Furthermore, they picked up twelve baskets filled with pieces of bread and some of the fish. Now there were five thousand men who ate this bread!

At that time, he required his disciples to board the ship and go ahead of him across the sea to Bethsaida while he dismissed the crowd. Once he had sent them away, he went out to the mountain to pray. When evening came, the ship was in the middle of the sea, and he was alone on the shore. He saw that they were having trouble making progress (because the wind was against them), so just before sunrise he went toward them—walking on the sea! He wanted to pass by them, but when they saw him walking on the sea, they thought, "It is a ghost!" and they shouted in fear. You see, everyone saw him and became worried.

So right away he spoke with them—telling them: "Cheer up; it is I. Do not be afraid." Then he got up into the ship with them, and the wind died down. They were completely beside themselves with amazement. You see, they did not understand about the pieces of bread, either. No, their hearts were hardened.

NOW WHEN THEY HAD CROSSED OVER TO THE SHORE, THEY arrived at Gennesaret and lowered the anchor. Immediately after they had gotten out of the ship, the people recognized Jesus, and that whole region ran out to where they heard he was. They began to bring out on mattresses the ones who had illnesses. Now wherever he entered a village, city, or countryside, the people would lay their sick in the marketplaces and beg him that they might even touch the edge of his robe—and whoever touched it was healed!

Also, the Pharisees and some of the scribes came from Jerusalem and gathered around him. Then they saw that some of his disciples were eating food with unclean (meaning unwashed) hands. You see, the Pharisees and all the Jews do not eat unless they wash their hands while making fists—thus adhering to the elders' tradition. Even when they come from the marketplace, they do not eat unless they dip their hands. They also adhere to many other things that they have received by tradition, such as the dipping of cups, pitchers, bowls, and reclining places.

So the Pharisees and scribes asked him, "Why do your disciples not live by the elders' tradition? No, they are eating food with unclean hands!"

Then he told them, "Isaiah prophesied about you hypocrites very well since it is written that:

> This people honors me with their lips,
> but their heart is very distant from me.
> So they worship me pointlessly
> because they teach the commands of people as their teaching!

You steer clear of God's command and adhere to people's tradition!" Then he told them, "You are good at ignoring God's command so that you can uphold your tradition. You see, Moses said, 'Honor your father and mother,' as well as 'Whoever insults his father or mother must be put to death.' But you say that if a man tells his father or mother, 'What you should have received from me is already Corban' (meaning an offering to God), you no longer allow him to do anything for his father or mother. You are voiding God's Word because of your traditions that you have received—and you do many other things like this!"

When he had returned to addressing the crowd, he told them, "Everyone listen to me and understand! Nothing outside of a person's body is able to make a person unclean by entering them. On the contrary, whatever comes out of a person is what makes that person unclean!"

Then when he went into the house away from the crowd, his disciples asked him about the allegory. Then he told them, "Can this be? Do you not understand, either? Do you not grasp that nothing that is outside the body can make a person unclean by entering them? You see, it does not go into their heart but into their stomach and then down the drain!" So he pronounced all foods to be clean.

Then he said, "What comes out of a person—that makes him unclean. You see, from inside—out of people's heart—come evil arguments, inappropriate sexual acts, thefts, murders, adulteries, greed, wickedness, deceit, lack of restraint, a jealous eye, blasphemies, arrogance, and foolishness. All these evil things come out from the inside and make a person unclean."

THEN HE GOT UP FROM THERE AND WENT AWAY TO THE BORDER of Tyre. As he entered into a house, he wanted no one to know it, but he could not escape notice. No, a woman heard about him right away. Her daughter was possessed by an unclean spirit, so she came and bowed down at his feet. Now the woman was a Greek (born in Phoenicia, Syria), and she asked him to cast the demon out of her daughter.

He told her, "Leave. Let the children be fed first because it is not right to take the children's food and throw it to the dogs."

Then she answered, "But Master, the dogs also eat the children's crumbs under the table!"

Then he replied to her, "Because of this statement, go back—the demon has gone out of your daughter."

When she returned to her house, she found the child lying down on the bed, and the demon had gone out.

He went back out from the border of Tyre to the Sea of Galilee, passing by Sidon and going along the borders of Decapolis. Then a deaf man with a speech impediment was brought to him, and they begged him to lay his hands on him. So he took him aside from the crowd and put his fingers into the man's ears. He spat and took hold of the man's tongue. Then he looked up to the sky, sighed, and said to him, "Ephatha" (which means "be opened"). Immediately the man's ears were opened, and his tongue's impediment was released so that he spoke correctly. Then he specifically warned them not to tell anyone; but the more he warned them, the more they proclaimed it. They were extremely surprised and said, "He has done everything well! He even makes the deaf hear and the speechless speak!"

Also, in those days, a large crowd had assembled and did not have anything to eat. So Jesus summoned the disciples and told them, "I feel sorry for the crowd because they have stayed with me for three days already and do not have anything to eat. Now if I dismiss them to their homes hungry, they will pass out on the way. Furthermore, some of them have come from far away."

Then his disciples answered him, "Where could anyone get enough bread here in the desert to satisfy these people?"

He asked them, "How much bread do you have?"

They answered, "Seven pieces."

Then he instructed the crowd to sit down on the ground. He took the seven pieces of bread and gave thanks for it. He broke it apart and gave it to his disciples so that they could distribute it. So they distributed it to the crowd. They also had a few small pieces of fish. He gave thanks for it and told them to distribute the pieces of fish also. So they ate and became full, and there were seven baskets full of leftover pieces. (And there were about four thousand people who were fed!) Then he dismissed them.

Right after this, he entered a ship with his disciples and went to the region of Dalmanutha. The Pharisees went out and began to argue with him, seeking from him a sign from heaven and testing him. He sighed with a deep breath and said, "Why does this generation seek a sign? I am truly telling you—a sign will not be given to this generation!" Then he left them, entered the ship again, and left for the other shore of the sea.

Now they had forgotten to bring bread, and except for one piece of bread, they had nothing with them on the ship. Jesus commanded them, "Pay attention! Look out for the yeast of the

Pharisees and the yeast of Herod." (They began arguing among themselves because they did not have any bread.) Since he knew this, he told them, "Why are you arguing because you do not have any bread? Do you not yet get it or understand? Do you have hardened hearts?

> Even though you have eyes, do you not see?
> Even though you have ears, do you not hear?

"Do you not remember, either? When I broke the five pieces of bread for the five thousand people—how many baskets full of leftover pieces did you pick up?"

They told him, "Twelve."

"When I broke the seven pieces of bread for the four thousand people—how many baskets full of leftover pieces did you pick up?"

They said, "Seven."

Then he told them, "Do you still not understand?"

They came into Bethsaida, and some people brought him a blind man and begged him to touch him. He took hold of the blind man's hand and led him out of the village. He spit into the man's eyes, placed his hands on him, and asked him: "Do you see anything?"

He looked up and said, "I see people, but they look like walking trees."

Then Jesus put his hands over the man's eyes again, and the man could see clearly—he was restored and could distinguish everything clearly from a long distance away. Then he sent the man home and said, "Do not enter into the village."

THEN JESUS AND HIS DISCIPLES WENT OUT INTO THE VILLAGE OF Caesarea Philippi. Now while they were on the way, he asked his disciples questions. He asked them, "Who do people say that I am?"

They told him, "John the Immerser. Others say Elijah, and still others say you are one of the prophets."

Then he asked them, "What about you—who do you say that I am?"

Peter answered him, "You are the Messiah."

Then Jesus warned them not to tell anyone about him. He began to teach them that the Son of Man must suffer many things—he must be rejected by the elders, high priests, and the scribes. He would be killed and resurrected after three days. He said these things plainly.

So Peter took him aside and began to rebuke him, but Jesus turned around, looked at his disciples, and rebuked Peter. He said, "Get behind me, Satan, because you are thinking about man's things instead of God's things!"

Then he summoned the crowd along with his disciples and told them, "If anyone wants to follow behind me, they must deny themselves, pick up their cross, and follow me! Whoever wants to save their own life will lose it, but whoever loses their life because of me and the gospel will save it! You see, what will a person profit if they win the whole world and forfeit their life? What will a person exchange for their life? So anyone in this adulterous and sinful generation who is ashamed of me and my words—the Son of Man will be ashamed of them when he comes with his Father's glory and the holy angels!" Then he told them, "I am truly telling you—some are standing here today who will not taste death until they see God's kingdom coming with power!"

Then, after six days, Jesus took Peter, James, and John along with him and led them up to a high mountain by themselves. Then he was transformed in front of them. His clothing began to shine white, very brightly—so white that no launderer on earth could have made them so white. Elijah and Moses also appeared among them, and they were conversing with Jesus.

Then Peter responded by telling Jesus, "Rabbi! It is good that we are here! We should also make three tents—one for you, one for Moses, and one for Elijah!" (You see, he did not know how he should respond because they were all terrified.)

Then a cloud appeared and overshadowed them, and a voice came from the cloud: "This is my dear Son! Listen to him!" Suddenly, they looked around and no longer saw anyone with them except for Jesus alone.

While they were coming down from the mountain, he commanded them not to tell anyone what they had seen until the Son of Man was to be raised from the dead. So they kept this matter to themselves, trying to figure out what the "resurrection from the dead" might mean.

Then they asked him, "Do the scribes not say that Elijah must come first?"

He told them, "Elijah does come first to restore everything—but how is it written about the Son of Man that he should suffer many things and be rejected? But I am telling you—Elijah has come, and they did to him whatever they wanted, just as it is written about him."

When they came to the disciples, they saw a large crowd around them, and the scribes were arguing with them. Right away, the whole crowd saw him, became excited, and ran to greet him.

He asked them, "Why are you arguing with one another?"

Someone from the crowd answered, "Teacher! I brought my son to you—he has a spirit that cannot speak. Whenever it seizes him, it causes him to fall down, and he foams at the mouth, grinds his teeth, and becomes stiff. I told your disciples to cast it out, but they were unable!"

Then he answered them, "You faithless generation! How long am I to be with you? How long am I to put up with you? Bring him to me."

Then they brought him to Jesus. When the spirit saw him, it immediately convulsed him, and he fell on the ground, rolling and foaming at the mouth.

He asked the boy's father, "How long has this been happening to him?"

He said, "Since childhood. It has often thrown him into fire and into water to kill him; but if you can, help us—show mercy to us!"

Then Jesus answered him, "If I can? All things are possible for someone who has faith."

Immediately the child's father cried out, "I have faith—help me with my lack of faith!"

When Jesus saw that a crowd was rushing back together, he rebuked the unclean spirit and said to it, "Speechless and deaf spirit! I command you to come out of him and never enter him again!"

Then it cried out and convulsed him even more, and then it went out. The child became like a dead person so that the crowd said, "He died!"

But Jesus took his hand and lifted him up, and he was raised.

When he had entered into the house, his disciples asked him privately, "Why were we unable to cast it out?"

He told them, "This kind is impossible to cast out with anything but prayer."

FROM THERE, HE WENT OUT TO PASS THROUGH GALILEE, AND HE did not want anyone to recognize him. You see, he was teaching his disciples and telling them that the Son of Man would be betrayed into the hands of men. He said they would kill him and that he would be resurrected three days after being killed. But they did not understand what he said and were afraid to ask him.

Then he came into Capernaum. While he was in the house, he asked them, "Why were you arguing on the way?"

They remained silent because they had been arguing with one another on the way about which of them was the most important.

He sat down, called for the twelve, and told them, "If anyone wants to be first, he will be the lowest of everyone and the servant of everyone." Then he took a little child, had him stand in front of them, and hugged him. He said to them, "Whoever welcomes one child like this one in my name—he welcomes me. Whoever welcomes me does not welcome me only but also the one who sent me."

John told him, "Teacher, we saw someone casting out demons in your name and told him to stop because he was not following us."

Jesus said, "Do not tell him to stop. You see, no one who performs a miracle in my name will also be able to speak evil of me quickly—whoever is not against us is for us! Whoever gives you a cup of water to drink simply because you belong to the Messiah—I am truly telling you—they will not lose their reward. Also, whoever causes one of these little ones who have faith in me to sin—it would be better for them for a heavy millstone to be tied around their neck and to be thrown into the sea. If your hand causes you to sin, cut it off. It would be better for you to enter into life deformed than to go away into hell—into the unquenchable fire—with both of your hands. If your foot causes you to sin, cut it off. It would be better for you to enter into life crippled than to be thrown into hell with both of your feet. If your eye causes you to sin, pull it out. It would be better for you to enter God's kingdom with one eye than to be thrown into hell with two eyes, where 'their worm does not die, and the fire is not quenched.' You see, everyone will be seasoned with fire. Salt is good, but if the salt loses its taste, how will you season it? Have salt in yourselves and be at peace with one another."

THEN HE GOT UP AND WENT TO THE BORDER OF JUDEA, THE BANK of the Jordan River, and again a crowd gathered around him. So he taught them, as it was his habit to do so.

Then the Pharisees came over to test him and asked him if it is right for a man to divorce his wife.

He answered them, "What did Moses command you?"

They said, "Moses permitted a man to write an annulment certificate and to divorce her."

Then Jesus said to them, "He wrote this command to you because of your hard-heartedness. No, from the beginning of creation, 'He made them male and female.' 'Because of this, a man will leave behind his father and mother and be united with his wife. The two of them will become one body.' So they are no longer two people but one body—so man must not separate what God has joined together."

Now when they were back in the house, the disciples asked him about this. He told them, "Whoever divorces his wife and marries another woman commits adultery with her. Furthermore, if she divorces her husband and marries another man, she commits adultery."

Then some young children were brought to him so that he would lay his hands on them. The disciples reprimanded them, but when Jesus saw this he became upset and told them, "Let the young children come to me. Do not get in their way because God's kingdom belongs to such people! I am truly telling you: whoever does not welcome God's kingdom like a young child will never enter it!" Then he hugged them, blessed them, and laid his hands on them.

Now when he had gone back out on the road, someone ran up to him, knelt down, and asked him, "Good Teacher, what must I do to inherit eternal life?"

Jesus said to him, "Why do you call me 'good?' No one is 'good' except God! You know the commands! 'Do not kill.' 'Do not commit adultery.' 'Do not steal.' 'Do not lie.' 'Do not cheat.' 'Honor your father and mother.'"

Then the man said to him, "Teacher, I have kept all of these since I was young!"

So Jesus looked at him, felt love for him, and told him, "You are missing one thing. Go sell everything you have and give it to the poor, and you will have treasure in heaven. Then come follow me."

But the man was devastated by what Jesus said and went away offended. You see, he had many possessions. Jesus looked around and told his disciples, "How difficult it is for those who have wealth to enter God's kingdom!"

The disciples were appalled at what he said, but Jesus again spoke up and told them, "Children, how difficult it is to enter God's kingdom! It is easier for a camel to pass through the eye of a needle than for a wealthy person to enter God's kingdom!"

They were even more surprised and said to one another, "So who can be saved?"

Jesus looked at them and said, "This is impossible with men but not with God. You see, everything is possible with God."

Peter began to say to him, "Look! We have left everything and followed you."

Jesus said, "I am truly telling you—as for those who have left a house, brothers, sisters, a mother, a father, children, or fields because of me and because of the gospel: no one has left these except to receive one hundred times more. At this present time, he will receive houses, brothers, sisters, mothers, children, fields, as well as persecution. Then in the coming age, he will receive eternal life. But many of the first ones will be last, and the last ones will be first."

SO THEY WERE GOING UP THE ROAD TO JERUSALEM, AND JESUS was walking ahead of them. Some of them were appalled, and others who followed him were afraid. Then he took the twelve aside again and began to tell them what was about to happen to him: "Look: we are going to Jerusalem, and the Son of Man will be betrayed to the chief priests and scribes. They will condemn him to death and will deliver him over to the gentiles. Then they will mock him, spit on him, flog him, and kill him, but he will rise up from the dead after three days."

So James and John (the sons of Zebedee) approached him and told him, "Teacher, we want you to do a favor for us that we ask of you."

He said to them, "What do you want me to do for you?"

They told him, "Grant us this: that one of us would sit at your right hand and the other on your left in your glory."

Then Jesus said to them, "You do not know what you are asking. Are you able to drink the cup that I drink or take the plunge that I take?"

They told him, "We are able!"

Then Jesus said to them, "You will drink the cup I drink and take the plunge that I take, but the rights to sit at my right and left hands are not mine to give. These rights belong to those for whom they have been prepared."

When the ten heard this, they began to get upset at James and John. Then Jesus summoned them and told them, "You know that those who think they rule over the nations tyrannize them, and their important ones domineer over them. This is not the case with you. On the contrary, whoever wants to become important among you must be your servant, and whoever wants to become the chief must be the slave of everyone. You see, the Son of Man did not even come to be served but instead to serve and give his life as a ransom for many."

Then they entered Jericho. While he, his disciples, and a large crowd were coming out of Jericho, a blind beggar (Bartimaeus, the son of Timaeus) was sitting beside the road. He heard, "It is Jesus the Nazarene," and began to cry out and speak: "Son of David! Jesus! Show compassion to me!"

Many people were reprimanding him, trying to keep him quiet, but he cried out even more: "Son of David! Show compassion to me!"

Then Jesus stopped and said, "Call for him."

They called for the blind man and said, "Cheer up! He is calling for you!" So he threw off his outer robe, leapt up, and went to Jesus.

Then Jesus answered him, "What do you want me to do for you?"

The blind man said to him, "Rabbi, I want to see!"

Then Jesus told him, "Go—your faith has delivered you." Immediately he received his sight and followed Jesus on the road.

WHEN HE HAD COME NEAR JERUSALEM TO BETHPHAGE AND Bethany, at the Mount of Olives, he sent two of his disciples and told them, "Go into the village in front of you. Immediately after you have entered it, you will find a harnessed foal no one has ever ridden. Untie it and bring it to me. If anyone asks you, 'What are you doing,' say: 'The Master needs it, and he will send it back here right away.'"

So they went and found a harnessed foal beside a door on the square, and they untied it. Some people standing there asked them, "What are you doing untying the foal?" So they told them just what Jesus had said, and they let them go. They brought the foal to Jesus and put their robes on it. Then Jesus sat on it.

Many of them spread their robes out on the road, while others cut down leafy branches from the field. They went in front of him and behind him, crying out,

> Save us! Blessed is the one who comes in the Master's name!

Blessed is the coming kingdom of David our father!
Save us in the highest heaven!

So he entered Jerusalem and the temple complex and looked around at everything, but since the time was already late, he went out to Bethany with the twelve.

The next morning, he was hungry as they were going out from Bethany. When he saw a fig tree in the distance in full leaf, he went toward it to try to find some fruit on it. But when he came up to it, he found nothing but leaves because it was not the season for figs. Then he spoke to it: "May no one ever eat fruit from you again—never!" Now his disciples heard him say this.

So he entered Jerusalem and went into the temple complex and began to throw out the people who were buying and selling in the temple. He overturned the tables belonging to the moneychangers, as well as the seats of those who were selling doves. Furthermore, he would not allow anyone to carry merchandise through the temple. He began to teach and tell them, "Is it not written that:

'My house will be called a house of prayer by all the nations?'
Yet you have made it a 'lair of thieves!'

Now the chief priests and scribes heard this and began to seek a way that they could kill him. You see, they were afraid of him because the whole crowd was amazed by his teaching.

When it had become very late, he went out from the city. Then, as they were passing by in the morning, they saw the fig tree—it had withered from the roots up!

Peter was reminded of what happened with the tree, and he said to Jesus, "Look, Rabbi! The tree that you cursed has withered!"

Then Jesus answered them, "Have faith in God! I am truly telling you: whoever tells this mountain, 'Get up and be thrown into the sea,' and does not doubt in their heart but instead believes that what they say will happen—it will happen for them! Because of this, I am telling you—believe that you have received everything you pray for or ask for, and it will happen for you. Furthermore, whenever you stop to pray, forgive anything that you might have against anyone so that your Father who is in heaven will also forgive you of the wrongs you have done."

THEN THEY AGAIN CAME TO JERUSALEM, AND WHILE HE WAS walking around in the temple, the chief priests, scribes, and elders approached him and asked him, "By what authority are you doing these things? Who has given you this authority so that you are doing these things?"

But Jesus said to them, "I will ask you one question; answer me, and I will tell you what authority I have for doing these things. John's immersion—was it from heaven or from men? Answer me."

Then they discussed among themselves. They said, "If we say, 'From heaven,' he will say, 'Then why did you not believe in him?' Yet, can we really say, 'From men?'" (You see, they were afraid of the crowd because everyone genuinely considered John to be a prophet.) So they answered Jesus by saying, "We do not know."

So Jesus said to them, "I will not tell you what authority I have for doing these things either."

Then he began to speak to them in allegories: "A man planted a vineyard. He set up a fence around it, dug a winepress, built a tower, and rented it out to farmers. Then he went away on a journey. In time, he sent a slave to the farmers so that he could receive some of the vineyard's fruit from the farmers. They took him, whipped him, and sent him away empty-handed. He sent another slave back to them, and they beat him on the head and insulted him. Then he sent another one, and they killed him. He sent many others. The farmers whipped some of them and killed others of them. The man still had one dear son. He finally sent him to them and said, "They will respect my son." But the farmers said to themselves, "This is the heir! Come on! Let's kill him, and the inheritance will be ours! So they took him, killed him, and threw him out of the vineyard. What will the master of the vineyard do? He will come, annihilate those farmers, and give the vineyard to others! Surely you have read this Scripture:

> The stone that the builders rejected—
> That very stone has become the chief cornerstone.
> This was brought about by the Master,
> And it is wonderful in our eyes!"

Then they sought to arrest him because they knew that he had spoken the allegory about them, but they were afraid of the crowd, so they released him and went away. They sent some of the Pharisees and Herod's sympathizers to him so that they could ensnare him by what he said. When they arrived, they said to him, "Teacher, we know that you are true and that you do not care about anyone's opinion because you are not partial toward people's appearances. No, you teach God's way with truth! Is it right to pay taxes to Caesar or not? Should we give it, or should we not?"

But he saw their hypocrisy and said to them, "Why are you testing me? Bring me a denarius so that I may look at it." Then they brought it, and he said, "Whose image and inscription is this?"

They said to him, "Caesar's."

Then Jesus told them, "Give back to Caesar what belongs to Caesar, and give back to God what belongs to God." They were amazed by him!

Next, some Sadducees approached him (they claim that there is no resurrection), and they asked him, "Teacher, Moses wrote to us: 'If some brother dies and leaves behind a wife without a child, his brother should take the wife and bring up a descendant for his brother.' There were seven brothers, and the first one took a wife and died leaving no descendant. Then the second brother took her and died without leaving a descendant. The same happened with the third, and so the seven brothers left no descendant. Last of all, the woman died too. In the resurrection, if they are ever raised, whose wife will she be? You see, all seven of them had her as a wife."

Jesus told them, "Is this not the reason you are misguided: because you do not know the Scriptures or God's power? You see, when the dead are raised, they neither marry nor give in marriage. Instead, they are like angels in heaven. Now as for the notion that the dead are not raised: have you never read in the book of Moses around the 'burning bush' passage that God told him, 'I am the God of Abraham, the God of Isaac, and the God of Jacob?' He is not a God of the dead, but of the living! You are greatly misguided!"

Then one of the scribes approached when he heard them debating. When he saw him answer them well, he asked him, "Which is the prime command of them all?"

Jesus answered him, "The primary command is: 'Listen, Israel! The Master—our God—is the only Master, and you are to love the Master your God with all your heart, with all your soul, with all your understanding, and with all your strength.' The second one is: 'You are to love your neighbor as yourself.' There is no greater command than these."

Then the scribe said to him, "Well said, Teacher! You have truthfully said that he is 'the only Master,' and 'there is no other beside him.' Also, to love him with all one's heart, with all one's understanding, and with all one's strength—and to love one's neighbor as himself—is worth more than all the burnt offerings and sacrifices!"

When Jesus saw that he had responded thoughtfully, he told him, "You are not far from God's kingdom!" Then no one dared to ask him questions anymore.

So when Jesus was teaching in the temple, he questioned in return: "How do the scribes say that the Messiah is David's son? David himself says by the Holy Spirit,

> The Master said to my Master: 'Sit at my right hand
> Until I put your enemies under your feet.'

"David himself calls him 'Master;' so how is he David's son?"

The huge crowd enjoyed listening to him.

While he was teaching, he also said, "Watch out for the scribes who want to walk around in long robes, who seek greetings in the marketplaces, the best seats in the assemblies, and the best places at the table at meals! They consume the houses of widows and make long prayers just for show. These will receive a greater condemnation!"

Now as he sat across from the contribution box, he watched as the crowd put coins into the box. Many rich people put in a lot of money. Then one poor widow came and put in two small coins that added up to the value of a penny. Jesus called for his disciples and told them, "I am truly telling you that this poor widow has put in more than anyone who has put money into the contribution box. You see, they have all put in money from their leftovers, but she has contributed everything she had from the money she needed—her whole livelihood!"

As he was going out of the temple complex, one of his disciples said to him, "Teacher! Look how magnificent the stones and buildings are!"

Jesus told him, "Do you see these large buildings? Not even one stone here will be left upon another stone—not one will escape destruction."

While he was sitting on the Mount of Olives across from the temple, Peter, James, John, and Andrew asked him privately, "Tell us: when will these things happen? What will be the sign when all these things are about to come to an end?"

Jesus began speaking to them: "Be careful that no one deceives you. Many will come in my name, saying 'I AM,' and they will deceive many people. But when you hear about wars and rumors of wars, do not be worried—this must happen, but it will not yet be the end. You see, one nation will rise up against another—one kingdom against another. There will be earthquakes everywhere—there will be famines. These are the beginning of the birth pains.

"Yet you need to look out for yourselves! They will hand you over to the courts, and you will be flogged in their assemblies. You will be presented before rulers and kings because of me to testify to them, and the Good Message must be preached to all nations first. So whenever they lead you to hand you over to them, do not be concerned what you will say. On the contrary, you are to speak precisely what you are given at that time. You see, you are not the ones who will be speaking—it is the Holy Spirit. A brother will betray his brother to death—and a father his son. Children will rebel against their parents and put them to death. Furthermore, you will be hated by everyone because of my name. Yet whoever is persistent to the end—that one will be saved!

"But when you see the 'desecrating sacrilege' standing where it is forbidden to be" (May the reader understand!), "then those who are in Judea must flee to the mountains. Whoever is on the top of their house must not go down or enter it to take anything from their house. Whoever is in the field must not even turn back to grab their robe. Those who are pregnant and nursing in those days are going to be in trouble!

"Pray that it will not happen in winter because those days will be a distress such as has never happened from the beginning of the world that God created until now—and it will never happen again! Unless the Master had cut short those days, not a single person would be saved. But because of the chosen ones whom he has chosen, those days have been shortened.

"So then, if someone tells you, 'Look! Here is the Messiah! Look over there!' do not believe them. You see, many false messiahs and false prophets will rise up and provide signs and wonders so that they might deceive the chosen ones, if possible. But you need to be careful because I have told you everything.

"No, in those days, after that distress,
The sun will be darkened, and the moon will not provide its light.
The stars will be falling from the sky,
And the forces that are in the sky will be shaken.

"Then they will see the Son of Man coming in clouds with great and glorious power. Then he will send the angels and gather up his chosen ones from the four winds, from the end of the earth to the end of the sky.

"Learn the allegory from the fig tree: when the branch has already become tender and sprouts leaves, you know that the summer is near. This is what you should do—when you see these things happening, know that it is near—at the door!

"I am truly telling you—this generation will not pass away until all these things happen. Heaven and earth will pass away, but my words will never pass away.

"But as for that day or hour, no one knows—neither the angels in heaven nor the Son—except for the Father.

"Watch out! Pay attention because you do not know when the time will be. Just like a man who left his house to go on a journey and gave authority to each one of his slaves over his business—he commanded the gatekeeper to keep watch. So you must be watchful because you do not know when the Master of the house is coming, whether it is evening, midnight, dawn, or in the morning. Otherwise, he may come suddenly and find you sleeping. What I am saying to you, I say to everyone—watch out!"

NOW THE PASSOVER AND THE FEAST OF UNLEAVENED BREAD were two days away, so the chief priests and scribes were looking for a way to arrest him underhandedly and kill him. You see, they said, "Not during the feast, or there will be a riot from the people."

So while he was reclining to eat in Bethany at the house of Simon the leper, a woman came in who had a flask of very expensive perfume (made of pure nard). She broke the flask and poured it onto Jesus's head.

Now some of the men expressed their anger toward one another: "Why has this perfume been wasted?" They reprimanded her harshly: "This perfume could have been sold for almost a year's salary and donated to the poor!"

But Jesus said, "Leave her alone! Why are you giving her a hard time? She has done a good thing for me. You see, you will always have the poor with you, and you can do good things for them whenever you want, but you will not always have me. She has done what she could—she has taken the initiative to anoint my body for burial. I am truly telling you: wherever the Good Message is proclaimed throughout the world, what this woman has done will also be told in memory of her."

Then Judas Iscariot (who was one of the twelve) went out to the chief priests to betray him to them. When they heard this, they were happy and promised to give him money. So he began to seek a convenient way to betray him.

On the first day of the Feast of Unleavened Bread, after they had sacrificed the Passover lamb, his disciples said to him, "Where do you want us to go and prepare for you to eat the Passover meal?"

Then he sent two of his disciples, telling them: "Go into the city, and a man will meet you carrying a ceramic jug of water. Follow him, and wherever he enters, tell the homeowner that the Teacher says, 'Where is my guest room, where I may eat the Passover meal with my disciples?' Then he will show you a large room upstairs, furnished and ready. Prepare the meal for us there."

So the disciples went out and entered the city. They found it just as he had told them and prepared the Passover meal.

When evening came, he arrived with the twelve. While they were seated and eating, Jesus said, "I am truly telling you—one of you who is eating with me will betray me."

They began to get upset, and one by one they asked him, "It is not I, is it?"

He said to them, "It is one of the twelve, one who is dipping bread into the dish with me. You see, the Son of Man will go away just as it has been written about him, but that man by whom the Son of man is betrayed will be in trouble—it would have been better for that man if he had not been born."

While they were still eating, he took bread, blessed it, broke it, and gave it to them. He said, "Take it: this is my body." Then he took the cup, gave thanks, and gave it to them, so they all drank from it. Then he said to them, "This is my blood of the covenant, which is being shed for many people. I am truly telling you—I will never again drink from the fruit of the vine until that day that I drink it in a new way in God's kingdom."

Then they sang praises and went out to the Mount of Olives. Jesus said to them, "You will all be turned against me because it is written:

I will strike the shepherd, and the sheep will be scattered.

"But after I have been raised, I will go ahead of you to Galilee."

Then Peter told him, "Even if everyone turns against you, I will not!"

Jesus said to him, "I am truly telling you: today—this very night, before the rooster crows twice—you will refuse to acknowledge me three times."

Then Peter began to speak more emphatically: "Even if I have to die with you, I will never refuse to acknowledge you." All the disciples spoke this way too.

THEN THEY CAME TO THE FIELD CALLED GETHSEMANE, AND Jesus said to his disciples: "Sit here while I pray." Then he took Peter, James, and John along with him and began to get nervous and anxious. He said to them, "My soul is very unhappy—to the point of death. Stay here and watch." Then he went on a little further and fell down upon the ground. He prayed that if possible, the hour would pass from him, and he said, "My Father: everything is possible for you. Take this cup away from me. But do not do merely what I want—but what you want."

Then he went back and found them sleeping. He said to Peter, "Simon—are you asleep? Are you unable to watch for a single hour? Watch and pray so that you will not enter into temptation. You see, the spirit is ready, but the body is weak." Then he again went and prayed the same prayer as before. He came back again and found them sleeping because their eyes were heavy, and they did not know how to answer him. He went the third time and said to them, "You are asleep and resting after everything? Enough! The time has come. Look! The Son of Man is being betrayed into the hands of sinners! Let's get up and go. Look! The one who betrays me is near!"

Immediately, while he was still speaking, Judas arrived (one of the twelve), and a crowd was with him, with swords and clubs. They came from the chief priests, scribes, and elders. Now the one betraying him had given them a signal by saying, "The one I kiss—he is the one. Arrest him and escort him away." So when he arrived, right away he approached him and said, "Rabbi!" and kissed him. Then they put their hands on him and arrested him. Then one of those who were present with Jesus drew a sword and struck the high priest's slave, cutting off his ear.

Then Jesus responded, telling them, "Have you come out with swords and clubs to apprehend me like an insurgent? Every day I was with you, teaching in the temple, and you did not arrest me! But this has happened so that the scriptures would be fulfilled."

Then everyone left him and ran away. One young man who followed him was wearing only fine-linen undergarments, and they grabbed him—but he left behind his undergarments and ran away naked.

They led Jesus away to the high priest, and all the chief priests, elders, and scribes had assembled. Peter also followed them from a distance until they entered the gates of the high priest's house, so he was sitting together with the court officers and warming himself by the fire.

Now the chief priests and all the Jewish Council were seeking testimony against Jesus so that they could put him to death, but they found none. You see, many people testified falsely about him, but their testimonies did not corroborate. Some even got up and testified falsely about him, saying: "We heard him saying, 'I will destroy this handmade sanctuary, and in three days I will build another one not made by hand!'" Yet their testimony did not even corroborate in this statement.

Then the high priest got up in front of them and asked Jesus, "Will you not answer any of the charges that these have brought against you?"

But he remained silent and did not answer anything. The high priest again asked him, "Are you the Messiah—the Son of the Blessed One?"

Jesus answered, "I AM, and you will see the Son of Man seated at the right hand of power and coming with the clouds of the sky."

Then the high priest tore his robe and said, "Why do we need any more witnesses? You have heard his blasphemy! What is your decision?"

They all condemned him as deserving of the death penalty. Then some people began to spit on him. They covered his face and began to beat him and said to him, "Prophesy!" Then the officers beat him as they took him.

Now while Peter was down past the gate, one of the high priest's servant girls came by and saw Peter warming himself. She looked at him and said, "You were with Jesus the Nazarene too!"

But he refused to acknowledge it. He said, "I do not know him! I do not even understand what you are saying!" Then he went outside to the courtyard, and a rooster crowed.

Then the servant girl saw him and again began to tell those who were standing there, "He is one of them!"

He again refused to acknowledge it.

Then after a little while, those who were standing there said to Peter again, "You really are one of them because you are a Galilean!"

Yet he refused to acknowledge it, calling down a curse on himself and swearing an oath, stating, "I do not know this man you are talking about."

Immediately the rooster crowed a second time, and Peter remembered what Jesus had said to him: "Before a rooster crows twice, you will refuse to acknowledge me three times." Then he threw himself down and wept.

THEN, FIRST THING IN THE MORNING, THE CHIEF PRIESTS FORMED an assembly with the elders, the scribes, and the entire Jewish Council. They tied Jesus up, led him away, and handed him over to Pilate.

So Pilate asked him, "Are you really the king of the Jews?"

Jesus answered him, "You said it."

The chief priests were also accusing him of many things, so Pilate asked him again, "Are you not going to answer me? You see how many things they are accusing you of doing!" Yet Jesus did not answer anything again.

Then Pilate was amazed. Now in conjunction with the Passover Feast, he used to release one prisoner—whomever they asked. There was one named Barabbas who was shackled with some insurgents who had committed murder during the previous insurrection. So the crowd came up and began to ask what he would do for them.

Pilate answered them, "Do you want me to release the king of the Jews to you?" (You see, he knew that the chief priests had turned him in because of jealousy.)

Yet the chief priests instigated the crowd to get him to release Barabbas for them instead. Then Pilate asked them again, "So what do you want me to do with the one you call the king of the Jews?"

Then they cried out again, "Crucify him!"

Pilate asked them, "What evil thing has he done?"

Yet they cried out even more: "Crucify him!"

So since Pilate's intent was to satisfy the crowd, he released Barabbas to them and handed Jesus over so that he would be flogged and then crucified.

The soldiers led him away into the court (the praetorium) and called together the entire company of soldiers. They clothed him in a purple military cloak and placed a crown woven from thorns on him. They began to salute him: "Hail, king of the Jews!" Then they beat him on the head with a reed and spit on him, and then they knelt down and worshiped him. When they had finished mocking him, they removed the military cloak from him and put his own clothes back on him.

Next, they led him out to crucify him. They forced a bystander who was coming from the field to carry his cross. This man was a Cyrenian named Simon, the father of Alexander and Rufus.

Then they brought him to the place called Golgotha (which is translated "Skull Place") and gave him wine mixed with myrrh, but he refused to take it. They crucified him and divvied up his clothes by casting lots for them to see who would get what. Now it was about 9:00 a.m. when they crucified him. The inscription of his charges was written:

> The King of the Jews.

Also, two insurgents were crucified with him—one on his right and one on his left. Those who passed by began to make fun of him, shaking their heads and saying, "Haha! The one who was going to destroy the sanctuary and rebuild it in three days! Save yourself by coming down from the cross!"

The chief priests likewise mocked him to one another, along with the scribes. They said, "Let this messiah—this king of Israel—come down from the cross now so that we can see it and believe!" Even the ones crucified with him insulted him.

When noon arrived, darkness came over the whole land until 3:00 p.m. Then at around 3:00 p.m., Jesus cried out with a loud voice: "Eli! Eli! Lema Sabachthani?"

This is translated, "My God! My God! Why have you abandoned me?"

Some of those who were standing there listening said, "Look! He is calling for Elijah!" Someone ran and filled a sponge with sour wine; they put it on a reed and gave it to him to drink. They said, "Leave him alone! Let us see if Elijah comes to take him down!" But Jesus let out a loud shout and breathed his last.

Then the sanctuary's curtain was ripped in two from top to bottom. When the centurion, who was standing right across from him, saw that he had breathed his last, he said: "This man really was a son of God!"

Now there were also some women who were watching from a distance. Among them were Mary (the one from Magdala), Mary (the mother of the younger James and Joseph), and

Salome. While they were following him in Galilee, they provided for him. Many others also were there who had come up to Jerusalem with him.

Now evening had already fallen, and since it was Friday—that is, the day before the Sabbath—Joseph from Arimathea took courage to go in to Pilate and ask for the body of Jesus. He was a reputable member of the Jewish Council, and he himself was waiting anxiously for God's kingdom. Pilate was amazed that Jesus had died so soon, and he summoned the centurion and asked him if Jesus was already dead. Once he had found out from the centurion, he presented the body to Joseph. So Joseph bought some fine-linen cloth, took him down from the cross, and rolled him up in the cloth. Then he placed him in a tomb that he had carved out of solid rock and rolled a stone against the entrance to the tomb. Mary (the one from Magdala) and Mary (the mother of Joseph) were watching where he placed him.

WHEN THE SABBATH HAD ENDED, MARY (OF MAGDALA), MARY (the mother of James), and Salome bought spices so that they could anoint him. So very early on the first day of the week—as the sun was rising—they went to the tomb. They were saying to one another, "Who will roll away the stone from the entrance to the tomb?" Then they looked up and saw that the stone had been rolled away! (It was a very large stone.)

After they had entered the tomb, they saw a young man sitting on their right, clothed in a long, white robe, and they were nervous.

Then he said to them, "Do not be nervous. You are looking for Jesus the Nazarene, who was crucified. He has been raised—he is not here! Look—this is where they laid him. Now—go tell his disciples, as well as Peter, that he is going ahead of you to Galilee. You will see him there, just as he told you."

Then they came out and ran away from the tomb because trembling and ecstasy had seized them. They said nothing to anyone because they were afraid.

After he had been raised, early on the first day of the week, he first appeared to Mary (the one from Magdala). He had cast seven demons out of her. She went and reported it to those who had come with him to Jerusalem, who were now mourning and weeping. Even when they heard that he was alive and had been seen by her, they did not believe.

After this, he appeared in a different form to two of them as they were walking in a field. They went away and reported it to the others—they did not believe them either.

Finally, he appeared to the eleven while they were sitting to eat and reprimanded them for their lack of faith and hard-heartedness because they did not believe those who had seen that he had risen from the dead. Then he said to them, "Go into the world—everywhere—and preach the Good Message to every creature. Whoever believes and is immersed will be saved, but whoever does not have faith will be condemned. These signs will accompany those who believe: they will cast out demons in my name. They will speak in foreign languages. They will pick up snakes with their hands. Even if they drink poison, it will not hurt them at all. They will lay their hands on sick people, and they will become well."

Then, after Jesus the Master had spoken to them, he was taken up into heaven and sat down at the right hand of God. Then they went out and preached everywhere—with the Master working alongside them, confirming the Message with the signs that accompanied them.

ACCORDING TO
LUKE

Most excellent Theophilus:

SINCE MANY HAVE ATTEMPTED TO ORGANIZE A NARRATIVE ABOUT the things that have been accomplished among us—as they were handed down by those who have been eyewitnesses and servants since the beginning—it seemed good to me that I should also write to you from the beginning because I have investigated everything meticulously. Thus, you may confidently be well informed about the statements that you have heard.

This happened in the days of King Herod of Judea. There was a priest named Zechariah who was from Abijah's division of priests. His wife was from among the daughters of Aaron, and her name was Elizabeth. Now they were both righteous in God's sight and conducted themselves faultlessly in all the Master's commands and regulations. Yet they did not have a child because Elizabeth was infertile, and both of them were advanced in years.

It happened while he was serving as priest in the order that his class of priests served before God. Per the priests' customs, he was appointed by lot to burn incense, so he entered the sanctuary of the Master. Also, the full number of the people were praying outside at the time to burn incense. So an angel from the Master appeared to him, standing to the right of the altar for burning incense. Zechariah became worried when he saw this, and fear fell over him.

Then the angel spoke to him, "Do not be afraid, Zechariah, because your prayer has been answered, and your wife Elizabeth will bear you a son. You will name him John. He will be a joy and celebration for you, and many will celebrate because of his birth. You see, he will be great before the Master. He will never drink wine or alcohol, and he will be filled with the Holy Spirit while he is still in his mother's womb. He will turn many of the sons of Israel back to their God. He himself will go before God in the spirit and power of Elijah so that he can turn the hearts of fathers to their children and the disobedient to the mindset of the righteous so that he can get the prepared nation ready for the Master."

Then Zechariah said to the angel, "How can I know this? You see, I am old, and my wife is also advanced in her age."

Then the angel responded to him, "I am Gabriel, who stands ready before God. I was sent to speak to you and give you this good message. Now look—you will be silent and unable to speak until the day this happens because you did not believe my words that will be fulfilled in their time."

Now the people were waiting for Zechariah and were wondering why he was staying in the sanctuary so long. Then, when he came out, he was unable to speak to them, so they recognized that he had seen a vision in the sanctuary. He was making gestures at them and remained unable to speak. Then, once the days of his service were completed, he went back to his house.

After those days, his wife Elizabeth conceived and kept herself hidden for five months, saying, "This is what the Master has done for me in the days when he took notice of me to take away my shame among men."

DURING THE SIXTH MONTH, THE ANGEL GABRIEL WAS SENT BY God to a city of Galilee called Nazareth, to a virgin who was engaged to a man named Joseph. He was of the house of David, and the virgin's name was Mary. The angel went inside to her and said, "Rejoice, favored one: the Master is with you." But she was worried by the message and wondered what kind of greeting this must be.

Then the angel said to her, "Do not be afraid, Mary, because you have found favor with God. Now look—you will conceive in your womb and bear a son, and you will name him Jesus. He will be great, and he will be called the Son of the Highest One, and God the Master will give him the throne of his father David, so he will reign over the house of Jacob forever, and his kingdom will not have an end."

Then Mary said to the angel, "How will this be since I have not been with a man?"

Then the angel said to her, "The Holy Spirit will come over you, and power from the Highest One will overshadow you; so the holy one who is born will be called the Son of God. Now look—your relative Elizabeth herself has also conceived a son in her old age, and this is the sixth month for her who was called barren. This is because nothing will be impossible for God."

Then Mary said, "See, I am the Master's servant. May it happen to me as you have said." Then the angel left her.

In those days, Mary got up and went in a hurry to the hill country, to a city in Judah. Then she went into the house of Zechariah and greeted Elizabeth. It just so happened that, when Elizabeth heard the greeting from Mary, the infant in her womb jumped, and Elizabeth became filled with the Holy Spirit. So she spoke up with a loud voice, "You are blessed among women, and the fruit of your womb is also blessed. Now how can it be that the mother of my Master has come to me? You see, as the sound of your greeting came to my ears, the infant in my womb jumped with joy. Blessed is she who believed that what was spoken to her by the Master will be fulfilled!"

Then Mary said:

> My soul magnifies the Master,
> And my spirit celebrates because of God my Savior,
> Because he has seen the humble circumstances of his servant.
> Look! From now on, all generations will bless me.
> Because the Powerful One has done great things for me.
> His name is holy,

and his mercy is for generation after generation
for those who revere him.
He has displayed strength with his arm;
and has scattered the arrogant because of what their hearts thought.
He has pulled rulers down from their thrones,
and has exalted the humble.
He has satisfied the hungry ones with good things,
and has left the wealthy ones empty.
He has come to the aid of Israel his servant,
To demonstrate mindfulness of his mercies.
Just as he said to our fathers,
To Abraham and to his posterity forever.

Then Mary stayed with her about three months and then returned to her house.

So the time for Elizabeth to bear her child was completed, and she gave birth to a son. Her neighbors and relatives heard that the Master had increased his mercy with her, and they celebrated with her. Now it happened on the eighth day, when they went to circumcise the child, that they named him after his father, Zechariah. So his mother responded, "No! He should be called John instead."

They said to her, "No one from your family is called by that name."

Then they motioned to his father to see what he might want to call him. So he asked for a writing tablet and wrote, "John is his name," and everyone was surprised. But then his mouth was opened instantly—and his tongue as well—and he began speaking, praising God. So it happened that fear came over all their neighbors, and all these things were talked about throughout all the hill country of Judea. Everyone who heard kept this in their hearts, saying, "So what will this child be because even the hand of the Master was with him!"

Then Zechariah, his father, was filled with the Holy Spirit and began to prophesy:

> Blessed is the Master, the God of Israel,
> Because he has looked after and provided a ransom for his nation,
> He has raised a horn of salvation for us
> in the house of his servant David.
> Just as he spoke through the mouth of his holy prophets of old—
> Salvation from our enemies and from the hand of all who hate us.
> He has treated our fathers mercifully,
> and has kept his holy covenant in mind.
> He has sworn an oath with Abraham our father
> to grant that we should be fearlessly rescued from the hand of our enemies,
> To serve him in holiness and righteousness
> In his presence all our days.
> And now you, child, will be called a prophet of the Highest One.
> because you will go before the presence of the Master to prepare his way,
> To share knowledge of salvation to his people,

> With the forgiveness of their sins.
> Because of the merciful compassion of our God,
> the dawn of heaven will look after us.
> To appear to those sitting in darkness and the shadow of death,
> So that it may strengthen our feet for the way of peace.

Now the child grew and developed a strong spirit, and he was in the desert until the day of his commission to Israel.

IT JUST SO HAPPENED IN THOSE DAYS THAT A DECREE CAME DOWN from Caesar Augustus that the whole empire should be registered. This was the first census that took place while Quirinius was governing Syria. So everyone went to be registered—each person went to their hometown. Now Joseph went up from the city of Nazareth, Galilee, to Judea—to the city of David, which is called Bethlehem—because he was from the house and family line of David. Thus he went to be registered with Mary, who was engaged to him and was pregnant. Well, it so happened while they were there that the days for her to give birth were completed, so she gave birth to her firstborn son. They swaddled him and laid him in a feeding trough because there was no room for them in the residential quarters.

Now some shepherds were staying outside in the same region, keeping watch over their flock during the night. So an angel from the Master appeared to them, and the Master's glory was shining around them, so they became extremely afraid.

Then the angel spoke to them, "Do not be afraid. Look! I am bringing a message of great joy to you that will be for the whole nation. You see, a savior has been born today in the City of David—he is the anointed Master! Also, this will be a sign for you—you will find an infant swaddled and placed in a feeding trough."

Then suddenly a large number of the army of heaven appeared with the angel, praising God and saying:

> Glory to God in the highest places, and peace on earth;
> Good will among mankind!

Then, as the angels went away from them into heaven, the shepherds talked with one another, "Let's go, now, to Bethlehem so that we can see this thing that has happened—which the Master has revealed to us."

They hurried on and found Mary and Joseph, as well as the infant placed in the feeding trough. When they saw this, they explained in detail the message that was told to them about this child. Then everyone who heard this was amazed at what the shepherds said to them, and Mary treasured all these things as she considered them in her heart. So the shepherds returned, giving glory and praise to God because everything that they had seen and heard was just as they were told.

After eight days had passed, when it was time to circumcise him, they named him Jesus, the name given to him by the angel before he was conceived.

Then, when the days of their purification had passed based on the Law of Moses, they brought him to Jerusalem to present him before the Master just as it is written in the Master's

ACCORDING TO LUKE

Law, "Every male who opens the womb will be called holy to the Master." They also went to offer a sacrifice, in accordance with what was said in the Master's Law, "A pair of turtledoves or two young pigeons."

Now get this—there was a man in Jerusalem whose name was Simeon. This man was righteous and devout, waiting for the consolation of Israel. The Holy Spirit was upon him, and he had been advised by the Holy Spirit that he would not see death before he would see the Master's Messiah. So he came by the Spirit into the temple. Now as the parents were bringing the little child Jesus inside so that they could fulfill the customs of the Law for him, Simeon took him up into his arms, praised God, and said:

> Now, Master, you can dismiss your servant in peace, just as you said,
> Because my eyes have seen your salvation, which you prepared in the presence of all nations;
> A light for enlightening the gentiles and glory for Israel your nation.

So his father and mother were amazed at the things that were being said about him. Simeon then blessed them and spoke to Mary, his mother, "Look, this one is destined to bring about the fall and rise of many in Israel and be a symbol that will face opposition—a sword will cut through your own very soul—so that the thoughts of many hearts will be revealed."

There was also a prophetess, Anna the daughter of Penuel, of the tribe of Asher. She was advanced in years, having lived with a husband for seven years from her virginity, and she had been a widow for the last eighty-four years. She never left the temple; she worshiped with fasting and praying night and day. At that very moment, she came up and praised God, talking about him to everyone who was waiting for the redemption of Jerusalem.

Then, when everything had been fulfilled according to the Master's Law, they headed back toward Galilee to their home city of Nazareth, and the child grew and gained strength and was filled with wisdom, and God's favor was on him.

Now his parents used to go to Jerusalem every year for the Passover Festival. When he was twelve years old, they went up to the festival according to that custom. When they had completed the days of the festival, and while they began going back, the boy Jesus stayed back in Jerusalem, but his parents did not know. You see, they thought he was with the caravan. They went a day's worth of travel and went looking for him among their relatives and acquaintances. When they could not find him, they returned to Jerusalem to look for him. As it happened, they found him after three days, sitting in the midst of the teachers in the temple, listening to them and asking them questions. Everyone who heard him was amazed at his understanding and answers. When his parents saw him, they were overwhelmed. His mother said to him, "Child, why have you treated us like this? Look! Your father and I have been worried sick looking for you."

Then he said to them, "Why were you looking for me? Did you not know that I needed to be involved in my Father's doings?"

They didn't understand what he had said to them.

Then he went down with them and arrived in Nazareth and was submissive to them. His mother treasured all these things in her heart. Then Jesus progressed in wisdom, age, and favor with God and people.

IT WAS THE FIFTEENTH YEAR OF THE REIGN OF TIBERIUS CAESAR, and Pontius Pilate was presiding over Judea. Herod was tetrarch of Galilee, his brother Philip was tetrarch of the region of Ituraea and Trachonitis, and Lysanias was tetrarch of Abilene. This was during the high priesthood of Annas and Caiaphas. The word of God came to John, the son of Zechariah, while he was in the desert. He went throughout all the neighboring region of the Jordan, preaching an immersion of repentance for the forgiveness of sins, just as it was written in the book of sayings of Isaiah the prophet:

> A voice cries out in the desert:
> Prepare the way for the Master.
> Make his paths straight.
> Every valley will be filled,
> And every mountain and hill will be lowered.
> What is crooked will become straight,
> And what is rough will become a smooth road.
> And all flesh will see God's salvation.

So he used to speak to the crowds that would come out to be immersed by him, "You spawn of snakes! Who showed you how to flee from the coming wrath? Then you need to bear fruit consistent with repentance and not begin saying among yourselves, 'We have Father Abraham.' You see, I am telling you that God is able to raise up children to Abraham from these stones. The ax is already set against the root of the trees. So every tree that does not produce good fruit will be cut down and thrown into the fire."

The crowd also asked him questions, "So what should we do?"

He answered them, "Whoever has two undershirts should share with someone who has none, and whoever has food should do the same."

Also, tax collectors came to be immersed. They asked him, "Teacher, what should we do?"

He told them, "Make a practice of taking nothing more than what is ordered of you."

Soldiers also asked him, "What about us—what should we do?"

He told them, "Do not extort anyone or give false accusations, and be satisfied with your wages."

At this time, the people were in anticipation, and they all were debating in their hearts about whether John himself might actually be the Messiah. John answered them all, "While I immerse you in water, one is coming who is stronger than I am—I am not worthy to untie the straps of his sandals. He will immerse you in the Holy Spirit and fire. The winnowing fork is in his hand so that he can clean out his threshing floor, gather the wheat into his barn, and consume the chaff with unquenchable fire."

In this way, he proclaimed the Good Message to the people with many other encouraging words. But when Herod the Tetrarch was reprimanded by him regarding Herod's brother Philip's wife Herodias and all the evil things that Herod did, he added this to them all—he locked John in a prison.

It just so happened when the whole nation was being immersed—and after Jesus also had been immersed and was praying—that the skies opened, and the Holy Spirit descended upon him in a physical form like a dove. A voice came from the sky, "You are my dear Son; I am very happy with you!"

Now Jesus, who was about thirty years old when he began his work, was (it was thought):

> Son of Joseph, son of Eli, son of Matthat,
> Son of Levi, son of Melchi, son of Jannai,
> Son of Joseph, son of Mattathias, son of Amos,
> Son of Nahum, son of Hesli, son of Naggai,
> Son of Maath, son of Mattathias, son of Semein,
> Son of Josech, son of Joda, son of Johana,
> Son of Rhesa, son of Zerubbabel, son of Salathiel,
> Son of Neri, son of Melchi, son of Addi,
> Son of Kosam, son of Elmadam, son of Her,
> Son of Jesus, son of Eliezer, son of Jorim,
> Son of Matthat, son of Levi, son of Simeon,
> Son of Judah, son of Joseph, son of Jonam,
> Son of Eliakim, son of Melea, son of Menna,
> Son of Mattatha, son of Nathan, son of David,
> Son of Jesse, son of Obed, son of Boaz,
> Son of Shelah, son of Nahshon, son of Aminadab,
> Son of Admin, son of Arni, son of Hezrom,
> Son of Phares, son of Judah, son of Jacob,
> Son of Isaac, son of Abraham, son of Terah,
> Son of Nahor, son of Serug, son of Reu,
> Son of Peleg, son of Heber, son of Shelah,
> Son of Kenan, son of Arphaxad, son of Shem,
> Son of Noah, son of Lamech, son of Methuselah,
> Son of Enoch, son of Jared, son of Mahalalel,
> Son of Kenan, son of Enosh, son of Seth,
> Son of Adam, son of God.

Then Jesus was filled with the Spirit and returned from the Jordan. By the Spirit, he went into the desert and was tempted by the devil for forty days. He did not eat anything in those days, and after they were completed, he was famished. Then the devil said to him, "If you are God's Son, tell this stone to become bread."

Jesus answered him, "It is written: 'Man does not live by bread only.'"

Then the devil led him up and showed him all the kingdoms of the world in a moment's time and said to him, "I will give you this authority and glory over them all because it has been given to me, and I will give it to whomever I want. So then, if you will bow down before me, it all will be yours."

Then Jesus answered him, "It is written: 'You must bow down to the Master your God and worship him alone.'"

Then he led him into Jerusalem and set him upon the pinnacle of the temple and told him,

"If you are God's Son, throw yourself down from here because it is written: 'Regarding you, it has been commanded to his angels that they must guard you,' and, 'They will lift you up in their hands so that you will not stub your toe against a stone.'"

Then Jesus answered him, "It has been said: 'Do not test God your Master.'"

Then, after the devil had finished every temptation, he went away from him for a while.

THEN JESUS RETURNED TO GALILEE BY THE POWER OF THE SPIRIT, and news about him went throughout all the surrounding area. So he began teaching in their synagogues and was praised by them all.

Then he went to Nazareth, where he was raised, and as was his custom, he entered the synagogue on the Sabbath day and stood up to read. The scroll of the prophet Isaiah was given to him, and he unrolled the scroll and found the place where it was written:

> The Spirit of the Master is upon me
> Because he has appointed me
> To bring good news to the poor,
> He has sent me
> To preach release to the captives
> And the restoration of sight to the blind,
> To send out the brokenhearted in freedom,
> To announce the year of the Master's welcome.

Then he rolled up the scroll, handed it back to the attendant, and sat down. The eyes of everyone in the synagogue were fixed on him. So he began to speak to them, "Today this Scripture has been fulfilled with you in the audience."

Everyone was talking about him and was amazed at the gracious words that came out of his mouth. They said, "Is this not Joseph's son?"

He said to them, "Surely you will quote this allegory to me: 'Physician, heal yourself.' Do here in your hometown what we heard happened in Capernaum!" Then he said, "I am truly telling you—no prophet is welcome in his hometown. I'm telling you the truth—there were many widows in Israel in the days of Elijah, when the sky was shut for three years and six months, and a severe famine came over all the land. But Elijah was not sent to any of them but instead to a widow of Zarephath, Sidon. Furthermore, there were many lepers in Israel in the time of the prophet Elisha, but none of them was cleansed—only Naaman the Syrian."

Then everyone listening to this in the synagogue was filled with rage, and they got up and threw him out of the city. They led him to the edge of the cliff of the mountain on which their city was built so that they could throw him off of it. But he passed through the midst of them and went away.

Then he went down to the city of Capernaum, Galilee. He began teaching them on the Sabbaths, and they were amazed at his teaching because his message was spoken with authority.

In that synagogue was a man who had spirits from an unclean demon. It cried out with a loud voice, "Ah! What do you have to do with us, Jesus of Nazareth? Have you come to destroy us? I know who you are—God's holy one!"

Then Jesus scolded him, saying, "Be quiet and come out of him!"

So the demon threw the man down in front of him and came out of him, doing him no harm. Amazement came over everyone, and they said to one another, "What kind of message is this? He even commands the unclean spirits with authority and power, and they come out!" News about him went out everywhere in the surrounding region.

Then he went up from the synagogue and entered the house of Simon. Simon's mother-in-law was suffering with a terrible fever, so they asked Jesus about her. He stood above her and rebuked the fever, and it left her. Immediately, she got up and began to serve them.

As the sun was going down, everyone who had someone who was sick—there were various kinds of diseases—brought them to him, and he put his hands on each one of them and healed them. Also, demons went out from many people, crying out, "You are the Son of God!" But he scolded them and would not let them say this because they knew he was the Messiah.

When day came, he went out to a deserted place. Then the crowds searched for him and came out to him and tried to hold onto him to prevent him from leaving them. He said to them, "I need to preach the Good Message of God's kingdom to the other cities as well because this is why I was sent." So he continued teaching in the Jews' synagogues.

AS THE CROWDS CAME AND PRESSED AROUND HIM TO HEAR God's message, he was standing beside the Sea of Gennesaret. He saw two boats moored beside the seashore, and the fishermen had stepped out of them and were washing their nets. So he stepped into one of the boats, which was Simon's, and asked him to push off a little from the shore. Then he sat and taught the crowd from the boat.

When he had finished speaking, he said to Simon, "Set out to the deep water and lower your nets to catch."

Simon answered by saying, "All night we struggled and caught nothing, but as you said, I will lower the nets."

When they did this, they caught a very large number of fish, and their nets began to break. They motioned to their partners from the other boat to come take it in with them. So they came and filled both of the boats so that they were beginning to sink. When Simon saw this, he bowed down at the knees of Jesus and said, "Leave me because I am a sinful man, Master!" You see, amazement had overcome him and all those who were with him because of the catch of fish that they had taken in. James and John, the sons of Zebedee who were Simon's partners, did the same thing.

Then Jesus said to Simon, "Do not be afraid—from now on you will catch people." So they brought their boats out onto the shore and followed him, leaving everything.

While he was in one city, get this—there was a man covered with leprosy. When he saw Jesus, he fell on his face and begged him, "Master, if you are willing, you are able to cleanse me!"

So he reached out his hand and touched him, saying, "I am willing—be cleansed!"

Immediately the leprosy left him. Jesus commanded him to tell no one, but instead, "Go show yourself to the priest and bring something for your cleansing, just as Moses commanded as a proof for them."

So the news about him spread all the more, and many crowds came together to hear him and to be healed from their sicknesses. Then he would retire back to the deserted places and pray.

ONE DAY, WHILE HE WAS TEACHING, THE PHARISEES AND teachers of the Law were also sitting there (from every town of Galilee and Judea, as well as Jerusalem), and the Master's power to heal was with him. Now get this—some men carried a man on a bed who was disabled, and they were trying to bring the man and set him down in front of Jesus. When they could not figure out how to bring him (because of the crowd), they lifted him up onto the house and lowered him with the small bed down through the roof tiles into the middle—in front of Jesus.

When he saw their faith he said, "Man, your sins are forgiven."

Then the scribes and Pharisees began to doubt, "Who is this? He is speaking blasphemy! Who is able to forgive sins, except God alone?"

But Jesus knew they were doubting and answered them, "Why are you doubting this in your hearts? Which is easier—to say, 'Your sins are forgiven,' or to say, 'Get up and walk'? Just so you know that the Son of Man has authority over the earth to forgive sins," he then said to the disabled man, "I tell you—get up, take your bed and go to your house."

Immediately the man got up in front of them, picked up the bed he had been lying on, and left for his house, praising God. Confusion gripped everyone, and they were praising God and were filled with fear, saying, "We have seen unexpected things today!"

After this, he left and saw a tax collector named Levi sitting at his tax booth. He said to him, "Follow me." So he left everything, got up, and followed him.

Then Levi hosted a great banquet for him at his house, and a large crowd of tax collectors and others who were reclining to eat with them were there. So the Pharisees and their scribes complained to his disciples, "Why do you eat and drink with the tax collectors and sinners?"

Jesus answered by telling them, "The healthy do not need a physician, but the sick do. I have not come to call the righteous—just sinners to repentance."

Then they said to him, "John's disciples fast frequently and offer prayers—and the Pharisees do the same—but you eat and drink."

Jesus said to them, "You are not able to make the bridegroom's attendants fast while the bridegroom is with them, are you? The days are coming when the bridegroom will be taken from them. Then, in those days, they will fast."

He also told an allegory to them, "No one cuts a patch from new clothing and sews it onto old clothing because if they did, it would tear the new clothing also. Furthermore, the old clothing would not match the patch that was taken from the new clothing. Also, no one puts fresh wine into old wineskins because if they did, the fresh wine would tear the wineskins, it would be poured out, and the wineskins would be ruined. On the contrary, fresh wine must be put into new wineskins, and no one wants fresh wine after drinking the old, because they say, 'The old is better.'"

On one Sabbath, when he was passing through some fields, his disciples began to pluck off and eat heads of grain, threshing it with their hands. Some of the Pharisees said, "Why are you doing what is not legal to do on the Sabbath?"

Jesus answered them, "Have you not read what David did when he and those who were with him were hungry—how he went into the house of God, took the Bread of the Presence, ate it, and then gave it to those who were with him? It was not legal for them to eat—it was for the priests only." Then he told them, "The Son of Man is Master over the Sabbath."

On another Sabbath, he went into the synagogue and began to teach. A man was there, and his right hand was paralyzed. The scribes and Pharisees followed him closely to see whether he would heal on the Sabbath so that they could find some cause for accusing him. But he knew their thoughts—he said to the man who had the paralyzed hand, "Get up and stand here in front." Then he stood there.

Jesus said to them, "I will ask you: is it right to do good or evil on the Sabbath—to save a life or to kill?" Then he looked around at them all and said to the man, "Reach out your hand."

Then he did, and his hand was restored. But they were filled with rage and discussed with one another what they should do to Jesus.

ON ONE OF THOSE DAYS, HE WENT OUT TO A MOUNTAIN TO PRAY, and he spent the night in prayer to God. When daylight came, he called for his disciples and chose twelve of them, whom he gave the title Apostles: Simon (whom he also named Peter); his brother, Andrew; James; John; Philip; Bartholemew; Matthew; Thomas; James Alphaeus; Simon (who was called the Patriot); Judas James; and Judas Iscariot (who became a traitor).

He came down and stood on a flat place with them and a large crowd of his disciples—a great number of people from throughout Judea, Jerusalem, and the seacoast of Tyre and Sidon. They came to hear him and to be healed from their diseases. Some who crowded together were cured of unclean spirits, and every crowd sought to touch him because power was coming out from him and healing everyone.

Then he raised his eyes to his disciples and began to speak:

> You who are poor are blessed,
> Because God's kingdom is yours.
> You who are now hungry are blessed,
> Because you will be satisfied.
> You who weep now are blessed,
> Because you will laugh.

You are blessed when people hate you, discriminate against you, insult you, and throw your name around as though you are evil because of the Son of Man.

Rejoice in that day and jump for joy! Look—their fathers acted in the same way toward the prophets!

> But you who are wealthy are in trouble,
> Because you are leaving your comfort.
> You who are full are in trouble,
> Because you will be hungry.
> You who are laughing now are in trouble,
> Because you will mourn and weep.
> Yare in trouble when all people speak well of you;

Their fathers acted in the same way toward the false prophets!

"In addition, I'm speaking to those who are listening: love your enemies; treat well those who hate you; bless those who curse you; pray for those who mistreat you. Turn the other cheek to the one who has hit you on one cheek. Do not withhold your undershirt from the one who takes away your outer garment. Give to the one who asks of you. Do not ask for anything back from someone who borrows from you.

"Also, whatever it is you want people to do for you, do it for them the same way. Now if you love those who love you, what kind of graciousness is that for you? You see, even sinners love those who love them. Further, if you do good for those who do good for you, what kind of graciousness is that for you? Even sinners do this. Also, if you lend to someone from whom you expect to receive it back, what kind of graciousness is that for you? Even sinners lend to sinners if they should receive an equal amount back. Instead, love your enemies, and treat them well, and lend without asking for anything in return. Then your reward will be great, and you will be sons of the Highest One because he is kind to the ungrateful and evil.

"Be compassionate just as your father is compassionate. Do not judge, and you will not be judged at all. Do not condemn, and you will not be condemned at all. Forgive and you will be forgiven. Give and it will be given to you—they will place into your lap a good measure, pressed down, shaken, and overflowing. You see, whatever measurement you use will be measured back to you."

He also told them an allegory, "A blind man cannot lead a blind man, can he? Will they not both fall into a pit? The disciple is not above his teacher. When everything has been completed, he will be like his teacher. Why do you see the splinter in your brother's eye but ignore the beam that is in your own eye? How can you tell your brother, 'Brother, let me take the splinter out of your eye,' when you yourself do not see the beam that is in your eye? You hypocrite! First, take the beam out of your eye, and then you will see clearly to take the splinter out of your brother's eye.

"You see, a good tree does not produce rotten fruit, and again, a rotten tree does not produce good fruit. Each tree is recognized by its fruit because they do not collect figs from thorns or grapes from a bramble bush. The good person produces what is good from the good treasury of their heart, and the evil person produces what is evil from the evil treasury of their heart. You see, their mouth speaks from the overflow of their heart.

"Why do you call me 'Lord, Lord,' yet you do not do what I say? Everyone who comes to me, hears my words, and does them, I will show you what they are like. They are like a man who was building a house—he dug down, went deep, and laid a foundation upon the bedrock. Then a flood came, and the surge broke against that house, but it was not able to shake the house because it was well built. But the one who hears and does not do it is like a man who was building a house upon the ground without a foundation. The surge broke against it, and immediately it fell—and the collapse of that house was intense."

NOW WHEN HE HAD FINISHED MAKING ALL THESE STATEMENTS in the audience of the people, he went to Capernaum. There was a centurion's slave who was doing so poorly he was about to die, and he was valued highly by him. When the centurion heard about Jesus, he sent him elders from the Jews, asking him to come and rescue the centurion's slave.

Then, when they came to Jesus, they called him hurriedly, saying, "He deserves for you to provide this because he loves our nation, and he himself built a synagogue for us."

So Jesus went with them. When he was not a long distance away from the house, the centurion sent friends to tell him, "Sir, do not trouble yourself—you see, I am not worthy for you to come under my roof, nor was I worthy to come to you. No—say the word and let my servant be healed. You see, I also am a man subjected to authority, and I have soldiers under my own. I tell this one, 'Go,' and he goes; and that one, 'Do this,' and he does it."

When Jesus heard this, he expressed amazement at him, turned to the crowd that was following him, and said, "I am telling you—I have not even found this kind of faith in Israel." Then he sent the envoy back to the house, and they found the slave healthy.

On the next day, he went to a city called Nain. His disciples also went with him, as well as a great crowd. As he approached the gate of the city, get this—an only son (whose mother was also a widow) had died, and he was being carried out for burial. A significant crowd of people from the city was with her. When the Master saw her, he was moved with compassion for her and told her, "Do not weep." Then he approached the coffin and touched it, and the men carrying it stopped. He said, "Young man, I tell you to get up." Then the dead man sat up and began to speak! Jesus presented him to his mother.

Fear seized everyone, and they praised God, saying, "A great prophet has come up among us!" and "God has visited his nation!" So this message about him spread throughout all Judea and all the surrounding region.

Now John's disciples reported to John about all these things, so John summoned two of his disciples and sent them to the Master, asking, "Are you the Coming One, or should we wait for another one?"

Then the men went to Jesus and said, "John the Immerser sent us to ask you—are you the Coming One, or should we wait for another one?"

During that time, he had healed many people of their illnesses, suffering, and evil spirits, and he gave many blind people the ability to see. He answered them, "Go tell John what you have seen and heard:

> The blind receive their sight, the paralyzed walk,
> Lepers are cleansed, the deaf hear,
> The dead are raised, and the poor have the Good Message preached to them.
> Blessed is the one who is not offended at me.

After John's messengers had gone, he began to tell the crowds about John, "What did you go out to the desert to see? A reed shaken by the wind? No—what did you go out to see? A man dressed in fine clothing? Look: those who are dressed in glorious clothing and luxury are among the nobility. So what did you go out to see? A prophet? Yes, I tell you, and more than a prophet. This is the one about whom was written:

> Look! I am sending my messenger into your presence.

He will prepare your way in front of you.

"I'm telling you—no one among those born of women is greater than John. But the least significant in God's kingdom is greater than he.

"Further, all people—even the tax collectors—who heard him praised the righteousness of God and were immersed with John's immersion. But the Pharisees and the lawyers disregarded God's advice for themselves and were not immersed by him.

"So to what should I compare the people of this generation, and what are they like? They are like children sitting in the marketplace and calling out to one another. They say, 'We played the flute, and you did not dance. We sang a funeral song, and you did not weep.' You see, John the Immerser came neither eating bread nor drinking wine, and you say, 'He has a demon.' The Son of Man came both eating and drinking, and you say, 'Look! That man is a glutton and drunk—a friend of tax collectors and sinners.' But wisdom is vindicated by all its children."

Someone from the Pharisees invited him to eat with him, so he went into the Pharisee's house and reclined to eat. Get this—a woman who was a sinner in the city discovered that he was reclining to eat in the Pharisee's house. She brought an alabaster jar of ointment and stood behind him, weeping beside his feet. She began to wash his feet with her tears, dry them with the hair of her head, kiss his feet, and apply the ointment.

Once the Pharisee who invited Jesus saw this, he said to himself, "This man—if he were a prophet—would have known who this woman is who is touching him and what kind of person she is because she is a sinner!"

Then Jesus answered him! He said, "Simon, I have something to say to you."

He said, "Say it, Teacher."

Jesus said, "Two debtors were indebted to one creditor. One owed five hundred days' wages, and the other, fifty. Because they did not have a way to pay, he forgave them both. So which of them will love him more?"

Simon responded, "I suppose that the one whom he forgave more would."

He said, "You have decided correctly." Then he turned toward the woman and told Simon, "Do you see this woman? I came into your house, but you have not provided me water for my feet. Yet she has rinsed my feet with her tears and dried them with her hair. You have not given me a kiss, but she—from the time I came in, she has not stopped kissing my feet. You did not anoint my head with oil, but she has anointed my feet with ointment. Because of this, I'm telling you, her many sins are forgiven—because she has loved a lot. On the other hand, the one who was forgiven a little loves little." Then he told her, "Your sins are forgiven."

Then those who were reclining at the table with him began to say to themselves, "Who is this—he also forgives sins?"

Then he told the woman, "Your faith has saved you; go in peace."

THEN ON THE NEXT DAY, HE HIMSELF TRAVELED THROUGH EVERY city and village, preaching and teaching the Good Message of God's kingdom. The twelve were with him, as well as some women who had been healed from evil spirits and illnesses: Mary, who was called Magdalene (from whom seven demons came out); Joanna (the wife of Chuza, who was an officer of Herod); Susanna; and many others. They took care of them when they needed anything.

When a large crowd had gathered, and people were coming out to him from every city, he spoke to them in allegories:

"A sower went out to sow his seed. While he was sowing it, some of it fell beside the path and was trampled underfoot. Then the birds of the sky devoured it. Other seed fell on the bedrock, and it sprouted and dried up because it did not have moisture. Yet other seed fell among thorns. Then the thorns sprouted with it and choked it out. Then other seed fell on good earth. It sprouted and produced fruit a hundred times what was sown." After he said this, he said, "Whoever has ears to hear needs to listen."

Then his disciples asked him, "What does this allegory mean?"

He said, "It has been granted to you to understand the secrets of God's kingdom, but to others it is given in allegories so that:

> Although they see, they would not see.
> Although they hear, they would not understand.

"This is the allegory: The seed is God's Word. Those that fell beside the path are those who hear, but afterward the devil comes and takes the Word out of their hearts so that they will not believe and become saved. Those that fell onto the bedrock are those who, when they hear, receive the message with joy. But these do not have roots, so they are faithful for a while, but in a time of testing they leave. Now for the seed that fell into the thorns: these are those who hear, but they are choked out because they live in anxiety, wealth, and life's pleasures, so they do not mature to the point of bringing fruit. And then what fell on good earth: these are the ones who hear the Message and hold onto it with beautiful and good hearts and bear fruit persistently.

"No one grabs a lamp and hides it in a basket or puts it under a couch. No, they put it on a lampstand so that whoever comes in can see the light. You see, nothing is hidden that will not be made clear, and nothing is secret that will not be known and come to light. So be careful how you listen because more will be given to whoever has, and whatever they only think they have will be taken away from them."

Then his mother and brothers came to see him, but they could not meet with him because of the crowd. So someone reported to him, "Your mother and your brothers are standing outside wanting to see you."

He answered them, "These are my mother and my brothers—the ones who listen to and do God's Word."

THEN ONE DAY, BOTH HE AND HIS DISCIPLES BOARDED A BOAT. HE said to them, "We are going to the other side of the sea."

So they went. While they were sailing, he fell asleep. Then a fierce gust of wind came down on the sea, and the ship began to fill up and was in danger. So they came to him and woke him, saying, "Master! Master! We are going to die!"

Once he was awake, he scolded the wind and the wave of water. They stopped, and the sea became calm. He asked them, "Where is your faith?"

Then they were afraid and amazed. They said to one another, "Just who is this? He gives orders to the winds and the water, and even they obey him!"

So they sailed to the region of the Gerasenes, which is on the opposite bank from Galilee. While he was getting out on the land, a man from the city came to meet him. He had demons and for a long time had not worn clothes or lived in a house but instead lived among the tombs. When he saw Jesus, he cried out, fell down in front of him, and shouted, "What business do you have with me, Jesus, Son of the Highest God? I beg you—do not torment me!" (You see, he had commanded the unclean spirit to come out of the man). Now it had seized him for a long time, and although he was imprisoned, bound in chains and shackles, he would shatter the restraints and be driven into the desert by the demon.

Jesus asked him, "What is your name?"

He said, "Legion," because many demons had possessed him. They begged him not to order them to go into the abyss. Now in that place was a large herd of pigs feeding on the mountainside. They begged him to allow them to possess them, and so he let them. Then the demons came out of the man and entered the pigs, and the herd rushed down the bank into the sea and drowned.

When the shepherds saw what happened, they fled to report to the city and its countryside. They came out to see what happened. Then they came to Jesus and found the man—the one from whom the demons had come out—sitting at Jesus's feet, clothed and in his right mind. They were afraid, and those who saw how he had saved the demon-possessed man told them what happened. Then the whole crowd from the Gerasene region asked him to get away from them because they were overcome by intense fear. So he got back into the boat and left.

The man from whom the demons had come out begged to come with him, but Jesus turned him back, saying, "Go back to your house and explain fully what God has done for you." Then he went back and proclaimed throughout the city what Jesus had done for him.

When Jesus returned, the crowd welcomed him because they all had been waiting for him. Get this—a man named Jairus, who was a ruler of the synagogue, came and fell at Jesus's feet, begging him to come to his house because his only daughter was dying. She was about twelve years old.

While he was on the way, the crowd was pressing against him. There was a woman with a twelve-year-old hemorrhage. She had spent all her livelihood on physicians but was not able to be cured in the slightest. She came up behind him and touched the hem of his clothes, and immediately her hemorrhage ceased.

Then Jesus asked, "Who touched me?"

While everyone denied it, Peter said, "Master—the crowd is pressing against you and pushing back."

Jesus said, "Someone touched me, because I know power went out from me."

When the woman knew that it had not escaped his notice, she came trembling and fell at his feet, and in front of all the people told the reason she touched him and that she was healed immediately.

Then Jesus told her, "Daughter, your faith has saved you; go in peace."

While he was still speaking, someone came from the ruler of the synagogue's house, saying, "Your daughter has died—do not trouble the Teacher anymore."

When Jesus heard this, he said, "Do not be afraid—just believe, and she will be saved."

When he went into the house, he did not let anyone enter with him except Peter, John, James, and the father and mother of the child. Everyone was weeping and demonstrating grief for her, but he said, "Do not weep, because she is not dead—only sleeping." They made fun of him because they knew that she had died. But he took her hand and called out, "Child, get up." Then her spirit returned, and she sat up immediately. He told them to give her something to eat. Then her parents were amazed, but he commanded them to tell no one what happened.

THEN HE SUMMONED THE TWELVE AND GAVE THEM POWER AND authority over all demons and to heal illnesses. He sent them to preach God's kingdom and heal the sick. He told them, "Take nothing for the road—do not carry a staff, bag, bread, money, or extra undershirt. When you enter into a house, stay there until you leave town. If anyone does not accept you, shake the dust off of your feet when you come out of that city as a testimony against them. Then go out and pass through all the villages, teaching the Good Message everywhere and healing."

Herod the Tetrarch heard about everything that was happening, and he was deeply concerned. You see, some said John had been raised from the dead, some said that Elijah had appeared, and others said that one of the old prophets had come back. But Herod said, "I myself had John beheaded—who is this person I am hearing so many things about?" He sought opportunity to see him.

When the apostles returned, they reported to Jesus what they had done. He took them aside and left alone with them for a city called Bethsaida, but the crowds were aware and followed him. While he greeted them, he spoke to them about God's kingdom and cured those who were in need of healing.

Daylight was beginning to fade, so the twelve approached him and said, "Dismiss the crowd so that they may go into the surrounding villages and towns, get a place to say, and find some food because we are in a deserted place here."

He said to them, "You give them something to eat."

Then they said, "We do not have enough—just five pieces of bread and two fish. That is, unless we were to go buy food for all these people." (You see, there were about five thousand men present.)

He said to his disciples, "Have them to sit down to eat in groups of about fifty." So that is what they did—they seated everyone.

Then he took the five pieces of bread and two fish, looked up toward the sky, blessed them, and then broke them apart and gave them to his disciples to distribute to the people. So everyone ate and was satisfied, and they picked up their leftovers—twelve baskets of pieces of food.

ONCE, WHILE HE WAS PRAYING PRIVATELY (ONLY HIS DISCIPLES were with him), he asked them, "Who do the crowds say that I am?"

They answered, "John the Immerser, but others say Elijah, and still others say that one of the ancient prophets has come back."

He asked them, "What about you? Who do you say that I am?"

Peter answered, "God's Messiah!"

Then he warned them, commanding them not to tell this to anyone because, he said, "The Son of Man must suffer; be rejected by the elders, chief priests, and scribes; be killed; and be raised on the third day."

Then he told everyone, "If anyone wants to follow behind me, they must deny themselves, take up their cross every day, and follow me. You see, whoever wishes to save their life will lose it, but whoever loses their life because of me will save it. What does it benefit someone to win the whole world but to lose their life or be injured? You see, whoever is ashamed of me and my words—the Son of Man will be ashamed of them when he comes in the glory that belongs to him, his father, and the holy angels. I'm telling you the truth—There are even some people standing here today who will not experience death before they see God's kingdom."

About eight days after he had said these words, he took Peter, John, and James up to the mountain to pray. While he was praying, the appearance of his face became different, and his clothing flashed like lightning. Get this—two men were speaking with him! They were Moses and Elijah, and they were displayed in glory as they talked about his departure that was about to be carried out in Jerusalem.

Now Peter and those who were with him had fallen deeply asleep. When they had awakened fully, they saw the glory of him and the two men who were standing there with him. Once the men were withdrawing themselves from Jesus, Peter told Jesus, "It is good that we are here! We should make three tents—one for you, one for Moses, and one for Elijah." (You see, he did not know what he was saying.)

While he was saying this, a cloud came and began to cover them. They became afraid as they were going into the cloud. Then a voice came from the cloud that said, "This is my Son—the chosen one. Listen to him." When the voice had spoken, Jesus was seen alone. Then they kept silent, and during those days, they did not tell anyone anything they had seen.

On the sixth day, as they came down from the mountain, a large crowd met them. Get this—a man from the crowd spoke out, "Teacher! I beg you to come see my son because he is my only one! Look! A spirit seizes him and cries out suddenly. It convulses him into foaming at the mouth, bruises him, and hardly ever comes out of him. I begged your disciples to cast it out, but they couldn't."

Then Jesus answered by saying, "Oh, faithless and twisted generation—how long will I be with you and put up with you? Bring your son here."

While he was still praying, the demon threw the boy down and convulsed him all over. Then Jesus scolded the unclean spirit, healed the child, and returned him to his father. So everyone was struck with astonishment at God's magnificence.

While everyone was in awe of everything he did, he said to his disciples, "You let these words settle into your ears—because the Son of Man is going to be betrayed into the hands of men." But they did not understand the statement; its meaning was kept hidden from them so that they did not get it, and they were afraid to ask him about this statement.

Then an argument came between them regarding who of them should hold the highest rank. Jesus knew of this argument in their hearts, and he picked up a child and set it down in front of himself. He told them, "Whoever welcomes this child in my name welcomes me, and whoever welcomes me welcomes the one who sent me. The lowest-ranked one of all of you—he is the greatest."

Then John answered, "Master—we saw someone casting out demons in your name and stopped him because he does not follow with us."

Jesus said to him, "Don't stop him; whoever is not against you is on your side."

So it happened that the number of days had been completed before he was to be taken up. He fixed his focus on going to Jerusalem. He sent messengers in front of him, so they went into a village of Samaritans to get things ready for him. But they did not welcome him there because his focus was fixed on going to Jerusalem. When the disciples James and John saw this, they said, "Master! Do you want us to tell fire to come down from the sky and consume them?"

He turned and corrected them, and they went to another village. While they were going along the road, someone told him, "I'll follow you wherever you go."

Then Jesus said to him, "Foxes have dens, and the birds of the sky have nests, but the Son of Man does not have anywhere to lay his head."

He told another person, "Follow me."

That one responded, "First, let me go back and bury my father."

Then he told him, "Let the dead bury their own dead—while you leave to publicize God's kingdom."

Still another one said, "I will follow you, Master, but first, let me tell those who live in my household goodbye."

Then Jesus told him, "No one who puts their hand on the plow and looks backward is ready for God's kingdom."

After that, the Master appointed seventy-two others and sent them in pairs ahead of him into every city and place where he was about to go himself. He told them, "The harvest is plenty, but there are few workers. So pray to the Master over the harvest that workers will be sent out for his harvest. Go, but look—I am sending you out like lambs in the midst of wolves. Do not carry a bag, a money sack, or extra sandals, and do not greet anyone along the way. Whatever house you enter, first say, 'Peace to this house.' Then, if a son of peace is there, your peace will rest on him. If not, it will return to you. Stay in that house, and eat and drink what is offered by them because the worker deserves his wages. Do not move on from house to house. Whatever city you enter that welcomes you, eat what is provided for you and heal those who are sick in that place. Tell them, 'God's kingdom has come near you.' Whatever city you enter that does not welcome you, go out into its streets and say, 'We wipe off on you even the dust of your city that is stuck to our feet, but know this: God's kingdom has come near.' I am telling you—in that day it will be more bearable for those of Sodom than for that city.

"You are in trouble, Chorazin—you are in trouble, Bethsaida! If the displays of power that appeared among you would have appeared among Tyre and Sidon, they would have repented a long time ago, sitting in sackcloth and ashes. No—in the Judgment, it will be more bearable for Tyre and Sidon than for you. As for you, Capernaum: you will not be lifted up to the sky, will you? You will be thrown down to the grave.

"Whoever hears you hears me, whoever disregards you disregards me, and whoever disregards me disregards the one who sent me."

Then the seventy-two returned joyfully and said, "Master, even the demons submitted to us in your name!"

He told them, "I saw Satan fall like lightning from heaven. Look—I have given you the power to walk all over snakes and scorpions and all over every power of the enemy, and nothing can harm you at all. But do not celebrate this—that the spirits are submissive to you—celebrate that your names have been written in heaven."

At that time, he expressed joy by the Holy Spirit and said, "I acknowledge you, Father, Master of heaven and earth, because you have hidden these things from the wise and intelligent and have revealed them to infants! Yes, Father, that is what was pleasing to you! Everything has been given to me by my father, and no one knows who the son is, except for the father. Who knows the father, except for the son and the one to whom the son wants to reveal him?"

Then he turned to the disciples alone and said, "Your eyes that see what they see are blessed. You see, I am telling you—many prophets and kings wanted to see what you see, but they did not see it. They wanted to hear what you hear but did not hear it."

GET THIS—A PARTICULAR LAWYER CAME UP TO TEST HIM BY saying, "What should I do to inherit eternal life?"

Then Jesus told him, "What is written in the Law? How do you interpret it?"

He answered, "You must love God your Master with all your heart, with all your soul, with all your strength, and with all your mind. You must also love your neighbor as yourself."

He then said, "You have answered correctly—do this and you will live."

But trying to justify himself, the lawyer asked Jesus, "And just who is my neighbor?"

Jesus resumed speaking, "There was a man going from Jerusalem to Jericho, and he happened upon some robbers. They stripped him, gave him bruises, and got away, leaving him half-dead. By chance, a priest was going down that road, but when he saw him, he crossed the road and passed by him. In the same way, when a Levite had come to the place, he saw him, crossed the road, and passed by him. Then a traveling Samaritan came to where he was, but he had mercy on him when he saw him. He approached him, bandaged his wounds after rinsing them with olive oil and wine, and placed him up on his own animal. Then he led him to an inn and took care of him. In the morning, he gave two days' wages to the host and said, 'Take care of him, and I will reimburse you for whatever else you spend when I return.'

"Which of these three do you think proved to be a neighbor to the man who happened upon the robbers?"

He said, "The one who treated him mercifully."

Then Jesus told him, "Go; you also must do that."

While they were going, he entered a certain village. Then a woman named Martha welcomed him. This woman had a sister, named Mary, who was seated at the Master's feet listening to what he said. Now Martha was distracted by many responsibilities. She stood up and said, "Master, is it not concerning to you that my sister has abandoned me to serve alone? Tell her that she needs to help me."

The Master told her in response, "Martha, Martha—you are worried and bothered by many things, but one thing is necessary. You see, Mary has chosen the good portion, and it will not be taken away from her."

ONE TIME, WHEN HE WAS PRAYING IN ANOTHER PLACE (AS HE stopped), one of his disciples said to him, "Master, teach us to pray, just as John taught his disciples."

Then he told them, "When you pray, say,

> Father:
> May your name be treated as holy.
> May your kingdom come.
> Give us our bread for the day—every day.
> Forgive us of our sins, because we forgive everyone indebted to us.
> Do not bring us into temptation."

Then he told them, "Say that one of you has a friend, and you go to him in the middle of the night and tell him, 'Friend, I need three pieces of bread because a friend of mine has come to me from the road, and I do not have anything to serve him.'

"Then he might say from inside, 'Do not give me trouble—the door has already been shut, and my children are with me in the bed. I cannot get up to give it to you.'

"I am telling you, even if he will not get up for them because he is their friend, he will give them whatever they need because of their persistence. So I am telling you—ask and it will be given to you. Seek and you will find. Knock and it will be opened for you. You see, whoever asks receives, and whoever seeks finds, and it will be open for whoever knocks. Say that a father among you has a son who asks for a fish—will he give him a snake instead of a fish? Or if he asks for an egg, will he give him a scorpion? Since you know that you—who have the capacity for evil—give good things to your children, how much more likely would the Father of heaven give the Holy Spirit to those who ask him?"

THEN HE WAS CASTING OUT A DEMON THAT WAS MUTE. IT happened that after the demon came out, the mute man spoke, and the crowd expressed amazement. But some of them said, "He casts out demons by Beelzebul, the ruler of demons!" Others were testing him, asking him for a sign from heaven.

But he knew their thoughts and told them, "Every kingdom divided against itself will be deserted, and a house divided against itself will fall. So if Satan also were divided against himself, how would his kingdom stand? You see, you are saying that I am casting out demons by Beelzebul. But if I cast out demons by Beelzebul, what about your sons—by whose authority do they cast them out? Because of this, even they will be your judges. On the other hand, if I cast out demons by the finger of God, then God's kingdom has taken over in front of you. When a strong man is fully armed, he protects his property, and his possessions are at peace. But when someone stronger than he goes to him and overcomes him, he confiscates the armor that the strong man trusted, so the man hands over his victory prize. Whoever is not with me is against me, and whoever does not gather with me scatters.

"When an unclean spirit leaves a man, it goes through dry places looking for rest but does not find it. Then it says, 'I will return to my house, where I came from.' So it comes and finds it swept and decorated. Then it goes and takes along seven other spirits more evil than itself and goes in to live there. That man's latest situation is worse than the first!"

Then, while he was saying these things, some woman from the crowd raised her voice and told him, "Blessed is the womb that carried you and the breasts where you nursed!"

But he said, "Even more blessed are those who listen to God's Word and keep watch!"

As the crowd continued to assemble, he began to speak, "This generation is an evil generation. It is looking for a sign, and no sign will be given to it except the sign of Jonah. You see, just as Jonah became a sign for those of Nineveh, in the same way the Son of Man will be for this generation. The Queen of the South will rise up in the Judgment with the men of this generation and condemn them because she came from the ends of the earth to listen to the wisdom of Solomon, but look—someone here is greater than Solomon. Men from Nineveh will rise up in the Judgment with this generation and condemn it because they repented at Jonah's message. Look—someone here is greater than Jonah.

"No one takes a lamp and puts it in a cellar or under a basket. No, they put it on a lampstand so that those who come in may see the light. The lamp of the body is your eye. When your eye is healthy, your whole body also is bright. But once it has become evil, your whole body also becomes dark. Be careful that the light in you does not become darkness. So then, if your whole body is bright and has no part that is darkened, it will be fully bright, just like the lamp that shines its brightness on you."

When he had finished speaking, a Pharisee asked him to have a meal with him, so he went in and sat down. When the Pharisee saw this, he expressed surprise that he did not first bathe before the meal. Then the Master said to him, "Currently, you Pharisees cleanse the outside of the cup and dish, but what is inside you is full of greediness and evil. Foolish people: did the one who made the outside not make the inside also? Give what is within you to charity, and look—everything will be pure for you.

"But you Pharisees are in trouble because you pay a tithe of mint, rue, and every herb, but you sidestep the judgment and love of God. You should have done these things without neglecting the others.

"You are in trouble, Pharisees, because you love the seat of honor in the synagogues and greetings in the marketplaces. You are in trouble because you are like unmarked graves; even people who walk around you do not know."

Then one of the lawyers answered him, "Teacher—when you say this, you are insulting us also!"

So he said, "You lawyers are also in trouble because you load people down with oppressive loads, and you will not touch even one of those burdens with your own fingers. You are in trouble because you erect monuments to the prophets, and your fathers killed them. So you are witnesses and join in condoning the actions of your fathers because they killed them and you erect the monuments. Because of this, God's wisdom also says, "I will send them prophets and messengers, and some of them they will kill and persecute so that for this generation there will be a reckoning for the blood of all the prophets that has been shed since the beginning of the world. From the blood of Abel until the blood of Zechariah, who was assassinated between the altar and the sanctuary—yes, I am telling you—there will be a reckoning for this generation!

"You are in trouble, lawyers, because you take away the key to knowledge. You do not enter it yourselves, and you forbid others to enter it."

When he had left from there, the scribes and Pharisees began treating him very terribly and interrogated him about many things. They devised plots to hunt down everything that came out of his mouth.

AS THOUSANDS OF PEOPLE WERE CROWDING AROUND THEM TO the point that they were trampling each other, he began to speak to his disciples first.

"Protect yourselves from the leaven of the Pharisees—that is, hypocrisy. Nothing has been covered up that will not be revealed, and nothing hidden that will not be known. Whatever you have said in the darkness will be heard in the light, and what you speak into someone's ear in a back room will be proclaimed from the housetops.

"I am telling you, my friends—do not be afraid of those who kill the body but have nothing more to do after that. I will show you whom to fear—fear the one who, after he kills, has the authority to throw into hell. Yes, I am telling you—fear this one! Are five sparrows not sold for an hour's wages? Not even one of them is forgotten by God. On the contrary, even the hairs of your head are all counted. Do not be afraid—you are more valuable than many sparrows.

"But I'm telling you—whoever acknowledges me in front of people, the Son of Man will also acknowledge them in front of God's angels. Also, whoever speaks a word against the Son of Man will be forgiven, but whoever slanders the Holy Spirit will not be forgiven.

"Whenever they carry you before the synagogues, the rulers, and the authorities, do not be worried about how you will answer or what you should say. You see, the Holy Spirit will teach you what you need to say at that time."

Someone from the crowd said to him, "Teacher! Tell my brother to share the inheritance with me."

Then he said, "Man, who appointed me as a judge or arbitrator over you?" Then he told them again, "Watch out, and protect yourselves from every bit of greediness because a person's life is not defined by the abundance of possessions."

Then he told them an allegory, "A rich man's land brought a good harvest. So he thought to himself, 'What should I do because I do not have anywhere to store my produce?' Then he said, 'This is what I will do—I will tear down my barns and build bigger ones, and I will store all the wheat and my goods there. I will tell myself, "You have many goods stored up for many years. Rest, eat, drink, and enjoy."'

"But God said to him, 'You fool! Tonight, your soul is demanded of you. The things you have prepared—whose will they be?' This is how it is for anyone who stores up for himself and yet is not rich by God's standard."

Then he told his disciples, "Because of this, I am telling you—do not be worried about your life: what you will eat or how you will clothe your body. You see, life is more than food, and the body is more than clothing. Consider the ravens—they do not sow or harvest, and they have no storage room or barn, but God feeds them. As for you, you are more valuable than birds! Say that one of you is worried—can you add even an hour to your lifespan? So if you cannot even do the smallest thing, why are you worried about the rest? Consider how the lilies grow—they do not work hard or spin a loom, but I am telling you—not even Solomon with all his glory was clothed like one of these. So you who are little in faith: if God clothes the grass in the field like this, even though it is here today and thrown into an oven tomorrow, how much more will he clothe you? As for you, do not question what you will eat or what you will drink, and do not keep yourself in suspense. You see, the nations of the world search for all these things, but your Father knows that you need them. Instead, seek his kingdom, and these things will be provided for you. Do not be afraid, little flock, because your Father is happy to give you the kingdom!

"Sell your possessions and give to charity, and make yourselves moneybags that do not wear out—infinite treasure in heaven, where a thief will not come, and a moth will not destroy. You see, wherever your treasure is, that is where your heart will be too.

Have your belts fastened and your lamps burning, and you will be like people waiting for their master to return from a wedding feast so that whenever he comes and knocks, they immediately open the door for him. Those servants will be blessed because, when the master comes, he will find them watching. I am truly telling you—he will get ready, have them sit down, and will come around to serve them. Even if he were to come in the second or third watch of the night and find them like this, they will be blessed! But know this: if the master of the house had known what time the thief would be coming, he would not have let him rummage through his house. As for you, you need to be ready, too, because the Son of Man is coming at a time that you do not expect!"

Then Peter said, "Master, are you telling this allegory to us or to everyone?"

The Master said, "Who is the faithful and wise manager of the house—the one whom the master will appoint over his servants to give them their rations at the right time? That servant is blessed if, when his master comes, he finds him doing this. I am truly telling you that he will appoint him over all his possessions. But say that this servant says in his heart, 'My master is going to take a while before coming,' and he begins to beat the serving boys and girls, as well as to eat, drink, and get drunk. The master of that servant will come on a day that he does not expect, and at a time that he does not know, and he will tear him in half. Then he will assign him to share in what is inherited by those who do not show faithfulness.

"Now that servant, who knows his master's will and does not prepare or do what he wants, will be beaten many times. The one who does not know but does something worthy of a beating will be beaten just a little. A lot will be asked of everyone who was given a lot, and more will be asked of the one who was entrusted with a lot.

"I have come to throw fire down onto the earth, and I wish that it were already on fire. I have a plunge to take—how it torments me until it has been finished! You think that I have arrived to give peace to the world. No, I'm telling you—instead, division. You see, from now on, five people in one house will be divided: three against two, and two against three. Father will be divided against son and son against father. Mother will be divided against daughter and daughter against mother. Mother-in-law will be divided against daughter-in-law and daughter-in-law against mother-in-law."

Then he told the crowd, "When you see the cloud rising in the west, you immediately say that rain is coming. That is what it will be. Whenever the south wind blows, you say that it will get really hot, and it does. Hypocrites! You know how to examine the appearance of the earth and sky, but how do you not know how to examine this time?

"Why do you also judge for yourselves what is right? You see, as you are going with your opponent to the ruler, make an effort along the way to come to a settlement with them so that they do not drag you away to the judge and the judge hand you over to the bailiff and the bailiff put you in prison. I am telling you—you will never get out of there until you have paid back the last penny."

AT THAT TIME, SOME FROM THE CROWD CAME TO HIM TO TELL him about the Galileans whose blood Pilate had mixed with their sacrifices. So he answered them, "Do you think that these Galileans were the worst sinners of all the Galileans—because they suffered these things? No, I am telling you! However, unless you repent, you all will die just the same. Or what about those eighteen people on whom the tower fell in Siloam and it killed them—do you think that they deserved this to happen to them more than all the people who live in Jerusalem? No, I am telling you! However, unless you repent, you all will die just the same."

Then he told this allegory, "Someone planted a fig tree in his vineyard, and he came looking for fruit on it but found none. So he told his gardener, 'Look—for three years now I have come looking for fruit on this fig tree and have not found any. Cut it down so that it does not cause the ground to be unproductive.' Then he answered, 'Master, leave it this year also, during which time I will dig around it and put fertilizer on it. Then it should bear fruit in the coming year, and if not, you will cut it down.'"

Then he was teaching in one of the synagogues on the Sabbath. Get this—there was a woman who had been sick for eighteen years and was bowed over and unable to stand up completely. When Jesus saw her, he called to her and said, "Ma'am, you have been set free from your weakness," and he put his hands on her. Then immediately she straightened up and praised God.

But the ruler of the synagogue responded, angry that Jesus had healed on the Sabbath. He told the crowd, "There are six days when you are supposed to work. So come on those days to be healed and not on the Sabbath Day."

Then Jesus answered, "Hypocrites! Every one of you lets your ox or donkey loose from the manger on the Sabbath Day and leads it to water. Yet this woman, who is a daughter of Abraham, whom Satan has restrained for—get this—eighteen years, should she not be released from these chains on the Sabbath Day?" When he said this, those who were protesting him were disgraced, and the whole crowd rejoiced at all the glorious things that he was causing to happen.

Then he said, "What is God's kingdom like? To what should I compare it? It is like a mustard seed that a man took and put into his garden. It grew and became a tree, and the birds of the sky made nests in its branches."

Again he said, "To what should I compare God's kingdom? It is like yeast that a woman took and buried in ten gallons of flour until the whole thing was leavened." So he traveled through every city and village teaching and making his way to Jerusalem.

Then someone said to him, "Master, will there be just a few who are saved?"

He said to them, "Strive to enter through the narrow gate because many, I tell you, will try to enter and will not be able to. Once the manager of the house has gotten up and closed the door, you will begin to stand outside and knock on the door, saying, 'Master, open for us!' He will answer you, 'I do not know where you have come from.' Then you will begin to say, 'We ate and drank with you, and you taught in our streets!' Then he will say, 'I do not know where you are from. Get away from me, everyone who does what is not right.' There will be weeping and clenched teeth when you see Abraham, Isaac, and Jacob, as well as all the prophets in God's kingdom, but you are thrown out. People will come from the east and west, from the north and south, and they will sit down to eat in God's kingdom, and look—the last will be first, and the first will be last."

At that time, some Pharisees approached him and said, "Go! Get out of here because Herod wants to kill you!"

Then he said, "Go tell that fox, 'Look! I am casting out demons and carrying out healings today and tomorrow, and the next day I will be finished. Yet, I must go today, tomorrow, and the next day because it is impossible for a prophet to be killed anywhere other than Jerusalem.

"Jerusalem, Jerusalem! The one that kills the prophets and stones those who are sent to it! How many times I wanted to gather your children together in the way that a mother bird gathers its young under her wings, and you were unwilling! Look! Your house is left to you. I am telling you—you will never see me until the day comes when you say, 'Blessed is the one who comes in the Master's name!'"

ONCE, HE WENT INTO THE HOUSE OF A RULER OF A CHIEF PHARISEE on a Sabbath to eat bread, and they were watching him meticulously. Then—get this—a man with severe swelling was in front of him. Then Jesus said to the lawyers and Pharisees, "Is it right to heal on the Sabbath, or not?" They remained silent, so he took hold of the man, healed him, and then let him go. Then he told them, "Who among you, if a son or ox were to fall into a well, would not immediately pull it up on the Sabbath Day?" They were unable to give an answer to this.

He told an allegory to those who had also been invited as he observed how they chose the seats of honor. He said, "When you have been invited by someone to a wedding feast, do not sit down in the seat of honor or else someone with more honor than yourself might have been invited by him, and then the one who invited you would come and tell you, 'Give this one your place.' Then you will begin to sit down with your shame at the least honorable seat. On the contrary, when you are invited, go and sit in the least honorable seat so that when the one who invited you comes, he will say, 'Friend, come up to a higher place!' Then your glory will be displayed before everyone who was sitting down to eat with you. You see, everyone who lifts himself up will be humiliated, and whoever humbles himself will be lifted up."

He also said to the one who invited him, "Whenever you prepare breakfast or supper, do not call your friends, brothers, relatives, or wealthy neighbors. Otherwise, they will also invite you in return, and you will have been repaid. On the contrary, when you prepare a banquet, invite the poor, crippled, paralyzed, and blind. Then you will be blessed because they have no way to repay you. You see, it will be repaid to you when the righteous are resurrected."

Upon hearing this, one of those sitting with him said to him, "Blessed is the one who eats bread in God's kingdom!"

Then he said, "There was a man who prepared a big banquet. He invited many people and sent his servant at the time of the meal to tell those who were invited, 'Come, because it has already been prepared!' Then one by one, they all began to ask to be excused. The first told him, 'I have bought a field, and I need to go look at it; I ask you to have me excused.' Another said, 'I have bought five yokes of oxen and am going to try them out. I ask you to have me excused.' Yet another said, 'I have married a woman, and because of this I cannot go.' Then the servant returned and reported this to his master. Then the manager of the house was enraged and told his servant, 'Go out quickly to the streets and alleys of the city and bring back the poor, crippled, blind, and paralyzed.' Then the servant said, 'Master, what you commanded has been done, and there is still room.' So the master told the servant, 'Go out into the roads and hedgerows and force people to come in so that my house may be full. I am telling you—none of those men who were invited will taste my supper!'"

Now a large crowd was traveling with him, and he turned to speak to them, "If someone comes to me and does not hate their own father and mother, wife and children, brothers and sisters, and even their own life, they cannot be my disciple. Whoever does not carry their own cross and follow after me cannot be my disciple.

"Say that one of you wants to build a tower—will you not first sit down and calculate the expense to see whether you can finish it? Otherwise, after you have laid the foundation and are unable to finish, everyone who sees it will begin to mock you by saying, 'This one started to build, and was not able to finish.'

"Or what king going out against another king to engage in battle does not first sit down to deliberate on whether he is able with ten thousand men to match up against one coming against him with twenty thousand? If he does not, while he is still far off, he will send an ambassador to ask for terms of peace. In the same way, every one of you who does not leave everything that you possess cannot be my disciple.

"Now salt is good, but if the salt were to lose its taste, how could it become seasoned again? It is not useful for the soil or the manure pile—it is thrown out. Whoever has ears to listen needs to listen!"

ALL OF THE TAX COLLECTORS AND SINNERS WERE COMING BY TO listen to him, and both the Pharisees and scribes were complaining, saying, "This man accepts sinners and eats with them!"

He told them this allegory, "Say that a man among you has one hundred sheep, and he loses one of them. Will he not leave the ninety-nine in the desert and go after the lost one until he has found it? Then, once he has found it, he puts it over his shoulder and rejoices. Then, when he has returned to his house, he calls his friends and neighbors and tells them, 'Celebrate with me, because I found my sheep that was lost.' I am telling you; just like this, there will be more joy in heaven over one sinner who repents than over ninety-nine righteous people who do not need repentance.

"Say that a woman has ten silver coins, and she loses one coin. Will she not take a lamp and sweep the house, looking carefully until she has found it? Then, when she has found it, she calls together her friends and neighbors, saying, 'Celebrate with me, because I have found the silver coin that I lost!' Just like this, I am telling you—there will be joy among the angels of God over one sinner who repents."

Then he said, "There was a man who had two sons. The younger son told the father, 'Give me the piece of property that comes to me.'

"So he distributed his property among them.

"Then, after a few days, the younger son collected everything and left for a distant country. There he wastefully squandered his possessions. After he had spent everything, a severe famine came over that whole country, and he began to be in need. As he traveled, he was hired out to a citizen of that country, and he sent him into his field to feed pigs. He wished to satisfy his appetite with the carob pods that the pigs were eating, but no one would give anything to him.

"When he came to himself, he said, 'How many of my father's hired servants have more than enough bread, while I am dying here of starvation? I will get up and go to my father and tell him, "Father, I have sinned against heaven and you—I am no longer worthy to be called your son. Treat me like one of your hired servants."' So he got up and went to his father.

"While he was still a long distance away, his father saw him and had compassion—he ran, fell on his neck, and kissed him.

"Then the son said to him, 'Father, I have sinned against heaven and you. I am no longer worthy to be called your son—'

"'Quickly!' the father told his servants, 'Bring the best robe and clothe him; put a ring on his hand and shoes on his feet! Bring the fattened calf, slaughter it, and we will eat and celebrate because this son of mine was dead and is now alive! He was lost but has been found!' And he began celebrating.

"Now his older son was in the field, and as he came near the house, he heard music and dancing. So he called over one of the servants and inquired what this was all about.

"He told him, 'Your brother has come, and your father has slaughtered the fattened calf because he has received your brother back alive.'

"But he was enraged and did not want to go in, so his father came out to beg him. He answered his father, 'Look—all these years I have served you and never sidestepped your command, and you have never given me even a young goat so that I could celebrate with my friends! But when this son of yours, who has consumed your goods with prostitutes, comes back, you slaughter the fattened calf for him!' Then he told him, 'Son, you have always been with me, and everything I have is yours, but it is necessary to celebrate and be happy because this brother of yours was dead but is alive. He was lost but is found!'"

Then Jesus said to his disciples, "There was a rich man who had a household manager and brought charges against him for wasting his possessions. So he called the manager and told him, 'What is this that I hear about you? Give an account for your management, because you cannot be my manager any longer.' Now the manager said to himself, 'What am I going to do, because my master is taking my administration away from me? I am not strong enough to dig, and I am ashamed to beg! I know what I will do so that when I have been removed from my office, they will welcome me into their homes.' So he called for each one of his master's borrowers. He asked the first one, 'How much do you owe my master?' He answered, 'One hundred jugs of olive oil.' Then he told him, 'Take your invoice, sit here, and quickly write "fifty."' Then to another, he said, 'And you—how much do you owe?' He said, 'One hundred baskets of wheat.' He told him, 'Take your invoice and write "eighty."' Then the master praised the unrighteous manager because he had acted wisely, saying: 'The sons of this age are wiser than the sons of light in their own generation.' Further, I am telling you—make friends for yourselves from unrighteous wealth so that when it runs out, they will welcome you into eternal dwelling places.

"Whoever is faithful with the least amount will also be faithful with a lot, and whoever is unrighteous with the least amount will be unrighteous with a lot. So if you are not faithful with unrighteous wealth, who will entrust you with the true kind? Also, if you are not faithful with something that belongs to someone else, who will give you something of your own?

"No one can serve two masters. You see, either they will hate this one and love that one, or they will devote themselves to this one and think little of the other one. You cannot serve both God and wealth."

The Pharisees (who loved money) heard all this and began to mock him.

So he told them, "You—you are justifying yourselves before people, but God knows your hearts because what is prized by people is disgusting to God.

"There was just the Law and the prophets until John—from then on, God's kingdom has been proclaimed, and everyone is being urged to enter it. It would be easier for heaven and earth to pass away than for one stroke of a letter in the Law to fall.

"Whoever divorces his wife and marries another commits adultery, and whoever marries one who was put away by a man commits adultery.

"There was a rich man who was clothed in purple and linen, and he was wonderfully happy every day. Also, there was a poor man named Lazarus, covered in sores, who was carried out to his gate. He wished to be fed from the crumbs that fell from the rich man's table. Furthermore, the dogs also came and licked all over his sores. It so happened that the poor man died and was carried by the angels to Abraham's lap. The rich man also died and was buried. Then in Hades, since he was being tortured, he lifted his eyes and saw Abraham from a distance—and Lazarus was in his lap. So he called out, 'Father Abraham, show mercy to me and send Lazarus so that he can dip the tip of his finger in water and cool my tongue because I am in agony in this flame.' Then Abraham said, 'Child, remember that you received your good things in your life and Lazarus received bad things; but now, here, he is comforted and you are suffering. Besides all this, between you and us, a large chasm has been put so that no one who might want to cross over from here to you is able to do so, and no one can cross over from there to here.' Then he said, 'I beg you then, Father: send him to my father's house because I have five brothers—so that he can testify to them so that they too will not come to this place of torture.' Then Abraham said, 'They have Moses and the prophets; they must listen to them.' But he said, "No, Father Abraham—but if someone were to go to them from the dead, they would repent.' Abraham told him, 'If they will not listen to Moses and the prophets, they will not be convinced even if someone were to rise from the dead.'"

Then he told his disciples, "It is impossible for temptations to sin not to come, but there will be trouble for the one by whom they come! It would be better for them if a millstone were tied around their neck and they were thrown out into the sea than for them to tempt one of these little ones to sin. Protect yourselves!

"If your brother sins, correct him, and if he repents, forgive him. Even if he were to sin against you seven times per day and come back to you seven times, saying, 'I repent,' forgive him."

Then his disciples said to the Master, "Increase our faith."

The Master said, "If you have faith like a mustard seed, you would say to this mulberry tree, 'Be uprooted and planted in the sea,' and it would obey you.

"Say that one of you has a servant plowing or shepherding. When he has come in from the field, would you tell him, 'Come in right away and rest?' Would you not tell him instead, 'Prepare something for me to eat and get dressed to serve me until I eat and drink, and after that you may eat and drink, too'? You do not do the servant a favor because the servant did what he was appointed to do. As for you, in the same way, when you have done everything you were appointed to do, say, 'We are unworthy servants; we have done what we ought to do.'"

AS HE TRAVELED TOWARD JERUSALEM, HE ALSO PASSED THROUGH the middle of Samaria and Galilee. As he was entering one village, ten men with leprosy met him. They stood far away, but they lifted their voices and said, "Jesus! Master! Have mercy on us!"

When he saw them, he said, "Go show yourselves to the priests."

So while they were on their way, they were cleansed. Then one of them, when he saw that he had been healed, turned and praised God with a loud voice. He fell down on his face at the feet of Jesus, thanking him. (He was a Samaritan.)

Jesus answered, "Weren't there ten who were cleansed? Where are the nine? Will none be found who will return to give glory to God, except for this one from another race?" Then he told him, "Arise and go—your faith has saved you."

After being asked by the Pharisees when God's kingdom would come, he answered them, "God's kingdom is not coming visibly. They will not say, 'Look! Here it is,' or 'There—Look!' You see, God's kingdom is within you."

He told his disciples, "Days are coming when you will want to see one of the days of the Son of Man, but do not pay attention to it. They will tell you, 'Look there!' or 'Look here!' Do not go out, and do not chase it. You see, it will be like lightning flashes streaking from horizon to horizon. This will be like the Son of Man on his day. But it is necessary that he first suffer many things and be rejected by this generation. Just as it happened in the days of Noah, that is how it will be in the days of the Son of Man too. They were eating, drinking, marrying, and giving in marriage until the day when Noah entered the ark, and the flood came and destroyed them all. It is also just as it was in the days of Lot. They were eating, drinking, buying, selling, planting, and building, but on the day Lot left Sodom, fire and sulfur rained down from heaven and destroyed them all. The day of the Son of Man will be revealed just like these. In that day, whoever is on the roof and their possessions are in the house, they should not go down to get them. Whoever is in the field likewise should not turn back—remember Lot's wife! Whoever tries to maintain possession of their life will lose it, and whoever loses it will save it! I am telling you—on that night, two will be in one bed. One will be taken, and the other left behind. Two will be working together at the mill. One will be taken, and the other left behind."

They answered him, "Where, Master?"

He told them, "Wherever the body is, that is where the vultures will gather."

He then told them an allegory to show the need for them to pray always and not give up, "There was this judge in a particular town who did not respect God or back down from anyone. There was also a widow in that city, and she came to him, saying, 'Give me justice against my opponent!' Now he did not want to do this for a while but afterward said to himself, 'Even though I don't respect God or back down from anyone, because this widow is causing me trouble, I will give her justice or else she might end up coming to blacken my eye.'"

Then the Master said, "Listen to what the unfair judge is saying—will God now also bring justice for his chosen ones who cry out to him day and night? Will he procrastinate acting in their behalf? I am telling you—he will bring justice for them quickly, but when the Son of Man comes, is he going to find this kind of faith on the earth?"

THEN HE TOLD THIS ALLEGORY TO SOME OF THOSE WHO WERE convinced they were righteous and looked down on the others, "Two men went up to the temple to pray. One was a Pharisee and the other a tax collector. The Pharisee stood by himself and prayed this: 'God, thank you that I am not like the rest of people—taking advantage, being unfair, adulterous, or even like this tax collector. I fast twice per week and pay a tithe for everything I earn.' But the tax collector stood far away and did not even want to raise his eyes toward heaven. Instead, he beat his chest and said, 'God, grant restitution for me, a sinner!' I am telling you—this one went to his house having been made righteous instead of the other one. You see, everyone who raises himself up will be humiliated, but whoever humbles himself will be lifted up."

Now they were bringing infants to him so that he would lay his hands on them, but when the disciples saw this, they scolded them. But Jesus called them aside and said, "Let the young children come to me—do not prevent them, because God's kingdom belongs to little ones like these. I am truly telling you: whoever doesn't accept God's kingdom like a young child, he will never enter it."

A ruler asked him, "Good Teacher, what should I do to inherit eternal life?"

Jesus said to him, "Why are you calling me 'good'? No one is good except one—God. You know the commands. Do not commit adultery, do not kill, do not steal, do not make false statements, and honor your father and mother."

Then he said, "I have kept all these since my youth."

Upon hearing that, Jesus told him, "You still lack one thing. Sell everything you have, and give the money to the poor. Then you will have treasure in heaven. Come follow me."

But when he heard this, he became very sad because he was extremely wealthy. Jesus looked at him and became sad.

He said, "How difficult it is for those who have wealth to enter God's kingdom! You see, it would be easier for a camel to pass through the eye of a needle than for a rich person to enter God's kingdom."

Those who were listening asked, "Then who can be saved?"

He said, "What is impossible for people is possible for God."

Then Peter said, "Look—we left our possessions to follow you."

Jesus told them, "I am truly telling you: of those who left house, wife, brothers, parents, or children because of God's kingdom, every single one will be repaid with many times more in this present time, as well as eternal life in the age to come."

Then he took aside the twelve and told them, "Look—we are going to Jerusalem, and everything that has been written by the prophets about the Son of Man will be done. You see, he will be handed over to the gentiles, made fun of, insulted, and spit upon. They will scourge him and kill him, and on the third day he will be raised." But they did not understand any of this, and this statement was hidden from them—they did not know what he was saying.

As he drew near to Jericho, a blind man was sitting beside the road, begging. Once he heard the crowd passing by, he inquired about what was happening. They told him that Jesus the Nazarene had arrived, so he cried out, "Jesus, Son of David—show mercy to me!" Those who were moving forward scolded him to be silent, but he shouted all the more, "Son of David! Show mercy to me!"

Then Jesus stopped and commanded him to be led to him. As he approached, Jesus asked him, "What do you want me to do for you?"

He said, "I want to regain my sight."

Then Jesus told him, "Receive your sight—your faith has saved you." Immediately he received his sight and followed him, praising God. Everyone who saw this also gave praise to God.

He entered and then passed through Jericho. Get this—there was a man named Zacchaeus. He was a chief tax collector and was very wealthy. He was trying to see who Jesus was, and he could not because of the crowd (you see, he was short in stature). So he ran ahead to the front and climbed up a sycamore tree so that he could see him since he was about to pass by there.

As Jesus arrived at that place, he looked up and said to him, "Zacchaeus, hurry and climb down because I need to stay at your house today." So he hurried and climbed down and greeted him joyfully.

But those who saw this complained, "He's stopped to stay with a sinful man!"

Then Zacchaeus stopped and told the Master, "Look—I am giving half of my possessions to the poor, Master, and if I have extorted anyone, I will pay back four times as much."

Jesus said to him, "Today, salvation has come to this house because this man is also a son of Abraham. See, the Son of Man came to seek out and save the lost."

As they were listening to this, he continued to tell them an allegory since he was getting closer to Jerusalem, and they thought that God's kingdom was going to appear immediately. He said, "A man of nobility went to a distant country to take over a kingdom for himself, and then he would return. So he called ten servants to him, distributed among them one thousand silver coins, and told them, 'Run the business until I return.' Now his citizens hated him, and they sent ambassadors after him, saying, 'We do not want this man to rule over us.' So after he had returned from taking over the kingdom, he told them to call for those servants to whom he had given the silver so that he could know how profitable the business had been. The first one stepped forward and said, 'Master, your one hundred silver coins has earned an additional one thousand silver coins.' He told him, 'Excellent, good servant! Since you were faithful with a little, assume authority over ten cities.' Then the second one came and said, 'Master, your one hundred silver coins have generated five hundred silver coins.' So he spoke to him also: 'You also—be in charge of five cities.' Yet another came and said, 'Master, look—here are your one hundred silver coins that I kept hidden in a handkerchief. You see, I was afraid of you because you are a harsh man. You take what you have not deposited and harvest what you did not sow.' Then he said to him, 'I will judge you by what came out of your own mouth, evil servant! You knew that I am a harsh man, that I take what I have not deposited, and harvest what I did not sow. Because of this, should you not have deposited my silver in the bank so that when I came, I could withdraw it with interest?' Then he told those who were standing guard, 'Take the one hundred silver coins from him and give them to the one who has one thousand silver coins. I am telling you—more will be given to the one who has, but what little someone has will be taken away when he does not have enough. Furthermore, bring me those enemies of mine who did not want me to rule over them and execute them in front of me.'"

WHEN HE HAD SAID THIS, HE ARRIVED AT THE ASCENT TO Jerusalem. As he drew near to Bethphage and Bethany, at the place called the Mount of Olives, he sent two disciples, telling them: 'Go into the village in front of you—when you get in, you will find a donkey tied there that no one has ever ridden. Untie it and bring it here. If someone asks you, 'Why are you untying it?' say this: 'Because the Master needs it.'"

When they went, the ones who were sent found this just as he told them. While they were untying the donkey, its owners asked them, "Why are you untying the donkey?"

They said, "Because the Master needs it." Then they led it to Jesus and threw their robes over the donkey and sat Jesus on it.

While he passed through, they spread their robes down on the road. As he was approaching the descent from the Mount of Olives, the whole crowd of disciples began celebrating and praising God with a loud voice for all the miracles that they had seen. They said,

> Blessed is the one who comes,
> The King, in the name of the Master!
> Peace in heaven and glory in the highest places!

Then some of the Pharisees from the crowd told him, "Teacher—reprimand your disciples!"

He answered, "I'm telling you—even if these were silent, the stones would cry out."

Then, as he approached and saw the city, he wept over it, saying, "If you had only known this day what would bring you peace! But now it has been hidden from your sight. You see, days will come upon you when your enemies will put sharpened stakes all around you, and they will surround you and press you down from every side. Then they will tear you to the ground with your children in you, and they will not leave one stone on another in you because you did not recognize the day of providence that was yours."

Then he went into the temple and began to throw out the moneychangers, telling them, "It is written that 'My house will be a house of prayer,' but you have made it a den of robbers!"

Then he continued teaching every day in the temple, but the chief priests, scribes, and leaders of the people were trying to kill him. They could not figure out what they should do because all the people were hanging on every word as they listened to him.

ONE OF THOSE DAYS, WHILE HE WAS TEACHING THE PEOPLE IN the temple and sharing the Good Message, the chief priests and scribes stood in front of him with the elders. They told him, "Tell us—by whose authority are you doing this? Who is the one who gave you this authority?"

Then he answered them, "I am going to ask you something too. Tell me—was John's immersion from heaven or from people?"

They debated among themselves, saying, "If we say, 'From heaven,' he will say, 'Then why did you not believe him?' But if we say, 'From people,' all these people will stone us to death because they are convinced that John was a prophet." So they answered him, saying that they did not know where it came from.

Then Jesus told them, "Neither will I tell you by whose authority I am doing these things."

Then he began to tell this allegory to the people, "There was a man who planted a vineyard, and he hired it out to farmers and left on a journey for a significant amount of time. In time, he sent a servant to the farmers so that they would give him some of the fruit from the vineyard. But the farmers sent him away empty-handed with a beating. So he proceeded to send another servant. They beat that one also and then dishonored him and sent him away empty-handed. So he proceeded to send a third. This one they injured and threw out. Then the master of the vineyard said, "What am I going to do? I will send my dear son. Perhaps they will show respect to him." But when they saw him, the farmers discussed with one another, "This is the heir! Let's kill him so that his inheritance can be ours!" Then they threw him out of the vineyard and killed him. So what will the master of the vineyard do to them? He will come back, destroy these farmers, and give the vineyard to others."

Those who were listening said, "Absolutely not!"

Then he looked at them and said, "Then why was this written:

> The stone that the builders rejected,
> It has become the chief cornerstone?
> Everyone who falls against that stone will be smashed into pieces,
> And if it falls on anyone, it will crush him.

Then the scribes and chief priests began trying to get their hands on him at that time because they knew he had told this allegory about them, but they were afraid of the people. So they watched him carefully and commissioned some spies to pretend to be righteous so that they could catch him by his message. That way, they could turn him over to the governor's rule and authority. So they asked him, "Teacher, we know that you speak and teach correctly and that you do not show favoritism. On the contrary, you teach God's way truthfully. Is it right for us to pay taxes to Caesar or not?"

But he recognized their willingness to do anything, and he told them, "Show me a denarius. Whose image and inscription does it have?"

They said, "Caesar's."

Then he told them, "Well then, give back to Caesar what is Caesar's and to God what is God's."

They were not able to catch him by his speech in front of the people, and because they were amazed at how he responded, they became silent.

Then some of the Sadducees (who say that there is no resurrection) came and asked him, "Teacher, Moses wrote to us: 'If someone's brother who has a wife dies, and he is childless, his brother should take her as a wife and bring up descendants for his brother.' Well, there were seven brothers. The first took a wife and died childless. The second and then the third took her as well, and likewise, all seven died and left no children. Finally, the woman also died. So then, in the resurrection, whose wife will she be? You see, all seven had her as a wife."

Then Jesus told them, "The sons of this age marry and give in marriage. But those who are deemed worthy to obtain that eternity and the resurrection from the dead—they do not marry or give in marriage. You see, they do not die any longer because they are like angels and sons of God because they are sons of the resurrection. As for the dead being raised, Moses also explained in the section about the bush that 'The Master is the God of Abraham, the God of Isaac, and the God of Jacob.' He is not the God of the dead but of the living. You see, they all are alive to him."

Then some of the scribes responded, "Teacher, you have spoken well," because none of them dared to ask him anything more.

Then he asked them, "How do they say that the Messiah would be the Son of David? You see, David himself says in the Book of Psalms:

> The Master said to my Master:
> Sit at my right hand,
> Until I set down your enemies
> As a footrest for your feet.

"Now David calls him 'Master,' so how is he his son?"

While all the people were listening, he told his disciples, "Be careful about the scribes, who want to walk around in robes and love greetings in the marketplaces, the best seats in the synagogues, and the seats of honor at banquets. They devour the houses of widows and pray long prayers for show. They will receive a stricter judgment."

Then he looked up and saw the wealthy men tossing their gifts into the treasury. Then he saw this impoverished widow toss two pennies in there. He said, "I am truly telling you—this poor widow has put in more than anyone. You see, they have tossed in their gifts from their overflow, but she, from what she did not have, has tossed in everything that she had to live on."

AS SOME WERE TALKING ABOUT THE TEMPLE, SAYING THAT IT was decorated with beautiful stones and gifts dedicated to God, he said, "Do you see these things? Days are coming when not a stone will be left on another stone that is not knocked down."

Then they asked him, "Teacher! So when will this be? What will be the sign that this is about to happen?"

Then he said, "Be careful that you are not deceived. You see, many will come in my name saying, 'I AM,' and 'The time has come'; but do not follow behind them. When you hear about wars and unrest, do not be terrified. You see, these things must happen first, but the end will not come right away."

Then he told them, "Nation will rise up against nation and kingdom against kingdom. There will also be severe earthquakes and famine everywhere, as well as disease. There will be terrifying and significant signs from the sky.

"Before these things happen, they will put their hands on you and persecute you—handing you over to synagogues, prisons; carrying you away to kings and governors because of my name. It will be given to you as an opportunity to offer testimony. So make up your mind not to rehearse your defense. You see, I will give you a mouth and wisdom, and no one who is opposed to you will be able to withstand it or speak against it. Now you will be betrayed by your parents, brothers, relatives, and friends, and they will kill some of you. You will be hated by everyone because of my name. Yet, not a hair of your head will be lost. You will regain your lives by your persistence!

"When you see Jerusalem surrounded by an army, then you know its devastation has come. At that time, those who are in Judea should flee to the mountains; those who are in the middle of the city should leave it, and those who are in its fields should not go back into it. You see, those are days of vengeance in order to fulfill everything that has been written. Those who are pregnant and nursing in those days will be in trouble because it will be immense pressure on the land and anger toward this nation. They will fall by the edge of the sword and will be taken captive into every nation, and Jerusalem will be trampled by gentiles until the gentiles' time has been completed.

"There will be signs among the sun, moon, and stars, as well as distress on the earth among the nations due to anxiety from the roar of the sea and waves. Meanwhile, people will hold their breath out of fear and anticipation for what is coming over the world because 'The celestial powers will be shaken.' Then they will see the Son of Man coming in a cloud, with significant power and glory. When these things begin to happen, get yourselves up and raise your heads, because your release is near."

Then he told them this allegory, "Observe the fig tree and all the other trees. When they have put out foliage, you can see for yourselves and know that summer has already come. As for you, in the same way, when you see these things happening, know that God's kingdom is near. I am truly telling you—this generation will never pass away until all this has happened. The sky and earth will pass away, but my words will never pass away.

"Protect yourselves so that your hearts do not weigh you down with indulgence, drunkenness, and anxiety about life, or that day will come and take you by surprise like a trap. You see, it will come upon everyone who lives, all over the face of the earth. So stay awake at all times, praying that you can power through and flee all these things that are going to happen and stand before the Son of Man."

So he was teaching in the temple during the day, but at night he would go out to spend the night in the place called the Mount of Olives. All the people would get up early and go hear him in the temple. Now the Feast of Unleavened Bread (also called Passover) was approaching, and the chief priests and scribes were trying to find a way to put an end to him because they were afraid of the people.

Then Satan entered the heart of Judas (the one called Iscariot), who was one of the ones numbered among the twelve. He went out and spoke with the chief priests and officers to see how he might hand him over to them. They were happy and agreed together to give him silver. Then he agreed to the terms and sought an opportunity to hand him over to them when he was away from the crowd.

SO THE DAY OF UNLEAVENED BREAD CAME, ON WHICH THEY WERE supposed to sacrifice the lamb. Jesus sent Peter and John, saying, "Go prepare the Passover for us so that we may eat it."

They asked him, "Where do you want us to prepare it?"

He told them, "Look—after you go into the city, a man carrying a clay jar of water will meet you. Follow him into the house that he enters, and tell the master of the house, 'The Teacher asks, "Where is the room where I am to eat the Passover meal with my disciples?"' Then he will show you a large, furnished upper room. You are to prepare it there." So they went and found this just as he told him, and they prepared the Passover meal.

Then, when the time came, he sat down, and his disciples sat with him. He told them, "I have wanted very much to eat this Passover meal with you before I am to suffer. You see, I am telling you—I will not eat it again until it has all been fulfilled in God's kingdom."

Then he took a cup, offered a blessing, and said, "Take this and divide it up among yourselves because I am telling you—I will not drink what is made from the vine from now until God's kingdom has come."

Then he took bread, offered a blessing, broke it apart, and gave it to them. He said, "This is my body, which has been given for you. Do this in my memory." Then he took the cup in the same way after the supper and said, "This cup is the new covenant with my blood, which is being shed for you.

"But look—the hand of the one who betrays me is with me at this table because the Son of Man truly will go just as it has been determined. Though, that man who betrays me is in trouble."

Then they began to argue among themselves about which of them might be the one who was going to do this. Now they also had the tendency among them to express opinions regarding which of them would be the greatest. So he told them, "The kings of the nations hold their lordship over them, and those who exercise authority over them are called benefactors. But you are not to be like this. On the contrary, whoever is the greatest among you must become like the youngest, and the leader needs to be like the one who serves. You see, which is greater—the one who is seated at the table or the one who serves? Is it not the one who is seated at the table? But I am with you as one who serves.

"You are the ones who have stayed with me throughout my trials, and I am making a covenant with you just as my Father made one with me regarding a kingdom. So you will eat and drink at my table in my kingdom, and you will sit on thrones to judge the twelve tribes of Israel.

"Simon, Simon! Look—Satan has asked for you all so that he can sift you like wheat. But I have prayed for you so that your faith will not be abandoned. As for you specifically, when you return, strengthen your brothers."

Peter told him, "Master, I'm ready to go with you, either to prison or to death."

Then he said, "I am telling you, Peter—the rooster will not crow today until you have denied knowing me three times." Then he asked them, "When I sent you without a moneybag, a sack, or shoes, did you lack anything?"

They said, "Not a thing."

He told them, "Now, on the other hand, whoever has a money bag needs to take it. The same goes for a sack, and whoever does not have a sword needs to sell his robe so that he can buy one. You see, I am telling you—this is what was written that must be accomplished by me: 'Then he will be considered like the criminals.' You see, what was written about me has a purpose."

Then they said, "Master, look—here are two swords."

He told them, "This is enough."

So he left and went to the Mount of Olives, as was their habit, and the disciples went with him too. Now when he had come to the place, he told them, "Pray so that you do not fall into temptation." Then he withdrew from them about a stone's throw away, bowed his knees, and prayed, "Father, if you are willing, take this cup from me, but your will must be done, not mine." Then an angel from heaven appeared to him to strengthen him. As he agonized, he prayed all the more enthusiastically, and get this—his sweat was like drops of blood falling to the ground.

Then, after he got up from his prayer and went to his disciples, he found them sleeping because of their sorrow. So he told them, "Why are you sleeping? Get up and pray so that you do not fall into temptation."

While he was still speaking, get this—a crowd assembled, and the one named Judas, who was one of the twelve, came ahead of them. He came up to Jesus and kissed him.

Then Jesus asked him, "Judas, you are betraying the Son of Man with a kiss?"

When those who were with him saw what was happening, they asked, "Master, should we attack with swords?" Then one of them attacked the servant of the high priest and severed his right ear.

Jesus said, "Stop—no more of this!" and he touched the servant's ear and healed it. Then Jesus asked the chief priests, the officers of the temple, and elders who had come out to him, "Have you come out with swords and clubs as if I were a robber? Every day while I was with you in the temple, you did not lay your hands on me, but this is your time and the power of darkness." So they took him and led him away. They brought him into the house of the chief priest.

Now Peter was following at a distance. After they had kindled a fire in the middle of the courtyard and sat around it, Peter sat among them. When a servant girl saw him sitting by the fire, she looked directly at him and said, "This one was with him too!"

But he denied it by saying, "Ma'am, I do not know him."

After a little while, someone else saw him and said, "You're one of them too!"

Peter said, "Sir, I am not."

After about an hour, another person affirmed confidently, "Truly this one was with him, too, because he is a Galilean!"

Then Peter said, "Sir, I do not know what you are talking about." Immediately, while he was still speaking, the rooster crowed, and the Master turned and looked at Peter. Then Peter remembered what the Master had said, how he told him, "Before the rooster crows today, you will deny me three times." Then he went out and wept inconsolably.

So the men who were holding Jesus began to make fun of him and beat him. They blindfolded him and then asked, "Prophesy! Who is the one who hit you?" They slandered him in many other ways as they spoke to him.

THEN, WHEN DAYLIGHT CAME, THE COUNCIL OF THE PEOPLE'S elders assembled, as well as the chief priests and scribes. They brought him before the council and said, "If you are the Messiah, tell us!"

Then he told them, "Even if I were to tell you, you would not believe me. If I were to ask questions, you would not answer. From now on, the Son of Man will be seated at the right hand of God's power."

Then they all asked, "So you are the Son of God?"

He then told them, "As you said yourselves, I am."

They said, "What witnesses do we still need? We've heard it ourselves from his own mouth!" So the whole assembly got up and brought him before Pilate.

They began to accuse him, "We found this man corrupting our nation, trying to keep people from paying taxes to Caesar, and claiming himself as the Messiah and king!"

Then Pilate asked him, "Are you the king of the Jews?"

Jesus answered, "Do you say so?"

Then Pilate said to the chief priests and the crowd, "I find no reason at all for charging this man."

But they became more emphatic, saying, "He stirs up the people as he teaches throughout Judea—all the way from Galilee to here."

When Pilate heard this, he asked whether the man was Galilean. When he realized that Jesus was under Herod's jurisdiction, he sent him along to Herod, who was also in Jerusalem in those days.

Herod became very happy when he saw Jesus because he had been wanting to see him for a long time. You see, Herod had heard about Jesus and hoped to see some kind of miracle performed by him. He interrogated him at considerable length, but Jesus did not respond to him at all.

Then the chief priests and scribes arrived, accusing him fiercely. Herod treated him disrespectfully (as did his company of soldiers), and he mocked him, clothed him in bright clothing, and sent him back to Pilate. So Herod and Pilate became friends with one another on that day. You see, they had previously been enemies of one another.

Then Pilate summoned the chief priests and rulers of the people and told them, "You have brought me this man as though he were causing the people to revolt. Now look—I investigated him right in front of you and found no reason at all for charging this man with the accusations you have brought against him. Neither did Herod because he sent him back to me, and look—no action has been committed by him that is deserving of death. So I will discipline him and release him."

So the whole crowd cried out, "Take him away! Release Barabbas to us!" (He had been imprisoned for an insurrection that had occurred in the city, as well as for murder.)

Pilate again called out to them, trying to release Jesus, but they kept shouting, "Crucify! Crucify him!"

So he said a third time, "Why? What bad thing has he done? After I have disciplined him, I will release him."

Then they confronted him forcefully with loud voices, demanding that he be crucified, and their voices were overpowering, so Pilate decided to grant what they demanded—he released the one they requested, who was imprisoned for insurrection and murder, and handed Jesus over for them to do as they wanted.

As they led him away, they grabbed Simon, a man from Cyrene who was on his way from the field, and they put the cross on him so that he could carry it behind Jesus. A very large number of people followed him, as well as some women who were hitting themselves in grief and mourning for him.

Jesus turned to them and said, "Daughters of Jerusalem: do not weep for me. Instead, weep for yourselves and for your children because days are coming when they will say, 'Blessed are those who are barren, as well as the wombs that have not given birth and the breasts that have never nursed.' Then they will begin to say to the mountains, 'Fall on us,' and to the hills, 'Hide us,' because if they will do this when the wood is green, what will happen when it is dry?"

They also were leading two other criminals to be executed with him, and when they came to the place that is called Skull, they crucified him there, along with the criminals—one on his right and one on his left.

Then Jesus said, "Father, forgive them because they do not know what they are doing."

Then they divided his clothes and cast lots, and the people stood there, watching. The rulers turned up their noses in ridicule and said, "He saved others—let him save himself if he is the chosen Messiah of God!" Then they mocked him.

The soldiers also came to him, offering him sour wine. They said, "If you are the king of the Jews, save yourself!" (You see, the inscription regarding him was "He was the King of the Jews.")

Then one of the criminals being hanged slandered him by saying, "Are you not the Messiah? Save yourself and us!"

But the other one scolded him and said, "Do you not even fear God? You are subjected to the same sentence! Furthermore, we are subjected to it fairly because we are getting what we deserve for what we have done—but he has done nothing out of place!" He then said, "Jesus, remember me when you come into your kingdom."

Jesus told him, "I am truly telling you—today you'll be with me in Paradise."

Now it was already about noon, and darkness came over the whole earth until mid-afternoon while the sun failed to shine. Then the inner curtain of the temple was torn in half, and Jesus said with a very loud voice, "Father! I place my spirit into your hands!" When he had said this, he died.

After the centurion saw what happened, he praised God and said, "This man was righteous after all!"

Then, when all the crowd that had gathered for this spectacle saw what happened, they beat their chests in grief and went back home. But the ones whom he knew stayed to watch these things at a distance, including the women who had followed him from Galilee.

Now get this: There was a man named Joseph who was on the Jew's council and was a good and righteous man—he was not in agreement with the verdict or what they did to him. He was from Arimathea, a city of the Jews, and he was waiting for God's kingdom. He approached Pilate and asked for the body of Jesus. Then he pulled it down, wrapped it in a linen cloth, and placed it in a tomb cut out of the stone, one where no one had ever been laid to rest. Now this was on a Friday, and the Sabbath was about to begin. The women also followed him (the ones who had come from Galilee with him). They saw the tomb and where his body was laid, and they returned to prepare spices and perfumes for the burial. Then, on the Sabbath, they rested in accordance with the command.

Very early in the morning on the first day of the week, they went to the tomb to bring the spices they had prepared, but they found the stone rolled away from the tomb. They went in but did not find the body of their Master, Jesus. Then, while they were very troubled by this, get this—two men appeared to them in radiant clothing. As the women became afraid and turned their faces toward the ground, the men said, "Why are you looking among the dead for the one who lives? He is not here. No, he has been raised! Remember how he told you while you were in Galilee, when he said that the Son of Man needed to be handed over into the hands of sinful men, to be crucified, and then to rise up on the third day?" Then they remembered what he had said.

So they returned from the tomb and reported all these things to the eleven and to the rest. This was Mary from Magdala, Joanna, and Mary wife of James, and the rest of the women who were with them. They told these things to the apostles, and in the apostles' opinions, these statements seemed like crazy talk—they did not believe them. But Peter got up, ran to the tomb, and bent down and saw only the linen cloth. Then he went back, thinking to himself with amazement about what had happened.

Get this: two of their group on that same day were going to a village called Emmaus, about seven miles from Jerusalem. They were conversing with one another about all these things that had happened. While they were conversing and debating, Jesus himself came up and began going with them, but their eyes were restrained from recognizing him.

He said to them, "What are these things that you are going back and forth about while you walk?"

Then they stopped and looked sad. One of them, named Cleopas, answered him, "Are you the only visitor to Jerusalem who did not know what happened there in recent days?"

He said to them, "What things?"

Then they told him, "About Jesus of Nazareth, a man who came here—a prophet who displayed power in action and word in front of God and all the people. Specifically, how our chief priests and rulers handed him over to be sentenced to death and crucified him. But we were hoping that he would be the one who would redeem Israel. On top of all this, today is the third day since the time this happened. Also, some women among us have astonished us—they went early in the morning to the tomb, and they said they did not find his body, but that they saw angels appear who said he was alive. So some of those who were with us went to the tomb and found it just as the women had said, but they did not see him."

Then he told them, "Oh, you are so foolish and so reluctant to believe everything that the prophets said about this! Was it not necessary for the Messiah to suffer these things and then enter into his glory?" Then he began at Moses and interpreted for them what was written about him in all the Scriptures by all the prophets.

As they came near the village where they were going, he pretended to keep going farther, but they urged him, "Stay with us because it is evening, and the sun has already gone down. So he went in to stay with them. While he was sitting with them, he took the bread, offered a blessing, broke it apart, and gave it out to them. Then their eyes were opened, and they recognized him, and he disappeared from in front of them. They said to one another, "Did our hearts not burn within us while he talked with us on the way, while he was explaining the Scriptures to us?"

They got up at that very moment and returned to Jerusalem. They found the eleven gathered, and others were with them. The eleven told them that the Master really had been raised and that he had appeared to Simon. Then the two men also reported what happened on the road, how that he made himself known to them when he was breaking apart the bread.

While they were saying this, Jesus himself appeared in their midst and told them, "Peace to you."

They became terrified and afraid, thinking that they had seen a ghost.

Then he asked them, "Why are you troubled—why have doubts overcome your heart? Look at my hands and my feet because I am he! Touch me and see because a ghost does not have flesh and bones, as you can see that I have!"

After he said this, he showed them his hands and feet. While they were still in disbelief because of their joy and amazement, he told them, "Bring some food here." They gave him a serving of roasted fish, and he ate it in front of them all.

He told them, "These are the words I told you while I was still with you—that it was necessary to fulfill everything that was written about me in the Law of Moses, the Prophets, and the psalms." Then he opened their minds to understand the Scriptures. He said to them, "This is what was written—the Messiah was to suffer and be raised from the dead on the third day, and then repentance for the forgiveness of sins can be preached in his name to all the nations, beginning at Jerusalem. You are witnesses of this, so look—I am sending the one my Father promised to you, and you will stay in the city until you are clothed with power from up high."

Then he led them out to Bethany, and he raised his hands and blessed them. While he was blessing them, he left them and was taken up into heaven. So they worshiped him and then returned to Jerusalem with great joy and were in the temple every day, praising God.

ACCORDING TO JOHN

In the beginning was the Word. The Word was with God, and the Word was God. This Word was in the beginning with God! Everything came to exist through him, and apart from him not a single thing has come to exist. What came to exist in him is life, and that life is the light for people! So the light shines in the darkness, and the darkness has been unable to prevail over it.

A man came along who was sent from God. His name was John. He came as a witness to give testimony about the light so that everyone would believe in it through him. This man was not the light—he only testified about the light.

The Word was the true light, who shines on every person as he comes into the world. He was in the world, and the world came to exist through him, but the world did not know him. He came to his own people, and his own people did not receive him. But he gave the right to become God's children to all who received him—to all who believed in his name. They were not born God's children by blood, by the will of the body, or by the will of a man, but by God's will!

So the Word became flesh and lived among us, and we saw his glory. It was glory like that of the uniquely born Son of the Father, filled with grace and truth. John testified about him—he cried out, "This is the one I was referring to—'One is coming after me who existed before me because he is my superior!' You see, we have all received grace on top of grace from his full abundance! For the Law was given through Moses, and grace and truth came to exist through Jesus the Messiah! No one has ever seen God; however, the uniquely-born God, who rests in the arms of the Father—he has shown the way!"

This is the testimony that John bore when the Jews of Jerusalem sent priests and Levites to him in order to ask him who he was. He acknowledged—he did not deny it—he acknowledged, "I am not the Messiah."

Then they asked him, "So who are you? Are you Elijah?"

So he said, "I am not."

"Are you a prophet?"

Then he answered, "No."

So they said to him, "Who are you? Tell us so that we can answer those who sent us! What do you have to say for yourself?"

Then he said: "I am the voice of someone crying in the desert, 'Prepare the Master's road!'"

(This was exactly what the prophet Isaiah said!)

Those who were sent were from among the Pharisees. They questioned him, saying, "So why do you immerse people if you are not the Messiah, Elijah, or the prophet?"

Then John answered them, "I immerse in water. Among you stands someone you do not recognize. He is coming after me, and I am not worthy to untie the straps of his sandals!" This happened in Bethany, on the bank of the Jordan River where John was immersing people.

THE NEXT MORNING, HE SAW JESUS COMING TOWARD HIM AND said, "Look! The Lamb of God who takes away the sins of the world! He is the one I was talking about: 'A man is coming after me who existed before me because he is my superior!' I myself did not know him, but I have come to immerse people in water for this reason: that he would be revealed to Israel."

Then John testified, "I have watched the Spirit come down from heaven like a dove and stay on him. I myself did not know him, but the one who sent me to immerse people in water told me himself: 'The one on whom you see the Spirit come down and stay—he is the one who immerses people in the Holy Spirit.' I have seen this, and I am testifying that this is God's Son!"

On the next day, John was again standing with two of his disciples and saw Jesus walking by. He said, "Look! The Lamb of God!" When his two disciples heard what he said, they followed Jesus. Now Jesus turned around and looked at them following him. Then he asked them, "What do you want?"

They asked him, "Rabbi" (which is translated "Teacher"), "where do you live?"

Jesus said to them, "Come and see." So they went and saw where he lived, and they stayed with him that day because it was about 4:00 p.m.

Andrew (the brother of Simon Peter) was one of the two who heard what John said and followed Jesus. The first thing he did was find his own brother, Simon, and tell him, "We have found the Messiah" (which is translated "Anointed"). Then he led him to Jesus. When Jesus saw him, he said, "You are Simon, John's son. You will be called 'Cephas'" (which means "Peter").

The next day, he wanted to leave for Galilee, and he found Philip. Jesus said to him, "Follow me." Philip was from Bethsaida (the same city as Andrew and Peter). Philip found Nathaniel and told him, "We have found the one that Moses and the prophets wrote about in the Law: Jesus, Joseph's son, from Nazareth!"

Then Nathaniel asked him, "Can anything good come from Nazareth?"

Philip said to him, "Come and see!"

Jesus saw Nathaniel coming toward him and talked about him, "Look! This is truly an Israelite in whom there is no deceit!"

Then Nathaniel asked him, "Where do you know me from?"

So Jesus answered him, "Before Philip called for you, when you were under a fig tree, I saw you."

Then Nathaniel said, "Rabbi, you are God's Son—you are the King of Israel!"

Jesus answered him, "Do you believe because I told you that I saw you under that fig tree? You will see better things than this!" Then he told him, "I am truly, truly telling you: you will see heaven opened and God's angels ascending and descending on the Son of Man."

ON THE THIRD DAY AFTER THAT, THERE WAS A WEDDING IN CANA, Galilee, and Jesus's mother was there. Jesus and his disciples were also invited to the wedding. When they had run out of wine, Jesus's mother said to him, "They do not have any more wine."

Then Jesus answered her, "What does that have to do with you or me, ma'am? My time has not come yet."

His mother said to the servers, "Do whatever he tells you to do."

Now there were six stone water pitchers placed nearby that were used for rites of cleansing for the Jews. Each one held about twenty to thirty gallons. Jesus told them, "Fill the pitchers with water," so they filled them to the brim. Then he said to them, "Now draw some out and take it to the head waiter," so they brought it.

Then the head waiter tasted the water that had become wine and did not know where it came from (although the servers who drew the water knew). So the head waiter called for the groom and said to him, "Everyone first serves the good wine; then, when they are drunk, he serves the inferior wine. But you have saved the good wine until now!"

Jesus did this—the first of his signs—in Cana, Galilee, and revealed his glory, so many of his disciples believed in him. After this, he went down to Capernaum (along with his mother, his brothers, and his disciples) and stayed there for many days.

THEN THE PASSOVER OF THE JEWS DREW NEAR, SO JESUS WENT up to Jerusalem. He found people in the temple who were selling cattle, sheep, and doves, and he saw the cashiers sitting there. So he made a whip from some rope and drove them all out of the temple, along with the sheep and cattle. He scattered the cashiers' coins and overturned the tables. Then he said to those who were selling doves, "Take these out of here! Do not make the house of my Father a place of business!" His disciples remembered that it had been written, "Zeal for your house has consumed me."

So the Jews asked him, "What sign are you showing us by doing these things?"

Jesus answered them, "Destroy this sanctuary, and I will raise it in three days."

Then the Jews said, "This sanctuary has been under construction for forty-six years, and you are going to raise it in three days?"

But he was talking about the sanctuary as his body. So when he was raised from the dead, his disciples remembered that he had said this, and they believed in the Scripture and the Message that Jesus spoke.

Now while he was among the residents of Jerusalem at the Passover feast, many people believed in his name once they saw the signs that he performed. But Jesus did not entrust himself to them because he knew everything—he did not need anyone to testify to him about a person because he knew what was in the minds of people.

There was a man from the Pharisees, whose name was Nicodemus. He was a leader among the Jews. He came to Jesus at night and said to him, "Rabbi, we know that you are a teacher who has come from God because no one could perform these signs that you perform unless God were with them."

Jesus answered him, "I am truly, truly telling you—unless someone is born again, they cannot see God's kingdom."

Nicodemus said to him, "How can a man be born when he is old? He cannot enter for the second time into his mother's womb and be born, can he?"

Jesus answered him, "I am truly, truly telling you—unless someone is born of water and the Spirit, they cannot enter into God's kingdom. Whatever is born of the body is physical. Whatever is born of the Spirit is spiritual. Do not be amazed that I have told you that you must be born again. The wind blows wherever it wants, and you recognize its sound, but you do not know where it comes from or where it is going. This is the way it is with the one who is born of the Spirit."

Nicodemus asked him, "How can this be true?"

Jesus answered him, "You are a teacher of Israel, and yet you do not know this? I am truly, truly telling you that we speak what we know and testify to what we see, but you do not receive our testimony. If I have spoken to you in earthly terms and you do not believe, how are you going to believe if I speak to you in heavenly terms? No one has ascended into heaven except the one who has descended from heaven—the Son of Man. Just as Moses lifted the serpent in the desert, the Son of Man must be lifted up—in the same way—so that everyone who believes in him will have eternal life! You see, this is how God loved the world—he gave his uniquely-born Son so that whoever believes in him will not be lost but have eternal life! For God did not send his Son into the world to condemn the world but that the world would be saved by him! Whoever believes in him is not condemned, but whoever does not believe is condemned already because they have not believed in the name of the uniquely born Son of God! This is the condemnation: the light has come into the world, but people have loved the darkness rather than the light because their actions have been evil. You see, everyone who practices despicable behavior hates the light and will not come to the light or else their actions will be exposed. On the other hand, whoever practices truth comes to the light so that it can be revealed that their actions are done with God!"

AFTER THIS, JESUS AND HIS DISCIPLES CAME TO THE LAND OF Judah. They spent some time there with those people and immersed them. Now John was in Aenon (near Salem) immersing people because there was a lot of water there, and the people were coming out and being immersed. (You see, John had not yet been thrown into prison.)

So a debate arose between the disciples of John and a Jew concerning purification. They came to John and said to him, "Rabbi, the one who was with you on the bank of the Jordan—the one about whom you bore witness—Look! He is immersing people, and everyone is going to him!"

John answered, "A man cannot receive anything except what has been given to him from heaven. You yourselves bear witness of me that I am not the Messiah. I only have been sent ahead of him! The one who has the bride is the groom. Now the groom's friend who stands and hears him rejoices gladly when he hears voice of the groom. So this joy of mine is complete! He must increase, and I must decrease."

The one who comes from above is over everything. Whoever is from the earth is from the earth, and they speak like they are from the earth. The one who comes from heaven is over everything. He bears witness of what he sees and hears, and no one receives his testimony. Whoever receives his testimony has certified that God is true! You see, the one God sent speaks God's words because he gives the Spirit without rations! The Father loves the Son and has given everything into his hand. Whoever believes in the Son has eternal life, but whoever does not obey the Son will not see life. On the contrary, God's wrath remains on him!

So since Jesus knew that the Pharisees heard he was making more disciples and immersing more people than John (although Jesus himself did not immerse anyone—his disciples did), he left Judah and went back to Galilee.

Now it was necessary for him to pass through Samaria, so he came to a Samaritan city called Shechem, near the property that Jacob gave to his son Joseph. One of Jacob's wells was there. So since Jesus was tired from the journey, he just sat down by the well. It was about noon. Then a woman from Samaria came to draw water. Jesus told her, "Give me something to drink." You see, his disciples had gone into the city to buy food. Then the Samaritan woman said to him, "How is it that you—a Jew—are asking from me—a Samaritan woman?" She said this because the Jews do not associate with the Samaritans.

Jesus answered her, "If you knew the gift of God and who it is who is telling you, 'Give me a drink,' you would have asked him, and he would have given you living water."

The woman said to him, "Sir, you do not have any way to draw the water, and the well is deep—so how do you have 'living water'? Are you any better than Jacob our ancestor? He gave us the well, and he and his sons and cattle drank from it."

Jesus answered her, "Whoever drinks this water will be thirsty again, but whoever drinks the water that I will give them will never thirst again. On the contrary, the water that I will give them will become a spring of water bubbling up in them that leads to eternal life."

The woman said to him, "Sir, give me this water so that I would not be thirsty or come here to draw water!"

He said to her, "Go call your husband and come back here."

She answered him, "I do not have a husband."

Jesus said to her, "You have well said, 'I do not have a husband,' because you have had five husbands, and the man you have now is not your husband—you have told the truth about this."

Then the woman said to him, "I see—you are a prophet! Our ancestors worshiped on this mountain, yet you Jews say that the place where we must worship is in Jerusalem."

Jesus said to her, "Believe me, ma'am; the time is coming when you will not worship the Father on this mountain or in Jerusalem. You do not know what you worship. We know what we worship because salvation comes from the Jews. But the time is coming—and is now here—when the true worshipers will worship the Father with spirit and truth. You see, the Father is seeking this kind of people to worship him. God is a spirit, and those who worship him must worship with spirit and truth."

The woman said to him, "I know that the Messiah is coming" (the one called Christ). "When he comes, he will explain everything to us."

Jesus said to her, "I AM—the one who is talking to you."

At that time, his disciples returned. They were amazed that he was talking to a woman. But no one asked, "What are you looking for?" or "Why are you talking to her?"

Then the woman left her water pitcher and went into the city and told the men of the city, "Come see a man who told me everything I have done! Could he be the Messiah?" They went out of the city and came to him.

Meanwhile, his disciples begged him, "Rabbi, eat!"

But he told them, "I have food to eat that you are not aware of."

Then his disciples said to one another, "No one brought him anything to eat, did they?"

Jesus told them, "My food is doing the will of the one who sent me and completing his work. Look, I am telling you—lift your eyes and look at the fields! They are white for harvesting. The one who harvests is already receiving wages and gathering produce for eternal life, so the one who plants has the same joy as the one who harvests. In this case, the saying is true: 'One plants, and another harvests.' I have sent you to harvest what you did not work for—on the contrary, others have worked it, and you have entered into their work!"

Many of the Samaritans who came from the city believed in him because of the woman's message, who testified, "He told me everything I have done." Then when the Samaritans came to him, they asked him to stay with them, so he stayed there for two days. Then many more believed because of his message and told the woman, "We no longer believe merely based on what you said because we have heard him for ourselves, and we know that he is truly the Savior of the world!"

After those two days, he left there for Galilee. You see, Jesus himself testified that a prophet does not have honor in his own homeland. So when he had gone to Galilee, the Galileans who saw everything he had done in Jerusalem at the feast received him. Then he came back to Cana of Galilee, where he made the water become wine.

There was a royal official in Capernaum whose son was sick. When he heard that Jesus had come from Judah to Galilee, he went to him and asked him to come down and heal his son because he was about to die. Then Jesus said to him, "You will never believe unless you see signs and wonders."

The official said to him, "Sir, come down before my child dies!"

Jesus said to him, "Go. Your son will live."

The man believed the statement that Jesus told him and went. By the time he was on his way back, his servants met him and told him that his child was alive. Then he asked them what time the child got better. Then they told him, "The fever left him yesterday at about 1:00 p.m."

Then the father understood: that was the time when Jesus told him, "Your son will live." So he and his whole household believed. This was the second sign that Jesus performed when he came from Judah to Galilee.

After this, there was a feast of the Jews, so Jesus went up to Jerusalem. Now there is a pool in Jerusalem by the Sheep Gate that is called "Bethesda" in Hebrew. It has five rows of pillars. All the sick, blind, lame, and crippled people used to lie down among them.

Well, there was a thirty-eight-year-old man who was there because of his sickness. Jesus saw him lying there and knew that he had been there a long time. He asked him, "Do you want to become healthy?"

The sick man answered him, "Sir, I do not have anyone who would put me in the pool when the waters are stirred up, and when I go, another goes down into it before I can."

Jesus said to him, "Get up, pick up your mattress, and walk." Immediately the man became healthy, so he picked up his mattress and began to walk!

Now that day was the Sabbath, so the Jews said to the man who had been healed, "It is the Sabbath, and you have no right to carry your mattress."

Then he answered them, "The one who made me healthy—he told me, 'Pick up your mattress and walk.'"

So they asked him, "Who told you to 'Pick it up and walk'?"

But the one who had been healed did not know who he was because Jesus had withdrawn from the crowd that was in that place.

After this, Jesus found him in the temple and said to him, "Look! You have become healthy! Do not sin anymore so that nothing worse will happen to you." The man left and reported to the Jews that it was Jesus who had made him healthy. So the Jews pursued Jesus because he did this on the Sabbath.

Yet Jesus answered them, "My Father has been working to this day, and I am working too." Because of this, they sought to kill him even more: "He not only makes light of the Sabbath—he also called God his Father, making himself equal to God."

So Jesus answered them, "I am truly, truly telling you—the Son is unable to do anything by himself other that what he sees the Father doing. You see, what the Father does, the Son will do in the same way. The Father loves the Son and shows him everything that he himself does. Furthermore, he will show him greater things to do than these so that you will be amazed. You see, just as the Father raises the dead and gives them life, the Son also gives life to whomever he wants. In addition, the Father does not condemn anyone—on the contrary, he has given the Son the right to condemn so that everyone will revere the Son as they honor the Father. Whoever does not honor the Son does not honor the Father who sent him.

"I am truly, truly telling you that whoever hears my message and believes in the one who sent me has eternal life and will not enter into condemnation. On the contrary, they have traveled over from death to life. I am truly, truly telling you that the time is coming (and is here now!) when the dead will hear the voice of God's Son, and those who hear will live again. You see, just as the Father has life-giving power in his grasp, he has also granted the Son to have it in his grasp. He also granted him the authority to execute judgment because he is the Son of Man. Do not be amazed about this, because the time is coming when everyone who is in the tombs will hear his voice. Then those who have done good things will go off to a living resurrection, but those who make a practice of despicable behavior will go off to a condemning resurrection.

"I am not able to do anything by myself. I judge based on what I hear, and my judgment is fair because I do not seek my own will. On the contrary, I seek the will of the one who sent me.

"As for me, if I were to give a testimony about myself, my testimony would not be true. There is another who bears witness about me, and I know that the testimony he bears about me is true. You have sent for John, and he has borne witness to the truth. (Now as for me, I do not accept the testimony of people, but I am saying this so that you can be saved!) He was the lamp that burned and shined, and you wanted to celebrate in his light for a little while.

"But I have a testimony that is better than John's. You see, the work that the Father has given me to complete—this work that I do testifies about me, saying that the Father has sent me. Also, the Father—who sent me—he has testified about me. You have never heard his voice or seen what he looks like, and his Word does not remain in you because you have not believed in the very one he sent. You search the Scriptures because you think you have eternal life in them, and they also bear witness about me. Yet you do not want to come to me in order to have life!

"I do not expect glory from men, but I have recognized you—you do not have God's love in you. I have come in my Father's name, but you have not received me. If another were to come in his own name, you would receive him. How are you able to trust the glory that you receive from one another, and yet you do not seek the glory that comes from the only God?

"Do not think that I will prosecute you before God. Moses is your prosecutor! You have set your hope in him. You see, if you had believed Moses, you would have believed me because he wrote about me. But since you do not believe what he wrote, how will you ever believe what I say?"

AFTER THIS, JESUS WENT TO THE AREA OF THE SEA OF GALILEE (Sea of Tiberius). A large crowd followed him because they had seen the signs that he had performed for the sick. But Jesus went up to a mountain and sat there with his disciples. The Passover (the Jewish feast) was near.

Then Jesus looked up and saw that the large crowd was coming to him. He said to Philip, "Where will we buy bread to feed these people?" (He said this to test him. You see, he knew what he was going to do.)

Philip answered him, "Two hundred days' wages would not be enough for each of them to have even a little to eat."

One of his disciples (Simon Peter's brother, Andrew) said to him, "Here is a child who has five pieces of barley bread and two pieces of fish, but what good are these for feeding such a crowd?"

Jesus said, "Have the people to sit down."

You see, there was a large field there, so the men sat down (there were about five thousand of them). Then Jesus took the pieces of bread, gave thanks for them, and distributed them to those who were lying down. He did the same thing with the pieces of fish. Everyone had as much as they wanted.

Once they were full, he said to his disciples, "Gather the leftover scraps so that they do not go to waste."

Then they gathered them and filled twelve baskets with the scraps of the five pieces of barley bread that were left by those who ate. Then the men who saw the sign that he performed said, "He is truly the Prophet who is coming into the world." Then Jesus went away to the mountain by himself because he knew that they were about to come seize him and make him king.

Since the evening was approaching, his disciples went down to the sea and boarded a ship going to Capernaum on the other side of the sea. Night was already falling, and Jesus had not yet come to them. The sea was getting rough because a strong wind was blowing. Then, after they had rowed about three or four miles, they saw Jesus walking on the sea—coming close to the ship—and they were afraid!

But he said to them, "I AM. Do not be afraid."

Then they sought to welcome him aboard the ship, and immediately the ship came to the shore at their destination.

IN THE MORNING, THE CROWD THAT WAS STANDING ON THE OTHER side of the sea saw that no other boat had been there—just the one. Furthermore, they knew that Jesus did not board the ship with his disciples. On the contrary, his disciples had left by themselves. Now some ships came from Tiberius to the place where they ate the bread that was blessed by the Master.

So when the crowd saw that neither Jesus nor his disciples were there, they boarded the ships and left for Capernaum, looking for Jesus. When they found him on the other side of the sea, they asked him, "Rabbi, how did you get here?"

Jesus answered them, "I am truly, truly telling you: you have been looking for me because you ate the bread and were satisfied, not because you saw signs. Do not work for perishable food. On the contrary, work for the enduring food (which leads to eternal life) that the Son of Man will give you. You see, the Father has put his seal on him!"

Then they asked him, "What can we do so that we can carry out God's work?"

Jesus answered them, "This is God's work: for you to believe in the one whom he sent."

Then they said to him, "So what sign will you perform so that we can see it and believe in you? What will you do? Our ancestors ate the manna in the desert, as it is written: 'He gave them bread from heaven to eat.'"

Then Jesus said to them, "I am truly, truly telling you: Moses did not give you the bread from heaven. On the contrary, my Father will give you the true bread from heaven. You see, God's bread has descended from heaven, and it gives life to the world."

Then they said to him, "Master, give us this bread always!"

Jesus said to them, "I am the bread of life. Whoever comes to me will never hunger, and whoever believes in me will never thirst again.

"But I told you that even though you have seen me, you do not believe. Everything that my Father gives me comes to me, and I will never throw away what comes to me. I have descended from heaven—not to do my will but to do the will of the one who sent me. Now this is the will of the one who sent me: that I would not lose anything that he has given to me. On the contrary, his will is for me to raise it up on the last day. You see, this is my Father's will: that everyone who sees the Son and believes in him would have eternal life, and that I would raise them up on the last day."

Then the Jews complained about him because he said, "I am the bread that descended from heaven." So, they said, "Is this not Jesus, the son of Joseph? We know his father and mother! How is it that he is now saying, 'I have descended from heaven'?"

Jesus answered them, "Do not complain among yourselves. No one can come to me unless the Father who sent me draws them. Then I will raise them up on the last day. It is written in the

Prophets: 'They all will be teachers for God.' Everyone who hears and learns from the Father comes to me. It is not as though anyone has seen the Father; yet the one who is from God has seen the Father. I am truly, truly telling you: whoever believes has eternal life. I am the bread of life. Your ancestors ate the manna in the desert, and yet they died. But this is the bread that has descended from heaven so that whoever ate it would not die. I am the living bread that has descended from heaven. Whoever eats this bread will live forever. Now the bread that I will give for the life of the world is my body."

Then the Jews argued among themselves, "How can he give us his body to eat?"

Then Jesus said to them, "I am truly, truly telling you: unless you eat the Son of Man's body and drink his blood, you do not have eternal life within you. Whoever eats my body and drinks my blood has eternal life, and I will raise him up on the last day. You see, my body really is food, and my blood really is something to drink. Whoever eats my body and drinks my blood remains in me, and I remain in him. In the same way that the living Father sent me—and I live because of the Father—the one who eats me will also live because of me. This is the bread that has descended from heaven. It is not like what your ancestors ate—they died. Whoever eats this bread will live forever." (He said this as he was teaching in the synagogue in Capernaum.)

Then many of his disciples who heard this said, "This is a hard message! Who can listen to it?"

But since Jesus knew in his heart that his disciples were complaining about this, he said to them, "Does this offend you? What if you were to see the Son of Man ascend to the place he was at first? The Spirit is what gives life—the body is not worth anything. The words that I have spoken to you are the Spirit and life, but there are some of you who do not believe them."

You see, Jesus knew from the beginning who would not believe and who would betray him. Then he said, "This was why I told you that no one can come to me unless it has been granted to them by the Father."

From that time, many of his disciples left his presence and did not walk with him anymore. Then Jesus asked the twelve, "Do you want to leave too?"

Simon Peter answered him, "Master, to whom will we go? You have the words of eternal life! Furthermore, we have believed and have come to know that you are God's Holy One."

Jesus answered them, "Did I not choose the twelve of you? Yet one of you is a devil." (He said this referring to Judas, the son of Simon Iscariot, because he was going to betray him—one of the twelve!)

AFTER THIS, JESUS BEGAN WALKING AROUND GALILEE. YOU SEE, he did not want to walk around in Judea because the Jews were seeking to kill him.

Now the Jews' Feast of Booths was approaching, so his brothers said to him, "Leave here and go to Judea so that your disciples may see the things that you are doing. No one does anything secretly while seeking public attention. If you are doing these things, reveal yourself to the world!" (You see, his brothers did not even believe in him.)

Then Jesus said to them, "My time has not yet come; but your time is always here. The world cannot hate you. It hates me because I testify about it—its actions are evil! You must go to the feast. I will not go to the feast because my time has not yet been completed." After saying this, he remained in Galilee.

So as his brothers went to the feast, then Jesus also went. But he did not go openly—he went secretly.

Then the Jews were looking for him at the feast. They asked, "Where is he?" There was a lot of gossip among the crowd about him. Some said, "He is a good man," while others said, "No! He deceives the crowd." But no one spoke publicly about him because they were afraid of the Jews.

Now the feast was already in progress when Jesus went to the temple and taught. Then the Jews were amazed and asked, "How does he know the Scriptures without having studied in a school?"

Then Jesus answered them, "My teaching is not in fact mine; rather, it belongs to the one who sent me. If someone wants to do his will, they will know (as far as the teaching is concerned) whether it is from God or I am speaking my own opinion. Whoever speaks their own opinion seeks their own glory. On the other hand, whoever seeks the glory of the one who sends them is genuine, and there is no unfairness with them.

"Did Moses not give you the Law? Yet none of you does what the Law says. Why are you seeking to kill me?"

The crowd answered, "You have a demon! Who is seeking to kill you?"

Jesus replied to them, "I have performed a miracle, and you are all shocked. This is why Moses has given you circumcision—not that it was from Moses; it came from the patriarchs. But you might circumcise a man on the Sabbath. If a man might receive circumcision on the Sabbath and yet the Law of Moses is not broken, are you going to become angry with me because I have made a person's whole body healthy on the Sabbath? Do not pass judgment based on outward appearance—pass a fair judgment!"

Then some of the citizens of Jerusalem said, "Is this not the one they are seeking to kill? Look! He is speaking publicly, and they are saying nothing to him. Might the religious authorities actually know that he is the Messiah? But we know where this man is from. When the Messiah comes, no one will know where he is from."

Then Jesus shouted in the temple as he was teaching, "You know me, as well as where I have come from. I have not come of my own accord. On the contrary, the one who sent me is trustworthy. You do not know him. I know him because I have come from him. He has sent me."

Then they sought to arrest him, but no one laid a hand on him because his time had not yet come. But some of the crowd believed in him and said, "When the Messiah comes, will he perform greater signs than the ones he has performed?" The Pharisees heard the crowd arguing this matter about him, and the chief priests and Pharisees sent servants to arrest him.

Then Jesus said, "I will be with you for a little while longer, and then I am going back to the one who sent me. You will seek me, but you will not find me. You are not able to go where I will be."

Then the Jews asked among themselves, "Where is he going to go so that we will not find him? Surely he is not going to go to the people who are dispersed among the Greeks and teach the Greeks, will he? What is this statement that he has made: 'You will seek me and not find me, and you cannot go where I will be'?"

ON THE FEAST'S LAST OBSERVED DAY, JESUS STOOD UP AND shouted, "Whoever is thirsty needs to come to me and drink! As the Scripture says, whoever believes in me—streams of living water will flow from their heart." (He said this referring to the Spirit, whom those who believed in him were going to receive. You see, the Spirit had not come yet because Jesus had not yet been glorified.)

Then those in the crowd who heard this statement said, "He really is a prophet!"

Others said, "He is the Messiah!"

Still others said, "No, he is not because the Messiah does not come from Galilee. Does the Scripture not say that the Messiah comes from David's lineage and from Bethlehem, the village where David was from?"

Then a division arose among the crowd because of him. Some of them wanted to arrest him, but no one laid a hand on him.

Then the assistants returned to the chief priests and Pharisees. The chief priests and Pharisees asked them, "Why did you not arrest him?"

The assistants answered, "No one has ever spoken like this man!"

Then the Pharisees replied to them, "You have not also been deceived, have you? None of the religious authorities or Pharisees have believed in him, have they? But this crowd who does not understand the Law—they are cursed!"

Nicodemus (who was one of them and had come to him earlier) said to them, "Our Law does not condemn the man until his case is heard and what he has done has been discovered, right?"

They answered him, "You are not also from Galilee, are you? Search the Scriptures and look: no prophet arises from Galilee!"

THEN EACH OF THEM WENT HOME, BUT JESUS WENT TO THE Mount of Olives. When morning came, he went to the temple again. All the people came to him, so he sat down to teach them. Now the scribes and Pharisees brought in a woman who was caught in the act of committing adultery. They stood her in between them and Jesus and said to him, "This woman was caught in the very act of committing adultery. Now Moses commanded us by the Law to stone such people to death. So what do you say?" (But they said this to test him so that they could have a reason to accuse him.)

But Jesus crouched down and wrote on the ground with his finger. As they continued to ask him, he stood up and said to them, "Whichever one of you who is sinless needs to throw the first stone at her." Then he again crouched down and wrote on the ground.

So when they heard this, they went away one at a time (starting with the older ones), and Jesus was left alone with the woman, who was in front of him. When he stood up, he said to her, "Ma'am, where are they? Did anyone condemn you?"

She said, "No one, sir."

So Jesus told her, "I do not condemn you, either. Go, and do not sin anymore."

THEN JESUS AGAIN TAUGHT THE PEOPLE, "I AM THE WORLD'S light. Whoever follows me will never walk in darkness. On the contrary, they will have the living light."

So, the Pharisees said to him, "You are testifying about yourself! Your testimony is not true."

Jesus answered them, "My testimony is true even if I testify about myself because I know where I have come from and where I am going. But you do not know where I have come from or where I am going. You condemn based on physical things—I am not condemning anyone. Even if I were to condemn someone, my judgment is true because I am not alone—it is I and the Father who sent me. Even in your Law, it is written that 'the testimony of two people is true.' I am the one who testifies about myself, and the Father who sent me testifies about me."

Then they said to him, "Where is your father?"

Jesus answered, "You do not know me or my Father. If you knew me, you would also know my Father." (He spoke these words in the treasury while he taught in the temple. Yet no one arrested him because his time had not yet come.)

Then he spoke to them again, "I am going away, and you will look for me, but you will die in your sin. You are not able to go where I am going."

Then the Jews said, "Will he kill himself? You see, he says, 'You are not able to go where I am going.'"

He said to them, "You are from below; I am from above. You are from this world; I am not from this world. So I said to you, 'You will die in your sins,' because if you do not believe that I AM, you will die in your sins."

Then they asked him, "Who are you?"

Jesus said to them, "What have I been saying to you from the beginning! I have a lot to say about you and a lot to condemn, but the one who sent me is true, and I speak in the world what I hear from him." (They did not know that he was speaking to them about the Father.)

Then Jesus said to them, "When you lift up the Son of Man, you will know that I AM and that I do nothing by myself. But I speak just as the Father has taught me. Furthermore, the one who sends me is with me. He has not left me alone because I always do what pleases him."

As he spoke these things, many people believed in him, so Jesus said to the Jews who had believed in him, "If you continue in what I say, you are truly my disciples. You will know the truth, and the truth will set you free."

They answered him, "We are descendants of Abraham, and no one has ever enslaved us. How can you say that you will set us free?"

Jesus answered them, "I am truly, truly telling you: everyone who commits sin is sin's slave. A servant does not stay in the household forever. On the contrary, a son does stay there forever. So if the Son sets you free, you really will be free!

"I know that you are Abraham's descendants. But you are seeking to kill me because what I am saying is not making any progress with you. I have spoken about what I have seen in the Father's presence, so you also must do what you have heard from the Father."

They answered him, "Our father is Abraham!"

Jesus said to them, "If you were Abraham's children, you would do what Abraham did. But you are now seeking to kill me—a man who has told you the truth that he heard from God. Abraham did not do this! You are doing what your father has done."

They said to him, "We were not born out of wedlock! We have one Father: God."

Jesus said to them, "If God were your Father, you would have loved me. You see, I have come from God—I am here! I have not come on my own accord. On the contrary, he has sent me. Why do you not understand what I have said? You see, you are not able to listen to my message. You belong to your father—the devil! You want to do what makes your father happy. He has been a murderer since the beginning. He has not remained with the truth because there is no truth in him. When he tells a lie, he speaks of his own accord because he is a liar (and a liar's father). But you do not believe me because I speak the truth. Who among you accuses me of sinning? If I tell the truth, why do you not believe me? Whoever belongs to God listens to his words. You do not listen because you do not belong to God."

The Jews answered him, "Did we not rightly say that you are a Samaritan and that you have a demon?"

Jesus answered them, "I do not have a demon. On the contrary, I honor my Father, and you dishonor me. I do not seek my own glory. There is one who seeks glory and passes judgment. I am truly, truly telling you: whoever keeps my message will never see death."

Then the Jews said to him, "Now we know you have a demon! Abraham died, as well as the prophets, and you say, 'Whoever keeps my message will never taste death.' You are not better than our father Abraham, are you? He died, and the prophets died too! Who are you claiming to be?"

Jesus answered, "If I were to glorify myself, my glory would be nothing. The Father, whom you call our God, is the one who glorifies me. You do not know him, but I know him. If I were to say that I did not know him, I would be lying to you. But I do know him, and I keep his message. Your father Abraham was thrilled that he would see my day; and he saw it and rejoiced."

Then the Jews said to him, "You are not yet fifty years old, and you have seen Abraham?"

Jesus said to them, "I am truly, truly telling you: before Abraham lived, I AM!"

Then they picked up stones to throw at him, but Jesus was hidden from them and left the temple.

Now as he went on from there, Jesus saw a man who had been blind since birth. His disciples asked him, "Who sinned—this man or his parents—causing him to be born blind?"

Jesus answered, "Neither this man nor his parents sinned. He was born blind so that God's work could be demonstrated in him. We must do the work of the one who sent me while it is still day. Night is coming, and then no one can work. As long as I am in the world, I am the world's light."

When he had said this, he spit on the ground, made mud from the spit, and smeared the mud on the man's eyes. He told him, "Go wash yourself in the Pool of Siloam" (which means "sent"). Then he went, washed himself, and came back seeing!

Then his neighbors and those who had previously seen him (you see, he was a beggar) asked, "Is this not the one who sat and begged?"

Some said, "It is he!" Others said, "No, but he looks like him!"

He said, "I am he!"

Then they asked him, "So how have your eyes been opened?"

He answered them, "The man named Jesus made mud and smeared it on my eyes. He told me to go to Siloam and wash myself. So I went, I washed myself, and I began to see!"

They said to him, "Who is he?"

He said, "I do not know."

They led the man who had been blind to the Pharisees. Now the day that Jesus made mud and opened the man's eyes was a Sabbath. So the Pharisees asked him how he began to see.

Then he said to them, "He put mud on my eyes, I washed myself, and now I see."

Then some of the Pharisees said, "This man is not from God because he does not keep the Sabbath!"

But others said, "How could he perform such signs if he were a sinful man?" Thus there was a division among them.

Then they asked the blind man again, "What do you say about him—the one who opened your eyes?"

He said, "He is a prophet."

Then many of the Jews did not believe that he had actually been blind before he began to see, until they called the parents of the man who could now see. They asked them, "Is this your son, who you say was born blind? How is it that he can see now?"

Then his parents answered them, "We know that he is our son and that he was born blind. But we do not know how it is that he can see now; furthermore, we do not know who opened his eyes. Ask him. He is an adult—he will speak for himself."

His parents said this because they were afraid of the Jews. You see, the Jews had already reached a decision that whoever confessed that he was the Messiah would be banned from the synagogue. So his parents said, "He is an adult—ask him."

Then, for the second time, they called the man who had been blind, and they said to him, "Give glory to God. We know that this man is a sinner!"

Then he answered, "Whether or not he is a sinner, I do not know. I do know one thing: I was blind, but now I can see."

They said to him, "What did he do to you? How did he open your eyes?"

He answered them, "I told you already, and you did not listen! Why do you want to hear it again? You do not want to be his disciples, do you?"

Then they ridiculed him and said, "You are his disciple, but we are disciples of Moses! We know God has spoken to Moses, but we do not know where this man is from."

The man answered them, "This is the amazing part: you do not know where he is from, and he opened my eyes. We know that God does not listen to sinners. But whoever is reverent to God and does his will—God will hear them. It has never been reported that anyone has opened the eyes of the blind. Unless this man were from God, he would not have been able to do anything!"

They answered him, "You were born in complete sin, and you are going to teach us?" So they threw him out.

Jesus heard that he had been thrown out. When he found him, he asked, "Do you believe in the Son of Man?"

He answered, "Who is he, sir, so that I could believe in him?"

Jesus said to him, "You have even seen him—It is he who is speaking with you."

Then he said, "I believe, Master!" Then he worshiped him.

Then Jesus said, "I have come to this world because of judgment so that those who cannot see may see and that those who see may become blind."

Some of the Pharisees who were with him heard this and said to him, "We are not blind, are we?"

Jesus answered them, "If you were blind, you would not have any sin. But now that you have said, 'We see,' your sin remains. I am truly, truly telling you: whoever does not enter the sheep's fold by the door (rather, he enters it from another place) is a thief and robber. But the one who enters through the door is the sheep's shepherd. The doorkeeper opens the door for him, and the sheep hear his voice. He calls his own sheep by name and leads them out. When he has brought out all his own sheep, he goes in front of them, and they follow behind him. They will not follow anyone else. On the contrary, they will flee from him because they do not recognize the other person's voice." Jesus spoke this allegory to them, but they did not know what he was saying to them.

Then Jesus spoke again, "I am truly, truly telling you: I am the sheep's door. All who have come prior to me have been thieves and robbers, but the sheep did not hear them. I am the door. If anyone enters through me, he will be saved—he will go in and out and find a place to graze. The thief comes only to steal, slaughter, and destroy. I have come so that they can have life—and that they can have it abundantly!

"I am the good shepherd. The good shepherd lays down his life for the sheep. The hired hand (who is not the shepherd, and the sheep do not belong to him) will see the wolf coming and then abandon the sheep and flee. Then the wolf will drag them away and chase them in every direction. You see, he is a hired hand and is not concerned about the sheep.

"I am the good shepherd. I know those who are mine, and those who are mine know me (in the same way that the Father knows me and I know the Father), and I am laying down my life for the sheep. Furthermore, I have sheep that are not part of this fold. I must also lead them, and they will hear my voice. They shall be one sheep fold, and there shall be one Shepherd.

"This is why the Father loves me, so that I will receive life again: because I am laying down my life. No one is taking it from me. On the contrary, I am laying it down on my own accord. I have the right to lay it down, and I have the authority to receive it again. I received this command from my Father."

There again arose a division among the Jews because of these statements. Many of them said, "He has a demon! He is crazy! Why are you listening to him?"

Others said, "These are not the words of someone who is demon-possessed. A demon-possessed man could not open the eyes of blind people, could he?"

AT THAT TIME, THE FESTIVAL OF HANUKKAH WAS TAKING PLACE in Jerusalem—it was winter. Jesus was walking in the temple, in Solomon's colonnade.

Then the Jews surrounded him and said to him, "How long will you keep us wondering? Are you the Messiah? Tell us publicly!"

Jesus answered them, "I have told you, and you do not believe. The things that I am doing in the name of my Father bear witness about me. But you do not believe because none of you are my sheep. My sheep hear my voice—I recognize them, and they follow me. Furthermore, I am giving them eternal life, and they will never perish. No one will snatch them from my hand. My Father, who gave them to me, is greater than everyone, and no one can snatch anything from his hand. I and the Father are one."

The Jews again picked up stones in order to stone him to death. Then Jesus replied to them, "I have shown you many good works from the Father. For which one of them are you now going to stone me to death?"

The Jews answered him, "It is not because of a good work that we are going to stone you to death—on the contrary, it is because of blasphemy. You—a man—make yourself out to be God!"

Jesus answered them, "Is it not written in your Law that 'I have said you are gods?' If he said 'gods,' referring to those to whom God's message came, and Scripture cannot be broken, will you say, 'You are blaspheming' to the one whom the Father sanctified and sent into the world because I said, 'I am the Son of God'? If I do not do my Father's work, do not believe me. But if I do his work and you will not believe me, believe because of what I have done so that you will know and understand that the Father is in me and I am in the Father."

Then they sought to arrest him again, but he escaped their hands. He came again to the bank of the Jordan, to the place where John was immersing earlier, and he stayed there. Many people came to him and said, "John did not perform a sign, but everything that John said about this man was true!" So many believed in him there.

NOW THERE WAS A SICK MAN NAMED LAZARUS FROM BETHANY— from the same village as Mary and her sister, Martha. (Mary was the one who anointed the Master with ointment and wiped his feet with her hair, and it was her brother, Lazarus, who was sick.) Then the sisters sent for him and said, "Look, Master, the one you love is sick."

But when Jesus heard this, he said, "This sickness will not end in death. On the contrary, it has happened for God's glory so that the Son of God will be glorified by it."

Now Jesus loved Martha, her sister, and Lazarus. When he heard that Lazarus was sick, he remained where he was for two days. After this, he said to his disciples, "Let us go to Judea again."

The disciples said to him, "Rabbi, the Jews are seeking to stone you to death now, and you want to go back there?"

Jesus answered, "Are there not twelve daylight hours? If someone walks during daylight, they will not stumble because they see by this world's light. But if they walk at night, they stumble because they do not have the light with them."

He said this, and afterward, he said to them, "Our friend Lazarus has fallen asleep, but I am going there to wake him."

Then the disciples said to him, "Master, if he has fallen asleep, he will recover."

Now Jesus was speaking about his death, but they thought he was talking about him resting—asleep. Then Jesus said to them clearly, "Lazarus has died, and I am excited for your benefit that I was not there so that you would believe. Now let us go to him."

Thomas (who was called "Twin") said to his fellow disciples, "Let us go so that we can die with him."

So when Jesus found him, he had already been in the tomb for four days. Now Bethany was near Jerusalem—about two miles away. Many of the Jews came to Martha and Mary to comfort them about their brother. When Martha heard that Jesus had come, she went to meet him, but Mary was sitting at home.

Then Martha said to Jesus, "Master, my brother would not have died if you had been here. But even now I know that God will give you whatever you ask of him."

Jesus said to her, "Your brother will be resurrected."

Martha said to him, "I know that he will be resurrected—during the resurrection on the last day."

Then Jesus said to her, "I am the resurrection and the life; whoever believes in me will live, even if they die. Everyone who lives and believes in me will never, ever die. Do you believe this?"

She said to him, "Yes, Master. I have believed that you are the Messiah—God's Son who has come into the world."

When she said this, she left and called her sister, Mary, and secretly told her, "The Teacher has come and is calling for you."

When she heard this, she got up quickly and went to him. Jesus had not yet come into the village; rather, he was still in the place where Martha met him. When the Jews who were in the house with her and comforting her saw that Mary had quickly gotten up and left, they followed her because they thought she was going to the tomb to weep.

When Mary came to the place where Jesus was, she saw him, fell down at his feet, and said to him, "My brother would not have died if you had been here."

When Jesus saw her (and the Jews who came with her) weeping, he became angry and upset and asked, "Where have you placed him?"

They said to him, "Master, come and look."

Jesus wept. Then the Jews said, "Look how much he loved him!"

But some of them asked, "Could this man, who opened the eyes of the blind man, not have done something to prevent Lazarus from dying?"

Then Jesus (again becoming angry) came to the tomb. It was a cave, and a stone was laid over its opening. Jesus said, "Take away the stone."

The dead man's sister Martha said to him, "Master, there will be a smell—it has already been four days!"

Jesus said to her, "Did I not tell you that if you believe you will see God's glory? Take away the stone."

Then Jesus looked upward and said, "Father, thank you for listening to me. I know that you always listen to me, but I said this because of the crowd that is present—so that they can believe that you have sent me."

When he had said this, he cried out with a loud voice, "Lazarus, come out!"

The man who had died came out, wrapped hand-and-foot with burial cloths, and his face was wrapped with a facecloth.

Jesus said to them, "Unwrap him, and let him go."

Then many of the Jews who had come to Mary and had seen what he did believed in him. But some of them went to the Pharisees and told them what Jesus had done.

Then the chief priests and Pharisees assembled the council and said, "What are we going to do? This man performs many signs! If we let him do this, everyone will believe in him, and the Romans will come and take us away, along with our place and nation!"

But one of them (Caiaphas, who was a chief priest that year) said to them, "You do not know anything! You also have not considered that it would be better for you that one man should die for the people rather than for the whole nation to perish." He did not say this as his own opinion. On the contrary, since he was a chief priest that year, he prophesied that Jesus was going to die for the nation—but not only for that nation. He also died so that God's children who were scattered would be brought together into a single group. So beginning that day, they decided to kill him.

Then Jesus no longer walked around in Judea publicly. On the contrary, he left there for the place called Ephraim, a city near the desert, and he stayed there with the disciples.

Now the Jews' Passover feast was approaching, so many people went up to Jerusalem before Passover from their places so that they could purify themselves. Then they looked for Jesus and spoke with one another as they stood in the temple, "What do you think? Will he actually come to the feast?" You see, the chief priests and Pharisees had given a command that whoever knew where he was must report it so that they could arrest him.

Then Jesus came to Bethany (where Lazarus lived, whom Jesus raised from the dead) six days before the Passover. They prepared supper for him there. Martha attended to him, and Lazarus was one of those reclining to eat with him.

Then Mary took a pound of perfumed ointment made from pure nard (which was very expensive) and anointed Jesus' feet. Then she wiped it dry with her hair, and the house became filled with the fragrance of the ointment.

One of his disciples, Judas Iscariot (the one who was going to betray him), asked, "Why was this ointment not sold for a year's worth of wages to give to the poor?" But he did not say this because he cared for the poor. On the contrary, he was a thief, and he was in charge of the money box that contained their contributions.

Then Jesus said, "Leave her alone because she has kept this for today so that she could prepare my body for burial. You always have the poor with you, but you will not always have me."

Then a large crowd of the Jews came to know where he was, and they came. But they did not come for Jesus alone but also that they could see Lazarus, whom he had raised from the dead. Now the chief priests had decided to put Lazarus to death, too, because many of the Jews abandoned them and believed in Jesus.

IN THE MORNING, WHEN THE LARGE CROWD THAT HAD COME TO the feast heard that Jesus had come to Jerusalem, they took palm branches and went out to meet him. They cried out:

> Hosanna!
> Blessed is the one who comes in the Master's name—
> The King of Israel!

Then Jesus found a young donkey and sat on it, just as it is written:

> Do not fear, daughter of Zion;
> Look! Your king is coming,
> Sitting on the foal of a donkey.

His disciples did not recognize this at the time. But when Jesus was glorified, they remembered that these things were written about him and were done for him.

Then the crowd (those who were with him when he called for Lazarus to come from the tomb and raised him from the dead) testified about him. Because of this, the crowd went to meet him because they heard that he had performed this sign.

Then the Pharisees said to one another, "Do you see that you are accomplishing nothing? Look! The whole world has followed him!"

Some Hellenists had come to worship at the feast. They came to Philip (who was from Bethsaida, Galilee), and asked him, "Sir, we want to see Jesus." Philip went and spoke with Andrew; then Andrew and Philip went and spoke with Jesus.

Then Jesus answered them, "The time has come for the Son of Man to be glorified. I am truly, truly telling you: unless the wheat seed falls to the ground and dies, it will remain alone. But if it dies, it will bear a lot of fruit. Whoever loves their own life will lose it, but whoever despises their own life in this world will preserve it for eternal life. Whoever wants to serve me must follow me. Then my servant will also be where I am. The Father will honor whoever serves me.

"Now my soul is troubled. What can I say? 'Father, save me from this time?' No, I have come *because* of this time. Father, glorify your name."

Then a voice came from heaven, "I have glorified it, and I will glorify it again."

The crowd that was standing there heard it, and they said, "It just thundered!"

Others said, "An angel has spoken to him!"

Jesus answered, "This voice did not come for my benefit but for yours. The judgment of this world has arrived—now the ruler of this world will be thrown out. Even if I am lifted up from the earth, I will draw everyone to me." (He said this to give a sign for what kind of death he was going to die.)

Then the crowd answered him, "We heard from the Law that the Messiah will stay forever. How can you say that the Son of Man must be lifted up? Who is this 'Son of Man'?"

Then Jesus said, "The light will be with you for a little while longer. Walk while you have the light so that darkness does not engulf you. Whoever walks in darkness does not know where they are going. Believe in the light while you have it so that you can become children of light." When Jesus had said this, he left and was hidden from them.

Although he performed these kinds of signs in front of them, they did not believe in him; so the message of Isaiah the prophet was fulfilled:

> Master, who has believed our report?
> To whom has the Master's power been revealed?

Because of this, they could not believe. You see, Isaiah also said:

> He has blinded their eyes and petrified their hearts,
> Or else they would see with their eyes, understand with their hearts,
> And return—then I would heal them.

Isaiah said this because he saw God's glory and spoke about it. But many of the religious authorities even believed in him, but they did not acknowledge it because of the Pharisees. You see, these authorities would have been expelled from the synagogue, and they loved glory from men more than God's glory.

Then Jesus cried out, "Whoever believes in me believes not only in me but also in the one who sent me. Whoever sees me also sees the one who sent me. I am the light that has come into the world so that whoever believes in me will not stay in darkness. If anyone hears my words and does not keep them, I do not condemn him. You see, I have not come to condemn the world. On the contrary, I have come to save the world! The one who does not listen to me and does not receive my words has something that condemns him. The message I have spoken will condemn him on the last day. You see, I have not spoken of my own accord. On the contrary, the Father, who sent me, has commanded me what I should say and what I should speak. I know that his command is eternal life. So I say what I say, exactly as the Father has told me."

NOW THIS HAPPENED BEFORE THE PASSOVER. JESUS KNEW THAT the time had come for him to pass from this life to the Father. He loved those who belonged to him in the world—he loved them to the end. Time had come for supper, and the devil had already put into the heart of Judas (the son of Simon Iscariot) to betray him. Jesus knew that the Father had given everything into his hands and that he had come from God and was going to God.

He got up from supper and laid down his robe, and then he picked up a towel and tied it around his waist. Then he put water into a basin and began to wash his disciples' feet and wipe them dry with the towel he was wearing around his waist.

When he came to Simon Peter, Peter asked him, "Master, are you actually going to wash my feet?"

Jesus answered him, "You do not know what I am doing now, but you will understand after this."

Peter said to him, "You will never wash my feet!"

Jesus answered them, "Unless I wash you, you will have no partnership with me."

Simon Peter said to him, "Master, do not wash only my feet—wash my hands and head too!"

Jesus said to him, "Whoever has bathed does not need to be washed except for their feet. On the contrary, they are completely clean. You guys are clean, but not all of you." (You see, he knew who was going to betray him. Because of this, he said "not all of you are clean.")

Then, after he washed their feet, picked up his robe, and reclined at the table again, he said to them, "Do you understand what I have done for you? You call me 'Teacher' and 'Master,' and you rightly say this because that is who I am. So since I—your master and teacher—have washed your feet, you also ought to wash one another's feet. You see, I have given you an example so that you may do exactly like what I have done for you. I am truly, truly telling you: The servant is no better than the master, and the one who is sent is no better than the one who sent them. Since you know these things, you are blessed if you do them.

"I am not talking about all of you. I know whom I have chosen. But the Scripture must be fulfilled. 'The one who ate my bread has lifted his heel against me.' I am telling you this before it happens so that after it does, you will believe that I AM. I am truly, truly telling you: whoever receives the one I send receives me. Also, whoever receives me receives the one who sent me."

After Jesus said this, he became inwardly upset and testified, "I am truly, truly telling you—one of you will betray me."

The disciples were looking at one another, at a loss as to which of them he was talking about. One of his disciples—the one Jesus loved—was reclining directly in front of Jesus. Simon Peter motioned to him to find out what Jesus was talking about, so he leaned back against Jesus' chest and asked him, "Master, who is it?"

Jesus answered, "He is the one with whom I dip my piece of bread and give it to him." When he had dipped his piece of bread, he took it and gave it to Judas, the son of Simon Iscariot. After this happened with the bread, Satan entered Judas.

Then Jesus said to him, "Do what you are going to do quickly." No one who was reclining to eat understood why he said this to him. You see, some of them thought that since Judas carried the money box, Jesus told him, "Buy what we need for the feast," or that he might give something to the poor. When he had taken the piece of bread, he left immediately. (It was nighttime.)

When he had left, Jesus said, "Now the Son of Man has been glorified, and God has been glorified with him. Since God has been glorified with him, God will also glorify him with himself and will glorify him immediately. Little children, I will be with you a little while longer. You will look for me, and just as I told the Jews that 'you cannot go where I am going,' now I am telling you too. I am giving you a new command: love one another exactly how I have loved you—so you should love one another also. This is how everyone will know that you are my disciples—you have love for one another."

Simon Peter asked him, "Master, where are you going?"

Jesus answered him, "You cannot yet follow me where I am going. But you will follow me later."

Peter asked him, "Master, why can I not follow you now? I will give my life for you!"

Jesus answered, "Will you really give your life for me? I am truly, truly telling you: The rooster will not crow until you have denied me three times.

"Do not let your hearts be upset. Believe in God, and believe in me too. There are many rooms in my Father's house—if that were not true, would I have said that I am going to prepare a place for you? So, since I am going to prepare a place for you, I will come back and take you along with me so that you will be where I am. You even know the way to where I am going!"

Thomas said to him, "Master, we do not know where you are going. How could we know the way?"

Jesus said to him, "I am the way, as well as the truth and the life. No one comes to the Father except through me. Since you have come to know me, you also will come to know my Father. Even now you have both known him and seen him."

Philip said to him, "Master, show us the Father, and that will be enough for us!"

Jesus said to him, "Have I been with you this long, and you do not yet know me, Philip? Whoever has seen me has seen the Father too! How can you say, 'Show us the Father'? Do you not believe that I am in the Father and he is in me? I do not say what I am telling you of my own accord—on the contrary, the Father who lives in me does his work. Believe in me because I am in the Father, and the Father is in me. Even if you do not believe because of this, believe because of what has been done!

"I am truly, truly telling you: whoever believes in me will do the work that I do—he will even do better work than this because I am going to my Father. So whatever you ask in my name, I will do it so that the Father will be glorified with the Son. If you ask me anything in my name, I will do it.

"If you love me, you will keep my commandments. Then I will ask the Father, and he will give you another Helper so that he will be with you forever: the Spirit of Truth. The world cannot receive him because it does not see or understand him. But you understand him because he remains with you and within you. I will not leave you like orphans—I am coming for you. In a little while, the world will no longer see me. But you will see me because I will live, and you will live. On that day, you will know that I am in my Father, as well as that you are in me and I am in you. Whoever has my commands—and keeps them—is the one who loves me. Whoever loves me will be loved by my Father, and I will love them and make myself visible to them."

Judas (not Iscariot) asked him, "Master, how can it be that you are going to make yourself visible to us and not to the world?"

Jesus answered him, "If someone loves me, they will keep my Word; then my Father will love them. Then we will come to them and set up our room with them. Whoever does not love me will not keep my Word, and the Word that you have heard is not mine—it belongs to the Father who sent me.

"I have spoken these things to you while I am with you. Now the Helper (the Holy Spirit whom the Father will send in my name) will teach you everything and remind you of everything that I have told you.

"I am leaving peace with you—I am giving my peace to you. I am not giving it to you as the world gives. Do not let your hearts be upset or afraid. You have heard (because I said it to you): 'I am going, and I will come back for you.' If you loved me, you would rejoice that I am going to the Father because the Father is better than me. Even now, I have told you before it happens so that when it happens you will believe. I will not speak with you much longer because the ruler of this world is coming. He has nothing to do with me. But I do exactly as the Father has commanded me so that the world may know that I love the Father. Get up—let us leave the table.

I AM THE TRUE VINE, AND MY FATHER IS THE FARMER. HE TAKES away every branch that is in me and does not bear fruit. Furthermore, he prunes every branch that bears fruit so that it can bear more fruit. You are already clean because of the Word that I have spoken to you. Stay with me, and I will stay with you. Just as the branch cannot bear fruit by itself—unless it stays with the vine—you cannot bear fruit unless you stay with me. I am the vine, and you are the branches. I will stay with whoever stays with me, and they will bear much fruit. You see, you can do nothing without me. Unless someone stayed with me, they would have been thrown out like a branch and withered. Then they are gathered and thrown into the fire to be burned up. If you stay with me, and my words stay with you, you will ask for whatever you want, and it will happen for you. My Father has been glorified in this way so that you can bear a lot of fruit and become my disciples.

"I have loved you just as the Father has loved me. Stay within my love. If you keep my commands, you will stay within my love—exactly how I have kept my Father's commands and stay within his love. I have spoken this to you so that my joy would be in you and that your joy would be complete. This is my command: that you love one another exactly as I have loved you. No one has a greater love than this—to lay down his life for his friends. You are my friends if you do what I am commanding you. I am no longer talking to you as if you were servants because the servant does not know what his master is doing. But I have called you friends because I have made known to you everything that I have heard from my Father. You did not choose me—I chose you, and I have appointed you to go and bear fruit. Your fruit will stay, so I will give you whatever you ask the Father in my name. I command you this: that you love one another.

"If the world hates you, understand that it hated me before it hated you. If you belonged to the world, the world loves those who belong to it. But you do not belong to the world (on the contrary, I have chosen you from the world). Because of this, the world will hate you. Remember the statement that I told you: 'The servant is no better than his master.' If they persecuted me, they will persecute you too. If they kept my Word, they will keep yours also. But they do all of this for you because of my name, because they do not know the one who sent me. If I had not come and spoken to them, they would not have any sin. But now they have no excuse for their sin. Whoever hates me hates my Father also. If I had not performed miracles among them that no one else had done, they would not have any sin. But now they have seen—and hated—both me and my Father. Yet they did this to fulfill the message that is written in their law: 'They hated me for no reason.'

"When the Helper comes, whom I am sending to you from the Father (the Spirit of Truth that comes from the Father), he will testify about me. Furthermore, you will testify because you have been with me since the beginning.

"I have said this to you so that you will not be led astray. They will ban you from the synagogue. But the time is coming when anyone who kills you will think that they are offering a service to God. They will do this because they have not known the Father or me. But I have told you this so that when their time comes, you will remember that I have told you about them. I have not told you this from the beginning because I have been with you. But now I am going to the one who sent me, and none of you is asking me, 'Where are you going?' But grief has filled your hearts because I have told you this. Now I am telling you the truth: you are better off because I am leaving. You see, if I did not leave, the Helper would not come to you. But if I go, I will send him to you. When he comes, he will convict the world as far as sin, righteousness, and condemnation are concerned. As far as sin is concerned, he will convict the world because they did not believe in me. As far as righteousness is concerned, he will convict the world because I am going to the Father, and you will not see me anymore. As far as condemnation is concerned, he will convict the world because this world's rulers are condemned.

"I still have a lot to tell you, but you are not able to put up with it now. When he (the Spirit of Truth) comes, he will guide you with all the truth. You see, he will not speak of his own accord, but he will speak what he hears and announce what is coming to you. He will glorify me because he will receive that glory from me and announce it to you. Everything the Father has is mine.

Because of this, I said that he receives it from me and announces it to you. In a little while, you will no longer see me, and after another little while, you will see me again."

Then some of his disciples asked one another, "What does he mean when he tells us, 'In a little while you will not see me, and after another little while, you will see me again,' and 'I am going to the Father'?"

Then they said, "What does he mean when he says 'a little while'? We do not understand what he is saying!"

Jesus knew that they wanted to ask him about this, so he said to them, "Are you seeking the answer for this from one another? 'In a little while, you will not see me, and after another little while, you will see me again.' I am truly, truly telling you: you will weep and wail, but the world will celebrate. You will grieve, but your grief will turn into joy. A woman experiences grief when she is giving birth because her time has come. But she no longer remembers her trouble when the child is born because of her joy that a person has been born into the world. So you will have grief now, but I will see you again and your heart will celebrate. No one will be able to take your joy away from you!

"On that day you will not be asking me anything. I am truly, truly telling you: the Father will give you whatever you ask him in my name. To this point, you have not asked for anything in my name. Ask and you will receive so that your joy may overflow.

"I have told you this with allegories, but the time is coming when I will no longer talk to you in allegories. On the contrary, I will openly deliver the message about the Father. On that day, you will ask in my name, and I will not tell you, 'I will ask the Father in your behalf.' You see, the Father himself loves you because you have loved me and have believed that I have come from the Father. I have come from the Father and into the world, and I will leave the world and go back to the Father."

His disciples said, "See? You are now speaking plainly, and you are not even using a single allegory. Now we know that you know everything and that you do not need anyone to ask you. Because of this, we have believed that you have come from God."

Jesus answered them, "Do you really believe now? Look: the time is coming—and it has come—when each of you will be scattered in his own direction, and you will leave me by myself. But I am not alone because the Father is with me. I have told you this so that you can have peace in me. You will have trouble in the world, but have courage: I have conquered the world!"

Jesus said this and then raised his eyes to heaven and said, "Father, the time has come. Glorify your Son so that your Son will glorify you in the same way that you gave him authority over all people so that he could give eternal life to the ones you gave him. This is eternal life: that they know you (the only true God) and the one you sent (Jesus the Messiah). I have glorified you on the earth by doing the work that you have given me to do. So now, Father, glorify me with the glory that I had with you before the world existed.

"I have revealed your name to the people you have given to me from the world. They belonged to you; so I gave them your Word and they kept it. Now they have come to know that everything you have given me is from you because I have given them the words you gave me. Furthermore, they received them and truly came to know that I came from you—they have believed that you sent me.

"I am asking on their behalf. I am not asking on behalf of the world but on behalf of the ones you have given to me because they belong to you. Everyone who belongs to me belongs to you, and whoever belongs to you belongs to me—and I have been glorified by them. I am no longer going to be in the world, but they will be in the world. I am coming to you. Holy Father, keep them in your name—the ones you gave me—so that they will be one just as we are. When I was with them, I kept them in your name that you had given me. I protected them, and none of them were lost except the lost son so that Scripture would be fulfilled. Now I am coming to you, and I am saying this in the world so that they will have my complete joy in them. I have given them your Word; and the world has hated them because they are not from the world—just as I am not from the world. I am not asking that you take them out of the world but that you keep them from the evil one. They do not belong to the world, just as I do not belong to the world. Sanctify them by the truth—your Word is truth. Just as you have sent me into the world, I have also sent them into the world. I sanctify myself for their sakes so that they also will be sanctified by truth.

"I am asking not only on their behalf but also on behalf of those who believe in me because of their message. I am asking that all of them will be one just like you, Father, are in me, and I am in you. I am asking that they might be one so that the world will believe that you have sent me. I have given them the glory that you gave to me so that they will be one just as we are one. I am in them and you are in me so that they will completely be one. So the world would know that you have sent me and have loved them just as you have loved me.

"As for those whom you have given me, Father, I desire that they may be where I am—with me. I desire that they see my glory, which you have given me because you have loved me since before the world was created. Righteous Father, even though the world has not known you, I have known you, and they have known that you have sent me. Furthermore, I have made your name known to them, and I will continue to make it known so that the love you gave to me will be in them and that I will be in them."

AFTER JESUS SAID THIS, HE WENT WITH HIS DISCIPLES TO KIDRON Valley. A garden was there, and he and his disciples entered it.

Now Judas (the one who betrayed him) was familiar with the place because Jesus often had met there with his disciples. So Judas took a cohort of soldiers and some assistants of the chief priests and Pharisees and came there with lanterns, torches, and weapons. When Jesus saw all of them coming for him, he went and asked them, "Whom do you seek?"

They answered him, "Jesus of Nazareth."

He said to them, "I am he." Now Judas (the one who betrayed him) was also standing there with them.

When he said, "I am he," they retreated and fell to the ground.

Then he asked them again, "Whom do you seek?"

They said, "Jesus of Nazareth."

Jesus answered, "I told you I am he. So if you are looking for me, let these people go."

So the statement was fulfilled:

I have not lost a single one of the people you have given to me.

Then Simon Peter, who had a sword, drew it, attacked the high priest's servant, and cut off his right ear (the servant's name was Malchus). Then Jesus said to Peter, "Put your sword into its sheath. Shall I not drink the cup that the Father has given to me?"

Then the cohort, its commander, and the Jews' assistants took Jesus and tied him up. They led him to Annas first. You see, he was the father-in-law of Caiaphas, who served as high priest that year. It was Caiaphas who advised the Jews that it would be better for one man to die for the benefit of the nation.

Simon Peter and another disciple followed Jesus. Now that disciple was recognized by the high priest, and he went into the high priest's courtyard with Jesus. But Peter stood outside by the door. Then the other disciple who was recognized by the high priest came out and talked with the doorkeeper, so Peter gained entrance. Then the doorkeeper's servant girl asked Peter, "Are you not also one of that man's disciples?"

He said, "No, I am not."

Now the servants and assistants were standing around, preparing a charcoal fire. You see, it was cold, and they were warming themselves. Now Peter was standing with them and warming himself too.

The high priest questioned Jesus about his disciples and his teaching.

Jesus answered him, "I have spoken publicly to the world. I have always taught in the synagogue and in the temple, where all the Jews had come together—I did not say anything secretly. Why are you asking me? Ask those who heard what I said to them. See? They know what I said."

When he said this, one of the assistants who was standing there slapped Jesus and said, "Is this how you are going to talk to the high priest?"

Jesus answered him, "If I have spoken inappropriately, state what was inappropriate! Why did you hit me?"

Then Annas sent him (tied up) to Caiaphas the high priest.

Now Simon Peter was standing by the fire and warming himself. Then someone asked him, "Are you not one of his disciples?"

He denied it, "I am not."

One of the high priest's servants (a relative of the one whose ear Peter had cut off) said, "Did I not see you in the garden with him?"

Peter denied it again, and immediately, a rooster crowed.

Then they led Jesus from Caiaphas to the governor's house. It was early in the morning. But they did not enter the governor's house because they would have become unclean. Thus, they could still eat the Passover meal.

Then Pilate came out to them and asked, "What accusation are you bringing against this man?"

They answered him, "If he had not committed any evil act, we would not have turned him over to you!"

Then Pilate said to them, "You take him; condemn him by your law."

The Jews said to him, "We do not have the right to put anyone to death." This happened so that what Jesus had said would be fulfilled, when he indicated what type of death he would die.

Then Pilate went back into his house and called for Jesus. He asked him, "Are you the king of the Jews?"

Jesus answered him, "Are you saying this of your own accord, or have others told you about me?"

Pilate answered, "I am not a Jew, am I? Your own nation and chief priests have turned you over to me! What have you done?"

Jesus answered, "My kingdom is not from this world. If my kingdom were from this world, my assistants would have fought so that I would not be arrested by the Jews. But my kingdom is not from here."

Then Pilate said to him, "So—you are a king?"

Jesus answered, "You said it. I am a king. I was born for this reason, and I have come into the world for this reason: to testify to the truth. Whoever belongs to the truth hears my voice."

Pilate asked him, "What is truth?"

So after he said this, he went to the Jews and said to them, "I do not find any guilt in him at all. It is a custom for you that I release someone to you at the Passover. So do you want me to release the king of the Jews for you?"

Then they shouted out again, "Not him—release Barabbas instead!" (Now Barabbas was an insurgent.)

So Pilate took Jesus and had him flogged. Then the soldiers wove a crown from thorns and put it on his head. They wrapped him in a purple robe and approached him, saying, "Hail: The king of the Jews!" Then they slapped him.

Pilate came back outside and said to the Jews, "Look! I am bringing him out to you so that you may know that I have not found any guilt in him."

Then Jesus came outside, wearing the crown made from thorns and the purple robe. Pilate said, "Look: here he is!"

When the chief priests and their assistants saw him, they shouted out, "Crucify! Crucify!"

Pilate said to them, "You take him and crucify him! I have not found any guilt in him."

The Jews answered, "We have a law; according to that law, he ought to die because he made himself out to be God's Son!"

When Pilate heard this statement, he became very afraid. He went back into his house and said to Jesus, "Where are you from?" But Jesus did not answer him.

Pilate said to him, "Are you not going to talk to me? Do you not know that I have the authority both to release and crucify you?"

Jesus answered him, "You do not have any authority at all over me except what has been given to you from above. Because of this, the one who turned me over to you has more sin."

From that point on, Pilate sought to release him. But the Jews shouted out, "If you release him, you are not Caesar's friend! Whoever makes himself out to be a king is against Caesar!"

When Pilate heard that statement, he led Jesus out and sat down on the platform in the place called The Stone Pavement ("Gabbatha" in Aramaic). Now this happened on the day of preparation for the Sabbath during the Passover, and it was about noon.

Pilate said to the Jews, "Look at your king!"

Then they shouted, "Take him! Take him and crucify him!"

Pilate asked them, "Shall I crucify your king?"

The chief priests answered, "We have no king except for Caesar!" He turned Jesus over to them to be crucified, and they took him.

Jesus went out, carrying his own cross, to the Skull Place (which is called "Golgotha" in Aramaic). They crucified him there with two others—one on either side, with Jesus in the middle.

Then Pilate wrote a notice and placed it on the cross. The notice said, "Jesus the Nazarene: the King of the Jews." So many of the Jews read this notice because the place where Jesus was crucified was near the city. Furthermore, it was written in Aramaic, Latin, and Greek.

Then the chief priests of the Jews said to Pilate, "Do not write, 'The King of the Jews'—instead it should be that He said, 'I am the King of the Jews.'"

Pilate answered, "I have written what I have written."

When the soldiers had crucified Jesus, they took his clothing and divided it into four parts—one part for each soldier. They also took his undershirt. The undershirt was seamless, woven completely from the top, so they said to one another, "Let us not tear it. On the contrary, let us cast lots for it to determine whose it will be." This happened in order to fulfill the Scripture:

> They divided up my clothing among themselves,
> And cast lots for my apparel.

So the soldiers actually did this!

Now Jesus' mother and her sister (along with Mary the wife of Clopas and Mary Magdalene) stood by his cross. When Jesus saw his mother and the disciple he loved standing there, he said to his mother, "Look: there is your son." Then he said to the disciple, "Look: there is your mother." From that time, the disciple took her into his own household.

Afterward, since Jesus knew that everything had already been done, he said (to fulfill Scripture), "I am thirsty."

A jar full of sour wine was lying around, so someone placed a sponge full of the sour wine on a hyssop stalk and brought it to Jesus' mouth.

When Jesus had taken a drink of the sour wine, he said, "It is done!" Then he bowed his head and yielded his last breath.

Since it was the day of preparation for the Sabbath (and that was an important Sabbath day), the Jews asked Pilate to break the legs of those who were crucified so that their bodies would not stay on the cross during the Sabbath—so that they would be taken away. So the soldiers came and broke the legs of the first criminal, as well as the other who was crucified with him. But when they came to Jesus, they did not break his legs because they saw that he was already dead. But one of the soldiers stabbed his spear into Jesus' side, and immediately blood and water flowed out. The disciple who saw this has testified of it, and his testimony is true—he knows he is telling the truth so that you can believe. You see, this happened so that the Scripture could be fulfilled:

> His bone will not be broken.

Again, another Scripture says:

> They will look at the one they have pierced.

After this, Joseph (a man from Arimathea who was secretly a disciple of Jesus because he was afraid of the Jews) asked Pilate if he could take the body of Jesus. Pilate permitted this, so he came and took Jesus' body. Nicodemus (the man who had come to him in the past at night) also came, carrying a mixture of ointment and aloe that was valued at about eight years' wages. Then they took Jesus' body and wrapped it in fine linen with those spices, as was the custom for Jews when burying someone. There was a garden at the place where he was crucified. In that garden was a new tomb—no one had yet been placed in it. So they buried Jesus there because it was nearby and the Jews' day of preparation for the Sabbath was approaching.

EARLY ON THE FIRST DAY OF THE WEEK (WHILE IT WAS STILL dark), Mary Magdalene came to the tomb and saw that the stone had been taken away from the tomb! Then she ran and went to Simon Peter and the other disciple (the one Jesus loved) and told them, "They have taken the Master out of the tomb, and we do not know where they have laid him!"

So Peter and the other disciple ran, and they came to the tomb. Now the two of them ran together, but the other disciple quickly outran Peter and came to the tomb first. He bent down and saw the fine-linen cloth lying there, but he did not go in. Then Simon Peter came after him and entered the tomb. He observed the fine-linen cloth lying there, as well as the facecloth that had been put on Jesus' head. Yet it was not lying beside the fine-linen cloth—it was folded up separately in its own place. Then the other disciple came inside also—he had arrived at the tomb first, and he saw this and believed. You see, they had not yet understood the Scripture that said it was necessary for Jesus to rise from the dead. Then the two disciples went back to the others.

But Mary stayed outside at the tomb and wept. As she was weeping, she bent over to look in the tomb and saw two angels in white sitting there! One was toward where the head of Jesus' body had been put, and the other was toward the feet.

They asked her, "Ma'am, why are you weeping?"

She said to them, "I am weeping because they have taken my Master away, and I do not know where they put him!" When she said this, she turned around and saw Jesus standing there—but she did not know it was Jesus.

Jesus asked her, "Ma'am, why are you weeping? Whom do you seek?"

She thought he was the keeper of the garden, so she said to him, "Sir, if you have moved him, tell me where you have put him, and I will take him off your hands."

Jesus said to her, "Mary."

She turned around and said to him in Aramaic, "Rabboni!" (This means "teacher").

Jesus said to her, "Stop clinging to me. You see, I have not yet ascended to the Father. Go instead to my brothers and tell them I am ascending to my Father and your Father, and my God and your God."

Mary Magdalene went and announced to the disciples that she had seen the Master and that he had told her that message.

When it was evening on that first day of the week, the doors were locked where the disciples were because they feared the Jews. Jesus came, stood in the middle of them, and said to them, "Peace to you." When he said this, he showed them his hands and his side. Then the disciples celebrated because they had seen the Master.

Then Jesus again said to them, "Peace to you. I am sending you, just as the Father has sent me." When he had said this, he breathed upon them and said to them, "Receive the Holy Spirit. If you forgive anyone's sins, they have been forgiven, and if you hold anyone's sins against them, they have been held against them."

But one of the twelve (Thomas, who was called the Twin) was not with them when Jesus came. The other disciples said to him, "We have seen the Master!"

But he said, "Unless I see the imprint of nails in his hands and I put my finger into his side, I will never believe it!"

Then after eight days, his disciples were again locked inside (and Thomas was with them). Jesus came—even though the doors were locked—and stood in the middle of them and said, "Peace to you." Then he said to Thomas, "Bring your finger here and look at my hands; bring your hand and put it into my side. Do not continue to disbelieve—on the contrary, believe!"

Thomas answered him, "My Master, and my God!"

Jesus said to him, "Have you believed because you have seen me? Blessed are those who have believed even though they have not seen me!"

Actually, Jesus performed many different kinds of signs in front of his disciples that have not been written in this book. But these have been written so that you could believe that Jesus is the Messiah—God's Son—and that you who believe could have life in his name.

AFTER THIS, JESUS AGAIN REVEALED HIMSELF TO HIS DISCIPLES by the Sea of Tiberius. The following tells how he revealed himself:

Simon Peter, Thomas (who is called the Twin), Nathanael from Cana in Galilee, the sons of Zebedee, and two other disciples were together.

Simon Peter said, "I am going to go fishing."

They said to him, "We are coming with you too."

Then they went and boarded a boat, but they caught nothing that night. When it had become morning, Jesus stood on the seashore, but the disciples did not know that it was Jesus.

Jesus asked them, "Children, do you not have anything to eat?"

They answered him, "No."

Then he said to them, "Cast the net on the right side of the boat—then you will find some."

Then they cast it, and they were not able to draw it in because of the number of fish.

The disciple whom Jesus loved said to Peter, "It is the Master!"

When Simon Peter heard that it was the Master, he put on his outer clothing (because he was stripped for fishing). He jumped into the sea, but the other disciples came on the boat, dragging the net full of fish. You see, they were not far from the land (they were about one hundred yards out). As they were going ashore, they saw a charcoal fire set up, and bread and fish were on it.

Jesus said to them, "Bring some of the fish that you just caught."

Then Simon Peter got up and dragged the net full of fish to the land—there were 153 of them, but the net did not break, even with this many fish!

Jesus said to them, "Come; eat breakfast."

None of the disciples dared to ask him, "Who are you?" They knew that he was the Master.

Jesus came, took the bread, and gave it to them. He did the same thing with the fish. This was the third time that Jesus was revealed to his disciples after being raised from the dead.

When they had eaten breakfast, Jesus asked Simon Peter, "Simon, son of John, do you love me more than these fish?"

He said to him, "Yes, Master. You know that I love you."

Jesus said to him, "Feed my lambs."

Then he asked him a second time, "Simon, son of John, do you love me?"

He said to him, "Yes, Master. You know that I love you."

Jesus said to him, "Shepherd my flock."

He asked him the third time, "Do you love me?" Then Peter was offended because he had asked him the third time, "Do you love me?"

He said to him, "Master—you know everything! You know that I love you!"

Jesus said to him, "Feed my flock. I am truly, truly telling you: When you were young, you clothed yourself and went wherever you wanted. But when you are old, you will reach out your hands, and then another person will clothe you and take you where you do not want to go." He said this in order to indicate how Peter would die to glorify God. When he had said this, he said, "Follow me."

Peter turned around and saw the disciple whom Jesus loved following them. (It was he who leaned back against Jesus' chest at supper and asked, "Master, who is the one who will betray you?") When Peter saw him, he asked Jesus, "Master, what about him?"

Jesus said to him, "If I wanted him to live until I return, what does that have to do with you? You just need to follow me."

Then what he said made it back to the brothers as, "That disciple is not going to die." But he did not say that the disciple would not die. Rather, he asked, "If I want him to live until I return, what does that have to do with you?"

It is that disciple who testifies about these things and who wrote this account. We know that his testimony is true. There are many other things that Jesus did. If every one of them had been written down, I do not think that the world itself could contain the books that would be written.

ACCORDING TO JOHN

THE WORD

THE APOSTLES' ACTS

THE APOSTLES'
ACTS

Theophilus,

I WROTE THE PREVIOUS DISSERTATION ABOUT EVERYTHING THAT Jesus began to do—both what he did and taught—until the day he commanded the apostles, whom he had chosen by the Holy Spirit, and was taken up on the cross. After he suffered, he presented himself alive to them with a lot of convincing evidence. He appeared to them for forty days and told them about God's kingdom.

While he was staying with them, he ordered them not to leave Jerusalem. On the contrary, they were to wait for what the Father promised, which "you heard from me. Indeed, John immersed with water, but you will be immersed with the Holy Spirit after a few more days."

So after they assembled together, they asked him, "Master, now are you going to restore the kingdom to Israel?"

Then he said to them, "It is not your right to understand the times and seasons that the Father has appointed by his authority. However, you will receive power after the Holy Spirit comes upon you. Then you will be my witnesses—in Jerusalem, all of Judea, Samaria, and to the farthest regions of the earth."

So after he said this—while they were watching—he was lifted up, and a cloud carried him out of their sight. As they were staring into the sky where he had gone—get this—two men in white clothing appeared to them and said, "Men of Galilee: why are you standing there staring at the sky? This Jesus, who was taken up into the sky from you, will come back in the same way that you watched him go into the sky!"

Then they returned to Jerusalem from the place called "The Mount of Olives," which is near Jerusalem (about three fifths of a mile away). When they entered the city, they went up to the upstairs room where they were staying (that is, Peter, John, James, Andrew, Philip, Thomas, Bartholomew, Matthew, James Alphaeus, Simon the Patriot, and Judas James were staying there). They all were unified in purpose, devoting themselves to prayer with their wives and with Jesus' mother, Mary, and his brothers.

In those days, Peter stood up in front of the brothers. (The group of people numbered about one hundred twenty.) He said, "Gentlemen! Brothers! It was necessary for the Scripture to be fulfilled that the Holy Spirit had spoken earlier by the mouth of David when he spoke about

Judas, who would become a guide for those who would arrest Jesus. You see, he belonged to our assembly and received this ministry by lot. This man then acquired a field by his unrighteous wages. He fell head-first and burst open in the middle, and all his entrails spilled out. This became known to everyone who lives in Jerusalem, and so that field in their language is called Aceldama, which means "bloody field." You see, it is written in the Book of Psalms:

> His residence should become deserted,
> And no one should live in it!"

Furthermore:

> Another person should take his office.

"So it needs to be one of the men who have accompanied us throughout the whole time that the Master went in and out among us (beginning at John's immersion until the day he was taken up from us)—one of these men must become a witness with us of his resurrection."

Then they proposed two men: Joseph, who is called Barsabbas (his last name was Justus), and Matthias. Then they prayed: "You, Master, who know everyone's hearts: reveal which one of these two you have chosen to take the position of this ministry and mission, from which Judas turned away to follow his own position." Then they cast lots for them, and the lot fell upon Matthias, so he was chosen to accompany the eleven apostles.

N OW WHEN THE DAY OF PENTECOST HAD ARRIVED, THEY ALL were together in the same place. Suddenly a sound came from the sky like a strong, rushing wind, and it filled the whole building where they were sitting. Then tongues that looked like fire appeared to them, which divided and came to rest on each one of them. They all were filled with the Holy Spirit and began to speak in other languages, as the Spirit gave them what to say.

Now there were Jews living in Jerusalem who were devout men from every nation under heaven. So when this sound came, the masses came together and were thrown into confusion because each one of them heard the apostles speaking in their own language. They were amazed and surprised, and they said, "Look! Are these not all Galileans? So how are we all hearing this in our own, native language? There are Parthians, Medes, and Elamites here, as well as some who live in Mesopotamia and Judea; others who live in Cappadocia, Pontus, and Asia; others who live in Phrygia and Pamphylia, Egypt, and the regions of Libya that are next to Cyrene; as well as Roman visitors. There are both Jews and converts to Judaism here—Cretans and Arabs— and we hear these men speaking these great things about God in our languages!" They all were amazed and did not know what to say. They asked one another, "What could this mean?" But others laughed at the apostles and said, "They are drunk on sweet wine!"

Then Peter stood up with the eleven, raised his voice, and spoke to them: "Gentlemen! Judeans and all of you who are staying in Jerusalem: you need to know this! Listen to what I am saying! You see, these men are not drunk as you are assuming, because it is only 9:00 a.m. On the contrary, this is what was spoken through Joel the prophet:

> God says, 'It will happen in the last days.
> I will pour out my Spirit on everybody,

> Then your sons and daughters will prophesy,
> Your young men will see visions,
> And your old men will have visions in dreams.
> Also in those days I will pour out my Spirit
> On both my male and female slaves, and they will prophesy.
> I will also provide omens in the sky above
> and signs on the earth below—
> Blood, fire, and smoky vapor.
> The sun will be changed into darkness, and the moon into blood,
> before the great and glorious day of the Master comes.
> It will happen that everyone who calls on the Master's name will be saved.'

"Men of Israel: listen to these words! Jesus of Nazareth is a man confirmed to you by God with miracles, omens, and signs that God performed through him in front of you—you know this yourselves! By God's established plan and foreknowledge, this man was betrayed; then you killed him by using lawless hands to nail him to a cross! God raised him up by breaking the stitches of death because it was impossible for him to be held by its power. You see, David says to him:

> I have seen the Master in front of me through everything,
> Because he is at my side so that I may not be shaken.
> Because of this, my heart has rejoiced, and my tongue has celebrated.
> So my body will still dwell with hopefulness.
> You see, you will not abandon my life in the grave
> Or allow your holy one to see decay.
> You have declared the ways of life to me.
> With your presence, you will make me completely happy.

"Gentlemen! Brothers! As for David our ancestor, I can confidently tell you that he died and was buried—and his tomb is with us to this day! So since he was a prophet and knew that God had sworn him an oath that he would install someone on his throne from the fruit of his loins, he spoke from his foresight about the resurrection of the Messiah (that he would not be abandoned to the grave and his body would not see decay). God has raised this Jesus, and all of us are witnesses of this! So, since he has ascended to God and received the promise (Holy Spirit) from the Father, He has poured this Spirit out, as you can both see and hear. You see, David did not ascend to the sky, but he says:

> The Master said to my Master,
> 'Sit at my side until I cause your enemies to be a footrest for your feet.'

"So the whole house of Israel needs to know without a doubt that God has made this Jesus—whom you crucified—both Master and Messiah!"

When they heard this, they felt stabbed in the heart. They said to Peter and the rest of the apostles, "Gentlemen! Brothers! What should we do?"

Then Peter said to them, "Repent; then each one of you needs to be immersed in the name of Jesus the Messiah for the forgiveness of your sins. Then you will receive the gift of the Holy Spirit. You see, this promise belongs to you, your children, and everyone who is far away, whom God our Master has called."

He urged and encouraged them with many more words. He said, "Be saved from this crooked generation!"

So those who accepted his message were immersed, and about three thousand souls were added to their group that day. They spent a lot of time in the apostles' teaching, eating in fellowship, and prayers. Reverence was present in everyone's life, and many omens and signs were performed through the apostles. So all the believers were together and shared everything. They sold their property and possessions and distributed the money to everyone as they needed it. They would spend a lot of time together in the temple every day. They would gather in every house and eat food together with celebration and openness in their hearts. They would praise God and show kindness to all people, and every day the Master would add those who were being saved to their group.

WELL PETER AND JOHN WENT UP TO THE TEMPLE AT THE TIME of prayer (3:00 p.m.). Now a man was carried there who was lame since birth. He was put there every day by the temple door that is called Beautiful so that he could beg for money from those who came into the temple. When he saw Peter and John approaching to enter the temple, he started begging to receive money from them.

Then Peter looked at him at the same time John did and said, "Look at us."

He fixed his attention on them, expecting to receive something from them.

Then Peter said, "I do not have silver or gold, but I am giving to you what I do have—in the name of Jesus the Messiah from Nazareth, get up and walk!"

Then he grabbed him by the right hand and helped him up, and instantly his feet and ankles were strengthened. He leaped to his feet and began to walk! He went inside the temple with them, walking, leaping, and praising God. All those people saw him walking and praising God. They recognized him: "He was the one who sat at Beautiful Gate in the temple to ask for money!" They were filled with amazement and surprise because of what had happened to him. While he was holding on to Peter and John, all the amazed people flocked to them at the colonnade named after Solomon.

When Peter saw this, he responded to the people, "Men of Israel: why are you amazed at this or at us? Why do you stare as if we have made him walk by our own power or religiousness? The God of Abraham—who is the God of Isaac, the God of Jacob, and our Father—has glorified Jesus his Son, whom you betrayed and rejected in front of Pilate, who had decided to set him free. But you rejected the holy and righteous person and asked that a murderer be released to you. You put to death the originator of life, and God raised him from the dead! We are witnesses of this!

"Now, brothers, I know that you were acting out of ignorance, just as your rulers did. But that is how God brought the sufferings of his Messiah (which he had previously proclaimed by the mouth of all the prophets) to fulfillment. So repent and be converted so that your sins can be scrubbed away so that times of rest can come from the presence of the Master and that he can send the hand-picked Messiah (Jesus) to you. It was necessary for the sky to take him up until the time comes for the restoration of all that God has spoken through his holy prophets a long time ago. Moses even said, 'God your Master will raise up a prophet like me for you from among your brothers. You must listen to him—to everything he says to you. This will happen: whoever does not listen to that prophet will be rooted out from among his people.' Every one of the prophets (from Samuel and those who followed him) spoke and announced the coming of these days. You are the descendants of the prophets and of the covenant that God decreed to your fathers when he said to Abraham: 'All the nations of the earth will receive a blessing because of your descendants.' God has raised up his Son and has sent him to be a blessing for you by turning each of you from your sins."

So Peter and John were talking to the people. The priests, the commander responsible for the temple, and the Sadducees were standing near them. They were annoyed because of what they were teaching the people, proclaiming the resurrection from the dead in the name of Jesus. They took hold of them and put them in prison until the next morning (because it was already evening). But many of the people who heard the message believed it. Then the number of men who were believers reached about five thousand.

THIS IS WHAT HAPPENED THE NEXT MORNING WHEN THEIR rulers, elders, and scribes assembled in Jerusalem (including Annas the high priest, Caiaphas, John, Alexander, and all who were from the high-priestly family). They stood Peter and John before them and interrogated them: "With what kind of power or in whose name did you do this?"

Then Peter (who was filled with the Holy Spirit) said to them, "Rulers of the people—elders! If we are being investigated today because of kindness shown to a handicapped man in the way he was healed, let it be known to all of you—and to all the people of Israel—that this man has been presented before you healthy in the name of Jesus the Messiah of Nazareth, whom you crucified and God raised from the dead! Jesus is the stone that was rejected by you builders, and he has become the chief cornerstone. Furthermore, there is no salvation at all in anyone else because, among the names given by people under heaven, there is no other name by which we must be saved!"

Now when they saw the confidence of Peter and John and understood that they were uneducated and untrained men, they were amazed and recognized that they had both been with Jesus. Plus, as they looked at the healed man who was present with them, they had nothing more to say in return. So they commanded them to go out from before the Sanhedrin and discussed with one another: "What should we do to these men? You see, for one thing it is obvious to everyone who lives in Jerusalem that a remarkable miracle has been done by them, and we cannot deny it! But so that no rumor worse than this is circulated among the people, let us threaten them so that they may not speak to anyone in this name again!"

So they called them and ordered them not to speak or teach anything at all in the name of Jesus.

But Peter and John responded to them, "Decide whether it is right in the sight of God to obey you rather than God. Yet as for us, we cannot help but speak what we have seen and heard."

Then they threatened them further and released them since they found no way to punish them because of the people. You see, they were all praising God because of what happened because the man who received this miraculous healing was more than forty years old!

When they had been released, they went to their group and reported everything that the high priests and elders had said. Then those who listened lifted their voices together to God and said, "Master, you are the one who created heaven, earth, the sea, and everything that is in them; you are the one who spoke by the mouth of our father—and your son—David through the Holy Spirit:

> Why are the nations arrogant, and why do the people conspire in vain?
> The kings of the earth have come,
> and the rulers have assembled together
> Against the Master and against his Anointed One.

"You see, in fact they have assembled in this city against your holy child, Jesus, whom you anointed—both Herod and Pontius Pilate, together with the nations and the people of Israel—to do everything that your hand and your plan predetermined would happen. So for now, Master, look at their threats and grant that your slaves would speak your word with complete confidence and that you would stretch out your hand for healing, miracles, and wonders by the name of your holy Son, Jesus."

As they were making this request, the place where they were gathered was shaken, and they were all filled with the Holy Spirit, so they spoke the Word of God with confidence.

NOW THE ENTIRE BODY OF THOSE WHO BELIEVED WAS OF ONE heart and one mind, and not one of them spoke of their possessions as if they were their own. On the contrary, everything was shared. The apostles were offering testimony of the resurrection of Jesus the Master with great power, and there was a lot of grace on all of them. You see, no one among them was in need because whoever owned property or houses sold them, brought the money from what was sold, and set it down at the apostles' feet. Then they distributed it to everyone according to their level of need.

There was a man named Joseph, who was a Levite born in Cyprus, and he was nicknamed Barnabas (translated as "Son of Encouragement") by the apostles. He owned a field but sold it and brought the money and set it at the apostles' feet.

Now there was a man named Ananias (with his wife, Sapphira) who sold his property and set aside some of the profit. With his wife as his accomplice, he brought part of it and set it at the apostles' feet.

Then Peter asked, "Ananias, why has Satan filled your heart like this so that you would lie to the Holy Spirit and set aside some of the profit from the field? When it remained in your possession—and even the money after you sold it—was it not rightfully yours? Why have you set your heart to do this? You have not lied to people but to God!"

When Ananias heard these words, he fell down and died! Great fear came over everyone who heard about it. Then some young men got up, wrapped him up, and carried him out to bury him.

About three hours later, it just so happened that his wife also came in (but she did not know what had happened). Peter addressed her, "Tell me—is this how much you were paid for the field?"

She said, "Yes, that is how much."

Then Peter asked her, "Why have you two agreed to test the Master's Spirit? Look—the feet of those who buried your husband are at the door, and they will carry you out!"

Immediately she fell down at his feet and died! Then the young men entered, found her dead, and carried her out to bury her beside her husband. So great fear came over the whole congregation—upon everyone who heard about this!

NOW MANY SIGNS AND WONDERS WERE BEING PERFORMED among the people by the hands of the apostles. They were all of a single mindset at Solomon's Colonnade. None of the rest of the Jews were bold enough to join them, but the people spoke highly of them. Still, even more believers were added to the Master—a large number of both men and women. So people were even carrying out the sick people into the streets and placing them on beds and mattresses so that when Peter came by, perhaps even just his shadow might come over some of them. Also, a large group of people came together from the cities surrounding Jerusalem. They brought sick people and those tormented by unclean spirits, and they were all healed.

Then the high priest and everyone who was with him got up (this refers to the Sadducee Party). They were filled with jealousy and laid hands on the apostles, publicly putting them in jail. But an angel from the Master opened the door of the prison during the night and led them out, telling them: "Go stand in the temple complex and speak to the people the entire message about this life." When they heard this, they went into the temple complex at about daybreak and taught.

When the high priest and those who were with him arrived, they called the Jewish Council to assemble, including the entire Council of Elders of the Sons of Israel. They sent into the jail to bring the apostles out. But when the officers got there, they could not find them in the prison. They went back and reported, "We found the jail locked with complete security and the guards standing at the doors, but when we opened them, we found no one inside!"

When the temple commander and chief priests heard these words, they were stumped about this—"What will come of this?"

Then someone came and reported to them, "Look! The men you put in prison are standing in the temple complex, teaching the people!"

Then the temple commander went with the officers and led them away, but without using force since they were afraid that the people would stone them to death. When they had led them out, they presented them to the Jewish Council.

The high priest asked them, "Did we not order you specifically not to teach in this name? Now look! You have filled Jerusalem with your teaching, and you intend to blame this man's spilled blood on us!"

Then Peter and the apostles answered, "We must submit to God's authority more so than man's! The God of our fathers raised Jesus, whom you seized and hanged on a tree. God has exalted this Ruler and Savior to a position at his right hand so that he could grant repentance and forgiveness of sins to Israel. We ourselves are witnesses of these things, as is the Holy Spirit whom God gave to those who submit to his authority."

When they heard this, they were stunned and wanted to kill them, but one of the Pharisees in the Jewish Council stood up. His name was Gamaliel, and he was a teacher of the Law who was respected by all the people. He commanded them to put the apostles outside for a minute. Then he spoke to the Council: "Gentlemen—Israelites! You need to be careful in what you are going to do with these men. You see, before these days Theudas rose up claiming to be someone important, and a number of men joined together with him—about four hundred. He was taken out; then all who were allied with him were split up, and it came to nothing. After that, Judas the Galilean rose up in the days of the census and incited the people to revolt behind him. Then he was killed, and all who were allied with him were scattered. Even now, I am telling you—stay away from these men and leave them alone. You see, if this plan or its enactment comes from men, it will be defeated, but if it comes from God, you will not be able to defeat them. You may even find yourselves fighting against God!"

They were persuaded by him, so they summoned the apostles, flogged them, and told them not to speak in the name of Jesus. Then they let them go.

So they went out from before the Jewish Council, celebrating because they were considered worthy to be dishonored on behalf of the Name. So every day—in the temple complex and at every house—they did not stop teaching and proclaiming the Good Message, that Jesus is the Messiah.

Now since the number of disciples was multiplying in those days, a complaint arose from the Greek-speaking Jews against the Aramaic-speaking Jews. You see, their widows were being overlooked in the daily distribution of food. So the twelve apostles summoned the crowd of disciples and said, "It would not be right for us to abandon God's Word in order to wait tables. Instead, brothers, select seven trustworthy men from among you who are full of the Holy Spirit and wisdom. We will appoint them to fill this need. As for us, we will devote ourselves to prayer and to distributing the Word."

The statement pleased the whole crowd, so they selected Stephen (a man who was full of faith and the Holy Spirit), Philip, Procorus, Nicanor, Timon, Parmenas, and Nicolaus (a convert from Antioch). They set these men before the apostles, and the apostles prayed and laid their hands on them. So the Word of God grew, and the number of disciples in Jerusalem multiplied remarkably. Even a large group of priests became obedient to the faith!

Now Stephen was full of graciousness and power, and he performed great miracles and signs among the people. Some people from the synagogue known as the Freedmen, as well as some of the Cyrenians, Alexandrians, Cilicians, and Asians, came up and were arguing with Stephen. They were not able to withstand the wisdom and spirit by which he spoke. Then they secretly instigated some men by saying, "We have heard him speaking blasphemous words against Moses and God!"

They upset both the people and the elders, as well as the scribes and others who were there. They grabbed him and carried him to the Jewish Council. They presented him and gave false testimonies, saying, "This man does not stop speaking words against this holy place and the Law!

You see, we have heard him say, 'This Jesus of Nazareth will destroy this place and change the customs that Moses has given to us!'" Everyone sitting among the Jewish Council was looking at him, and they saw his face look like the face of an angel!

Then the high priest asked, "Are these things true?"

So he spoke: "Gentlemen—brothers and fathers—listen! The God of glory appeared to our ancestor Abraham while he was in Mesopotamia, before he lived in Haran, and said to him, 'Go out of your land, from your relatives, and go to the land that I will show you.' Then he went out from the land of the Chaldeans and lived in Haran. From there, after his father died, he migrated to this land in which you live now. Well, God did not give him an inheritance in it—not even one foot. He promised to give it to him—and to his descendants as well—as a possession, even though Abraham had no child at that time. But this is what God said: 'His descendants will be foreigners in a different land, and they will enslave them and mistreat them for four hundred years. Then I will judge the nation for which they slaved,' said God, 'and after this they will go out and worship me at this place.'

"Then he gave him the covenant of circumcision. So he fathered Isaac and circumcised him on the eighth day. Isaac did the same with Jacob, and Jacob did the same with the twelve patriarchs. Now the patriarchs were jealous of Joseph and sold him into Egypt, but God was with him. He delivered him from all his troubles and gave him favor and wisdom in the presence of Pharaoh, the king of Egypt. So Pharaoh set him up as a ruler over Egypt and over his entire household. Then a famine and great difficulty came over all of Egypt and Canaan, and our ancestors could not find any food. But Jacob heard that there was wheat in Egypt, and he sent our ancestors the first time. Then on the second journey, Joseph revealed himself to his brothers, and Joseph's family was pointed out to Pharaoh. So Joseph sent and summoned his father, Jacob, and all his relatives (which included seventy-five people). Jacob went down to Egypt, and that is where he died—both he and our ancestors. They were buried in Shechem—placed in the tomb that Abraham bought for a sum of money from the sons of Hamor in Shechem.

"As the promised time drew near, of which God had assured Abraham, the people grew and multiplied in Egypt until 'a different king arose in Egypt who did not know Joseph.' He acted shrewdly with our family and mistreated our ancestors by making them leave their babies outside so that they would not survive. At that time, Moses was born—and he was beautiful to God. He was nursed for three months in his father's house. When he was put outside, the daughter of Pharaoh took him up and raised him as her own son. So Moses was trained with all the wisdom of Egypt, and he was capable in his words and actions. As he completed his fortieth birthday, it entered his mind to go see his brothers, the sons of Israel. When he saw one of them being wronged, he retaliated and brought justice for the man who had been mistreated—killing the Egyptian. He thought his brothers would understand that God would grant deliverance to them by his hand, but they did not understand. On the next day, he saw two of them fighting and took it upon himself to reconcile them peacefully by saying, 'Gentlemen, you are brothers! Why are you hurting one another?'

"But the one who was hurting his neighbor pushed him away and asked, 'Who set you up as a ruler and judge over us? Do you want to kill me in the same way that you killed that Egyptian yesterday?' Then Moses fled because of that statement and went to live in the land of Midian (where he fathered two sons).

"After another forty years passed, an angel appeared to him in the desert of Mount Sinai—in a blazing bush. When Moses saw it, he was amazed by the sight, and as he drew near to look closer, the voice of the Master came: 'I am the God of your ancestors—the God of Abraham, Isaac, and Jacob.' Then Moses, terrified, would not dare to look at it. Then the Master said to him, 'Remove your shoes from your feet because the place where you are standing is holy ground. I have watched and have seen the mistreatment of my people in Egypt, and I have heard their moans, so I have come down to deliver them. Now go—I will send you to Egypt!'

"God sent that same Moses (whom they had refused to acknowledge by asking, 'Who appointed you as a ruler and judge?') to be a ruler and deliverer by using the angel that appeared to him in the bush. He led them out, performing wonders and signs in the land of Egypt, at the Red Sea, and in the desert for forty years. This is the same Moses who told the sons of Israel, 'God will raise up a prophet like me from among your brothers!' This is the same one who was in the assembly in the desert—with the angel who spoke to him on Mount Sinai and with our ancestors—who received the living words that were given to us!

"But our ancestors did not want to obey him—instead they pushed him away and returned to Egypt in their hearts by telling Aaron: 'Make us gods who will go before us! As for this Moses who led us out of Egypt, we do not know what has happened to him.' So they made a calf in those days and offered a sacrifice to the idol, celebrating what they did with their hands. But God turned from them too—he handed them over to worship the hosts of the sky, just as it is written in the book of the prophets:

> Did you not bring me offerings and sacrifices
> for forty years in the desert, house of Israel?
> Then you set up a sanctuary for Molech
> and the star of your god Rephan,
> Whose statues you made, in order to worship them,
> so I will resettle you beyond Babylon.

"The tent of testimony was with our ancestors in the desert, just like the one who spoke with Moses instructed him to make it, 'according to the pattern that he saw.' Our ancestors inherited it and carried it when they—with Joshua—took possession of the land of the gentiles, whom God pushed out from the presence of our ancestors until the days of David. He was the one who found favor before God and requested to provide a dwelling for the God of Jacob. Then Solomon built him a house. Yet, the Most High does not live in handmade dwellings, just as the prophet says:

> Heaven is my throne, and earth is my footrest;
> What kind of house will you build for me? says the Master.
> What place will you build for me to rest?
> Did my hand not make all these things?"

"You are stubborn, and your hearts and ears are uncircumcised! You always fight against the Holy Spirit—you are just like your ancestors! Which of the prophets did your ancestors not persecute? Then they killed those who were sent to proclaim about the coming of the Righteous One—and you have now become his traitors and murderers since you received the Law by the instruction of angels and have not kept it!"

When they heard this, they were infuriated and clenched their teeth at him. As he was filled with the Holy Spirit, he looked into heaven and saw God's glory and Jesus standing on God's right side. He said, "Look! I see the heavens opened and the Son of Man standing at God's right side!"

Then they cried out with a loud voice, covered their ears, and rushed on him all at once. They threw him out of the city and stoned him. Those who testified against him put their coats down at the feet of a young man named Saul. Then they stoned Stephen as he was calling out, "Master Jesus! Receive my spirit!" He fell on his knees and cried out with a loud voice, "Master, do not hold this sin against them!" When he had said this, he died. now Saul had voted for his death.

ON THAT DAY, A MAJOR PERSECUTION AROSE AGAINST THE congregation that was in Jerusalem, and they were all scattered throughout the regions of Judea and Samaria (except for the apostles). Some God-respecting men prepared Stephen's body for burial and had a loud funeral for him. But Saul began trying to destroy the congregation—going into every house and dragging out both men and women to put them in prison.

So those who were scattered went everywhere proclaiming the Good Message. For example, Philip went down to the city of Samaria and preached about the Messiah to them. The crowds paid close attention to what was being said by Philip—they were completely focused as they listened to him and saw the signs he performed. You see, many of them had unclean spirits, which cried out with loud voices and came out. Many others who were weak or crippled were healed. There was a lot of celebration in that city!

Now a man named Simon previously had practiced magic and amazed the nation of Samaritans. He claimed to be someone—the Magnificent. Everyone paid attention to him—from the least to the greatest—and they said, "This is the power of God—he is called 'the Magnificent!'" They paid attention to him because for a long time he had amazed them with magic. But when they believed Philip (who was proclaiming the Good Message about God's kingdom and the name of Jesus the Messiah), both men and women were being immersed. Simon himself believed and was immersed, and then he followed Philip. He was amazed as he watched the signs and great miracles that were happening.

When the apostles in Jerusalem heard that Samaria had received God's Word, they sent Peter and John to them. These men came down and prayed for them so that they would receive the Holy Spirit. You see, he had not yet fallen on any of them—they were only immersed in the name of Jesus the Master. Then the apostles laid their hands on them, and they received the Holy Spirit. When Simon saw that the Spirit was granted by the apostles laying their hands on them, he offered them money. He said, "Give me this power, too, so that whenever I lay my hands on someone, they will receive the Holy Spirit."

Peter told him, "May your silver be destroyed with you because you thought that God's gift could be purchased with money! You have no part or inheritance in this Message because your heart is not right in God's sight. So repent from this wickedness of yours and beg the Master so that your heart's intentions will be forgiven. I see that you are in bitter poison and the chains of sin!"

Then Simon responded by saying, "You—beg the Master on my behalf so that nothing that you have said will happen to me!"

SO AFTER THEY HAD TESTIFIED AND DELIVERED THE MASTER'S Message, they returned to Jerusalem—but on their way, they preached the Good Message in many Samaritan villages.

Now an angel from the Master spoke to Philip: "Get up and go south to the road that descends from Jerusalem toward Gaza—the deserted place." So he arose and went.

Now get this—an Ethiopian eunuch (a court official for Candace, Queen of Ethiopians) who was in charge of her entire treasury had come to Jerusalem to worship. He was returning home, seated in his chariot and reading Isaiah the Prophet.

The Spirit said to Philip, "Go grab onto this chariot."

So while Philip was running, he heard him reading Isaiah the Prophet and said, "Hey! Do you understand what you are reading?"

The eunuch asked, "How would I be able to understand it unless someone were to guide me?" Then he invited Philip to come up and sit with him. This was the passage of Scripture that he was reading:

> He was led like a sheep to be slaughtered,
> But just as a lamb is silent in front of the one who shears it,
> He did not open his mouth.
> His condemnation was carried out with humiliation—
> Who will tell the story of his family?
> You see, his life was taken from the earth.

Then the eunuch responded to Philip, "I beg you—about whom does the prophet say this: himself or some other person?"

So Philip opened his mouth and began with this very passage to preach to him the Good Message about Jesus. Now while they were going down the road, they came upon some water.

Then the eunuch said, "Look! Water! What is keeping me from being immersed?" So he commanded the chariot to stop, and they both went down into the water (Philip and the eunuch), and he immersed him. When they came up out of the water, the Spirit of the Master carried Philip away, and the eunuch did not see him anymore. He went down the road celebrating. But Philip made an appearance in Azotus. As he passed through, he preached the Good Message to all those cities until he came to Caesarea.

NOW SAUL CONTINUED TO ISSUE MURDEROUS THREATS AGAINST the Master's disciples. He approached the high priest and asked for letters from him to Damascus for the synagogues so that if he found anyone belonging to The Way (whether men or women), he could bring them to Jerusalem in chains.

It happened while he was on his way—he was coming near to Damascus—that suddenly a light from the sky flashed all around him. As he fell to the ground, he heard a voice speak to him: "Saul! Saul! Why are you persecuting me?"

He asked, "Who are you, sir?"

"I am Jesus—the one you are persecuting! Now—get up and enter the city, and what you must do will be told to you."

The men who were traveling with him had been standing there speechless—they heard a sound but did not witness anything. So Saul got up from the ground, but when he opened his eyes, he could not see anything. They led him by the hand into Damascus, and he stayed there for three days without being able to see—and he did not eat or drink anything.

Now there was a disciple named Ananias in Damascus. The Master spoke to him in a vision, "Ananias!"

Then he said, "Here I am, Master!"

The Master said to him, "Get up and go to Straight Street, and search in Judas' house for someone named Saul, from Tarsus. He is praying, you see, and in a vision he has seen a man named Ananias coming and placing his hands on him so that he would become able to see."

Ananias answered, "Master, I have heard about this man from many people—he has done so many evil things to your holy people in Jerusalem. Furthermore, he has authority from the chief priests to come here and put everyone who calls on your name into prison!"

Then the Master said to him, "Go, because that man is an instrument chosen by me to carry my name in front of both nations and rulers of the sons of Israel. You see, I will show him how many things he must suffer because of my name."

Then Ananias went. He entered the house, placed his hands on him, and said, "Saul, my brother: the Master—Jesus, who appeared to you on the road while you came—he has sent me so that you would become able to see and be filled with the Holy Spirit."

Immediately something like scales fell from Saul's eyes, so he became able to see. Then he got up and was immersed. He accepted some food and regained his strength. He stayed with the disciples in Damascus for several days, and right away he began to preach in their synagogues about Jesus—that he is the Son of God.

Now everyone who heard this was shocked. They asked, "Is this not the one who made havoc in Jerusalem on the ones who call on this name? Has he not also come here to chain them up and carry them to the chief priests?"

As for Saul, he continued to grow even stronger, and he baffled the Jews who were living in Damascus by demonstrating that Jesus is the Messiah.

As a considerable number of days came to an end, the Jews met in council to execute him. But their plot was made known to him. They carefully watched the gates day and night so that they could execute him. So during the night, his disciples lifted him up and lowered him from a window by letting him go down in a basket.

Now when he arrived in Jerusalem, he tried to join the disciples, but they were afraid of him—not believing that he was truly a disciple. But Barnabas took him aside and led him to the apostles. He explained to them that Saul saw the Master on the road and spoke with him and that he had spoken openly at Damascus in the Master's name. So he stayed with them, going in and out of Jerusalem and speaking openly in the Master's name. He spoke with—and then debated—the Hellenistic Jews, so they tried to kill him. When the brothers realized this, they led him down to Caesarea and then sent him to Tarsus.

As a result of this, the whole assembly throughout Judea, Galilee, and Samaria had peace. It was being built up and living with reverence for the Master, and it was filled the encouragement of the Holy Spirit.

NOW IT JUST SO HAPPENED THAT, WHILE PETER WAS TRAVELING all around, he went to the saints who lived in Lydda. While there he found a man named Aeneas, who was paralyzed. He had been confined to his bed for eight years. Peter told him, "Aeneas: Jesus the Messiah heals you! Get up and make your bed." Then he got up immediately, and everyone who lived in Lydda and Sharon saw him—and they all converted to follow the Master!

Meanwhile, there was a disciple in Joppa named Tabitha (in translation, she was called Dorcas). She was full of good works and acts of charity that she performed. It just so happened in those days that she became sick and died. Once they had rinsed her body, they placed her in an upper room. Now since Lydda was near Joppa, and the disciples had heard that Peter was there, they sent two men to him, begging: "Do not hesitate—come to where we live."

So Peter got up and went with them. When they arrived, they led him up to the upper room. All the widows presented before him—they showed him all the shirts and robes that she had made for them while Dorcas was alive.

Then Peter sent them all outside. He bowed his knees and prayed and then turned toward the body and said, "Tabitha: Get up!"

Then she opened her eyes and sat up when she saw Peter. He offered her a hand and helped her stand up. He called for the saints and widows and presented her alive. This was reported throughout all of Joppa, and many believed in the Master. He spent a significant number of days in Joppa with a man named Simon—a tanner.

Now there was a man named Cornelius in Caesarea. He was a centurion from what was called the Italian Cohort. He was religious and revered God with his entire household—he performed many acts of charity for the people and prayed to God all the time. In a vision at about 3:00 p.m., he distinctly saw an angel from God coming toward him and calling him: "Cornelius!"

Then Cornelius stared at him and became very afraid. He asked, "What is it, Master?"

The angel said to him, "Your prayers and charitable actions have risen before God like a memorial offering. Now send men to Joppa and ask for a particular Simon—the one called Peter. He is living as a guest with another Simon (a tanner), whose house is beside the sea."

So as the angel who spoke with him went away, Cornelius called two household servants and a religious soldier among those who stayed by his side. He repeated everything to them and sent them to Joppa.

The next day, while they were on their way and coming close to the city, Peter went up onto the roof to pray at about noon. He became hungry and wanted to eat something. As they were preparing it, a trance came over him, and he saw the sky opened up. Something came down like a large linen cloth being lowered onto the ground by its four corners. In it were all kinds of four-footed animals, reptiles of the ground, and birds from the sky.

A voice came to him: "Get up, Peter! Kill and eat."

Then Peter said, "No way, Master! You see, I have never eaten anything profane or unclean!"

The voice came to him a second time: "Do not call what God has cleansed profane!"

It came a third time, and immediately the object was lifted up into the sky. While Peter was inwardly confused about what this vision he had seen could mean, get this—those men who were sent by Cornelius to seek Simon's house arrived at the gates! They called someone and asked if the Simon who is called Peter lived there. While Peter was reflecting on the vision, the Spirit said to him, "Look! Three men are looking for you—get up, climb down, and go with them without hesitation because I have sent them myself."

So Peter went down to the men and said, "Hey! I am the one you are looking for; what is the reason you have come here?"

They said, "The centurion Cornelius—a righteous man who reveres God, and this is attested by the whole nation of the Jews—was divinely instructed by an angel of the Master to send for you to be brought into his house so that he could listen to your words."

Then Peter invited them in as guests. On the next day, he got up and left with them, and some of the brothers who were from Joppa went with him. On the following day, they entered Caesarea. Now Cornelius was anticipating their arrival—he invited his relatives and closest friends. Just as Peter came near to enter, Cornelius met him, fell down at his feet, and worshiped him.

Peter lifted him up and said, "Get up! I am only a man myself!" Then as he was talking with him, he entered and found many people who had come together. He said to them, "You understand that it is forbidden for a Jewish man to associate with or approach someone of another race, but God has shown even me not to call people profane or unclean. As a result, without any objection I have come as I have been requested. So now I am asking—why did you send for me?"

Then Cornelius said, "Four days ago at this exact time—3:00 p.m.—I was praying in my house. Get this: a man stood in front of me in bright clothing and said, 'Cornelius, your prayer has been answered, and your charitable actions have been mentioned before God. So send to Joppa and summon Simon—the one called Peter. He is staying in the house of Simon the tanner beside the sea.' So I sent for you at once, and you have done well by coming—you see, now we all have come before God to hear everything that you have been commanded by the Master."

Then Peter opened his mouth to speak: "I genuinely understand that God is not prejudiced! No—in every nation, whoever reveres him and does what is right is accepted by him. He sent this message to the sons of Israel, bringing good news of peace through Jesus the Messiah—he is the Master of everyone! You yourselves are aware of the things that have happened throughout Judea—starting at Galilee after the immersion that John preached. You are aware of Jesus from Nazareth, how God anointed him by the Holy Spirit and power. He passed through doing good things and healing all who were oppressed by the devil because God was with him. We also are witnesses of everything that he did in the country of the Jews and in Jerusalem. They executed him by hanging him on a tree. God raised this man up on the third day and permitted him to be seen—not by just any people but by witnesses who were hand-selected by God—us! We ate and drank with him after he was raised from the dead. Then he sent us to preach to the people and attest to the fact that this man is the one appointed by God to be the judge of the living and the dead! All the prophets testified of this—that all who believe through his name would receive the forgiveness of sins!"

While Peter was still speaking these words, the Holy Spirit fell upon all who were listening to the message. Everyone in the group of faithful Jewish men who had gone with Peter was shocked because the gift of the Holy Spirit had been poured out onto the gentiles! You see, they heard them speaking in other languages and glorifying God.

Then Peter asked, "Can anyone withhold water so as to prevent these from being immersed? They have received the Holy Spirit just as we did!" Then he instructed them to be immersed in the name of Jesus the Messiah, and they asked him to stay there for a few more days.

WELL, THE APOSTLES AND THE BROTHERS WHO WERE IN JUDEA heard that the gentiles had received God's Message. So when Peter went up to Jerusalem, the members of the circumcision party disagreed with him. They said, "You went to uncircumcised men and ate with them!"

Then Peter began to lay out for them what happened, point by point. He said, "I was praying in the city of Joppa, and I saw a vision while in a trance—an object came down from the sky like a large linen cloth being placed down by its four corners. It came right to me. I stared at it, watching it, and I saw four-footed animals from the earth, as well as beasts, reptiles, and birds of the sky. Now I also heard a voice call to me and say, 'Get up, Peter! Slaughter and eat!'

"But I said, 'No way, Master, because never has anything profane or unclean entered my mouth!'

"Then the voice from the sky answered me a second time: 'You must not call what God has cleansed profane!'

"This happened three times, and then all these things were pulled up into the sky. Now get this: immediately three men arrived at the house where I was staying—sent to me from Caesarea. The Spirit told me to go with them without hesitation. There also were six brothers who went with me, and we entered the man's house. He told us that he had seen an angel standing in his house who said, 'Send to Joppa and summon Simon—the one called Peter. He will speak words to you through which you and all of your household will be saved.'

"Now, as I began to speak, the Holy Spirit fell on them just as he did on us at the beginning. Then I remembered the Master's statement when he said, 'Yes, John immersed in water, but you will be immersed in the Holy Spirit.' So if God gave them the same gift that he gave us when we believed in the Master, Jesus the Messiah, who was I to be able to withstand God?"

When they heard this, they became quiet and then praised God. They said, "Well, God has also granted opportunity for repentance to the gentiles!"

NOW THOSE WHO WERE SCATTERED BECAUSE OF THE OPPRESSION that began with Stephen went as far as Phoenicia, Cypress, and Antioch; but they did not speak the message except to Jews only. Some of these were men from Cypress and Cyrene who had come to speak to the Hellenistic Jews in Antioch and to preach the Good Message of Jesus the Master. This report about them reached the ears of the congregation in Jerusalem, so they sent Barnabas to journey to Antioch. When he arrived and saw the display of God's grace, he celebrated and encouraged them all to stay with the Master with heartfelt devotion. You see, he was a good man who was full of the Holy Spirit and faith, and a significant crowd of people was added to the Master. Then he went out to Tarsus and searched out Saul. When he had found him, he brought him to Antioch and stayed with them for an entire year, gathering with the congregation and teaching a significant crowd of people. The disciples were first called Christians at Antioch.

During those days, prophets went down to Antioch from Jerusalem. One of them—named Agabus—got up and demonstrated a sign by the Holy Spirit that a severe famine was about to come upon the whole world (which happened during the reign of Claudius). So each of the disciples—as much as each was able to spare—set apart money for support to send to the brothers who lived in Judea. They sent what they had prepared to the elders by the hand of Barnabas and Saul.

AT ABOUT THAT TIME, KING HEROD GOT HIS HANDS ON SOME people from the congregation so that he could mistreat them. He executed James (John's brother) by sword. When he saw that it pleased the Jews, he proceeded to arrest Peter. By the way, this was during the feast days of Unleavened Bread. Once he had captured him, he put him into prison and set four teams of four soldiers each to guard him—intending to bring him before the people after the Passover. So Peter was kept in prison, but passionate prayer was being offered to God for him by the congregation.

So on the very night that Herod was about to bring him before the people, Peter was sleeping between two soldiers, tied with two chains, and they were standing guard in front of the prison door. Now get this: an angel of the Master appeared, and a light shone within the room. He hit Peter in his side and got him up, saying, "Get up quickly." Then his chains fell off from his hands. The angel said to him, "Get dressed and put on your sandals," so that is what he did. Then he told him, "Put your robe around you and follow me." So Peter followed him out but did not know that what was done by the angel was really happening. You see, he thought he was seeing a vision. They passed through the prison first, and secondly went to the iron gate that led into the city. It automatically opened for them, so they came out and went down one street.

Then the angel left him, and Peter came to himself and said, "Now I really know that the Master has sent out his angel and rescued me from the hand of Herod and all of what the Jewish people expected!" So once he comprehended this, he went to the house of Mary (the mother of John Mark), where several were gathered together to pray. While he was knocking on the door at the gate, a young girl named Rhoda came near to listen, and she recognized Peter's voice. Out of joy she neglected to open the gate, instead running inside to report that Peter was standing in front of the gate!

But they told her, "You are crazy!" Yet she insisted that she was right. Then they said, "It is his angel."

Well, Peter kept knocking, and when they had opened the door, they saw him and were shocked! Then he waved his hand to quiet them and told them how the Master had led him out of the prison and proceeded to say, "Tell James and the brothers these things." Then he went out and walked to another place.

When daylight came, there was a significant disturbance among the soldiers as to where Peter had gone. So when Herod inquired about him and did not find him, he interrogated the guards and commanded that they be taken away. Then he went down from Judea to Caesarea and stayed there.

Now he had been very angry with the residents of Tyre and Sidon. So they appeared before him unified in purpose and convinced Blastus (who was in charge of the king's bedroom) to ask for peace because their country had been fed by the king's country.

So on an appointed day, Herod put on his royal clothing. Once he had taken his seat at the judicial bench, he delivered a speech to them.

Then the people cried out, "This is the voice of a god—not of man!"

Instantly an angel of the Master struck him because he neglected to give glory to God. He became sick because of worms and died.

SO GOD'S MESSAGE GREW AND MULTIPLIED. BARNABAS AND SAUL returned to Jerusalem to complete the support offering, and they took John Mark with them.

There were prophets and teachers in the congregation at Antioch, including: Barnabas, Simon (the one called Black), Luke (the Cyrenian one), Manaen (who was also a close friend of Herod the Tetrarch), and Saul. While they were offering a worship service to the Master and fasting, the Holy Spirit said: "Appoint Barnabas and Saul to me now for the work that I have called them to do." Then after they had fasted, prayed, and laid their hands on them, they sent them away.

So these men who were sent by the Holy Spirit went down to Seleucia, and from there they sailed off to Cypress. When they arrived in Salamis, they proclaimed God's Message in the Jews' synagogues, and they had John as an aide. They traveled throughout the entire island all the way to Paphos and found a man—some Jewish magician/false prophet named Bar-Jesus. He was with the proconsul, Sergius Paulus, a very intelligent man. Sergius Paulus had invited Barnabas and Saul, requesting to hear God's Message, but the magician Elymas (that is actually the translation of his name) stood up to them, trying to mislead the proconsul away from the faith.

Then Saul (who is also called Paul) was filled with the Spirit and stared at him. He said, "You son of the devil—full of all deceit, full of fraud, and enemy of all that is right! Will you ever stop twisting the straight ways of the Master? Look now! The Master's hand is against you, and you will be blind—unable to see the sun for a while!"

Immediately a haze and darkness fell upon him, and he went around looking for someone to lead him by the hand. Then the proconsul saw what happened and believed, overwhelmed by the Master's teaching.

Then the people who were with Paul went up from Paphos and came to Perga, Pamphylia (but John abandoned them and returned to Jerusalem). They traveled from Perga and arrived in Antioch, Pisidia, where they entered the synagogue on the Sabbath Day and took a seat. After the reading of the Law and Prophets, the ruler of the synagogue sent for them and said, "Gentlemen!

Brothers! Do you have some message of encouragement for the people? Say it!"

So Paul stood up and motioned with his hand. He said, "Gentlemen—Israelites and you who respect God—listen! The God of this nation of Israel chose our fathers and nation. He lifted them up during their stay in Egypt and led them out of it with a raised arm. Then for about forty years, he put up with them in the desert. He took down seven nations in the land of Canaan and gave Israel their land as an inheritance for about 450 years. After this, he gave them judges until Samuel the prophet. At that time, they asked for a king, and God gave them Saul, the son of Kish—a man from the tribe of Benjamin—for forty years. After removing him, he raised up David as a king for them. He gave testimony about him: 'I have found David, the son of Jesse, to be a man with a heart like mine. He will do everything that I want.'

"As promised, from this man's own lineage God brought Israel a savior—Jesus. Before he arrived on the scene, John proclaimed an immersion of repentance for all the nation of Israel. Then once John completed his mission, he asked, "Who do you think I am? I am not he, but someone is coming after me, and I am not worthy to untie the sandals on his feet." Gentlemen! Brothers! Sons of Abraham's family and you who respect God: the message of this salvation has been sent to us! You see, those who live in Jerusalem—and their rulers too—did not recognize this or the voices of the prophets who are read every Sabbath, so they fulfilled them by condemning him. Even though they found no reason to put him to death, they begged Pilate to execute him. Furthermore, after they had brought everything written about him to reality, they pulled him down from the cross and put him in a tomb. But God raised him from the dead, and he appeared for many days to those who had gone up to Jerusalem from Galilee—and now they are his witnesses for the people. We ourselves have proclaimed the Good Message to you—that the promise made to our ancestors has come to happen—because God has fulfilled this promise to us, their children, by raising Jesus just as it has been written in the second psalm:

> You are my son; today I have fathered you.

"So since he raised him from the dead, no longer to return to decomposition, then he said, 'I will give you David's trustworthy divine assurances.' You see, in another psalm he says,

> You will not cause your holy one to experience decomposition.

"Now even though David served as an assistant to his own generation by the will of God, he passed away and was buried with his ancestors—and he saw decomposition. On the other hand, the one whom God raised did not experience decomposition. So let this be known to you, gentlemen and brothers: that through him the forgiveness of sins is proclaimed to you—even forgiveness of everything that prevented you from being made righteous through the Law of Moses. In him, everyone who believes will be made righteous! So be careful that what was spoken in the prophets does not happen:

> Look, scoffers! Be amazed and destroyed
> Because I am doing a work in your days that you would never believe,
> even if someone told you in great detail.'

As they were going out of the synagogue, they begged him to speak to them about these things on the following Sabbath. Once the synagogue meeting had been dismissed, many of the

Jews and religious converts followed Paul and Barnabas, who spoke to them, trying to convince them to continue in God's grace. On the next Sabbath, almost the entire city was assembled to listen to the Master's Message. When the Jews saw the crowds, they were overcome with jealousy and fought against what Paul was saying, slandering it. Then both Paul and Barnabas spoke out boldly: "It was necessary for God's Message to have been spoken to you first, but since you have thrown it away and do not consider yourselves deserving of eternal life, then look—we are turning to the gentiles. You see, this is what the Master has commanded us:

> I have appointed you to be a light to the gentiles
> so that you may bring salvation to the ends of the earth.

When the gentiles heard this, they celebrated and praised the Master's Message. Everyone who was appointed for eternal life believed, and so the Master's Message spread throughout the country. Then the Jews riled up the religious women who were prominent figures, as well as the important men of the city, and they stirred up a persecution against Paul and Barnabas, driving them out of the area. But they shook off the dust from their feet at them and went to Iconium. Meanwhile, the disciples were filled with joy and the Holy Spirit.

THE SAME THING HAPPENED IN ICONIUM—THEY WENT INTO THE Jews' synagogue and spoke this message so that a great number of both Jews and Greeks believed. But the Jews who refused the message riled up and poisoned the minds of the gentiles against the brothers. So for a good while they spent their time speaking openly about the Master, who attested to the message by his grace—providing signs and miracles to be performed by their hands. So a lot of the city was divided—some sided with the Jews and others with the apostles. When they became aware of an attempt made by both the gentiles and the Jews (along with their rulers) to insult and stone them to death, they fled to the cities of Lycaonia—Lystra, Derbe, and the surrounding cities—and preached the Good Message there.

Now there was a man sitting in Lystra who was paralyzed in his feet—he had been crippled from his mother's womb and had never walked. He listened while Paul speaking. Paul stared at him and saw that he had the faith to be saved, so he said with a loud voice, "Stand up straight onto your feet." Then he got up and walked!

The crowd saw what Paul had done and raised their voices in the Lycaonian language and said, "The gods have taken on human form and have come down to us!" They called Barnabas "Zeus" and Paul "Hermes" since he was the primary speaker. Then the priest of Zeus, who served in behalf of the city, brought bulls and wreaths to the gates because he wanted to offer a sacrifice with the crowd.

But when the apostles Barnabas and Paul heard about this, they tore their robes, jumped out into the crowd, and cried out: "Gentlemen! Why are you doing this? We also are men with similar struggles like you! We are preaching the Good Message to you in order to turn you from these worthless things to the living God, 'who made the heaven, the earth, the sea, and everything that is in them.' In past generations, he has allowed all the nations to live their own way, but even then he did not leave himself without evidence! He did good works from heaven—giving you rain and seasons of fruitfulness and satisfying your hearts with food and happiness!" Even after saying this, they could barely keep the crowd from sacrificing to them.

Then some Jews arrived from Antioch and Iconium and won over the crowd—they stoned Paul and dragged him out of the city, thinking that he was dead. But after the disciples surrounded him, he got up and entered the city. Then in the morning, he left with Barnabas for Derbe. They preached the Good Message to that city and made several disciples and then returned to Lystra, then to Iconium, and then Antioch. Meanwhile, they strengthened the minds of the disciples, encouraging them to continue in the faith and saying, "We must enter God's kingdom through many hardships."

When they had hand-selected for themselves elders for every congregation, they prayed (with fasting) and committed them to the Master in whom they had believed. Then after they traveled through Pisidia, they came to Pamphylia and spoke the Message in Perga. They went down to Attalia, and from there they sailed away to Antioch, from where they had been set apart by God's grace for the work that they had now accomplished. So when they arrived, they assembled the congregation and reported everything that God had done with them and how he had opened faith's door to the gentiles. Then they spent a lot of time with the disciples.

NOW SOME PEOPLE WHO CAME DOWN FROM JERUSALEM WERE teaching the brothers, "Unless you are circumcised by the statute of Moses, you cannot be saved." Once a significant uproar and argument came to Paul and Barnabas about them, they arranged for Paul and Barnabas (and some others with them) to go up to Jerusalem, to the apostles and elders, about this argument. So when they had been sent away by the congregation, they traveled through Phoenicia and Samaria, explaining in detail the conversion of the gentiles and producing considerable joy among all the brothers.

Then when they arrived in Jerusalem, they were welcomed by the congregation, the apostles, and the elders. They reported everything that God had done with them. Then some men from the Pharisees' sect who had become believers stood up and said, "They must be commanded to be circumcised and to keep the Law of Moses!"

Both the apostles and elders assembled to attend to this matter, and after much arguing had taken place, Peter stood up and said to them, "Gentlemen! Brothers! You know that a long time ago, among all of you, God chose for the gentiles to hear the Message of the gospel by my mouth and to have faith. Furthermore, you know that the heart-knowing God attested this by giving the Holy Spirit to them just as he had done to us. He did not make a distinction at all between us or them as he purified their hearts by faith. So why are you now tempting God by putting a yoke on the disciples' necks that neither our ancestors nor we have been able to carry? No! By the grace of the Master Jesus, we believe and are saved—the same way they are!"

Then the whole crowd stopped speaking and listened as Barnabas and Paul explained how God had performed through them so many signs and miracles among the gentiles.

Once they had finished speaking, James responded, "Gentlemen, brothers: listen to me. Simon has explained how God first saw to it that he received a nation from among the gentiles to wear his name. Plus the words of the prophets agree with this, as it was written:

> After this I will return and rebuild the tent of David that has fallen;

I will rebuild its parts that have fallen down and restore it,
That way, the rest of mankind may seek the Master,
even all the gentiles who are called by my name.
So says the Master who makes these things known from forever ago.

"So I think we should not cause trouble for those of the gentiles who have converted to God. On the contrary, we should send them a message to avoid defilement by idols, illicit sexual behavior, and food that was strangled or eaten with blood. You see, since a long time ago, Moses has had people who preach his message in every city, and he is read in synagogues on every single Sabbath."

Then he decided, along with the apostles and elders (together with the whole congregation), to select men from among them and send them to Antioch with Paul and Barnabas. They chose Judas (who was called Barsabbas) and Silas, who were leading men among the brothers, and through them they wrote:

"The brothers—the apostles and elders—to the gentile brothers who are in Antioch, Syria, and Cilicia: Hello!

"Since we have heard that some have come from us and have caused you trouble with their words and have upset your minds without us sending them, it seemed best to us to unanimously select men and send them to you with our dear friends Barnabas and Paul—men who have put their lives on the line for the name of our Master, Jesus the Messiah. So we have sent Judas, Silas, and them to announce these things through their message. You see, it seemed best to the Holy Spirit and to us not to put any further pressure on you except for what is necessary: avoid food sacrificed to idols, as well as food with its blood or that has been strangled, and illicit sexual behavior. It would be a good practice for you to keep yourselves away from these. Stay strong!"

So once they were dismissed, they went down to Antioch, assembled the crowd, and relayed the letter. When the people read it, they were joyful because of its encouragement. Both Judas and Silas (who were also prophets themselves) encouraged and strengthened the brothers with a lengthy message. They spent some time there and then were released back to those who had sent them, with peace from the brothers. But Paul and Barnabas (and many others) stayed in Antioch, teaching and preaching the good news of the Master's Message.

AFTER SEVERAL DAYS, PAUL SAID TO BARNABAS: "LET'S GO BACK and check on the brothers in every city where we proclaimed the Master's Message, to see how they are doing."

Now Barnabas wanted to take John (the one called Mark) along with them. But Paul did not think it was acceptable to take him along with them because he had abandoned them in Pamphylia and did not go and work with them. So there was a sharp disagreement, and they parted ways from one another—Barnabas took Mark along with him and sailed away for Cypress while Paul chose Silas and went out, entrusted by the brothers to the Master's grace. He traveled through Syria and Cilicia and strengthened the congregations.

Then he reached Derbe and Lystra. Now get this—a disciple named Timothy was there. He was the son of a woman who was a Jewish believer, but his father was Greek. He was commended by the brothers in Lystra and Iconium. Paul wanted to take him with him and go out, so he took him aside and circumcised him because of the Jews who were in those places. You see, everyone knew that his father was Greek. So then they traveled through the cities and relayed the message for them to abide by the decisions made by the apostles and elders who were in Jerusalem. As a result, the congregations were strengthened in faith, and they increased in number every day.

Then they traveled through the regions of Phrygia and Galatia but were prevented by the Holy Spirit from preaching the Message in Asia. As they approached Mysia, they tried to go to Bithynia, but the Spirit of Jesus did not allow them. So they went through Mysia and went down to Troas. Now a vision appeared to Paul during the night: a Macedonian man was standing there and begging him, "Travel to Macedonia! Help us!"

So once he had seen the vision, we immediately sought to leave for Macedonia because we had put it together that God was summoning us to preach the Good Message to them.

When we had carried on from Troas, we ran straight to Samothrace and then to New City. From there we went to Philippi, a Roman colony that is an important city of the Macedonian province. We stayed in that city for several days. Now on the Sabbath Day, we went outside the gate beside a river where we thought there would be a place for prayer, so we sat down and spoke with the women who had assembled. One woman was named Lydia. She was a merchant of purple goods from the city of Thyatira, and she respected God. She listened, and the Master completely opened her heart to accept the things being said by Paul. Once she had been immersed (and her household as well), she begged us, "If you have considered me to be faithful to the Master, come into my house and stay," and she urged us strongly.

It just so happened, while we were going to the place for prayer, that some slave girl who had a spirit of fortunetelling met us. She netted her masters a lot of profit by her fortunetelling. She followed Paul and us, crying out, "These men are slaves of God the Highest, and they are proclaiming the way of salvation to you!" She kept doing this for several days.

Well, Paul became annoyed and turned to the spirit, saying, "I command you in the name of Jesus the Messiah to come out of her!" Then it came out of her at that exact time. When her masters saw that their hope for profit was gone, they seized Paul and Silas, dragged them to the square before their rulers, and carried them to the generals, saying, "These men are causing a lot of trouble in our city! They are Jews, and they preach habits that are not right for us to accept or do because we are Romans."

So the crowd joined in against them, and the generals stripped them of their robes and commanded for them to be beaten with rods. They laid many blows on them and threw them into prison, telling the prison guard to keep them carefully. When he had received this command, he threw them into the inner prison and secured their feet in the wooden stocks.

At about midnight, Paul and Silas were praying and singing hymns to God, and the prisoners were listening to them. Suddenly there was a strong earthquake, and so the foundations of the prison were shaken. Instantly all the doors were opened and the restraints were released. The prison guard was awakened from sleep, and he saw the prison's doors opened, so he drew his sword. He was about to kill himself because he thought the prisoners had escaped.

Then Paul cried out with a loud voice, "Do not harm yourself because we are all here."

Then the prison guard called for a torch and rushed in, overcome with terror, and fell down in front of Paul and Silas. He led them outside and asked, "Sirs, what do I need to do to be saved?"

They said, "Believe in Jesus the Master, and you will be saved—your household too!" Then they told him (with all his household) the Master's Message. He took them at that very hour during the night and washed their wounds, and then right away he was immersed—he and all his household. Then he led them up to the house and prepared a table for them, and he celebrated because he had believed in God with his entire household.

When daybreak came, the generals sent the officers, who said, "Release those men."

The prison guard told these words to Paul: "The generals have sent to release you, so come out and go in peace!"

But Paul said to them, "They flogged us publicly when we had not been condemned—we are Roman citizens! Then they threw us into prison, and now they are sending us away secretly? No! See, let them come themselves and lead us out!"

So the officers told the generals these things, and when they heard that they were Roman citizens, they became afraid. They went and begged them, and as they led them out, they asked them to leave the city. So when they had left the prison, they went into Lydia's house. They saw the brothers, encouraged them, and then left.

AFTER TRAVELING THROUGH AMPHIPOLIS AND APOLLONIA, THEY came to Thessalonica, where there was a Jewish synagogue. So consistent with Paul's habit, he went inside to them and debated with them from the Scriptures for three weeks. He explained and demonstrated that the Messiah had to suffer and rise from the dead and that "the Jesus I am proclaiming to you is that Messiah." Some of them were convinced and sided with Paul and Silas; from the religious Greeks there was a large crowd and not just a few of the influential women!

But the Jews became jealous and took bad guys from the marketplace as reinforcements, and then they assembled a crowd to start a riot in the city. They showed up at Jason's house, looking for Paul and Silas so that they could bring them to court, but when they did not find them, they dragged Jason and some brothers before the city magistrate. They cried out, "These men who have disrupted the entire world have now come here, and they have been given refuge by Jason!" They are all acting contrary to Caesar's decrees, saying that there is another king named Jesus!" So they upset the crowd and the magistrates who heard this, and they took bail money from Jason and the others and let them go.

So when night fell, the brothers immediately sent Paul and Silas to Berea. When they arrived, they went to the Jews' synagogue. Now these people were more open-minded than the ones from Thessalonica—they accepted the message with complete readiness and read the Scriptures every day to see if these things held up. As a result, many of them believed, including more than a few prominent Greek men and women.

But once the Jews from Thessalonica knew that God's Message had also been proclaimed by Paul in Berea, they went there too to disturb and stir up the crowd. As a result, the brothers immediately sent Paul off so that he could go to the sea (meanwhile, Silas and Timothy stayed there). They escorted Paul, going as far as Athens, and were given instruction for Silas and

Timothy to leave quickly and come to him.

So while Paul was waiting for them in Athens, he was inwardly bothered in spirit because the whole city was full of idols. He went so far as to preach in the synagogue to the Jews and the gentiles who worshiped God and also every day in the marketplace to those who happened to be there. Even some of the Epicurean and Stoic philosophers debated with him. Some of them asked, "What is this 'proverb collector' trying to say?" Others said, "He seems to be a preacher of foreign deities," because he was proclaiming the Good Message of Jesus and the resurrection.

They even took him aside and led him to the Areopagus. They asked, "May we know what this new teaching is that has been spoken by you? You have brought some surprising things to our ears, so we would like to know what these things are supposed to mean." You see, many Athenians and foreign residents used to have nothing better to do than to say or listen to something new.

So Paul stood in the middle of the Areopagus and said, "Men of Athens—I have seen that you revere deities in everything because as I passed through and was looking around, I came across your objects of worship, including an altar on which was written: TO AN UNKNOWN GOD. So this very God you worship without knowing is the one I proclaim to you. The God who created the world and everything in it—since he is the Master of heaven and earth—does not live in hand-made sanctuaries, and he is not cared for by human hands as if he needed something. He gave life, breath, and everything to everyone—he made every nation of people from one man so that they would inhabit the whole earth. He appointed and determined the times and places where they would live, that they would seek God, so that they would feel around for him and find him—even though he is not far from any one of us. You see, 'In him we live, move, and exist'—like some of your own poets have said—'for we also are his descendants.' So since we are descendants of God, we should not think that the Divine Being is anything resembling gold, silver, or stone formed by human artistry and reasoning. Indeed, God overlooked these times of ignorance, but now he commands people—everyone and everywhere—to repent. You see, he has set a day when he is going to judge the world with justice by a man he has appointed, and he has presented evidence to everyone by raising him from the dead."

When they heard about resurrection from the dead, some of them made fun of it, but others said, "We will listen to you again about this." So Paul went out from among them. Some men joined themselves to him and believed; among them were Dionysius the Areopagite, a woman named Damaris, and others with them.

After this, he left Athens and arrived in Corinth. He found a particular Jew named Aquila and his wife, Priscilla. Aquila was a native of Pontus who had recently come from Italy because Claudius had ordered all the Jews to leave Rome. Paul approached them, and because he was in the same profession, he lived and worked with them. You see, they were in the business of making tents. He preached in the synagogue every Sabbath, winning over both Jews and Greeks. Once Silas and Timothy had come down from Macedonia, Paul was completely absorbed in preaching the Message, attesting to the Jews that Jesus was the Messiah. Because the Jews were resisting and slandering, he shook out his robe at them. "May your blood fall on your own heads—I am guiltless! From now on, I will go to the gentiles!"

So he went on from there and into the house of someone named Titius Justus, a worshiper of God whose house shared a property line with the synagogue. Now the ruler of the synagogue, Crispus, believed in the Master, along with his entire household. Furthermore, many of the Corinthians who listened also believed and were immersed.

Then the Master spoke to Paul during the night through a vision: "Do not be afraid; just speak and do not be silent, because I am with you, and no one will lay a hand on you to harm you. You see, I have many people in this city."

So he stayed there a year and six months, teaching God's Message among them.

WHILE GALLIO WAS THE PROCONSUL OF ACHAIA, THE JEWS wholeheartedly rose up against Paul and carried him to court. They said, "This man is convincing people to worship God in a manner that is against the law!"

Paul was going to open his mouth, but Gallio said to the Jews, "If there were some injustice or heinous crime, Jews, I would carefully listen to your every word. But since this is a lawsuit concerning a message and names and your law, see to it yourselves. I do not want to be an arbitrator over these things." Then he drove them away from the courtroom. So they all seized Sosthenes, the ruler of the synagogue, and beat him in front of the court, but none of this was a concern to Gallio.

Now Paul continued to stay a few more days with the brothers, but then he took leave of them and sailed to Syria. Priscilla and Aquila went with him. He shaved his head in Cenchrea because of a vow he had taken. Then they reached Ephesus, and that is where he left them as he went on into the synagogue to preach to the Jews. Although they asked him to stay for a longer time, he did not consent. Instead, he took leave of them, saying, "By the will of God, I will come back to you." So he went up from Ephesus, traveled down to Caesarea, and then he went down to Antioch to greet the congregation. Then after spending a while there, he left, traveling systematically through the Galatian province and Phrygia, strengthening the disciples.

NOW THERE WAS A PARTICULAR JEW NAMED APOLLOS WHO traveled to Ephesus. He was a native of Alexandria who was very educated and powerful with the Scriptures. He was teaching the Master's Way, and his spirit was on fire as he spoke and taught in detail about the account of Jesus—but he knew only of John's immersion—and he began to preach openly in the synagogue. So when Priscilla and Aquila heard him, they took him aside and explained to him in better detail about God's Way. When he decided to pass through to Achaia, the brothers wrote to the disciples there, encouraging them to welcome him. Once he arrived, he met often with those who had believed by grace. You see, he was vigorously engaging the Jews in debate in public, proving by the Scriptures that Jesus was the Messiah.

While Apollos was in Corinth and Paul passed through the inland country to go to Ephesus, it just so happened that Paul found some disciples. He said to them, "Did you receive the Holy Spirit after you believed?"

But they said, "No, we have not even heard of the Holy Spirit."

So he asked, "Into what were you immersed, then?"

They said, "Into John's immersion."

Then Paul said, "John performed an immersion of repentance, telling the people that they should have faith in the one who was coming after him—that is, Jesus."

Now when they heard this, they were immersed in the name of Jesus the Master, and then Paul laid his hands on them, and the Holy Spirit came over them so that they began to speak in other languages and prophesy. The total number of men was about twelve.

Then he went into the synagogue and spoke publicly for three months, discussing and persuading them about God's kingdom. But since some were hardened and unpersuaded, they spoke evil about the Way in front of the crowds; he left them and separated out the disciples, and then he discussed it every day in the School of Tyrannus. This went on for another two years, and so everyone who lived in Asia heard the Master's Message—both Jews and Greeks. God performed extraordinary, powerful miracles by Paul's hand so that even when handkerchiefs or aprons that had touched his skin were carried and placed on sick people, their illnesses left them and their evil spirits came out.

Now some exorcists from the Jews also went around, laying their hands on people and invoking the name of Jesus the Master on those who had evil spirits. They said, "I subpoena you," and proclaimed the names of Jesus and Paul. There were seven sons of Sceva, the Jews' high priest, who were doing this.

One evil spirit then answered them, "I know Jesus, and I am familiar with Paul, but just who are you?" Then the man who was possessed by the evil spirit jumped them and overpowered every one of them so that they ran away from that house, naked and injured. After this happened, it became known to all Jews and Greeks who lived in Ephesus, and fear came over them all so that they glorified the name of Jesus the Master.

Many who believed came and confessed, admitting what they had done. Numerous practitioners of sorcery collected their books and burned them in front of everyone. They counted their value and found it to be fifty thousand pieces of silver. That is how powerfully the Master's Message grew and exercised influence.

ONCE THESE THINGS HAD FINISHED THEIR COURSE, PAUL decided to pass through Macedonia and Achaia on his way to Jerusalem. He said, "After I have been there, I must also see Rome." Then he sent two of his assistants, Timothy and Erastus, to Macedonia while he stayed for a while in Asia.

Now around that time, there arose a significant uproar regarding the Way. You see, there was a man named Demetrius, a silversmith who built shrines for Artemis out of silver, which provided the craftsmen with more than a few job opportunities. He gathered them and others who worked in similar trades and said, "Gentlemen, you know that our prosperity comes from this type of work, and you have seen and heard that this Paul has converted—corrupted—a significant number of people from not only Ephesus, but also throughout all of Asia. He has convinced them that gods cannot be made by hand, and not only has he risked making a mockery of our area of business, but also he has put the temple of the great goddess Artemis at risk for becoming nothing, and its magnificence is going to be ruined—and it is respected throughout all of Asia and the world!"

When they heard this, they were filled with rage and began shouting, "Great is Artemis of the Ephesians!" So the city was filled with chaos, and they rushed headlong into the theater, seizing Gaius and Aristarchus from Macedonia, who was a fellow traveler with Paul.

Now Paul wanted to enter where the people had assembled, but the disciples did not let him. So some of the Asian officials who were friends of his sent a message to him, begging him not to turn himself in at the theater. Others were shouting something else because the whole assembly was in chaos, and most of them did not know why they had come together.

Then several from the crowd instructed Alexander to speak as the Jews pushed him forward, so Alexander waved his hand, wanting to give a defense before the people.

But when they realized that he was a Jew, there came a unified shout from all of them for about two hours—"Great is Artemis of the Ephesians!"

Then the secretary of the state quieted the crowd and said, "Gentlemen, Ephesians: who is there among men who does not know that the city of the Ephesians is the honorary caretaker of the great Artemis and the idol that fell from the gods? So since these things are undeniable, you must be quiet and not become reckless because you have abducted these men who are neither stealing from temples nor slandering our god. So if Demetrius and the craftsmen who are with him have something to say, the courts are in session, and there are proconsuls—they must bring it to them. But if you are asking for something more, then by law the assembly must be dismissed. We risk being accused of a riot because of today's events. There is no reason that we are able to give for this that would account for this commotion." When he had said this, he dismissed the assembly.

AFTER THE UPROAR CAME TO AN END, PAUL SENT FOR THE disciples and encouraged them. Then he said goodbye to them and left to go to Macedonia. As he passed through those regions and encouraged them with many messages, he entered Greece and spent three months there. When a conspiracy against him was made by the Jews as he was preparing to go to Syria, he came to a decision to go back through Macedonia. Now Sopater (Pyrrhus's son from Berea) was accompanying him, as were the Thessalonians Aristarchus and Secundus, Gaius from Derbe, Timothy, and Tychicus and Trophimus, who were from Asia. They arrived first and waited for us at Troas. After the days of the Feast of Unleavened Bread, we set sail from Philippi and came to them at Troas (within five days), and we spent seven days there.

Then on the first day of the week, we got together to break bread. Paul preached to them, and since he planned to leave the next morning, he extended his message until midnight. There were several torches in the upper story where we were assembled.

Now a young man in particular, named Eutychus, was sitting at the window. He was overcome by deep sleep while Paul was talking so much, and once he had fallen asleep, he fell down from the third floor and was picked up dead.

But Paul went down, got down over him, and embraced him. He said, "Do not be upset because his life is still with him." So Paul got up, broke bread, and ate. Then he socialized quite a bit until daybreak, and then he left. They brought the young man back alive and were more than comforted.

So we went on to the boat and were taken to Assos. From there we planned to pick up Paul because that is what he directed, as he planned to go on foot. Once he met with us in Assos, we picked him up and went to Mitylene, and from there we sailed out on the next day and arrived on the other side of Chios. On the next day, we landed at Samos, and the next day in Miletus. Now Paul had decided to sail past Ephesus so that he would not lose time in Asia. You see, he was hurrying so that it would be possible for him to be in Jerusalem for the Day of Pentecost.

He sent a message to Ephesus from Miletus, summoning the elders of the congregation. So when they arrived, he said to them, "You know for yourselves that from the first day that I set foot in Asia I have been with you the whole time, serving the Master with complete humility—with tears and trials that have come over me in the form of the conspiracies of the Jews. These came about because I did not hold back from telling you anything beneficial, and I taught you publicly and from house to house. To both Jews and Greeks, I stated my case for repentance back to God and faith in Jesus our Master. Now look: my own hands are tied by the Spirit—I am going to Jerusalem, not knowing what will happen to me there except that in every city the Holy Spirit has been stating his case to me, saying that shackles and oppression are waiting for me. But I do not place any value at all on precious life for myself so that I may finish my race and the responsibility that I received from Jesus the Master to state my case for the Good Message of God's grace. Even now, look—I know that you, everyone among whom I went around preaching about the kingdom, will not see my face again. So I promise you on this very day that I am pure from the bloodguilt of everyone. You see, I have not held back from telling you the entire plan of God. Take care of yourselves and all the flock, among whom the Holy Spirit has appointed you as supervisors to shepherd God's congregation, which he purchased with his own blood. I know that after my departure, savage wolves will come in among you and will not spare the flock. Even from among yourselves. men will rise up and say misrepresentations in order to pull away the disciples to follow them. As a result, pay attention, because you know that night and day for three years, I did not cease to warn every single one through tears. Even so, now I am entrusting you to God and to his message of grace, to the one who can strengthen you and give you that inheritance with all the purified ones. I have not been greedy for anyone's silver, gold, or clothing. You know for yourselves that these hands have served to provide for my needs and for those who are with me. In every way I have shown you—by working hard, you must come to the assistance of the weak and remember the words of the Master Jesus since he said, 'It is more of a blessing to give than to receive.'"

When he had finished saying this, he bowed his knees with all of them and prayed. A significant amount of weeping came over everyone, and they fell upon Paul's neck and kissed him. They were pained most of all by what he said—that they were not going to see his face again. Then they accompanied him to the ship.

Once it became time for us to take up anchor and sail away from them, we took a straight course and went to Cos. The next day we went to Rhodes, and from there to Patara. We located a ship crossing over to Phoenicia, so we boarded and set sail. We spotted Cypress and passed by it on the left, and then sailed to Syria and docked in Tyre because the ship was unloading its cargo there. So we searched out some of the disciples and stayed with them for seven days. They told Paul (via the Spirit) not to go to Jerusalem. When the time came that our days there were finished, we left and went as they all accompanied us—with their women and children—until we were outside the city. Then we got down on our knees on the shore and prayed. We told them goodbye and boarded the ship, and they returned to their homes.

Having completed our voyage from Tyre, we arrived at Ptolemais. We greeted the brothers and stayed one day with them. In the morning, we left and came to Caesarea. There we entered the house of Philip the evangelist (who was one of the seven), and we stayed with him. Now he had four virgin daughters who prophesied. During the many days we stayed there, a prophet named Agabus came down from Judea. He came to us and took Paul's belt, tying it around his feet and hands.

He said, "This is what the Holy Spirit says: 'The man whose belt this is—this is how the Jews in Jerusalem will tie him up and turn him over to the hands of gentiles.'"

So once we heard this, both we and those who lived there begged Paul not to go up to Jerusalem.

Then Paul asked in response, "What are you doing—weeping and breaking my heart? You see, I am prepared not only to be tied up but also to die in Jerusalem for the name of Jesus the Master."

Since he would not be persuaded, we quieted down, saying, "May the Master's will be done."

AFTER THOSE DAYS, WE MADE PREPARATIONS TO GO UP TO Jerusalem. Some of the disciples from Caesarea came with us and led us to Mnason, a Cyprian and early disciple, so that we could stay with him. Then after we came to Jerusalem, the brothers gladly welcomed us.

On the next day, Paul was going with us to see James, and all the elders were present. So he greeted them and demonstrated each and every thing that God had done among the gentiles through his ministry.

Those who were listening praised God and then told Paul, "You see, brother, how many tens of thousands of people among the Jews have become believers, and all are passionate about the Law of Moses. They have been taught about you—that you teach all Jews who live among the gentiles to abandon Moses—telling them not to circumcise their children or walk according to his customs. So what is the plan? Surely they will hear that you have come. Now this is what we are saying for you to do—among us are four men who are under a vow. Take these men with you, and be purified with them; pay for them to have their heads shaven. Then everyone will know that what they have been taught about you is nothing—instead, that even you walk by the principles of the Law and keep it. As for the gentiles who have believed, we have decided and sent to them to keep themselves from food sacrificed to idols, from blood, from eating strangled things, and from illicit sexual behavior."

Then Paul took those men the next day and was purified with them. He went into the temple and proclaimed when the days of purification would be fulfilled, the time when the offering was to be made for each one of them.

Now as the seven days were about to be completed, some Jews from Asia saw him in the temple and threw the whole crowd into an uproar. They laid hands on him and cried out, "Gentlemen! Israelites! Listen! This is that man who teaches everyone—everywhere—against the people, the Law, and this place! He has even led Greeks into the sanctuary and defiled this holy place!" (You see, they had previously seen the Ephesian Trophimus in the city with him, and they thought that Paul had led him into the sanctuary.)

Then the whole crowd was stirred up, and protesting began among the people. They grabbed Paul and dragged him out of the temple, and immediately the doors were shut. As they were trying to kill him, news reached the commander of the regiment that Jerusalem was in complete chaos. At once he took soldiers and centurions and ran down to meet them. When the people saw the commander and the soldiers, they stopped beating Paul. The commander approached and arrested Paul and commanded that he be bound with two chains. Then he asked him who he was and what he had done.

Some among the crowd were shouting one thing and others another. The commander was not able to understand with certainty because of the uproar, so he commanded that they take Paul to the headquarters. When Paul came to the steps, he had to be carried by the soldiers as a result of the violence of the crowd. You see, a great number of people had followed, crying out: "Take him away!"

As he was about to be carried into headquarters, Paul asked the commander, "Is it allowed for me to say something to you?"

He asked, "You know Greek? Now—aren't you the Egyptian who was recently stirring up trouble and led out to the wilderness some four thousand men who were terrorists?"

Paul said, "I am a Jewish man from Tarsus of Cilicia—not some obscure city. I beg you—permit me to speak to the people."

Once he permitted him, Paul stood up on the steps and waved his hand to the people. When many of them had become quiet, he called out to them in the Aramaic language:

"Gentlemen—brothers and fathers: listen to the defense I am now giving you."

When they heard that he called out to them in the Aramaic language, they became even more silent.

Then he said, "I am a man of the Jews—born in Tarsus of Cilicia, raised in this city, and instructed under the feet of Gamaliel, strictly by the Law of our fathers. I am as passionate about God as all of you are today! I persecuted this Way to death, chaining up and putting both men and women into prison, as even the high priest and all the elders testify about me. I received letters from him and went to the brothers in Damascus also to bring them to Jerusalem in chains so that they could be punished.

"Here is what happened: as I went and approached Damascus around noon, suddenly a bright light from the sky flashed around me. I fell to the ground and heard a voice saying to me, 'Saul! Saul! Why are you persecuting me?'

"I asked, 'Who are you, sir?'

"Then he said to me, 'I am Jesus of Nazareth, the one you are persecuting.'

"Now, those who were with me saw the light too. But they did not hear the voice that was speaking to me. I asked, 'What should I do, sir?'

"So the Master said to me, 'Get up, go into Damascus, and there you will be told about everything that I have planned for you to do.'

"Since I couldn't see because of the brightness of that light, I was led by the hand of those who went with me, and we came to Damascus. Someone named Ananias—a man who was devout to keep the Law, and everyone who lives among the Jews confirms it—he came and stood with me and said, 'Saul, brother, regain your sight.' And at that exact time, I looked up at him. Then he said, 'The God of our fathers has handpicked you to know his will and to see the Righteous One and hear the sound of his voice. You see, you will be his witness of what you have seen and heard to all people. So now—why are you waiting? Get up, be immersed, and wash away your sins, calling on his name!'

"It just so happened that when I returned to Jerusalem and was praying in the temple, I fell into a trance and saw him speaking to me: 'Hurry and get out of Jerusalem quickly because they will not accept your testimony about me.'

"So I said, 'Master, they know that I was imprisoning and beating those who believe in you in every single synagogue. Also, when your martyr Stephen's blood was shed, I myself was present—I cast my approval and looked after the coats of those who were executing him.'

"Then he said to me, 'Go, because I will send you far away to the gentiles.'"

Now they heard him up to this statement, but then raised their voices, saying, "Wipe this man off the face of the earth because he doesn't deserve to live!"

While they were crying out and tearing their coats and throwing dust into the air, the commander commanded that he should be taken into the headquarters. He ordered Paul to be interrogated with a flogging so that he may come to know the exact reason they were shouting out at him like this.

But as they were extending the whip, Paul asked the presiding centurion, "Is it legal for you to scourge a man who is a Roman citizen and has not been condemned?"

When the centurion heard this, he approached the commander and informed him: "What are you going to do? You see, this man is a Roman citizen!"

So the commander approached Paul and asked, "Tell me—are you a Roman citizen?"

He answered, "Yes."

Then the commander responded, "I acquired this citizenship with a substantial amount of money."

Paul responded, "And yet I was born a citizen."

Then immediately, those who were about to interrogate him backed away, and the commander became afraid once he recognized that Paul was a Roman citizen and that he had put him in chains.

THE NEXT MORNING, BECAUSE HE WANTED TO KNOW THE TRUTH about why he had been accused by the Jews, he unchained him and summoned the chief priests and the entire Sanhedrin to assemble so that Paul could be carried down to stand before them.

Paul looked around at the Sanhedrin and said, "Gentlemen! Brothers! I have acted completely with a good conscience before God to this very day."

The high priest, Ananias, ordered one of those standing next to him to slap Paul on the mouth.

Then Paul said to him, "God is going to slap you, you whitewashed wall! Are you actually sitting to judge me by the Law and yet command me to be slapped illegally?"

Those standing next to him said, "Are you insulting God's high priest?"

Then Paul said, "Brothers, I did not know that he was the high priest—and it is written that 'You must not speak evil of the ruler of your people.'"

Once Paul recognized that one part of them were Sadducees and the others were Pharisees, he cried out among the Sanhedrin, "Gentlemen! Brothers! I am a Pharisee—the son of a Pharisee. I am being tried because of the hope and resurrection from the dead!"

After he said this, an argument broke out between the Pharisees and Sadducees—the whole group was divided. You see, the Sadducees claim that there is no resurrection from the dead, no angels, and no spirit. But the Pharisees acknowledge all these.

So a large outcry erupted, and some of the scribes from the party of Pharisees stood up and protested, "We find nothing wrong with this man. What if a spirit or an angel has spoken to him?"

As the argument was becoming heated, the commander became afraid that they might tear Paul in half, so he commanded the soldiers to go down and take him out from in front of them and put him back in the headquarters. On the next night, the Master appeared to Paul and said, "Cheer up—just as you testified about me in Jerusalem, you also must testify in Rome."

ONCE MORNING CAME, THE JEWS DEVISED A CONSPIRACY AND invoked a curse on themselves, swearing neither to eat nor drink until they had killed Paul (there were more than forty who swore this oath together). These men went before the high priest and the elders and said, "We have invoked a solemn curse on ourselves to eat nothing until we have killed Paul. So now you must go appear before the commander with the Sanhedrin so that he will bring him out to you as though you are going to examine the evidence about him more carefully. Then before they bring him, we will be ready to kill him."

But when Paul's nephew heard about the ambush, he came to the rescue, and he entered the barracks and relayed it to Paul. Then Paul called for one of the centurions and said, "Take this young man to the commander because he has something to tell him."

So he took him along and led him to the commander, saying, "The prisoner, Paul, called for me, asking me to bring you this young man who has something to tell you."

The commander took his hand, led him to a private place, and asked, "What is it that you have to report to me?"

Then he said, "The Jews assembled to ask you to bring Paul down to the Sanhedrin tomorrow as though they are going to more closely interrogate him. So do not trust them. You see, some of their men—more than forty of them—are ambushing him. They have invoked a curse on themselves not to eat or drink until they have killed him, and now they are ready, waiting for your approval."

Then the commander let the young man go, ordering him, "Do not disclose to anyone that you have brought this information to me."

Then he called two of the centurions and said, "Prepare two hundred soldiers to go to Caesarea, as well as seventy horses and two hundred spearmen, starting at the third hour of the night. Also, have an animal standing by so that you can put Paul on it to carry him safely to Felix the governor. Write a letter having this stamp:

Claudius Lysias, to the most excellent Felix: Greetings!

This man was seized by the Jews and was about to be killed by them when I arrived with the army. I brought him out, having learned that he is a Roman citizen. Since I was planning to investigate the case they were bringing against him, I took him down to the Sanhedrin and found that he was being accused about trivial matters of their Law but no charge that was deserving of death or imprisonment. Once it was revealed to me that there was a plot against the man, I immediately sent him to you and ordered that his accusers bring their case against him to you.

So the soldiers did as he directed, getting Paul and taking him by night to Antipatris. Then in the morning, they released the horses to go with him and returned to the barracks. When they arrived at Caesarea and delivered the letter to the governor, they also presented Paul to him. He read it and then asked what province Paul was from. When he learned that he was from Cilicia, he said, "I will grant you a hearing when your accusers have also arrived." Then he commanded that Paul be kept in Herod's headquarters.

AFTER FIVE DAYS, ANANIAS THE HIGH PRIEST CAME DOWN WITH some of the elders and an orator named Tertullus. They appeared against Paul before the governor. When he was called upon, Tertullus began to accuse him, saying, "Since we have enjoyed substantial peace through you and reformations are taking place in this nation because of your foresight, we appreciate this in everything and everywhere with utmost thankfulness, most excellent Felix. So that I do not weary you any further, I beg you by your graciousness to hear us briefly. You see, we have found this man to be a pest who causes insurrection among all the Jews in the world. He also is a ringleader of the sect of Nazarenes. He even tried to profane the temple, so we seized him—after investigating, you will be able to see for yourself all these things about which we are accusing him." The Jews also joined in, affirming that this was true.

Then when the governor nodded to him, Paul responded, "Since you have been judge of this nation for many years, you know immediately what I will answer for myself—you are able to know that it has not been more than twelve days since I went up to worship in Jerusalem. Further, they did not find me arguing in the temple or attempting to draw a crowd—neither in the synagogues nor in the city. They are unable to present anything to you about which they are accusing me. But I confess this to you—I worship my ancestors' God in the way that they are calling a sect, having faith in everything that is written according to the Law and the prophets. I have hope in God, which all these men themselves uphold, of a resurrection that is going to happen for both the righteous and unrighteous. In this also I myself strive to have a clear conscience through everything toward God and men. After many years I came back to present a charitable donation and offering for my nation. With these they found me sanctified in the temple—not with a crowd or an uproar. On the other hand, there are some Jews from Asia who also should have appeared before you and given accusation if they were to have anything against me. Either these men themselves need to say what injustice they have found with me when I was before the Sanhedrin or with this one statement that I exclaimed while standing among them—that I am being judged before you today because of the resurrection from the dead."

So Felix adjourned them because he was well informed about the Way, saying, "When Commander Lysias comes down, I will render a decision in your case." So he appointed the centurion to keep Paul in custody (but he could have some freedom) and gave instructions not to forbid any of his people from attending to him.

AFTER SEVERAL DAYS, FELIX ARRIVED WITH HIS WIFE, DRUSILLA, who was a Jewish woman. He sent for Paul and listened to him speak about the faith of Jesus the Messiah. But as Paul discussed righteousness, self-control, and the coming judgment, Felix became afraid and responded, "Hold on for now, and go; when I have an opportunity, I will summon you." He was also hoping that he might be given money from Paul, so he sent for him frequently to converse with him. After two years, his term was completed, and Felix received a successor: Porcius Festus. And because he wanted to do the Jews a favor, Felix left Paul imprisoned.

So three days after Festus set foot in the province, he went up to Jerusalem from Caesarea. There the high priest and the leaders of the Jews stood before him against Paul and begged him, asking for a favor at Paul's expense—that he would summon him to Jerusalem so that they could wait to ambush and kill him on the way.

Then Festus responded that he would keep Paul in Caesarea and that he was soon going to go there himself. He said, "The powerful men among you can go down with me to see whether there is anything out of order with the man; and if so, they may make an accusation against him."

After he had spent no more than eight or ten days with them, he went down to Caesarea. The next morning he sat at the judge's bench and commanded for Paul to be brought. When he arrived, the Jews who had come down from Jerusalem stood around him and laid serious accusations that they were unable to prove. Meanwhile, Paul was defending himself, saying that he had not sinned against the Jews' Law or the temple or against Caesarea.

Then Festus (wanting to do the Jews a favor) responded to Paul by asking, "Do you want to go up to Jerusalem to be judged by me for these matters?"

Paul said, "I stand before the judgment bench in Caesarea, where I should be judged. I have wronged none of the Jews, as you well know for yourself. So if I have committed an injustice and done something deserving of death, I do not seek to avoid the death penalty. But since I have done nothing that these people are accusing me of doing, no one can give me to them—I appeal to Caesar!"

Then Festus consulted with his advisors and answered, "To Caesar you have appealed; to Caesar you will go."

AFTER A FEW DAYS HAD PASSED, KING AGRIPPA AND BERNICE traveled to Caesarea and greeted Festus. Since they would be spending several days there, Festus laid out Paul's case for the king: "There is this man left behind as a prisoner by Felix. While I was in Jerusalem, the high priests and elders of the Jews appeared before me regarding him, asking for his condemnation. I answered them that it is not the custom for Romans to hand over any man before the accused could have opportunity to face his accusers and give a defense for the accusation. Then when they assembled here, I did not postpone the trial—the next session at the judge's bench, I commanded the man to be brought. The accusers stood around him but brought no complaint that I considered to be bad. They just had trivial matters about their own religious beliefs against him and against some Jesus—who was dead, but Paul claimed that he is alive. Since I was at a loss about these questions, I asked if he would like to go to Jerusalem and be judged there about these things. But once Paul appealed that he would be kept in custody for His Majesty's arbitration, I commanded him to be kept until I could send him to Caesar."

Then Agrippa said to Festus, "I myself would like to hear this man."

"Tomorrow," he said, "you will hear him."

On the next day, after Agrippa and Bernice had come with great fanfare and had entered the auditorium with the commanders and preeminent men of the city, Festus again commanded Paul to be brought. Festus said, "King Agrippa and all men who are present here with us: See this man, of whom the whole horde of Jews has begged me—both in Jerusalem and here—crying out that he should not live any longer! I have found that he has done nothing worthy of death, but since he has appealed to His Majesty, I have decided to send him. I am uncertain what I should write to my master about him, and so I have brought him before you all—and especially before you, King Agrippa, so that once you have examined him, I may have something to write. You see, it seems absurd to me to send a prisoner without also indicating what charges are filed against him."

So Agrippa said to Paul, "You are permitted to speak for yourself."

Then Paul saluted with his hand and gave his defense: "Having been accused by the Jews of everything, King Agrippa, I consider myself blessed that I am going to give my defense before you today, especially since you know all the Jews' customs and controversies. So I beg you to hear me patiently. All the Jews know that I have lived my entire life from my youth—since the beginning—among my nation and in Jerusalem. If they were willing to admit it—since they have known me for some time—they know that I lived as a Pharisee according to the strictest sect of our religion. Even now, I am standing on trial because of my hope in a promise made by God to our fathers. Because of this, our twelve tribes strive night and day in service, hoping to attain it—because of this hope, I am being called to account by the Jews, King Agrippa. Why is it considered unbelievable by you that God raises the dead? Even so, in my own opinion, I felt I needed to do many things to oppose the name of Jesus of Nazareth. I even did these things in Jerusalem, and many of those saints I myself locked up into prison on the authority I received from the chief priests—and when the prisoners were executed, I cast my vote for it. Also, throughout all the synagogues on many occasions, I punished them, trying to force them to blaspheme. I became so furious with them that I chased them to distant cities.

"While I was doing this, I traveled to Damascus by the authority and commission of the chief priests. In the midday on the day I was on the road, King Agrippa, I saw this brightness of sunlight shine down from the sky on me and those traveling with me.

"As we were falling to the ground, I heard a voice speak to me in the Aramaic language: 'Saul! Saul! Why are you persecuting me? It is hard for you to kick against the spur.'

"I asked, 'Who are you, sir?'

"Then the Master said, 'I am Jesus—the one you are persecuting. Now get up and stand on your feet—this is why I have appeared to you: to handpick you as a servant and witness of the things you have seen about me and what I am going to show you. I am separating you from the people and the nations so that I can send you to them myself to open their eyes, redirect them from darkness to light—from Satan's authority to God's—and to help them receive forgiveness of sins and an inheritance with the saints in the faith that rests in me.'

"Based on this, King Agrippa, I have not been disobedient to that heavenly vision. On the contrary, for those living in Damascus first, and then in Jerusalem—for all in the region of Judea and for all gentiles—I have proclaimed repentance and redirection toward God through performing actions befitting repentance. Because of this, the Jews arrested me while I was in the temple and were trying to kill me. So to this very day since I have obtained the help of God, to both small and great I stand to bear witness of nothing except what the prophets and Moses said when they spoke about things to come—that the Messiah would suffer, that as the first to be raised from the dead, he would come to proclaim light to both the nation of Jews and the gentiles."

When Paul had finished giving his defense, Festus spoke with out loud voice, "You are crazy, Paul! Your extent of study has driven you crazy!"

Then Paul said, "I am not crazy, most excellent Festus—I have spoken out with true and soundly spoken words. You see, the king understands these things, so I have been encouraged to speak to him. I am sure he has not forgotten any of these things because this was not done in a corner.

"Do you believe the prophets, King Agrippa? I know that you believe them."

Agrippa said to Paul, "With little time you are trying to convince me to be a Christian."

Then Paul said, "I pray to God that—whether with a little or a lot—not only you but also everyone who hears me today would be exactly as I am—except for these chains."

So the king arose, as did the governor, Bernice, and those who were seated with them. They withdrew to speak among themselves and said, "This man has done nothing deserving of death or imprisonment."

Agrippa even said to Festus, "It would have been possible to set him free if the man himself had not appealed to Caesar."

NOW SINCE IT HAD BEEN DECIDED THAT WE WOULD SAIL AWAY to Italy, they transferred custody of Paul and some of the other prisoners over to a centurion named Julius from the emperor's cohort. So we boarded a ship from Adramyttium and hoisted anchor, planning to sail toward the Asian ports. Aristarchus (a Macedonian from Thessalonica) was with us. On the next day, we dropped anchor in Sidon. Julius even treated Paul kindly, sending him to his friends to receive care. From there we lifted anchor and sailed under the lee of Cypress because the winds were against us. We sailed across the deep sea along Cilicia and Pamphylia and came to Myra of Lycia. There the centurion found a ship from Alexandria sailing for Italy, so he put us on board. After several days of slow sailing, we barely made it to Cnidus. Since we were unable to go farther because of the wind, we sailed under the lee of Crete along Salmone. With difficulty we sailed past there and came to a place that was called Beautiful, a harbor that was near the city Lasea.

By now a lot of time had passed, and the voyage was already dangerous. Since the fast had already happened, Paul offered advice. He told them, "Gentlemen, I have seen that this voyage will be met with disaster and a lot of damage—not only to cargo and the ship but also to our lives."

But the centurion had more confidence in the pilot and captain than in what Paul had said. Since the harbor was not a suitable place for them to spend the winter, the majority voted to depart from there so that they would perhaps arrive at Phoenix and spend the winter in that harbor of Crete, which faces both to the southwest and northwest.

When a south wind came up, they thought they had achieved their plan and lifted anchor near the coast along Crete. But it was not long before a hurricane-force wind (called the Northeaster) came down from the coast. Since the ship was caught and unable to face into the wind, we yielded trying to control and were carried away. We sailed under the lee of a small island called Cauda; we were barely able to maintain control of the skiff. They hoisted it up, using supports to brace the ship, afraid that they would run aground on the Syrtis shoals. They released the driving anchor and so were carried away. Since we were being battered by the storm, the next day they began jettisoning the cargo. Then on the third day, they picked up the ship's equipment and threw it overboard. Since we had seen neither the sun nor the stars for several days and the storm continued to bear down heavily, we abandoned all hope of being saved.

We had been without food for a long time when Paul stood amid them and said, "Gentlemen, you should have listened to me and not left Crete so that you would have been spared this disaster and damage. Even now I advise you to take courage. You see, not a single one of your lives will be lost—only the ship—because an angel of the God that I belong to and serve has appeared to me tonight. He said, 'Do not be afraid, Paul; you must appear before Caesar, and look: God has granted to you all those who are sailing with you.'

"So take courage, men! You see, I trust God that this will happen just in the way it was told to me, but we will have to run aground on some island."

So it happened on the fourteenth night while we were being carried along in the Adriatic—in the middle of the night the sailors began to suspect that land was near them. They measured the depth and found it to be 120 feet. They waited a short time and then measured the depth again, finding it to be ninety feet. Because they were afraid we would run aground along a rocky place, they threw four anchors out from the stern and prayed for daylight to come.

Some of the sailors tried to escape the ship and lowered the skiff into the sea, pretending to be putting out an anchor from the bow of the ship.

Then Paul said to the centurion and the soldiers, "Unless these men stay on the ship, you will not be able to be saved." So the soldiers cut away the ropes from the skiff and let it fall.

Just as day was about to break, Paul encouraged everyone to eat some food, saying, "Today is the fourteenth day that you have gone without food, and you have eaten nothing. So I beg you to eat some food. You see, this is to be done to keep you alive because not even one of the hairs of your head will be lost."

When he had said this, he took some bread, gave thanks to God for it in front of all of them, and broke it and began to eat. Then everyone was encouraged, so they also took some food. Now we had a total number of 276 souls on the ship. Once they had eaten their fill, they began to lighten the load on the ship by throwing the grain into the sea.

When day had arrived, they did not recognize the land but noticed a bay that had a beach. They planned to drive the ship onto it if they could. They cast off the anchors and left them in the sea, and at the same time they loosened the ropes on the rudders. Then they raised the foresail in the wind and held course for the beach. But they struck a sandbar and ran the ship into the ground—the bow was stuck firm and remained immovable, but the stern was being broken up by the force of the waves.

Some of the soldiers had a plan to kill the prisoners so that none of them would swim away and escape, but the centurion planned to save Paul. He prevented them from carrying out their plan, commanding those who could swim to jump down into the water first and get out. As for the rest, some were to go out on boards and others on other things from the ship. So that is how it happened, and everyone made it safely to land.

After we had made it safely, we discovered that the island was called Melitus. Now the natives showed us extraordinary kindness, in that they lit a fire and took us all in because of the rain that was falling and the cold.

Then as Paul was gathering a lot of sticks and placing them on the fire, a viper came out from the heat and fastened onto his hand. The natives who saw this animal hanging from his hand said to one another, "This man surely must be a murderer because he made it safely from the sea, but Justice did not let him live!"

So even though Paul shook the animal off into the fire and suffered no harm, they were waiting to see him swell or suddenly fall down dead. After they had waited a good while and had seen nothing surprising happen to him, they changed their minds and said that he must be a god.

Now near that place, there was an estate belonging to the chief of the island, named Publius. He welcomed us and showed us gracious hospitality for three days. It so happened that Publius's father was confined to the bed, overcome with fever and dysentery. Paul went in to him and prayed, put his hands on him, and healed him. Once this happened, the rest of the inhabitants of the island who were sick came to him, and he healed them. So they honored us with many acts of reverence and donated items we would need as we were setting sail.

AFTER THREE MONTHS, HAVING SPENT THE WINTER ON THAT island, we set sail on a ship from Alexandria decorated with the symbol of the Twin Sons of Zeus. We went down to Syracuse and stayed three days, and from there we sailed on an arc and reached Rhegium. After one day, we encountered a south wind, so we got to Puteoli on the second day. There we found some brothers and were asked by them to stay seven days, so then we went to Rome.

There the brothers heard the news about us and came to meet us at the Forum of Appius and the Three Taverns. When Paul saw them, he thanked God and cheered up. Once we had entered Rome, Paul was allowed to stay by himself with the soldier who was guarding him.

So after three days had passed, he called together the leaders of the Jews. Once they had assembled, he began speaking to them: "Gentlemen—brothers—although I have done nothing against our people or the customs passed down from our ancestors, I am a prisoner transferred from Jerusalem to the hands of Romans. And they, once they had examined me, wanted to release me because there was nothing found on me worthy of the death penalty. But since the

Jews were protesting, I have been forced to appeal to Caesar without having any charges against my people. For this reason, I have asked to see you and speak with you. You see, I am kept in chains because of the hope of Israel."

Then they told him, "We have not so much as received a letter from the Judeans regarding you, and none of the brothers traveling through has announced it or even said any bad thing about you. Further, we think it is worth hearing directly from you what you think. You see, we are aware that this sect is being protested all over the world."

So they set an appointment for a day with him, and many of them came to him in that guest room. Then he laid it out for them, trying to convince them about Jesus from both the Law of Moses and the Prophets. He did this from early in the day until late and did convince some of them—but some did not believe. They were disagreeing with one another and began to leave when Paul said one particular thing: "The Holy Spirit said it well when Isaiah spoke to your fathers:

> Go to this nation and say,
> Although you hear, you hear without understanding.
> Although you see, you see without comprehending.
> Because the heart of this nation has become fat,
> Their ears are hard of hearing,
> And they have shut their eyes,
> Or else they would see with their eyes,
> And hear with their ears,
> And turn back, and I would heal them.

"So be aware that this salvation from God has been sent to the gentiles, and even they will hear!"

So he stayed two full years in his own rented house and welcomed everyone who came to see him, and boldly and without interference he proclaimed God's kingdom and taught about the Master, Jesus the Messiah.

ACTS

THE
WORD

PAUL'S LETTERS

TO THE
ROMANS

From Paul, a servant of Jesus the Messiah who was called to be an apostle and set apart for God's Message. He previously promised this Message through his prophets in the Holy Scriptures about his Son. His Son was born physically of the lineage of David but was appointed powerfully by the Holy Spirit to be God's Son by his resurrection from the dead. His Son is Jesus the Messiah, through whom we have received God's favor and mission: faithful obedience among the nations in representation of his name.

To all who are loved by God and called to be saints in Rome: May grace and peace be yours from God our Father and the Master, Jesus the Messiah!

BEFORE I BEGIN, I THANK MY GOD THROUGH JESUS THE MESSIAH for all of you because your faith is renowned throughout the world! You see, God (whom I worship with my spirit with the Message of his Son) is my witness as I constantly mention you in my prayers—begging that perhaps I will at last be granted by the will of God to come to you. You see, I want to see you so that I can share a spiritual gift with you to strengthen you. But this would be a joint encouragement with you through the faith that is in each of you as well as in me! Brothers, I do not want you to be unaware that I have often planned to come to you so that I could have some fruit with you as I have had with the rest of the nations (but to this day, I have been prevented from doing so). I am obligated both to Greeks and non-Greeks—both to wise and uneducated people—and my eagerness to preach the Good Message to you who are in Rome is no different!

You see, I am not ashamed of the Good Message because it is God's power for salvation to everyone who believes—first the Jew but also the Greek. You see, God's righteousness is revealed in it—by faith, for faith—just as it is written, "The righteous will live by faith."

Now God's wrath is revealed from heaven against all the ungodliness and unrighteousness of people who suffocate the truth with unrighteousness. You see, what is known about God is clear to them because God revealed it to them: his invisible characteristics (such as his invisible power and deity) have been clearly visible from the creation of the world because they are implied by what he has done. So they are without an excuse. You see, although they knew God, they did not praise or thank him as God. Rather, they became foolish because of their thought processes, and their foolish hearts were darkened. They claimed to be wise, but they were foolish—they even traded the glory of the immortal God for idols that resemble mortal men, birds, livestock, and reptiles. Because of this, God left them in their filthiness with their hearts' desires so that they would dishonor their bodies with them.

They traded the truth about God for a lie and then honored and worshiped what was created rather than the one who created it—the one who is praised forever and ever, amen! Because of this, God left them in their humiliating passion. You see, the women were not the only ones among them to trade the natural sexual relationship for one that was against nature—the men among them also abandoned the natural sexual relationship (one with women) and became inflamed with their desires for one another—these men did shameful things with men and received in their own bodies a fair repayment for their wrong beliefs.

Furthermore, just as they did not consider God to be worth keeping in their appreciation, God left them with a worthless mindset so that they would do what is improper. They are completely unrighteous, wicked, greedy, and evil. They are full of jealousy, murder, division, lying, and mean-spiritedness. They are gossips, slanderers, God-haters, violent, arrogant, boastful, engineers of evil, and disobedient to parents. They are mindless, faithless, loveless, and merciless. Although they know God's condemnation—that whoever practices these things deserves to die—they not only do them but also take sides with those who do these things!

So those of you who pass judgment are without an excuse. You see, while you are passing judgment on others, you are condemning yourselves because you are passing judgment and practicing the same things that you condemn. Now, we know that God's judgment on those who do these things is consistent with truth, but do you think—you who judge those who do these things but do them yourself—that you will escape God's judgment? Or is it the case that you think nothing of his rich kindness, tolerance, and patience, unaware that God's kindness is meant to lead you to repentance? Because of your stubbornness and the lack of repentance in your heart, you are storing up wrath for yourself for the day of the wrath and the revelation of God's righteous judgment. "He will repay everyone in accordance with each one's actions." He will repay eternal life to those who persistently seek glory, honor, and immortality by doing good things. On the other hand, he will repay wrath and fury to those who chase after unrighteousness by being divisive and not obeying the truth. Struggle and difficulty will overcome the soul of everyone who does what is evil—first the Jew but also the Greek. But glory, honor, and peace belong to everyone who does what is good—first to the Jew but also to the Greek—because there is no favoritism with God!

You see, whoever has sinned who did not have the Law will also be lost without having the Law. Whoever sinned with the Law will be judged by the Law. You see, it is not those who hear the Law who are righteous in God's sight. On the contrary, those who do what the Law says will be made righteous. Whenever the Gentiles (who do not have the Law) naturally do what the Law says, these people who do not have the Law are a law for themselves! Such people demonstrate the doing of the Law written in their hearts, and their consciences bear witness with them—their thoughts will either accuse or excuse them on the day when God judges the hidden thoughts of people, according to the Good Message that is mine through Jesus the Messiah.

Now if you are called a Jew and find comfort in the Law, applaud God, know his will, and have found the exceptional teachings of the Law to be genuine—if you have become convinced that you are a guide to the blind, a light to those who are in darkness, a corrector of foolish people, and a teacher of infants—if you think you have the embodiment of knowledge and truth in the Law—then as you teach others, do you not teach yourself? As you preach, "Do not steal," do you steal? As you say, "Do not commit adultery," do you commit adultery? As you voice your disgust of idolatry, do you commit sacrilege? You applaud the Law, but you dishonor God by breaking the Law! You see, "God's name is ridiculed by the nations because of you," just as it is written!

Now circumcision is beneficial if you practice the Law, but if you are a lawbreaker, your circumcision has become uncircumcision! If one who is uncircumcised keeps the regulations of the Law, is his uncircumcision not considered to be circumcision? Furthermore, the one who is uncircumcised and naturally keeps the Law will condemn you—you are a lawbreaker, even though you have Scripture and circumcision. You see, it is not the appearance that makes one a Jew, and circumcision is not what is visible in the body. On the contrary, what is done secretly makes one a Jew, and circumcision affects the heart because of the Spirit (not the Scripture). Such a person seeks praise from God, not from people.

So what is the benefit of being a Jew? What is gained by circumcision? Much is gained—in every way! Primarily, it means that God's sayings were believed! So what if some were unfaithful? Would their faithlessness really cancel out God's faithfulness? Absolutely not! May God be true even if every man is a liar! This is what was written:

> So that you will be vindicated by your words,
> And overcome when you are criticized.

Now if our unrighteousness merely proves God's righteousness, what are we going to say? "Is God not unfair to bring wrath against us?" (I am talking like a mere human!) Absolutely not! Otherwise, how could God judge the world? Furthermore, if because of my lie God's truth excels, resulting in his glory, why would I still be judged as a sinner? It is not like the way we are slandered—as some claim that we say, "We will do what is evil so that good may come out of it." Their condemnation is deserved!

So what? Are we any better off? Not at all! You see, we have already reached the verdict: both Jews and Greeks—all of them—are under sin. This is what was written:

> No one is righteous—not even one.
> No one understands, no one seeks God.
> All of them have turned away at the same time and become worthless.
> No one acts with kindness—there is not even one!
> Their throat is an opened tomb,
> They deceive with their tongues.
> The venom of Egyptian cobras is under their lips.
> Their mouths are full of curses and bitterness.
> Their feet are quick to shed blood.
> Destruction and difficulty are in their lives.
> And they have not known the life of peace.
> There is no respect for God in their viewpoint.

Besides this, we know that the Law says what it says to those who are under the Law so that every mouth may be shut and all the world may be brought to trial before God. You see, no human is made righteous before him by doing what the Law says because recognition of sin comes by the Law!

Now God's righteousness has been revealed without the Law, even though it was verified by the Law and the Prophets. Indeed, God's righteousness has been revealed by faith in Jesus the Messiah to everyone who has that faith. You see, there is no difference—everyone has sinned and is without God's glory! All are made righteous as a gift (by his grace) through the redemption that is in Jesus the Messiah. God set him forth to be a peacemaker through faith in his blood as an example of his righteousness at that time (you see, God overlooked those previously committed sins by his tolerance) and as an example of his righteousness at this time (so that he would be righteous, as well as the one who makes those who have faith in Jesus righteous).

So where is bragging? It is excluded! By what law is it excluded—a law of works? No! On the contrary, it is excluded by a law of grace! You see, we have established that a person is made righteous by faith without keeping the Law. Is God only the God of the Jews? Is he not also the God of the Gentiles? Yes, he is God of the Gentiles too! Since there is only one God, he will make the circumcised righteous by faith and the uncircumcised righteous through faith. So do we cancel out the Law by this faith? Absolutely not! On the contrary, we validate it!

What are we going to say that Abraham, our physical ancestor, discovered? You see, if Abraham were made righteous by doing what the Law says, he would have a reason to brag—although not before God. You see, the Scripture says, "Abraham had faith in God, and this was credited to him as righteousness." Now wages are not considered a gift to the one who works; rather, it is what is owed. But as for the one who does not work, and whose ungodly actions are made righteous, his faith is credited as righteousness. This is just like what David said, too, about the blessing of the one to whom God credits righteousness apart from their actions:

> Blessed is the one whose law-breaking actions are forgiven,
> And whose sins are covered up.
> Blessed is the one to whom the Master does not credit sin.

So is this blessing offered only for the circumcised, or is it also for the uncircumcised? You see, we say, "Faith was credited to Abraham as righteousness." So how was it credited—when he was circumcised or when he was uncircumcised? It was not when he was circumcised, but when he was uncircumcised! Then he received circumcision as a symbol—a seal of the righteousness that came by faith while he was uncircumcised—so that he could be the father of everyone who has faith and is uncircumcised. Thus their faith could also be credited as righteousness. He also received circumcision so that he could be the father of the circumcised—to those who not only have been circumcised but also follow in the footprints of the faith that our ancestor Abraham had when he was uncircumcised. You see, the promise was not made to Abraham or to his descendants that he would inherit the world by the Law, but rather by the righteousness that comes by faith. You see, if they were heirs by the Law, faith would have no purpose; then the promise would be canceled out because the Law produces wrath. Where there is no law, there is no lawbreaking. Because of this, it comes by faith so that it could be based on God's favor. So the promise could be confirmed to all his descendants (not only to those who live by the Law, but also to those who live by the faith of Abraham, who is the father of all of us!). This is what was written, "I have made you the father of many nations." Based on this, he believed God, who gives life to the dead and calls into existence things that do not exist. He believed contrary to hope—but based on hope—so that he could become the father of all nations as it was said, "This is how your descendants will be." He considered his body to be as good as dead (because he was around one hundred years old) and knew of the infertility of Sarah's womb, but he was not weakened in faith. Now, he did not waver from a lack of faith in God's promise—on the contrary, he was empowered by faith and gave glory to God. So it was credited to him as righteousness. Now, "It was credited to him" was written not only for him but also for us, to whom it is about to be credited—who believe in the one who raised Jesus our Master from the dead.

He was betrayed because of our sins and raised for our righteousness.

So since we have been made righteous by faith, we have peace with God through our Master, Jesus the Messiah. By faith we have received access through him into this favor in which we stand and take pride in the hope of God's glory! Not only that, but we also take pride in our struggles because we know that struggle produces persistence. Then persistence produces confirmation, and confirmation produces hope. This hope does not bring shame because God's love has been poured out in our hearts through the Holy Spirit, who has been given to us. You see, the Messiah died for the ungodly while we were still weak. Now someone would scarcely die for a righteous person, and perhaps someone would have the courage to die for a good man. But God proves his love for us because the Messiah died for us while we were still sinners! So now that we have been made righteous by his blood, we will most certainly be saved through him from God's wrath! You see, if we were reconciled to God through the death of his Son while we were enemies, we will most certainly be saved by his life now that we are reconciled! Not only that, but we also take pride in God through our Master, Jesus the Messiah, through whom we have now received this reconciliation.

Now, because sin entered the world through one person and death entered through sin, death likewise passed through to all people because everyone has sinned. You see, sin existed in the world before the Law existed in the world, but sin is not credited where there is no law. But death reigned from Adam until Moses even on those who did not sin in a way that resembled Adam's violation (he is an example of the one who is coming). Yet the gift is not like the violation. You see, if many people died because of one man's violation, most certainly God's favor would overflow to many people because of the kind gift of one man (Jesus the Messiah). Furthermore, the gift is not like what followed the single sin of that man. You see, the judgment that followed one violation resulted in condemnation, but the gift that follows many violations results in righteousness. You see, if death reigned through one man because of that man's violation, then most certainly those who receive the abundance of kindness and the gift of righteousness will reign in life through the one and only Jesus the Messiah. So in conclusion, since one man's violation resulted in condemnation for all people, also one man's righteous action results in a righteous life for all people. You see, since many were declared to be sinners through the disobedience of one man, many will also be declared righteous through the obedience of one man. Now the Law came into the picture so that the violation would overflow. But when sin overflowed, God's favor overflowed even more. So since sin reigned in death, God's favor would also reign through righteousness, resulting in eternal life through our Master, Jesus the Messiah.

So what are we going to say? Should we continue living in sin so that grace would overflow? Absolutely not! How shall we—who have died to sin—still live in it anymore? Are you not aware that all of us who were immersed into the Messiah have been immersed into his death? So we have been buried with him into his death by immersion, so that in the same way that he was raised from the dead (by the Father's glory), we also should walk in newness of life. You see, if we have been united with him by a representation of his death, we shall also be united with him by a representation of his resurrection! We know that our old self was crucified with him so that the sinful body would be canceled out and that we would no longer be enslaved to sin. You see, whoever has died has been released from sin. Now if we have died with the Messiah, we believe that we will also live with him because we know that the Messiah has been raised from the dead, never to die again. Death no longer has authority over him. You see, he died the death that he died to sin, once and for all, and he lives the life that he lives to God. In the same way, you must consider yourselves to be dead to sin and alive to God in Jesus the Messiah.

So sin must not reign in your mortal body, which would mean that you would obey its desires. Also, do not make your body parts available to sin as tools for unrighteousness. On the contrary, make yourselves available to God—since you have come alive from the dead—and your body parts available to God as tools for righteousness. You see, sin does not have authority over you because you are not under the Law—you are under God's favor. So what? Should we sin since we are under God's favor and not under the Law? Absolutely not! Do you not know that when you make yourselves available as servants to obey something, you are slaves to whatever you obey? This is true whether you are slaves of sin (which leads to death) or obedience (which leads to righteousness)! Thank God that although you were slaves of sin, from your heart you have obeyed the pattern of teaching that you have been given. Since you have been set free from sin, you have become slaves of righteousness. (I am speaking in human terms because of the weakness of your body.) You see, since you have made your body parts available as servants to filthiness and lawbreaking (which leads to more lawbreaking), now you must likewise make your body parts available as slaves of righteousness (which leads to purification). You see, when you were slaves to sin, you were free from righteousness. So what fruit did you produce then? You are now ashamed of these things because the destination of those things is death. But since you have now been set free from sin and have become servants to God, you produce your fruit that leads to purification, and the destination is eternal life. You see, the compensation paid by sin is death, but God's free gift is eternal life in our Master, Jesus the Messiah.

Or is it, brothers (I am talking to those who know the Law), that you do not know that the Law has authority over a person as long as they are alive? You see, the married woman is bound by the Law to her husband as long as he is alive. But if that husband dies, she is set free from the law concerning her husband. Also, if her husband is alive, she is labeled as an adulteress if she becomes married to another man. But if her husband were to die, she would be free from that law and would not be an adulteress, even if she were to marry another man. So, my brothers, you also have been executed (as far as the Law is concerned) by the body of the Messiah so that you could be married to another—to the one who was raised from the dead—so we could bear fruit for God. You see, when we were physically focused, the sinful passions that were aroused by the Law were active in the parts of our body so that we would bear fruit for death. But now we have been set free from the Law so that we could be servants by the new spiritual way and not with the old written way.

So what will we say? Is the Law sin? Absolutely not! But I did not know sin except through the Law. You see, I did not understand selfish desire except for what the Law said, "You must not desire selfishly." No, sin took advantage of the command and brought about all kinds of selfish desire in me. You see, without the Law, sin is dead. At one time I was alive without the Law, but when the command came, sin came alive and I died—the command that was meant for life resulted in death. You see, sin took advantage of the command, deceived me, and killed me through it. So the Law is holy, and the command is holy, right, and good. So did something good become death for me? Absolutely not! On the contrary, sin (so that it would be exposed as sin) brought about death in me through something good so that sin would become extremely sinful through the command.

You see, we know that the Law is spiritual, but since I am human, I am sold as a slave to sin. You see, I do not know what I am doing. I do not practice what I want to do, but I do precisely what I hate to do. So if I do what I do not want to do, I agree with the Law—the Law is good. But now I no longer accomplish the Law; on the contrary, the sin that resides in me is active. You see, I know that nothing good resides in me—that is, in my human tendencies. Actually, the desire for what is good is present with me, but the accomplishment of what is good is not present with me. You see, I do not do the good things that I want to do, but I make a practice of precisely the evil things that I do not want to do. So if I do what I do not want to do, I am no longer the one doing it—it is sin, which resides in me. So I discover this law: when I have the desire to do what is good, evil is present with me. You see, I relish in God's Law with my inner self, but I see another law in the parts of my body that is waging war with the law that is in my mind, and it takes me captive by the law of sin that is in the parts of my body. What a miserable person I am! Who will rescue me from this body of death? Thank God, through our Master, Jesus the Messiah! So I myself am a servant of God's Law with my mind but a servant of sin's law with my human tendencies.

So now there is no condemnation for those who are in Jesus the Messiah because the law of spiritual life in Jesus the Messiah has set you free from the law of sin and death. You see, God has done what was impossible for the Law (because it was weakened by the body) by sending his own Son in the likeness of a sinful body. As for sin, he condemned it with his body so that the Law's requirement could be accomplished by us who do not live with a bodily focus (on the contrary, we live spiritually!). You see, those who live with a bodily focus set their minds on the body, and those who live spiritually set their minds on the Spirit. Now, the physically focused mindset results in death. But the spiritually focused mindset results in life and peace. You see, the physically focused mindset is hostile toward God because it does not submit itself to God's Law (it is not even able to do so). Furthermore, those who live focused on physical things cannot please God. But you are not focused on physical things. On the contrary, you are focused on spiritual things if God's Spirit really resides in you. But if anyone does not have the Messiah's

Spirit, they do not belong to the Messiah. But if the Messiah resides in you, even though your body may be dead because of sin, your spirit is alive because of righteousness. But if the Spirit of the one who raised Jesus from the dead resides within you, then the one who raised the Messiah from the dead will bring your dead bodies to life through his Spirit, who resides in you.

As a result, brothers, we are not obligated to live with a physical focus so that we should live like mere humans. You see, if you live with a physical focus, you are going to die. But if you put the body's practices to death by the Spirit, you will live because everyone who is led by God's Spirit is a child of God. You see, you have not received a spirit of slavery, which would result in a return to fear. On the contrary, you have received a spirit of adoption, by which we cry out, "My Father!" The Spirit himself testifies with our spirit that we are God's children. So if we are children, we are also heirs (God's heirs, for one thing, and fellow heirs with the Messiah, for another—that is, if we suffer with him so that we can also be glorified with him).

You see, I figure that the passions of this present time are not worth comparing to the glory that is going to be revealed to us! Nature eagerly anticipates the unveiling of God's children because nature has been subjected to worthlessness. This was not voluntarily—on the contrary, it was forced into subjection in hopes that nature itself would be set free from slavery to destruction for the glorious freedom of God's children. You see, we know that all of nature groans and suffers together to this day. Not only that, but also we who have the initial offering of the Spirit groan within ourselves, too, and wait for that adoption: the deliverance of our bodies. You see, we are saved by this hope! But hope is not something that is seen—I mean, who hopes for what they already see? On the other hand, since we hope for something we do not see, we wait patiently for it. The Spirit comes to help with our weakness in the same way. You see, we do not know how to pray as we are supposed to, but the Spirit himself speaks on our behalf with unspeakable groans. Now the one who examines hearts knows what the Spirit's mindset is because it appeals to God for the saints. Furthermore, we know that he orchestrates everything for the benefit of those who love God and are called by God's plan. As for those that he knew beforehand: he predetermined them to be conformed to the image of his Son so that he would become the firstborn among many brothers. He called the ones he had predetermined, he made righteous the ones whom he had called, and he glorified the ones he made righteous.

What are we going to say about this? If God is for us, who could be against us? Frankly, he did not spare his own Son—he gave him up for all of us. How could he not also give us everything with him? Who can bring charges against God's chosen people? God is the one who makes us righteous! Who can condemn us? Jesus the Messiah (the one who died—but more importantly the one who was raised) is on God's good side, and he is speaking on our behalf! Who can separate us from the Messiah's love—struggle, difficulty, persecution, lack of food and clothing, danger, or violence? This is what was written:

> We are being killed all day long because of you—
> We are treated like sheep to be slaughtered.

But we more than succeed despite all of this through the one who loved us. You see, I am convinced that nothing—death, life, angels, authorities, present circumstances, future circumstances, powers in the sky above or on the earth below, or any other creature—can separate us from God's love that is in our Master, Jesus the Messiah!

I am speaking the truth in the Messiah—I am not lying; my conscience is bearing witness with me by the Holy Spirit. You see, I have much grief and constant pain in my heart because I wish that I myself could be separated from the Messiah for the sake of my brothers (my physical relatives). They are Israelites, and they possess the adoption, glory, covenants, receiving of the Law, worship, and promises. Among them were our ancestors, and from them came the Messiah (physically speaking), who is God, forever blessed above everything, amen!

Yet it is not as though God's word has failed. You see, not all of those who are from Israel are truly part of Israel! In the same way, not all the descendants of Abraham are his children. On the contrary, "Only through Isaac will your descendants be called." That is, his physical children are not necessarily God's children; rather, the promised children are considered to be his descendants. You see, this is the statement of the promise, "At this time next year, I will come to you, and Sarah will have a son."

Not only that, but also Rebekah conceived twins by one man—our ancestor Isaac. You see, they had not yet been born or done anything (good or bad) so that God's plan could continue as he chose. What was said ("The older will serve the younger") was not said based on works of the Law, but on the one who called them. This is what was written, "I have loved Jacob, but I have hated Esau."

What are we going to say? Is God unfair? Absolutely not! You see, he said to Moses, "I will show mercy to whomever I show mercy, and I will show compassion to whomever I will show compassion." As a result, it was not done by the one who wanted it or who gave the effort, but by God, who shows mercy. You see, the Scripture says to Pharaoh, "I have elevated your status for this reason: so that I could show my power using you and that my name could be proclaimed throughout the land." As a result, he shows mercy to whomever he wants to show it, but he causes whomever he wants to resist. "So what are you telling me? Why does he still blame anyone? You see, who can resist his will?" On the contrary, sir, who are you to talk back to God? Will something that was designed ask its designer, "Why have you done this?" Does the potter not have authority over the clay to make one bowl for honorable use and another for dishonorable use—from the same lump of clay? What if God wanted to demonstrate his wrath and announce his power, so he has very patiently put up with bowls of wrath that he has prepared for destruction? What if he did this also to announce the wealth of his glory upon bowls of mercy that he prepared for a glorious purpose? (This includes us whom he called— not only from the Jews but also from the Gentiles.) This is just what he says in Hosea too:

> I will call Not-Mine, "Mine," and Not-Loved, "Loved."
> In the place where they were told, "You are not my nation,"
> This will happen—they will be called "Sons of the Living God."

Isaiah also cries out in Israel's behalf:

> If the number of the children of Israel were like the sand on the seashore, only a small group would be saved.

You see, the Master will close the case quickly and decisively in the land. This is just like what Isaiah also prophesied beforehand:

> If the Master of Armies had not let descendants remain for us,
> We would have become like Sodom,
> And we would have been like Gomorrah.

So what are we going to say? The Gentiles (who were not pursuing righteousness) achieved righteousness—but it was a righteousness that came by faith. But Israel pursued the righteous Law, but they did not obtain righteousness. Why not? They did not obtain righteousness because they pursued it based on works and not by faith. They tripped over the obstacle just as it was written:

> Look! I am laying a stone in Zion that will be an obstacle—
> A rock causing temptation—
> And whoever believes in it will not be humiliated.

Brothers, my heart's desire and my prayer to God are for them to be saved. You see, I am vouching for them—they have a zeal for God, but not based on knowledge. And since they were ignorant of God's righteousness and sought to set up their own, they did not submit to God's righteousness. You see, the Messiah is the goal of the Law—to bring righteousness to everyone who is faithful. Moses wrote about the righteousness that comes from the Law, "The person who does these things will live by them." But the righteousness that comes by faith says this, "Do not say in your heart, 'Who will ascend to heaven?'" (that is, to bring the Messiah down from there), "'Or who will descend into the underworld?'" (that is, to bring the Messiah back from the dead). No, what does it say? "The message is near you—in your mouth and in your heart" (that is, the message that we preach about faith). You see, if with your mouth you confess Jesus to be the Master, and with your heart you believe that God raised him from the dead, you will be saved. You see, this is believed by the heart, leading to righteousness, and it is confessed by the mouth, leading to salvation. Now, the Scripture says, "No one who believes in him will be humiliated." You see, there is no difference between a Jew and a Greek—the same one is Master of everyone, and he is generous to everyone who calls on him because "everyone who calls on the Master's name will be saved."

Still, how will they call on someone they have never believed in? How will they believe in someone they have never heard of? How will they hear without someone proclaiming it? How will they proclaim it if they are not sent? This is what was written, "How beautiful are the feet of those who bring a good message about good things!" But not all of them have obeyed the Message! You see, Isaiah says, "Master, who has believed our proclamation?" So faith comes from what is proclaimed, and the proclamation came from the Messiah's Message! Yet I am asking: did they not hear anything? Of course they did!

> Their voice has gone out into the whole earth,
> And their words have gone out to the farthest parts of the world.

Again I am asking, "Did Israel not know?" First Moses says:

> I will make you jealous by one that is not a nation,

And I will frustrate you, using a nation that has no understanding.

Isaiah also had the audacity to say:

I was found by those who were not looking for me;
I appeared to those who were not asking for me.

Then he says to Israel:

I have stretched out my hand all day long
To a disobedient and defiant nation.

So am I saying that God has disowned his nation? Absolutely not! You see, I am also an Israelite—from the lineage of Abraham and the tribe of Benjamin! God has not disowned his nation—the one he had previously chosen. Are you not aware of what the Scripture says in the passage about Elijah (as he was pleading with God against Israel), "Master, they have killed your prophets and torn down your altars—I am the only one left, and they are seeking to take my life!" What was the divine answer given to him? "I have reserved for myself seven thousand men who have not knelt down to Baal." In the same way, a remnant exists even now—chosen by God's kindness. Now since it is left by kindness, it is not based on works of the Law, or else the kindness would not have been kindness. So what? Israel did not obtain what it was seeking, but those who were chosen did obtain it. The rest became resistant just as it was written:

God gave them a spirit of disorientation:
Disoriented eyes so that they would not see
And disoriented ears so that they would not hear, to this very day."

David also says:

May their table become a trap and an ambush,
As well as a temptation and punishment for them.
May their eyes be darkened so that they cannot see,
And may you completely double them over!

So am I saying that they have tripped and have fallen away? Absolutely not! But because of their slip-up, salvation has come to the Gentiles so that the Jews would become jealous of them. Now if their wrongdoing results in profit for the world and their loss results in profit for the Gentiles, to a much greater degree their inclusion will too! I am speaking to those of you who are Gentiles: as long as I am an apostle for the Gentiles, I will emphasize my ministry so that perhaps I can make my physical relatives jealous and save some of them. You see, if their rejection means reconciliation for the world, what would their acceptance mean—if not life from the dead? Furthermore, if the first batch of dough is holy, the dough mixture will be too. If the root is holy, so are the branches. Now if some of the branches were broken off and you (like a wild olive branch) were grafted among them and began to take a helping of the olive sap from the root, do not be arrogant toward the branches. If you are arrogant, remember that you do not support the root—the root supports you! What are you going to say? "Branches were broken off so that I could be grafted in?" Good for you! They were broken off because of a lack of faith, but you remain because of faith. Do not become high and mighty—be afraid! You see, if God did not spare the branches that grew naturally, he would not spare you, either, if you do not remain faithful. So observe God's kindness and ruthlessness. He shows ruthlessness to those who fell away and kindness to you—provided that you remain in his kindness. Otherwise you, too, would be cut off. Now as for them: if they were to stop persisting in faithlessness, they would be grafted back in. You see, God can graft them back in! If you, a branch naturally growing on a wild olive tree, were cut down and grafted unnaturally to a cultivated olive tree, then certainly these who are natural branches will be grafted into their own tree!

You see, brothers, I do not want you to be unaware of this secret, or else you could become smart alecks. You see, a partially closed mind has come over Israel until the full number of Gentiles enters in—this is how all of Israel will come to be saved! This is what was written:

> A rescuer will come from Zion;
> He will remove ungodliness from Jacob.
> This is the covenant I will make with them when I take away their sins.

As far as the Message is concerned, they are God's enemies because of you. But as far as their choosing is concerned, they are dearly loved because of their ancestors. You see, God's gifts and calling are irrevocable. In the same way that you once were faithless toward God and have now received mercy because of their faithlessness, these have now become faithless because of the mercy you received so that they could now be shown mercy. You see, God has incarcerated everyone for disobedience so that he could show mercy to everyone.

> Oh, the depth of God's riches, wisdom, and knowledge!
> How immeasurable his judgments are!
> How undetectable his ways are!
> You see, "who has understood the Master's mind?
> Who has become his adviser?
> Who gave to him first? Who will repay him?"
> For everything comes from him, through him, and for him.
> Glory belongs to him forever, amen!

So, brothers, I beg you through God's compassion: offer your bodies to God as living, holy, and pleasing sacrifices—this is a thoughtful act of worship for you. Also, do not model yourself after this world. On the contrary, be transformed by renewing your mind so that you can be able to determine what God's will is: what is good, pleasing, and perfect.

You see, I am speaking to everyone who is with you by the gift that was given to me: no one is to think more highly of themselves than is necessary. On the contrary, they must think reasonably in the same way that God has distributed an allotment of the teaching of the faith to each person. You see, just as we have many body parts in one body (and the parts do not all have the same function), we also are many people but one body in the Messiah—we are each members of one another's body! Now we have different gifts because of the favor that has been shown to us. If it is prophecy, it must agree with the faith. If it is serving, it must be done with faith's service; if it is teaching, it must be with faith's teaching. Whoever encourages must do so with faith's encouragement. Whoever shares must do so generously. Whoever presides over an

TO THE ROMANS

administration must do so diligently. Whoever shows mercy must do so wholeheartedly.

Love must be without hypocrisy. Despise what is evil, and unite yourself with what is good. Love one another dearly with brotherly love. Outdo one another in showing respect. Diligently prevent yourself from being lazy. Maintain a spiritual excitement. Serve the Master. Rejoice in hope. Be persistent when you struggle. Spend much time in prayer. Take interest in the needs of the saints. Aspire to hospitality. Bless whoever persecutes you. Bless—do not curse! Rejoice with those who are rejoicing, and weep with those who are weeping. Agree with one another. Do not think highly of yourselves. On the contrary, go out of your way to assist those who are underprivileged. Do not be a smart aleck. Do not repay evil for evil. Take into consideration what is good in everyone's opinion. If you can, keep the peace with everyone. Do not retaliate for yourselves. On the contrary, give God's wrath that opportunity. You see, it is written, "The Master says, 'Retaliation is mine—I will get them back.'" On the contrary:

> If your enemy is hungry, give them something to eat.
> If they are thirsty, give them something to drink.
> You see, by doing this you will pile up burning coals on their head.

Do not be defeated by evil. On the contrary, beat evil with good!

Every person must be submissive to the ruling authorities. You see, there is no authority except for what has come from God. Furthermore, those who are currently in authority have been appointed by God. So whoever resists that authority has set themselves against God's decree. Plus, those who set themselves against it will receive judgment for themselves. You see, the authorities are terrifying to those who do what is evil—not to those who do what is good. So do you want to be unafraid of their authority? Do what is good, and you will receive praise from it! You see, whoever is in authority is God's servant for your benefit! Now if you do what is evil, be afraid because they do not carry a sword for no reason! They are God's avengers so that they can inflict wrath upon those who make a practice of evil. So you must be submissive to them—not only because of that wrath, but also because of your conscience. You see, this is why you also pay taxes—because they are God's attendants who are busy doing this very thing. Pay what you owe to everyone—taxes to whom you owe taxes, dues to whom you owe dues, fear to whom you owe fear, and respect to whom you owe respect.

Do not be indebted to anyone for anything except in love for one another. You see, whoever loves another person has fulfilled the Law's requirement. For example, "You must not commit adultery, you must not murder, you must not steal, you must not desire selfishly," and whatever other command there is, it is summed up in this statement, "You must love your neighbor as yourself." Love does not commit a crime against a neighbor, so love is the fulfillment of the Law's requirement.

Be aware of the time because it is already time for you to wake up from your sleep. You see, now our salvation is closer than when we began to have faith. The night has already passed, and daybreak has drawn near, so we need to take off the actions of darkness and put on the armor for daylight. Let us behave appropriately since it is daytime—not with wild partying or drunkenness, not with sexual exploits or inappropriate behavior, not with divisiveness or jealousy. On the contrary, clothe yourselves with the Master, Jesus the Messiah, and do not give the body any opportunity to accomplish what it wants.

Welcome someone who is conscientious with their faith, but not for arguments over opinions. One believes in eating everything, but the conscientious brother may eat only vegetables. The one who eats must not look down on the one who refuses to eat, but the one who refuses to eat must not criticize the one who eats, because God has welcomed them both! Who are you to criticize someone else's servant? They stand or fall by their Master! They will stand because the Master can cause them to stand.

One person values one day above another, but another values every day. Each of them must be fully convinced in their mind. Whoever observes a holiday observes it for the Master, and the one who eats does so for the Master because they give thanks to God. Also, the one who refuses to eat does so for the Master and gives thanks to God because none of us lives for themselves, and no one dies for themselves. You see, if we live, we live for the Master, and if we die, we die for the Master. So whether we live or die, we belong to the Master. The Messiah died and came back to life because of this—so that he could be the Master of the living and the dead. But who are you to criticize your brother? Who are you to look down on your brother? You see, we will all present ourselves before God's judgment seat because it is written:

> The Master says, "As I live, every knee will bow to me,
> And every tongue will acknowledge God."

As you can see, each of us will give an account of themselves to God, so let us no longer criticize one another. Decide to do this instead: do not lay an obstacle or temptation in front of your brother. I know (and I have been convinced in Jesus the Master) that nothing is vulgar in and of itself. But if someone considers it to be vulgar, it is vulgar to them. You see, if your brother is offended because of food, you are no longer walking in love! Do not destroy that person (for whom the Messiah died) because of your food! Do not allow your good behavior to be slandered in this way. You see, God's kingdom is not a matter of food and drink. On the contrary, it is a matter of righteousness, peace, and joy in the Holy Spirit. You see, whoever serves the Messiah in this way is pleasing to God and accepted by people. As a result, we must seek what leads to peace and encouragement for one another. Do not ruin God's work because of food. Anything could be pure, but it is evil to the one who eats it despite their hesitation. It is better not to eat meat or drink wine or do anything else by which your brother is offended. You have the faith that you have in God's presence. Blessed is the one who does not condemn themselves by what they accept. But if someone eats when they are unsure, they are condemned because this was not done by faith. Everything that is not done by faith is sin.

Now those of us who are capable ought to put up with the weaknesses of those who are not capable, rather than pleasing ourselves. Each of us needs to please our neighbor—to encourage them for their benefit. You see, the Messiah did not even please himself. On the contrary, as it is written, "The insults of those who are insulting you have fallen on me." You see, whatever was written earlier was written for our instruction so that we could have hope through the persistence and comfort of the Scriptures. Now may the God of persistence and comfort grant you the ability to agree with one another in step with Jesus the Messiah so that with one purpose and one mouth you can glorify God—the Father of our Master, Jesus the Messiah!

So accept one another—just as the Messiah has accepted you—so that it may result in God's glory. You see, I am saying that the Messiah became a servant of the circumcised as a demonstration of God's truth. Thus he could confirm the promises made to our ancestors, and the Gentiles could glorify God as a demonstration of God's mercy. As it is written:

> Because of this, I will acknowledge you among the Gentiles
> and praise your name.

It also says,

> Gentiles: celebrate with his people.

And also,

> All nations: praise the Master—may all the people praise him!

Then Isaiah also says:

> He will be the root of Jesse—the one who rises to rule Gentiles,
> The Gentiles will put their hope in him.

Now may the God of hope fill you with complete joy and peace in your faith so that you overflow with hope by the power of the Holy Spirit!

My brothers, as for me, I have become convinced about you—you are full of goodness, overflowing with complete knowledge, and you are able to instruct each other. I have written quite boldly to you. This was intended in part to be a reminder for you because of the kindness that was given to me by God. Because of that kindness, I have become an attendant to Jesus the Messiah for the nations, acting as a priest of God's Message so that the Gentiles' offering can become acceptable to God once it has been sanctified by the Holy Spirit. So in Jesus the Messiah I take pride in working for God. You see, I would not dare to speak of anything except what the Messiah has accomplished through me, resulting in the Gentiles' obedience—with speech and action, with the power of signs and wonders, and with the power of God's Spirit. Thus from Jerusalem and its surrounding area to Illyricum, I have completed the preaching of the Message of the Messiah. So I also make it my ambition to preach the Message where the Messiah is not yet known so that I am not building on another person's foundation. On the contrary, as it is written:

> Those who have not received the message about him will see,
> And those who have not heard will understand.

Because of this, I have often been prevented from coming to you. But now, I do not have any more opportunities in these regions. So since I have had the desire to come to you for many years, I hope to pass through Rome and see you when I go to Spain so that I can be assisted on my way there by you after I have first enjoyed your company for a while. But I am now going to Jerusalem to give assistance to the saints. You see, Macedonia and Achaia wished to make a fellowship offering of sorts to the impoverished saints who are in Jerusalem. They wished to do this—and they owe it to them—because if they have taken part with them in spiritual things, they ought to offer a service to them in physical things too. So after I have completed this and have confirmed delivery of this fruit to them, I will leave for Spain by way of you. I know that when I come to you, I will do so with the complete blessing of the Messiah.

Now, brothers, I beg you by our Master, Jesus the Messiah, and by the love of the Spirit: join me in the fray by offering prayers to God on my behalf. Pray that I will be rescued from those in Judea who are disobedient, and that my service that is done in Jerusalem will be accepted by the saints. Pray so that by the will of God I may come to you joyfully and relax with you. May the God of peace be with all of you, amen!

I recommend Phoebe our sister to you. She is a servant of the congregation in Cenchrea. I recommend that you receive her by the Master in a way that is worthy for the saints, and that you help her with whatever need she has because she has been a supporter of many people—myself included.

Greet Prisca and Aquila, who are my fellow workers in Jesus the Messiah. They risked their own necks to save my life. I am not the only one who thanks them—all the Gentile congregations do too. Greet the congregation that meets in their house. Greet my dear friend Epaenetus, who is the first produce for the Messiah in Asia. Greet Mary, who has often worked hard for you. Greet my relatives and fellow prisoners, Andronicus and Junias, who are considered by the apostles to be outstanding; they came to be in the Messiah before I did. Greet Ampliatus; he is dear to me in the Messiah. Greet my fellow worker Urban and my dear friend Stachys. Greet Apelles, who is accepted in the Messiah. Greet those who are part of Aristobulus' household. Greet my relative Herodion. Greet the members of Narcissus' household who are in the Master. Greet Tryphaena and Tryphosa, who work hard with the Master. Greet my dear friend Persis, who has often worked hard with the Master. Greet Rufus, who is chosen in the Master, and his mother (who is also mine!). Greet Asyncritus, Phlegon, Hermes, Patrobas, Hermas, and the brothers who are with them. Greet Philologus and Julia, Nereus and his sister, and Olympas and all the saints who are with them. Greet one another with a holy kiss. All the Messiah's congregations greet you.

Brothers, I beg you to look out for those who cause division and temptation to turn from the teaching that you have learned. Avoid them because these kinds of people do not serve our Master the Messiah, but their own bellies! They deceive the hearts of gullible people with smooth speech and flattery. The news of your obedience has reached everyone, so I celebrate because of you. But I want you to be skilled in doing what is good, but innocent of doing what is evil. Now may the God of peace quickly crush Satan under your feet! May the grace of Jesus our Master be with you!

My fellow worker Timothy greets you—as do my relatives Lucius, Jason, and Sosipater. I, Tertius, who penned this letter by the Master, greet you. Gaius, a guest of mine and of the whole congregation, greets you. Erastus, the city's treasurer, greets you, as does our brother Quartus.

To the one who can strengthen you according to my Message and the proclamation about Jesus the Messiah—He can do this because he unveiled the secret that had been kept hidden for the longest time; it has now been revealed through the prophetic Scriptures by the command of the eternal God so that faithful obedience could be announced to all of the Gentiles:

May the glory belong to the only wise God through Jesus the Messiah forever, amen!

TO THE
CORINTHIANS (I)

From Paul (who was called as an apostle of Jesus the Messiah by the will of God) and Brother Sosthenes,

To God's congregation that is in Corinth—to those who are sanctified in Jesus the Messiah and called to be saints together with everyone in every place who calls on the name of our Master, Jesus the Messiah (He is both theirs and ours!): grace and peace to you from God our Father and the Master, Jesus the Messiah.

I ALWAYS THANK MY GOD FOR YOU BECAUSE OF GOD'S GRACE THAT has been given to you in Jesus the Messiah. You see, you have become wealthy in every way because of it—in every word and in all knowledge, just like the testimony about the Messiah has been confirmed in you. So you do not lack any spiritual gift as you wait for the appearance of our Master, Jesus the Messiah. Furthermore, he will confirm you until you are completely guiltless on the day of our Master, Jesus the Messiah. God is faithful—you have been called by him into a partnership with his Son, our Master, Jesus the Messiah.

Brothers, I am begging all of you by the name of our Master, Jesus the Messiah, to agree and not have any divisions among you so that you will be in proper condition: with the same mind and with the same purpose. You see, my brothers, it has been disclosed to me by people from Chloe about you—there is strife among you! This is what I am talking about: each one of you says, "I belong to Paul," "I belong to Apollos," "I belong to Cephas," or "I belong to the Messiah." Is the Messiah divided? Was Paul crucified for you? Were you immersed in the name of Paul? I thank God that I did not immerse any of you except for Crispus and Gaius! Otherwise, some might have claimed that you were immersed in my name! (I also immersed the household of Stephanus, but I do not know that I have immersed anyone else besides these.) You see, the Messiah did not send me to immerse, but rather to preach the Good Message—and not with wisdom of speech or else the Messiah's cross would have no effect!

Now the message of the cross is foolishness to those who are being destroyed. But it is God's power to us who are being saved! It is written, "I will destroy the wisdom of the wise, and I will remove the intellect of the intelligent."

Where is the wise person? Where is the scribe? Where is the debater from this age? Has God not made the "wisdom" of the world foolishness? You see, since the world did not recognize God by using wisdom, with his wisdom God was delighted to save those who believe—by the foolishness of what was proclaimed! Now the Jews look for signs and Greeks seek "wisdom," yet we preach, "The Messiah has been crucified," which is scandalous to the Jews and foolishness to the Gentiles. But to those who are called, both Jews and Greeks, we preach "The Messiah: God's Power and God's Wisdom." You see, even God's "foolishness" is wiser than mankind, and his "weakness" is stronger than mankind!

Look at your invitation, brothers, because not many of you were "wise" according to human standards; not many of you were "strong," and not many of you were "of noble birth." But God chose those who were "foolish" in the world to humiliate the wise. God chose those who were "weak" in the world to humiliate the strong. God chose those who were "insignificant" and "despised" in the world (who are "nobodies") to remove the power of those who are "somebody." So no one can boast in God's presence! You also exist by him in Jesus the Messiah, who became "wisdom" from God to us, as well as "righteousness," "sanctification," and "redemption." So as it is written: "Whoever boasts must boast in the Master!"

Now, brothers, when I came to you, I did not come announcing God's secret to you with eloquence in speech or wisdom. You see, I determined not to know anything among you except Jesus the Messiah and that he was crucified. So I came to you with weakness, fear, and a lot of trembling. Furthermore, my message—like my preaching—was not with wise, persuasive words; rather, it was with the demonstration of the Spirit and power so that your faith would rest in God's power and not in the wisdom of men.

So we speak wisdom among those who are mature—a wisdom that is not from this age or from the rulers of this age who are going to be wiped out. On the contrary, we speak God's wisdom that is hidden in a secret that God ordained before the ages for our glory! None of the rulers of this age recognized it, because if they had recognized it, they would not have crucified the glorious Master. But it has been written:

> There are things that the eye has not seen, and the ear has not heard;
> It has not entered man's heart
> What God has prepared for those who love him!

Yet God has revealed it to us through the Spirit! You see, the Spirit examines everything, including the depths of God! Who knows a person's thoughts except for the spirit of the person who lives in them? Likewise, no one knows God's thoughts except God's Spirit! We have not received the world's spirit, but rather God's Spirit so that we can know the things that have been given to us by God! Furthermore, we do not say what we say with words that have been taught by human wisdom. On the contrary, we speak with words taught by the Spirit—we explain a spiritual message with spiritual words! But a worldly person does not receive this from God's Spirit because it is foolishness to them. They are not able to come to know it because it is only investigated spiritually. On the other hand, the spiritual person investigates everything, but they are not under investigation by anyone. "Who knows the Master's mind so as to teach him?" Yet we have the Messiah's mind!

Yet, brothers, I was not able to speak with you as spiritual people, but as worldly people—as infants in the Messiah! I gave you milk to drink, not food, because you were not strong enough for it yet. But even now, you are not yet strong enough for it. You are still worldly! You see, where there is jealousy and strife among you, are you not being worldly and living like the rest of mankind? When someone says, "I belong to Paul," while another says, "I belong to Apollos," are you not behaving like the rest of mankind? So who is Apollos, and who is Paul? They are merely ministers through whom you have come to believe in the Messiah! The ministry belongs to each as the Master has granted: I planted, and Apollos watered, but God caused the growth! So it is neither the one who plants nor the one who waters, but God who caused it to grow! The one who plants and the one who waters are equal, and each will receive their own reward based on their labor. You see, we are fellow workers for God, and you are God's field—God's building!

Because of God's grace that was given to me, I have laid the foundation like a wise master of carpentry. Another person builds upon it, but each one who builds must be careful how they build upon it! You see, no one can lay any other foundation that what has been laid—it is "Jesus is the Messiah." If anyone builds upon the foundation with gold, silver, precious stones, wood, grass, or straw, the work of each person will become apparent. You see, the Day will reveal it because it will be tested by fire. If the work that someone has done remains, they will receive a reward. If someone's work is burned up, they will suffer damage, but they themselves will be saved. Thus it will be like being saved through fire. Do you not know that you are God's sanctuary and that God's Spirit dwells in you? If anyone destroys God's sanctuary, God will destroy them! You see, God's sanctuary is holy, as you yourselves are!

Do not let anyone deceive you. If someone among you seems to be wise in this current age, they must become a fool so that they can become wise! You see, the wisdom of this world is foolishness to God because it is written: "He catches the wise with their craftiness," and also, "The Master knows that the thoughts of the wise are worthless." So no one must boast in human matters because everything belongs to you—whether it is Paul, Apollos, Cephas, the world, life, death, the present, or what is to come—everything belongs to you! You also belong to the Messiah, and the Messiah belongs to God.

So everyone should think of us as the Messiah's servants and managers of God's secret. Furthermore, in this case it is a requirement that managers are to be found faithful. Now to me, it is insignificant that I might be under investigation by you or by some human day of judgment—I do not even investigate myself. You see, I am not aware of anything lacking in myself. But I am not justified by this because the Master is the one who investigates me! So do not judge anyone prematurely until the Master comes—he will illuminate what is hidden in darkness and reveal the intentions of the hearts of people. Then honor will be given to each one from God.

Brothers, I have applied this to Apollos and myself for your benefit so that you could learn not to go beyond what is written, or else someone might become arrogant in favor of one and against the other. What makes you different? What do you have that you have not been given? So if you have been given everything, why do you boast as though you earned it? You have already "had enough." You are already "wealthy." If not for us, you "would be kings!" I would prefer that you were kings so that we could also reign with you! It seems to me that God has presented us apostles as the last in line like those who have been condemned to die in the arena because we have become a performance for the world, angels, and people. We are fools because of the Messiah, but you are wise in the Messiah! We are weak, but you are strong! You are held in honor, but we are held in contempt. To this very day, we are hungry, thirsty, naked, beaten, and homeless—and we work very hard with our hands! When we are insulted, we bless. When we are persecuted, we put up with it. When we are slandered, we encourage. To this day, we have become like the filth that the world wipes off, like what everyone scrubs away!

I am not writing this to you in order to shame you. On the contrary, I am warning you like my dear children, because although you may have ten thousand guardians in the Messiah, you do not have many fathers. You see, I fathered you through the Message in Jesus the Messiah. So I encourage you—imitate me! For this reason, I have sent Timothy to you. He is my dear and faithful child in the Master, and he will remind you of my ways in Jesus the Messiah, like I teach in every congregation everywhere. Some of you have become arrogant as though I am not coming to you, but I will come to you soon if the Master wants me to. Then I will gain knowledge of the power of these arrogant people and not their words. You see, God's kingdom does not consist of mere words, but of power. What do you want? Should I come to you with a rod—or with love and a courteous spirit?

It is actually rumored that there is prohibited sexual activity among you—the kind of sexual activity that is not even rumored among the Gentiles—that one of you has his father's wife! Furthermore, you have become arrogant! Should you not rather be upset to the extent that the one who has done this would be removed from among you? You see, even though I am physically absent from you, I am spiritually present, and I have already cast my absentee vote against the one who has done this! When you are gathered in the name of Jesus our Master (my spirit will also be with you by the power of Jesus our Master), deliver this person to Satan to destroy his focus on the body so that his spirit might be saved on the Day of the Master. Your bragging is not a good thing. Do you not know that a little yeast will leaven the whole batch of dough? Thoroughly clean out the old yeast so that you can be a new batch, unleavened like you should be! You see, our Passover Lamb (the Messiah) has already been offered. So let us feast—but not with old leavened bread or the leaven of evil and wickedness. On the contrary, let us feast on the unleavened bread of pure and true motives. I have written to you by letter not to associate with those who practice prohibited sexual behavior. I was not at all referring to those in the world who are sexually immoral, greedy, swindlers, or idol worshipers. You see, otherwise you would have to leave the world. But I have now written to you not to associate with someone who is called a brother who is sexually immoral, greedy, an idol worshiper, abusive, a drunk, or a swindler—do not even eat with such people! You see, what business do I have judging those who are outside the body of the Messiah? Do you not judge those who are within the body? God will judge those who are outside the body. Clean out the evil person from among you!

When one of you has a lawsuit against another, how can any of you bring yourself to go to court before the unrighteous and not before the saints? Is it that you are unaware that the saints will judge the world? So if the world is to be judged by you, are you not worthy to judge even the least of cases? Are you not aware that we will judge angels? Can you not judge everyday matters? So if you have lawsuits about everyday matters, are you really going to select judges who have no standing in the congregation? I am saying this to embarrass you. Is there not even one of you who is wise who could decide a case between their brothers? It is already a complete failure for you to have lawsuits with one another. Why would you not prefer to be mistreated? Why would you not prefer to be cheated? On the contrary, you are the ones mistreating and cheating—you do this to your own brothers, no less! Now are you not aware that those who mistreat others will not inherit God's kingdom? Do not be deceived! No one who participates in prohibited sexual practices, idolatry, adultery, homosexuality (as active or passive partners), stealing, greed, drunkenness, abuse, or swindling—none of these will inherit God's kingdom! Some of you were these kinds of people, but you were washed! You were sanctified! You were made righteous by the name of the Master, Jesus the Messiah, and by the Spirit of our God!

"I have the right to do anything," but not everything is helpful! "I have the right to do anything," but I will not be controlled by anything! "Food is for the belly, and the belly is for food," but God will do away with both the belly and food!

Now God raised the Master, and he will also raise us by his power. Do you not know that your bodies are parts of the Messiah's body? Would I actually take the parts of the Messiah's body and cause them to be parts of a prostitute's body? Absolutely not! Are you not aware that whoever unites himself with a prostitute becomes one body with her? You see, it says, "The two of them will become one body." On the other hand, whoever unites himself with the Master becomes one spirit with him. Flee from prohibited sexual practices. "Every sin that a person commits is outside of their body," but whoever engages in prohibited sexual practices sins within their own body. Are you not aware that your body is the sanctuary that you have received from God for the Holy Spirit who dwells in you? Are you not aware that you do not belong to yourself? You see, you have been bought at an expensive price! So glorify God with your body!

Now about what you wrote to me: it is better for a man not to have a sexual relationship with a woman. But because prohibited sexual practices are being committed, each man needs to have his own wife, and each woman needs to have her own husband. The husband needs to fulfill an obligation to his wife, just as the wife needs to do for her husband. The wife does not have the right to her own body—no, her husband has that right. In the same way, the husband does not have the right to his own body—no, the wife has that right. Do not deprive one another unless it is for a limited time by agreement (so that you can take time for prayer). Then you should come back together to prevent Satan from tempting you because of your lack of self-control. Now I am saying this to give you permission—not to command you. On the contrary, I would prefer everyone to be like me, but each person has their own gift from God. One has this one, and another has that one.

I am now speaking to those who are unmarried and to the widows: it would be better for them to continue that way—like I do. But they need to get married if they do not have self-control because it would be better to get married than to burn with passion. Now I (not I, but the Master) command those who are married: a woman must not leave her husband. But if she does leave, she needs to remain unmarried or be reconciled to her husband. A husband also must not divorce his wife. To the rest of you, I (not the Master) say: if a brother has a wife who does not have faith and she is happy to live with him, he must not divorce her. Also, if a woman has a husband who does not believe, and he is happy to live with her, she must not divorce her husband. You see, the husband who does not have faith is sanctified by his wife, and the wife who does not have faith is sanctified by that brother. Otherwise, your children would be unclean—but they are clean now. On the other hand, if the one who does not have faith leaves, let them leave. The brother or sister is not bound in such cases. Yet God has called you in peace. Ma'am, how do you know whether you will save your husband? Or you, sir: how do you know whether you will save your wife?

It is just that everyone should live how the Master assigned them to live—how God called them to live. This is what I command in all the other congregations too. Whoever was called after being circumcised should not conceal his circumcision. Whoever was called while he was uncircumcised should not be circumcised. Circumcision does not matter, and uncircumcision does not matter. But keeping God's commands does matter! Each person should remain in the condition they were in when they were called. If you were a slave when you were called, do not let it bother you. But if you can obtain your freedom, that would be better. You see, a slave who is called by the Master is the Master's free person just as the one who is free when they were called is the Messiah's slave. You have been bought at an expensive price—do not become slaves to people. Brothers, in God's presence each of you should remain in the condition you were in when you were called.

Now I do not have a command from the Master about virgins, but I offer an opinion as one who has become trustworthy by the mercy of the Master. Because of our current crisis, it is better for a person to remain as they are. Have you been united with a wife? Do not seek a divorce. Are you divorced from your wife? Do not seek a wife. But if you were to marry, you would not be sinning. Also, if a virgin were to marry, she would not be sinning either. These will have a physical struggle, and I am trying to spare you! But, brothers, I am telling you this: time is limited. So from now on, those who have wives should be like those who do not have them; those who weep should be like those who are not weeping; those who celebrate should be like those who are not celebrating; those who are buying should be like those who do not have anything; and those who have power over the world should be like those who have no power at all. You see, the way of this world is passing away. Now I want you to be carefree. An unmarried man is concerned about the Master (i.e., how to please the Master), but a married man is concerned about this world (i.e., how to please his wife). He is divided! Also, the unmarried and virgin women are concerned about the Master so that they might be holy—both in body and spirit. But a married woman is concerned about this world (i.e., how to please her husband). I am saying this for your benefit—not to put a restriction on you. On the contrary, I say this so that you may be presentable and devoted to the Master without distractions. But if someone feels like he is behaving shamefully toward his fiancée and is gripped in passion and it must be this way, he should do what he wants to do—he is not sinning. They should get married. On the other hand, whoever stands firm in his heart and does not feel this obligation—he has power over his own will and has decided this in his own heart (i.e., to keep her as his fiancée), he will do well. So the one who marries his fiancée does well, and the one who does not marry does even better! A woman is bound to her husband as long as he lives. But if her husband were to die, she would be free to marry whomever she wanted—but only in the Master. Yet she would be happier if she remained a widow, in my opinion (and I think I have God's Spirit!).

TO THE CORINTHIANS (I)

Now about what is sacrificed to idols: we know that all of us have knowledge. Knowledge makes one arrogant, but love builds someone else up! If someone thinks they know something, they do not yet know what they need to know. But if someone loves God, they will be recognized by him. So as for this food that is sacrificed to idols: we know that an idol is nothing in the world and that there is no God but one. You see, although there are many things called "gods" (whether they are in the sky or on earth) just as there are many "gods" and many "masters,"

> Yet for us, there is one God, the Father—
> Everything came from him, and we live for him;
> And one Master, Jesus the Messiah—
> Everything came through him, and we live through him.

But this knowledge is not shared by everyone. Out of habit, some people to this day eat that idol's food like a sacrifice to an idol, and their conscience is ruined because it is fragile. Food will not cause us to be approved by God! If we do not eat, we will not lack his approval—if we eat, we will not have more of it. Be careful that this right of yours does not somehow become an obstacle for those who are fragile. You see, if someone sees that you know you are reclining to eat in an idol's temple, will their fragile conscience not be encouraged to eat what is offered to an idol? You see, the one who is fragile—this brother for whom the Messiah died—has been destroyed by your "knowledge"! So by sinning against your brothers and assaulting their fragile consciences, you are sinning against the Messiah! Because of this, if food causes my brother to sin, I will never again eat meat—never again—so that I will not cause my brother to sin.

Am I not a free man? Am I not an apostle? Have I not seen Jesus our Master? Are you not my accomplishment in the Master? Even if I am not an apostle to others, am I not at least an apostle to you? This is my defense to those who criticize me. Do we not have the right to eat and drink? Do we not have the right to take along a sister as a wife like the rest of the apostles, the Master's brothers, or Cephas? Furthermore, are Barnabas and I the only ones who do not have the right to preach without working? Who serves as a soldier at his own expense? Who plants a vineyard but does not eat from its fruit? Who shepherds a flock but does not drink the flock's milk? I am saying this like a mere human, aren't I? Yet does the Law not also say this? You see, it is written in the Law of Moses: "Do not muzzle an ox that is threshing grain." God is not concerned about the ox, is he? Does it not say this completely for our benefit? You see, it is written for our benefit that "Whoever plows should do so with an expectation to share in the crop, and whoever threshes the grain should do so with that same expectation." Since we have sown spiritual things with you, is it too much to ask that we reap material things from you? Since others are sharing in these rights with you, certainly should we not also share in them? But we have not taken advantage of this right. On the contrary, we have put up with everything so that we would not cause a difficulty for the Messiah's Message. Are you not aware that those who work in temples eat what is sacrificed by the temple? Those who take care of the altar share with the altar in what was sacrificed on it! In the same way, the Master commanded those who proclaim the Message to get their living from the Message. Now, I have not taken advantage of any of these rights—and I have not written this to make these things happen for me. You see, it would surely be better for me to die—no one will deprive me of my sense of accomplishment. You see, when I preach the Message, I have no sense of accomplishment because obligation confronts me. It would be upsetting to me if I did not preach the Message! You see, if I am making this a practice voluntarily, I have a reward! But if it is involuntary, it is because I have been entrusted with a task. So what is my reward? My reward is that when I preach the Message, I can offer it free of charge so that I do not take full advantage of my right with the Message.

You see, even though I was free from everyone, I have made myself a slave to everyone so that I can win the majority of them. I have also become like a Jew for the Jews so that I can win Jews. I have become like someone under the Law for those who are under the Law (even though I myself am not under the Law) so that I can win those who are under the Law. I have become like those who are not subject to the Law for those who are not subject to the Law (I'm not saying that I am not subject to God's law; on the contrary, I am subject to the Messiah's law!). Thus I can win those who are not subject to the Law. I have become fragile for those who are fragile so that I can win those who are fragile. I have become everything to everyone so that by all means I can save some of them! But I do all of this for the Message so that I can become a participant in it.

Are you not aware that all of those who run in a stadium may run, but only one receives the prize? That is how you should run so that you can take hold of it! Furthermore, whoever engages in competition exercises self-control in everything. Now they do this to receive a perishable crown, but we do it to receive an immortal one! So I run like this and not without purpose. I fight, and I do not miss. On the contrary, I blacken the eye of my body and make it obey me so that I myself do not fail the test after preaching to others.

You see, brothers, I do not want you to be unaware that all our ancestors went under the cloud and passed through the sea, so all of them were immersed into Moses in the cloud and in the sea. Then all of them ate the same spiritual food, and all of them drank the same spiritual drink. You see, they drank from the spiritual rock that followed them (that rock was the Messiah). But God was not pleased with the majority of them because they were killed in the desert. Now these people became examples for us so that we would not have evil desires like they did. Do not worship idols, either, like some of them did. Then as it is written, "The nation sat down to eat and drink, and got up to amuse themselves." Do not commit prohibited sexual practices, either, like some of them did. Then twenty-three thousand of them fell in one day. Do not try the Messiah's patience, either, like some of them did. Then they were destroyed by snakes. Do not complain, either, like some of them did. Then they were destroyed by the angel of destruction. These things happened to them as warnings. Then they were written down to caution us (to whom the end of the ages have come). So whoever thinks they are standing firm needs to be careful that they do not fall. No temptation has seized you that is not common to humanity. But God is faithful—he will not allow you to be tempted beyond your ability. On the contrary, he will also provide an escape with the temptation so that you can put up with it.

Because of this, my brothers, flee from idolatry. I am talking to you like wise people—decide for yourselves what I am saying! Is the cup of blessing that we bless not fellowship with the Messiah's blood? Is the bread that we break not fellowship with the Messiah's body? Because there is one piece of bread, the many of us are one body. You see, we take a part of the same bread! Be careful about the physical Israel. Are those who eat the sacrifices not associated with the altar? So what am I saying? Am I saying that what is sacrificed to an idol is significant—that an idol is significant? No, I am saying that they sacrifice what they sacrifice to demons and not to God. I do not want you to be associated with demons. You cannot drink from both the Master's cup and the demons' cup. You cannot eat from both the Master's table and the demons' table. Should we provoke the Master to jealousy? We are not stronger than he, are we?

"I have the right to do everything," but not everything is helpful! "I have the right to do everything," but not everything encourages! No one should seek to benefit themselves. Rather, they should seek to benefit the other person. Eat anything that is sold at the market, but do not ask any questions (because of your integrity). You see, "The earth and everything in it belongs to the Master." If a nonbeliever invites you to eat and you want to go, eat anything that is set before you, and do not ask any questions (because of your integrity). But if someone says, "This is offered to an idol," do not eat it because of the one who informed you and because of their integrity. Now, I am not talking about your integrity in this case but that of the other person. You see, why is my freedom criticized by another person's integrity? If I eat with thankfulness, why am I slandered because of something for which I gave thanks? So whether you are eating, drinking, or doing anything else, do everything for God's glory. Do not be offensive to Jews, Greeks, or to God's congregation; just like I do: in everything I accommodate everyone. I am not seeking my own benefit but rather the benefit of others (so that they can be saved). Imitate me like I imitate the Messiah.

I applaud you for remembering me in everything and for holding on to the tradition that I delivered to you. Now I want you to understand that the Messiah is head over every man. Man is head over woman, and God is head over the Messiah. Every man who prays or prophesies with his head covered dishonors his head. But every woman who prays or prophesies with her head unveiled dishonors her head. You see, that is one and the same as having her head shaved. You see, if a woman is not veiled, she should also cut her hair. But if it is shameful for a woman to cut her hair or shave her head, she needs to wear a veil. Now a man should not veil his head since he is God's image and glory, but woman is man's glory. You see, man was not created from woman (on the contrary, woman was created from man), and man was not created for woman (on the contrary, woman was created for man). Because of this, the woman needs to have a symbol of her husband's authority on her head because of the angels. On the other hand, woman is nothing without man, and man is nothing in the Master without woman. You see, although woman was created from man, man was also born through woman (and everything came from God). Decide for yourselves—is it proper for a woman to pray to God without a veil? Does nature itself not teach you that it is shameful for a man to have long hair, but if a woman has long hair, it is her glory? You see, her long hair has been given to her as a covering. So if someone seems to be argumentative, neither we nor God's congregations have this kind of standard.

Now I do not applaud you as I am giving you these instructions because you are meeting together for the worse, not for the better. Primarily, I hear that when you come together in the assembly, there are divisions among you—and I believe it to an extent! You see, there just have to be some differing opinions among you so that those who are genuine may be revealed to you. So when you come together, you are not doing so to eat the Master's meal. You see, each of you breaks line to eat that meal, so one of you is thirsty while another is drunk. Do you not have houses in which you can eat and drink? Or is it the case that you think nothing of God's assembly, so you dishonor those who do not get anything? What can I tell you? Am I going to applaud you? I do not applaud this!

You see, what I delivered to you, I received from the Master—that Jesus the Master picked up bread on the night he was betrayed. He gave thanks for it and broke it and then said, "This is my body that is given for you. Eat this in memory of me." In the same way, he picked up the cup after they ate; he said, "This cup is the new covenant with my blood. As often as you drink this, do it in memory of me." You see, as often as you eat that bread and drink that cup, you are proclaiming the Master's death until he comes.

So whoever eats the bread or drinks the cup in a careless manner will be guilty of the Master's body and blood. So a person must examine themselves, and that is how they are to eat the bread and drink the cup. You see, whoever eats and drinks without paying careful attention to the body is eating and drinking to their own condemnation. Because of this, many of you are weak and sick, and some of you have fallen asleep. But if we are paying careful attention to ourselves, we will not be condemned! So we are disciplined when we are criticized by the Master so that we will not be condemned with the world. So, my brothers, wait for one another when you come together to eat. If someone is hungry, they need to eat at home so that you are not assembling for your condemnation. But I will set the other things right whenever I come.

Now, brothers, I do not want you to be unaware as far as spiritual gifts are concerned. You know that when you were still Gentiles, you were led away (as you were inclined to be) to idols that do not speak. So I announce to you that no one speaking with God's Spirit says, "Jesus is cursed." Also, no one can say, "Jesus is the Master," unless it is with the Holy Spirit.

Now there are different gifts, but there is only one Spirit. There are different ministries, but the same Master directs them. There are different activities, but the same God activates everything in everyone. So an exhibition of the Spirit is given to each person to help them. You see, a message of wisdom is given to one person by the Spirit, but a message of understanding is given to another person that is in agreement with the same Spirit. Faithfulness is given to someone else by the same Spirit, but gifts of healing are given to another person by the one and only Spirit. Furthermore, the ability to perform miraculous powers is given to another person, the ability to prophesy is given to another, the ability to evaluate spirits is given to another, the ability to speak in various languages is given to another, and the ability to interpret languages is given to another. But the Spirit who activates all these abilities is one and the same, and he distributes them individually to each person as he desires.

You see, it is the same way. There is one body that has many parts, but all the body's parts constitute one body even though there are many of them. The Messiah is the same way! You see, we were all immersed by one Spirit into one body. We also have all come to drink from one Spirit. You see, a body is not composed of one part, but many. If its foot were to say, "I am not a hand, so I am not part of the body," does that prevent it from belonging to the body? Also, if its ear were to say, "I am not an eye, so I am not part of the body," does that prevent it from belonging to the body? If the whole body were made of eyes, what part would hear? If all of it were for hearing, what part would sense smell? As it stands, though, God has placed each one of those parts in the body just like he wanted to do. Now if everything were composed of one part, there would be no body! As it stands, though, there are many parts but only one body.

So the eye cannot say to the hand, "I do not need you," and likewise the head cannot say to the feet, "I do not need you." On the contrary, to a great extent the parts of the body that seem to be weak are vital. Also, we clothe the parts of the body that we consider to be shameful with greater respect, and our private parts are treated with greater modesty, but our presentable parts do not require this. Certainly, God has composed the body so as to give greater honor to the part that had no honor so that there should be no divisions in the body. On the contrary, he composed it so that those very parts would be concerned for one another. So if one part were to suffer, all the body's parts suffer. If one part were to be clothed in glory, all the body's parts would celebrate together. Now you are the Messiah's body (and individually you are only parts of that body). God has placed these body parts into the congregation: apostles first, prophets second, teachers third, then miracle workers, then those with gifts to heal, help others, administrate, and speak in various languages. Are all these apostles? Are all of them prophets? Are all of them teachers? Are all of them miracle workers? Do all of them have the gift of healing? Do all of them have the gift of speaking in other languages? Are all of them interpreters? You are enthusiastic about the better gifts, but I will still show you a better way.

Even if I were to speak in the languages of people and angels, I have become a ringing gong or a crashing cymbal if I do not have love. Even if I were to prophesy, understand every divine secret, and have complete understanding—even if I were to have faith that would relocate mountains—I would be nothing if I did not have love. Even if I were to give away all my possessions—even if I were to surrender my body to be burned, I gain nothing if I do not have love.

Love is patient. Love is kind. It is not jealous. Love does not brag about itself. Love does not have an exaggerated self-image. It does not behave inappropriately. It does not behave selfishly. It is not irritable. It does not think about evil things. It does not celebrate because of injustice; on the contrary, it celebrates in what is true. It puts up with everything. It is faithful in everything. It is hopeful in everything. It is persistent in everything.

Love never ends. But if gifts of prophecy exist, they will come to an end. If gifts of speaking in languages exist, they will be silenced. If gifts of understanding exist, they will come to an end. You see, we understand in pieces and prophesy in pieces. But when the complete picture comes, what was once in pieces will come to an end. When I was a child, I talked like a child, understood like a child, and thought about things like a child. But I have put away childish ways now that I have become a man. You see, we currently see indirectly—through a mirror. But when the complete picture comes, we will see face to face. We currently recognize it in pieces, but then we will recognize it fully just like we have been recognized. These three things currently continue: faith, hope, and love. But love is the greatest among these.

Pursue love, but also be enthusiastic about spiritual gifts (especially that you might prophesy). You see, whoever speaks in another language does not speak to people, but only to God. You see, no one hears them—the Spirit is speaking secrets! On the other hand, whoever prophesies speaks so that he can encourage, comfort, and reassure people. Whoever speaks in another language encourages themselves, but whoever prophesies encourages the congregation. So I do not want all of you to speak in other languages. I would prefer that you prophesy! The one who prophesies is more important than the person who speaks in another language except when he interprets so that the congregation may receive encouragement.

Now, brothers, if I were to come to you to speak in other languages, how would I benefit you unless I also spoke to you with revelation, knowledge, prophecy, or teaching? Even with inanimate objects that make sounds (like the flute or harp), if they do not make distinguishable sounds, how can what is being played on the flute or harp be recognized? You see, if the trumpet were to blast indistinctly, who would prepare for war? In the same way, unless you are giving a recognizable speech with your language, how can what you are saying be understood? You see, you are just talking to the air! Surely there are many families of languages in the world, and none of them is without meaning! So unless I understand the meaning of what is said, I will be a foreigner to the person who is speaking, and the person speaking will be a foreigner to me. It is the same way with you: because you are enthusiastic about gifts of the Spirit, seek to encourage the congregation so that you can grow.

So whoever speaks in another language needs to pray for the ability to interpret. You see, if I pray in another language, my spirit may pray, but my mind is not being useful. So what is my point? I will pray with my spirit, but I will also pray with my mind. I will sing with my spirit, but I will also sing with my mind. You see, if you offer a blessing with your spirit, how will the person sitting there who is uninitiated say amen to your prayer of thanksgiving if they do not understand what you are saying? You see, you may very well be giving thanks, but the other person is not encouraged. I thank God that I speak in other languages more than all of you. But during the assembly, I would prefer to speak five words with my mind than ten thousand words with another language so that I can also teach others by what I say.

Brothers, do not be childish in the way you think. Actually, you should be infants as far as evil is concerned, but you should be mature in your thinking. It is written in the Law:

"I will speak to this nation with different languages and with different lips; Thus they will not listen to me," the Master says.

So these languages are a sign to those who are unfaithful—not to those who are faithful. And prophecy is a sign to those who are faithful—not to those who are unfaithful. So let us say your whole assembly comes together in one place, and everyone is speaking in other languages. If those who are uninitiated or are unfaithful come in, will they not say that you are crazy? On the other hand, if everyone is prophesying and someone who is unfaithful or uninitiated comes in, they will be convinced by everyone and called to account by everyone. The secrets of their heart will become known, and so they will fall on their face and worship God, proclaiming, "God is really here!"

So what is my point, brothers? When you come together, each of you has a song, a teaching, a revelation, something in another language, and an interpretation. Everything needs to be intended for encouragement!

So if someone is speaking in another language, it should be done two at a time (three at the most), and one after the other—and one needs to interpret. But if there is no interpreter, he needs to be silent during the assembly. He needs to speak to himself and to God.

Two or three prophets should also speak, and the others need to evaluate the authenticity of the prophecy. But if something is revealed to another prophet who is sitting there, the first one needs to be silent. You see, then all of you can prophesy one at a time so everyone can learn and be comforted. Furthermore, the prophets' spiritual gifts are under the prophets' control. You see, he is not a God of disorder, but of peace!

As is the case in all the assemblies of the saints, women are to be silent during the assemblies. You see, it is not appropriate for them to speak up. On the contrary, they need to be in submission like the Law also says. So if they want to learn something, they need to ask their husbands at home. You see, it is shameful for a woman to speak up during the assembly. Is it the case that God's message came from you or that it came only to you?

If someone claims to be a prophet or to be spiritual, they need to recognize that what I am writing to you is a command from the Master. But if someone ignores this, they are to be ignored. So, my brothers, be enthusiastic about prophesying—and do not prevent others from speaking in other languages—but everything needs to be done in the right way and with proper procedure.

Now, brothers, I want you to be aware of something concerning the Good Message that I preached to you. You received it and have stood firm in it. You will be saved by it if you hold on to the message that I preached to you—unless you believed for no reason. You see, I delivered this message to you at first (and it is what I received): the Messiah died for our sins (according to the Scriptures). He was buried. He rose on the third day (according to the Scriptures). He appeared to Cephas and then to the twelve apostles. Then he appeared to over five hundred brothers at the same time. Many of them are still living today even though some have fallen into death's sleep. Then he appeared to James and then to all the apostles. Last of all, he also appeared to me, as if to one who was born at the wrong time. You see, I am the least significant of the apostles—I am not worthy of being called an apostle because I persecuted God's congregation. But I am what I am because of God's grace, and his grace toward me was not shown for nothing. On the contrary, I have worked harder than all of them (although it was not me—it was God's grace working with me). So whether I preached it or they did, this is what we preach, and this is what you have believed.

So if it is preached that the Messiah was raised from the dead, how can some of you say that there is no resurrection from the dead? Now if there is no resurrection from the dead, the Messiah has not been raised either! Furthermore, if the Messiah has not been raised, then our preaching is useless (and your faith is useless too). Also, we have been discovered to be liars about God because we testified about God that he raised the Messiah. He did not raise him if it is the case that the dead are not raised! You see, if the dead are not raised, then the Messiah has not been raised either! Furthermore, if the Messiah has not been raised, your faith is worthless—you are still in your sins, and those who were in the Messiah and have fallen into death's sleep are lost. If we have put our hope in the Messiah for this life only, we are more pathetic than any other people!

But it is the case that the Messiah has been raised from the dead—the first of those who have fallen into death's sleep. You see, since death came because of a man, resurrection from the dead also came through a man. You see, just like everyone who is in Adam dies, everyone in the Messiah will be brought back to life. But each one will be brought back to life when it is their turn—the Messiah was first, but then those who belong to the Messiah will be brought back to life when he comes. Then the end comes, when he will hand over the kingdom to our God and Father (when he has destroyed all power as well as all authority and might). You see, he must reign until "He has put all of his enemies under his feet." Death is the last enemy that will be destroyed. You see, "He has subjected everything under his feet." But although it says that everything is subjected to him, it is clear that the one who subjected everything to him is exempt from being subject to him. On the contrary, when everything is subjected to him, then the Son himself will be subject to the one who subjected everything under him so that God can be over everything in every way.

Otherwise, why are those who are being immersed for the dead doing it? If the dead are not actually raised, why are they being immersed for them? Also, why are we endangered every hour of the day? Brothers, as sure as the sense of accomplishment that I have for you because of our Master, Jesus the Messiah—I die every day! If I have fought wild animals in Ephesus with human motives, what good is that to me? If the dead are not raised, "Let us eat and drink because we die tomorrow!" Do not be deceived: "Evil companions ruin good habits." Come to your senses like you ought to do and do not sin! Some people have no knowledge of God! I am saying this to shame you!

Yet someone will ask, "How are the dead raised? With what kind of body will they come back to life?" You fool! The seed that you sow does not come to life unless it dies first. Also, you do not sow the body that will sprout from the ground; on the contrary, you sow a bare kernel, perhaps of wheat or of some of the rest of the grains. Now God gave it a body just like he wanted, and he gave each of the seeds its own body. Not all physical bodies are the same: some belong to humans, some to livestock, some to birds, and others to fish. There are also celestial bodies and earthly bodies. But the splendor of celestial beings is different from that of earthly ones. The sun's splendor is one kind, the moon's splendor is another, and the stars' splendor is another. You see, each star is different in splendor. The resurrection from the dead is the same way. It is sown with mortality, but it is raised with immortality. It is sown with humiliation, but it is raised with splendor. It is sown with weakness, but it is raised with power. It is sown as a physical body, but is raised as a spiritual body. Since there is a physical body, there is also a spiritual one. This is what was written too: "The first man, Adam, became a living soul." The last "Adam" has become a life-giving Spirit. The spiritual body does not come first. On the contrary, the physical comes first and then the spiritual. The first man came from the dust of the earth, but the second man came from heaven. Those who are made of that dust are like the one who was made of dust, and those who are from heaven are like the one who was from heaven. Also, just like we have borne the resemblance of the one who was made of dust, we will also bear the resemblance of the one who was from heaven.

Now, brothers, this is what I am saying: flesh and blood cannot inherit God's kingdom. Furthermore, mortality cannot inherit immortality. Look! I am telling you a secret—not all of us will fall into death's sleep, but we will all be changed in an instant—the blink of an eye—at the last trumpet. You see, it will sound, the dead will be raised as immortal beings, and we will be changed (because this decaying body must be clothed with a non-decaying nature, and this mortal body must be clothed with immortality). When this decaying body is clothed with that non-decaying nature, and this mortal body is clothed with immortality, then the statement that was written will happen:

> Death has been swallowed up in victory.
> Death, where is your victory?
> Death, where is your sting?

Now death's sting is sin, and sin's power is the Law. Thank God, who gives us the victory through our Master, Jesus the Messiah! So, my dear brothers, be firm and immovable, always excelling in the Master's work, because you know that your hard work in the Master is not pointless!

Now, about the collection for the saints: you need to do just what I commanded the congregations of Galatia. On the first day of the week, each of you individually needs to set aside and save money based on their financial success so that there will be no collections when I come. So when I arrive, I will send whomever you consider to be adequate for the task with letters to carry your gift to Jerusalem. If you deem it worthy for me to go, I will accompany them.

Now, I will come to you when I have passed through Macedonia (because I am going through Macedonia). Perhaps I will stay with you or even spend the winter with you so that you can send me wherever I end up going. You see, I do not want to see you only in passing because if the Master permits me, I hope to stay with you for some time. But I will stay in Ephesus until Pentecost because a large and powerful door has opened for me, and there are many adversaries here.

Now, if Timothy comes, be careful to ensure that he can be courageous around you because he is doing the work of the Master just like I am. So no one needs to look down on him. On the contrary, you need to send him off peacefully so that he can come to me. You see, I am waiting for him with the brothers.

Now, as for our brother Apollos, I have invited him to go to you many times with the brothers, but he was quite unwilling to go at this time. But he will come when he has an opportunity.

Watch out! Stand firm in the faith, conduct yourselves courageously, and be strengthened. May everything you do be done with love.

I am begging you, brothers: acknowledge the household of Stephanas because they are the first converts of Achaia, and they have devoted themselves to serving the saints. Acknowledge them to the extent that you submit yourselves to such people and to everyone who helps them or works hard with them. Now I am rejoicing at the coming of Stephanas, Fortunatus, and Achaicus because they have filled the gap left by your absence. You see, they provided rest for my spirit (and yours as well). Give recognition to such people!

The congregations of Asia greet you. Aquila and Priscilla (with the congregation that meets in their house) greet you repeatedly in the Master. All the brothers greet you. Greet one another with a holy kiss.

This is my handwritten greeting: Paul. If anyone does not love the Master, may God put a curse on them! May our Lord come! May the grace of Jesus our Master be with you! My love is with all of you in Jesus the Messiah.

TO THE
CORINTHIANS (II)

From Paul (an apostle of Jesus the Messiah by God's will) and Brother Timothy,
To God's congregation that lives in Corinth, as well as all the saints who live anywhere in Achaia: may grace and peace be yours from God our Father and the Master, Jesus the Messiah!

MAY GOD BE PRAISED: THE FATHER OF OUR MASTER, JESUS THE Messiah; the Father of compassion; the God of complete comfort! He comforted us throughout every one of our struggles so that we would be able to comfort others throughout every one of their struggles. This is because of the comfort that we ourselves received from God. You see, in the same way that the Messiah's sufferings spilled over to us, this comfort of ours also spilled over through the Messiah. Even when we are struggling, it is for your comfort and salvation. Even when we are comforted, it is for your comfort that operates in persistence through these same sufferings that we ourselves have suffered. So our expectation about you has been confirmed because we know that you are partners in these sufferings just as much as you are in this comfort!

You see, brothers, I do not want you to be unaware of our struggles that have taken place in Asia because we were extremely overloaded beyond our power so that we doubted that we would even live through it! Yet we have carried the death sentence in ourselves so that we would not trust in our own ability but in God, who raises the dead. He has rescued us from this great threat of death, and he will continue to rescue us. We have placed our confidence in him that he will continue to rescue us as you join in helping us by your prayers. Then thankfulness may be expressed by many people because of the blessing given to us through the prayers of many people.

You see, this is what we are proud of: the testimony of our consciences. We have conducted ourselves with sincerity and pure, godly motives in the world (not with merely physical wisdom, but with God's grace)—especially toward you. We are not writing anything to you except for what you have read and recognized. I hope you will recognize it fully (much like you recognized us in part) so that you will be just as proud of us as we are of you on the Day of Jesus our Master.

Now, at first I wanted to come to you with this confidence so that you would receive a second gift. Then I would have journeyed from you to Macedonia and then come back to you from Macedonia so that I could be sent by you to Judea. So since I wanted to do this, was I perhaps just being fickle? Do I plan to do what I selfishly want to do so that I can be ready to say, "Yes! Yes!" and, "No! No!" at the same time? God is faithful because our message to you was not yes and no. You see, God's Son—Jesus the Messiah—who was preached among you by us (by Silas, Timothy, and myself), did not come as a yes and no. On the contrary, in him it is always yes because as many of God's promises as there are, they are yes in him. So we offer an "Amen!" through him for glory to God, who strengthened us with you in the Messiah, anointed us, and also sealed us and gave us a down payment in our hearts—the Spirit!

Now I summon God as a witness against me because I refrained from coming to Corinth so that I would spare you. It is not as if we are controlling of your faith. Rather, we are fellow workers in your joy because you continue in faith. You see, I determined for myself not to come back to you with hurt feelings. You see, if I hurt your feelings, who then can cheer me up except for the ones whose feelings I hurt? So I wrote that very letter so that I would not come to you while I was hurt by those who should have caused me to celebrate. I was convinced about you—my joy could be the joy of you all as well. You see, I wrote to you with much difficulty and distress—through many tears. I did not do this to hurt you, but to let you know of the love that I have overflowing toward you.

Now, if a certain one has hurt anyone, he has not hurt me. Rather (not to put this bluntly), he has somewhat hurt all of you, and this punishment administered by the majority of you is enough. So on the contrary, you should rather forgive and encourage him so that he will not be swallowed up by such overwhelming hurt. So I beg you to reaffirm your love for him. You see, this is why I wrote to you: so that I could know your character (whether you will be obedient in everything). I forgive whomever you forgive. Indeed, I have forgiven what I have forgiven in the presence of the Messiah for your benefit. That way, we will not be taken advantage of by Satan. You see, we are not ignorant of his plan!

So when I had come to Troas to work in the Good Message of the Messiah (because a door of opportunity was opened to me in the Master), my spirit was restless because I had not found Titus my brother. So I said goodbye to them and went to Macedonia.

Thank God always, who leads us in victory in the Messiah and in the fragrance of knowing him that is revealed everywhere by us! You see, we are the Messiah's fragrance to God among those who are being saved, as well as among those who are perishing. Truly to some we are the smell of death that leads to death, and to others we are the smell of life that leads to life. Who is worthy of this? You see, we are not like many of those who make a business out of God's word. Rather, we (like those who have pure motives) speak before God in the Messiah as though we were sent from God.

Are we starting to recommend ourselves again? Do we really need (like some do) letters of recommendation to you or from you? You yourselves are our letter! It is written in your hearts—recognized and read by all people. You show that you are a letter from the Messiah and delivered by us. It was not written with ink, but with the Spirit of the Living God. It was not written on stone tablets, but on tablets made of heart—flesh!

We have that kind of confidence toward God because of the Messiah. It is not that we are worthy in and of ourselves to consider anything to be coming from us—we were given this qualification by God! He has also qualified us to become ministers of the New Covenant (not by written words, but by the Spirit). You see, the written code kills, but the Spirit brings life!

So if the ministry of death (which was written with words engraved on stone) appeared gloriously—to the extent that the sons of Israel could not look at Moses' face because of the temporary radiance of his face—how could the ministry of the Spirit not come with much more glory? You see, if glory belonged to the ministry of condemnation, certainly the ministry of righteousness will overflow with much more glory! In this case, what was glorified is no longer glorified because of this excellent glory. You see, if the temporary covenant appeared with glory, certainly the permanent one will also appear with glory!

So since we have this expectation, we can act with great boldness—unlike Moses, who put a veil over his face because the sons of Israel could not look at it at all until the end of its temporary radiance. Furthermore, their minds were blinded. You see, to this very day the same veil remains when the Old Covenant that was read by Moses is read. It is a veil over their hearts. Whenever they turn to the Master, the veil is taken away. Now the Master is the Spirit, and where the Master's Spirit is, there is freedom. So we are all reflecting the Master's radiance with unveiled faces! We are being transformed from one kind of radiance to another just like the Spirit who came from the Master!

So since we have been shown the mercy to have this ministry, we do not give up! Instead, we renounce shameful secrets—we do not conduct ourselves with trickery or tamper with God's Word. Rather, we conduct ourselves with disclosure of the truth by showing ourselves to every person's conscience in God's presence. Even if our Message is veiled, it is veiled only to those who are perishing. (As for them, the god of this world has blinded the eyes of the unfaithful so that the illumination from the radiance of the Messiah's Message does not shine on them.) This illumination is the very image of God! You see, we do not proclaim ourselves to be anything, but rather we proclaim Jesus the Messiah to be the Master, and we are your servants because of Jesus. You see, God is the one who said, "A light will shine out of the darkness." It has shined in our hearts as an illumination of the knowledge of God's glory in the presence of the Messiah!

Furthermore, we have this treasure stored in clay jars so that this extraordinary power comes from God—not from us. We face difficulty in everything, but we are not crushed. We are uncertain, but not desperate. We are persecuted, but not abandoned. We are thrown down, but not destroyed. We carry the death of Jesus everywhere in our bodies so that the life of Jesus will also be revealed in our bodies. You see, even though we are alive, we are continually delivered over to death because of Jesus so that the life of Jesus will be revealed in our mortal bodies. So death is at work within us, but life is at work within you. So we have the same attitude of faithfulness that was written, "I believed; so I spoke." We also believe, and so we also speak because we know that the one who raised Jesus the Master will also raise us with Jesus. Then he will present us alive with you. You see, this is all because of you—so that the grace that has overflowed because of the abundance of thankfulness might spill over into praise for God.

So we do not give up! On the contrary, even though our outer person is wasting away, at the same time our inner self is renewed day after day. You see, this weightless, temporary affliction of ours is extraordinarily working in us to produce an extraordinary weight of glory! We are not paying attention to what is visible, but rather to what is invisible. You see, what is visible is also temporary, but what is invisible is eternal! You see, we know that if our earthly tent where we live is destroyed, we have a building that we will receive from God. It is an eternal house that was built in heaven without hands. In this tent, we complain because we long to be sheltered by our heavenly dwelling so that when we put it on, we will not be found uncovered. You see, as long as we are in this tent, we complain because we are burdened. Because of this, we do not want to be uncovered, but rather covered even more so that mortality will be swallowed up by life. God is the one who also prepares us for this very thing, and he gives us the down payment—the Spirit!

So we are always courageous, and we know that as long as we are present in the body, we are absent from the Master. You see, we walk by faith, not by sight. So we are courageous and content instead to leave the body and be at home with the Master. As a result, I make it my ambition (whether present or absent) to be acceptable to him. You see, we must all appear before the Messiah's judicial bench so that each person will receive a retribution for what they have done with their body (whether it was good or evil).

So since we know the fearsomeness of the Master, we convince people. What we are is clear to God, and I hope that it is also clear in your consciences. We are not recommending ourselves to you again—we are only giving you a reason to be proud of us so that you will have something for those who take pride in appearances and not in the heart. You see, even if we are out of our minds, it is for God. If we are sensible, it is for you. You see, the love of the Messiah controls us because we consider this fact: one person died for everyone, and so everyone has died. He died for everyone so that those who live would no longer live for themselves but for the one who died and was raised for them.

So from now on, we do not recognize anyone based on physical things. Even though we have recognized the Messiah based on physical things, we no longer recognize him as such. So anyone who is in the Messiah is a new creation. The old things have passed away. Look! It has become new! Now all of this comes from God, who reconciled us to himself through the Messiah and gave us this ministry of reconciling others. That is, God is reconciling the world to himself in the Messiah, and he is not keeping a record of their sins. He then placed this message of reconciliation within us! So we are representatives for the Messiah as if God is speaking through us. We are begging on behalf of the Messiah: "Be reconciled to God!" He made the one who did not experience sin to become a sin offering for us so that we could become God's righteousness in him! So we are working together and encouraging you not to receive God's grace in vain!

> In a pleasant time, I listened to you;
> On the Day of Salvation, I helped you.

Look! Now is that pleasant time. Look! Today is that day of salvation! We have not tripped up anyone in any way so that the ministry would not be blamed for it. On the contrary, we proved ourselves to be God's ministers in every way—with much persistence, struggles, hardships, difficult situations, bruises, imprisonments, volatile situations, labors, sleeplessness, and hunger. We have proven this with purity, understanding, patience, kindness, the Holy Spirit, sincere love, the word of truth, and the power of God. We have proven this by the weapons of righteousness that are in our right and left hands through glory and dishonor and through bad and good reports. Even though we were slandered as liars, we were true. Even though we were slandered as unknowns, we were recognized. Even though we were slandered as dying, look—we are alive! Even though we are being chastised, we are not put to death. Even though we are constantly hurt, we rejoice. Even though we are poor, we have plenty in many ways. Even though we have nothing, we possess everything.

Corinthians, we have spoken openly with you; our hearts are wide open for you. Do not restrain us—restrain your emotions instead. Now respond in the same way (I am talking like I would to children)—be open toward us!

Do not get mixed up with unbelievers. You see, what do righteousness and lawlessness have in common? What fellowship do light and darkness have? What agreement is between the Messiah and Satan? What do the faithful and unfaithful people share? What union does God's temple have with idols? You see, we are the living God's temple, just like God said:

> I will live among them and walk around among them.
> I will be their God, and they will be my people.

So

> "Come out from among them and separate yourselves from them," says the Master,
> "and do not touch what is unclean. Then I'll accept you."

Also

> "I will be like a father to you,
> And you will be like sons and daughters to me," says the almighty Master.

So, dear loved ones, since we have these promises, we need to cleanse ourselves from every physical and spiritual defilement so as to achieve holiness with the fear of God.

Accept us because we have not hurt anyone. We have not taken advantage of anyone, and we have not exploited anyone. I am not saying this as a condemnation. You see, I have already said that you are in our hearts to the extent that you die and live together with us. I am very confident about you. I am very proud of you. I am filled with comfort and overflowing with joy despite all our struggles.

You see, when we came to Macedonia, our bodies had not rested at all—we were distressed in every way. There was fighting outside and fear inside. But God (who comforts the humble) comforted us with Titus' arrival. Not only were we comforted by his arrival, but also received comfort because of you when he told us of your desire, remorse, and zeal for me (so that I could rejoice even more). You see, if I hurt you by that letter, I do not regret it (even though I did regret it). This is because I see that, even though that letter hurt you for a little while, I can now rejoice. Now, I do not rejoice that you were hurt, but that your hurt led to repentance—you felt godly pain so that you would not suffer loss in anything by us. You see, godly pain produces repentance, which leads to a salvation that is free from regret. On the contrary, worldly hurt produces death. When you were hurt with this particular godly pain, look how much diligence it produced in you! How it made you answer for yourselves! How angry it made you! How fearful it made you! What desire it produced! What zeal it produced! What punishment it inflicted! In every way, you have proven yourselves to be innocent in this matter. So even though I wrote to you, it was not because of the one who committed injustice or was treated unjustly. Rather, it was written to show you your diligence for us in the presence of God. This is why we have been comforted.

Furthermore, we have rejoiced even more now that we have been comforted by Titus' joy because his spirit was calmed by all of you. You see, even though I bragged to him about you, I was not put to shame. Rather (just like we told you the truth about everything), our bragging to Titus was proven to be true. Also, he has a lot more compassion for you when he remembers the obedience of all of you because you received him with fear and trembling. I am rejoicing because I am proud of you in every way.

Now, brothers, we want you to know God's grace that has been given by the Macedonian congregations. You see, despite their struggle, their overflowing joy and deep poverty swelled up (with a lot of proof) to an abundance of generosity from them. I am a witness of it: they gave as much as they could—more than they could—willingly! They begged us with a lot of encouragement for a favor—that they could take part in the ministry that reached out to the saints. This was not what we were expecting! But they first gave themselves to the Master and to us by God's will. So we encouraged Titus to accomplish this act of grace with you just like he had started to do. Now since you excel in every way—in faithfulness, speech, understanding, complete diligence, and your love for us—you need to excel also in this act of grace.

I am not saying this as a command. On the contrary, I am just testing the authenticity of your love based on the diligence of others. You see, you are familiar with the grace of our Master, Jesus the Messiah: even though he was rich, he became poor for you so that you could become rich because of his poverty. I offer my opinion in this matter because it is helpful to you. A year ago, you started not only doing this, but also wanting to do this! But now you need to complete it, too, so that the completion of this with what you have to give can be equal to the willingness that you expressed. You see, if willingness is present, it is acceptable based on what someone has to give and not on what they do not have. You see, this is not intended to let others rest while you are burdened—it is based on fairness. Currently, your surplus should meet their need so that eventually their surplus can meet your need. So it is fair, just as it is written:

> The one who had a lot did not have anything left over,
> And the one who had little did not lack anything.

Thank God, who put this same diligence into the heart of Titus for our benefit! You see, he received this encouragement and became more diligent. Thus he took it upon himself to come to you. Now with him, we sent the brother who is famous for preaching the Message throughout all the congregations. Not only that, but also he was appointed by the congregations to be our traveling companion with this gift that will be administered by us in order to show the glory of the Master and the willingness that we have. We are trying to avoid one thing—anyone finding fault with this generous gift that will be administered by us. You see, we were already very careful—not only before the Master, but also before people. We have also sent with them our brother, whom we have often proven to be diligent in many ways (and he is now more diligent than ever because of his great confidence in you). As for Titus, he is my partner and fellow worker for you. As for our brothers, they are messengers of the congregations—the Messiah's glory. So show proof in the presence of the congregations of your love and of what we bragged to these men about you.

Indeed, as far as this ministry to the saints is concerned, I do not need to write to you. You see, I am aware of your willingness—I bragged to the Macedonians about it: "Achaia has been ready since a year ago." Your zeal has spurred many people to action. I sent those brothers so that our bragging about you in this matter would not be in vain. So since I said you were preparing, the Macedonians should not come with me and discover that you are unprepared (causing us to be ashamed because of this confidence we have in you, to say nothing of your shame). So I considered it necessary to encourage those brothers to go to you before we did and get this promised offering of yours ready. Thus it can be ready like an offering instead of a forced collection.

Now this is what I am saying: whoever sows sparingly will harvest sparingly, and whoever sows freely will also harvest freely. Each person should give as they have made up their mind to do. It should not be done because of hurt feelings or being forced. You see, God loves a person who gives cheerfully! Furthermore, God can overflow every gift to you so that you can always have perfect contentment in everything since you were overflowing for every good work when you had opportunity. As it is written:

> He has distributed—he has given to the poor;
> His righteousness continues forever.

So the one who supplies seed to the one who sows and bread for food will also supply—and multiply—your seed. Then he will cause the produce of your righteousness to grow. You will be rich in every way for the purpose of generosity, which is done because of our thankfulness to God. You see, the administration of this ministry is not only going to supply what is needed for the saints—but also it will overflow by many offerings of thankfulness to God. Because of the character of this ministry, they will praise God for your obedience to what you professed regarding the Messiah's Message and for your generous fellowship toward them and everyone else. Then they will pray for you because they long for you on account of God's overflowing grace toward you. Thank God for his indescribable gift!

Now I—Paul myself, who am humble when I am with you in person but bold toward you when I am absent—beg you by the courtesy and graciousness of the Messiah. I beg you that I will not have to be bold with you when I arrive—with the confidence that I have the audacity to show toward those who think that we are living with a focus on physical things. You see, even though we conduct ourselves in a physical body, we do not wage war in a physical way because the weapons of our warfare are not physical. Rather, they are God's powers to be used for tearing down fortresses—tearing down arguments and every exalted opinion that is lifted up against the knowledge of God—and forcing every thought into obedience to the Messiah by being ready to punish every act of disobedience when your obedience has been accomplished.

Look right in front of your face! If anyone is confident that they belong to the Messiah, they need to think again about themselves because we belong to the Messiah just as much as they do! Even if I am bragging too much about the authority that the Master has given us (which is for building up, not for tearing down), I will not be ashamed of it. Otherwise, I would seem as though I were trying to terrify you by those letters. You see, they are saying, "His letters are forceful and powerful, but his bodily presence is weak, and his speaking ability is laughable." This kind of person needs to consider this: what we say by our letters when we are absent is what we do when we are present. You see, we do not take it upon ourselves to classify or compare ourselves to any of these who recommend themselves. But these people measure themselves with one another and compare themselves to one another. They do not understand! Furthermore, we do not brag infinitely; rather, only within the territory that God has distributed to us, which even reaches you! You see, we were not trespassing out of our territory by reaching out to you because we were the first to come all the way to you with the Good Message of the Messiah! We do not brag infinitely in the work that others have done. Rather, we have hope that as your faith grows, our territory among you would also expand abundantly. Thus we could preach the Good Message in places farther away than you without bragging in another person's territory that has already been worked. So "whoever brags must brag in the Master." You see, it is not the one who recommends themselves who is proven, but the one whom the Master recommends!

I wish you would put up with my foolishness for a little while. Really—put up with me! You see, I am jealous for you with God's jealousy because I joined you in marriage to one man (I presented you like a pure virgin to the Messiah). Yet I am afraid that your minds have been swindled out of the simplicity and innocence that you should have toward the Messiah, just like the serpent deceived Eve with his trickery. You see, even if someone comes and proclaims a different Jesus from the one we preached or a different Spirit from the one you received or a different message from the one you accepted, you allow it just as well! You see, I do not consider myself to be inferior to these "special apostles" in any way. Even if I have the speaking ability of an idiot, I do not have the understanding of one. We have made this clear to you in everything and in every way.

Did I commit sin by becoming humble so that you could be exalted because I preached God's Good Message to you free of charge? I robbed from other congregations—receiving wages for ministry to you. Then when I was there with you and was in need, I did not burden anyone. You see, the brothers who came from Macedonia supplied what I needed, and I kept myself from being burdensome to you in any way (and I will continue to do so). As sure as the truth of the Messiah is in me, the pride in this that I have had will not be silenced in the regions of Achaia. Why? Because I do not love you? God knows that answer!

But I will continue to do what I do so that I can exterminate the claims of those who are trying to claim that they should be regarded equal to us in what they brag about. You see, these kinds of people are false apostles—workers in lies who are disguised as apostles of the Messiah. No wonder! You see, Satan himself is disguised as an angel of light! So it is not a big deal if his servants are disguised as servants of righteousness. Their outcome will be based on what they have done.

Again I am telling you—no one needs to think that I am being foolish. But even if you do, then accept me as a fool so that I can brag a little. What I am saying with this demonstration of bragging is not said based on the Master. I am speaking as if with foolishness. Since many others are bragging about physical things, I will too. You see, you are happy to put up with fools since you are so wise! You put up with it even if someone forces you into slavery, devours you, steals from you, takes control of you, or hits you in the face! Shamefully, I am telling you, we were too weak to do that!

I am talking like a fool, but I also will take it upon myself to brag about everything any of them brags about. Are they Hebrews? So am I. Are they Israelites? So am I. Are they Abraham's descendants? So am I. Are they servants of the Messiah? I am talking foolishly—I am more than they are! I have served with far more labor, with far more imprisonments, with immeasurable bruises, often in deadly situations. Five times I have received thirty-nine lashes from the Jews. I have been beaten with rods three times. I have been beaten with stones once. I have been shipwrecked three times. I have spent a night and a day in the open sea. I have served with frequent journeys, endangered by rivers, endangered by thieves, endangered by my nation, endangered by other nations, endangered by cities, endangered by deserts, endangered by the sea, and endangered by false brothers. I have served with toil and hardship, frequently without sleep, with hunger and thirst, going without food frequently, with cold and no covering. Furthermore, besides all of this, there is daily pressure on me—concern for all the congregations. Who is weak if I am not weak? Who is offended if I am not even angry?

If bragging is necessary, I will brag of my weaknesses. God—the Father of Jesus the Master, who is blessed forever—knows that I am not lying. In Damascus, the governor under King Aretas was guarding the city and arrested me. Then I was lowered in a basket through a window in the wall, so I escaped his hands.

Bragging is necessary, but it does no good, so I will proceed to visions and revelations from the Master. I know a man in the Messiah who was taken up fourteen years ago into the third heaven (whether in the body or out of body I do not know—God knows). I know that this man (whether in the body or out of body, I do not know—God knows) was taken up into Paradise. He heard unmentionable words that no human can speak. I will brag about this man, but I will not brag about myself except in my weaknesses.

You see, even if I wanted to brag, I would not be foolish because I am telling the truth. But I refrain from it so that no one will consider me to be better than what they see in me or hear from me. Furthermore, because of these excessive visions (so that I would not become conceited), a thorn was given to me in my body. It was a messenger from Satan sent to torture me and prevent me from becoming conceited. I begged the Master three times that it would be taken away from me. Then he said to me, "My grace is enough for you because power is perfected in weakness." So I brag even more about my weaknesses so that the Messiah's power can rest upon me. So I am happy about my weaknesses, insults, difficulties, persecutions, and struggles on behalf of the Messiah. You see, when I am weak, that is when I am strong!

I have been foolish, but you forced me to it! You see, I ought to be recommended by you. I was not at all inferior to these "special apostles," even though I am nothing. Indeed, the signs of apostleship were performed among you with complete persistence—with signs, wonders, and miracles. You see, how were you treated worse than the rest of the congregations except that I myself did not burden you? Forgive me for that pain!

Look—this is the third time I have made preparations to come to you, and I will not be a burden to you. You see, I am not looking for what you have—I am looking for you. Children should not save up to care for their parents. Rather, parents should do so for their children. I would gladly spend (or even be spent) for your lives. If I have overflowed in love for you, should I be loved less? So it must be the case that, even though I did not burden you, I stole from you by using cunning deceit. Yet did I take advantage of you by using any of the people I sent to you? I encouraged Titus to go, and I sent that brother with him—did Titus take advantage of you? Have Titus and I not conducted ourselves with the same attitude? Are our footprints not the same?

You have long thought that we have been giving a defense of ourselves to you. But we speak in the Messiah in the presence of God. Brothers, we do everything to build you up. You see, I am afraid that when I come, perhaps I will not find you to be as I would like. Perhaps also I will not be found to be as you would like. I am afraid that perhaps there will be strife, jealousy, rage, selfishness, evil speech, gossip, arrogance, and volatile situations. I am afraid that when I come to you again, God might humiliate me, and I will mourn the loss of many who sinned earlier and have not repented of the filthiness, prohibited sexual practices, and lack of restraint that they have exercised.

This is the third time that I am coming to you. "By the mouth of two or three witnesses, each fact is to be established." Earlier when I was there the second time, I told those who sinned before and all the rest of you (and I continue to say it in advance now that I am absent): if I come, I will not spare you again since you seek proof of the Messiah speaking in me. He was not weak toward you; he was powerful among you! You see, even though he was crucified out of weakness, he lives by God's power. We also were weak in him, but we will live with him by God's power he has demonstrated toward you.

Examine yourselves to determine whether you are in the faith. Test yourselves. Do you not know about yourselves—that Jesus the Messiah is in you (that is, unless you fail the test)? I hope you know that we have not failed the test. We pray to God that you will not do anything wrong—not so that we appear to pass the test, but that you will do what is good even if we were to fail the test. You see, we cannot do anything against the truth—it is done for the truth. We celebrate when we are weak and you are strong. We also pray for this: your preparation. Because of this, I am writing these things while I am absent so that, when I arrive, I will not have to take it upon myself to be blunt on account of the authority that the Master has given me—it is for building up, not for tearing down.

Finally, brothers, rejoice. Get ready. Be encouragers. Get along. Live peacefully. Then the God of love and peace will be with you. Greet one another with a holy kiss. All the saints here greet you.

May the grace of our Master, Jesus the Messiah, as well as the love of God and the fellowship of the Spirit, be with all of you!

TO THE
GALATIANS

From Paul (an apostle sent not by men nor by way of men, but instead through Jesus the Messiah and God the Father, who raised him from the dead) and all the brothers who are with me,

To the congregations of Galatia: may grace and peace be given to you by God our Father and the Master, Jesus the Messiah, who gave himself for our sins so that he could rescue us from this current wicked age according to God our Father's will—to him be glory forever and ever, amen!

I AM AMAZED THAT YOU HAVE SO QUICKLY TURNED ON THE ONE who called you by the Messiah's grace and have followed another message. It is not really another one—yet there are some who are causing you trouble who want to pervert the message of the Messiah. But even if we or an angel from heaven preach anything to you other than what we have preached to you, may God put a curse on them! As I have just said, I am telling you now again: if anyone preaches something to you that is different from what you received, may God put a curse on them!

Now do I try to persuade men or God? Do I seek to please men? If I still sought to please men, I would not be a servant of the Messiah.

Brothers, I am letting you know that the message that was preached by me was not human because I neither received it from a man nor was I taught it. On the contrary, I received it through revelation from Jesus the Messiah.

You heard about my conduct when I was affiliated with Judaism, that I obsessively persecuted God's congregation and tried to destroy it. I advanced in Judaism beyond many people my age in my nation because I was overly zealous for my forefathers' tradition. But when God (who set me apart from my mother's womb and called me by his grace) determined to reveal his Son using me so that I could preach him among the Gentiles, I did not immediately consult with flesh and blood, and I did not go up to Jerusalem to those who were apostles before me. On the contrary, I went up to Arabia and then returned a second time to Damascus.

Then after three years, I went up to Jerusalem to consult with Cephas and remained with him for fifteen days. I did not see the other apostles except for James, the Master's brother. I am writing this to you in God's presence—I am not lying. Then I went to the regions of Syria and Cilicia, but I was not recognized by the Jewish congregations in the Messiah. They had only heard that "the one who once persecuted us now preaches the faith he once tried to destroy." Then they praised God because of me.

Then after fourteen years, I went up to Jerusalem again with Barnabas (and I also took Titus along with me). I went up based on a revelation and privately explained to those who were influential the Message that I preach among the Gentiles to make sure that I was not running (or had not run) in vain. And Titus, who was with me, was not even forced to be circumcised even though he was a Greek. Yet false brothers slipped in to spy on the freedom that we have in Jesus the Messiah so that they could enslave us. But we did not give in to them, even for a moment, so that the Message's truth could continue with you. What did these influential men amount to? It makes no difference to me what kind of people they were—God does not show favoritism with people—for it seems to me that the influential men did not contribute anything. On the other hand, they saw that I had been entrusted with the message for the uncircumcised in the same way that Peter was entrusted with the message for the circumcised. The one who empowered Peter for a mission to the circumcised also empowered me for a mission to the Gentiles! When James, Cephas, and John (those considered to be pillars) realized the grace that was given to me, they extended to me and Barnabas the right hand of partnership so that we may go to the Gentiles and they may go to the circumcised. They just advised us to remember the poor—which I also am very diligent to do.

But when Cephas came to Antioch, I got in his face and opposed him because he was to blame. Before some people came from James, he ate with the Gentiles, but when they came, he withdrew from them and separated himself because he was afraid of the Jews. Then the rest of the Jews committed this hypocrisy with him, to the point that even Barnabas was carried away with them in hypocrisy. When I saw that they were not acting right with regard to the truth, I told Peter in front of all of them, "If you—a Jew—live like a Gentile and not a Jew, how could you force the Gentiles to live like Jews?"

We are Jews by birth and not "sinners" from Gentile descent. We know that a man is not made righteous by doing what the Law says, but instead by the faith of Jesus the Messiah. We ourselves have also believed in Jesus the Messiah so that we could be made righteous by that faith in the Messiah and not by doing what the Law says. No one will be made righteous by doing what the Law says. But if we are seeking to be made righteous in the Messiah and we are found to be sinners ourselves, then is the Messiah a servant for sin? Absolutely not! If I rebuild what I have destroyed, I prove myself to be a sinner! You see, I died to the Law, through the Law, so that I could live to God—I have been crucified with the Messiah. I no longer live—it is the Messiah who lives in me. I live the life that I live in this body by faith in God's Son, who loved me and gave himself for me. I am not careless about God's grace. You see, if righteousness comes from the Law, the Messiah has died for nothing.

You foolish Galatians! Who has tricked you? Before your very eyes, Jesus the Messiah was publicly portrayed as crucified! I just want to learn one thing from you: did you receive the Spirit by doing what the Law says or by hearing—by faith? Have you experienced this remarkable thing for nothing (if indeed it was for nothing)? So as for the One who gives you the Spirit and performs miracles using you: does he do this based on your doing what the Law says or based on your hearing by faith? It was the same way with Abraham: "He believed God, and it was credited to him for righteousness."

From this you know that those who live by faith—those are the sons of Abraham! The Scripture saw beforehand that God would make the Gentiles righteous by faith because it previously had proclaimed to Abraham: "All the Gentiles will be blessed in you." So those who live by faith are blessed together with Abraham's faith. Everyone who lives by doing what the Law says is under a curse, because it is written: "Everyone who does not continue to do the things written in this book of the Law is cursed." It is clear that no one is made righteous before God by the Law because "the righteous will live by faith." But the Law is not based on faith because it is written: "Whoever does these things will live by them." The Messiah redeemed us from the Law's curse by becoming a curse for us because it is written: "Everyone who is hanged on a tree is cursed." So the blessing of Abraham could come to the Gentiles in Jesus the Messiah so that we could receive the promise of the Spirit through faith.

Brothers, I am speaking in human terms, but no one disregards or modifies a human covenant that has been ratified. Now these promises were spoken to Abraham and to his offspring. It does not say "and to offsprings," referring to many, but referring to one: "and to your offspring." That one is the Messiah! So I say this: a law that was enacted four hundred thirty years after a covenant was ratified by God will not revoke that covenant or make its promise worthless. If the inheritance is based on the Law, it is no longer based on the promise. Yet God has shown favor to Abraham by a promise! So why does the Law exist? It was added to the covenant because of trespasses until the promised offspring would come who was appointed by the hand of a mediator, using angels. Now a mediator implies that there are more than one—but there is one God!

So is the Law opposed to God's promises? Absolutely not! If there were a law given that could create life, righteousness really would have been based on law. But the Scripture has locked everything together under sin so that the promise would be given to those who are faithful based on the faithfulness of Jesus the Messiah.

Now, before faith came, we were all locked together under the Law's custody until that anticipated faith should be revealed. So the Law had become our guardian until the Messiah so that we would be made righteous based on faith. Now that faith has come, we are no longer under a guardian because, in Jesus the Messiah, all of you are God's sons through faith. Every one of you who has been immersed into the Messiah has put on the Messiah. There is no Jew or Greek; there is no slave or free person; there is no male or female—you are all one in Jesus the Messiah! And if you belong to the Messiah, you are Abraham's offspring: heirs as far as the promise is concerned!

I am telling you: as long as the heir is a child, he is no different from a servant, even though he is the master of all of them. Instead, he is placed under guardians and managers until the time that his father has set. We are like this too! When we were children, we were enslaved to the fundamental principles of the world. But when the time had fully come, God sent his Son, who was born of a woman. He was born under the Law so that he could redeem those who were under the Law and that we could receive adoption. So because you are sons, God has sent his Son's Spirit into our hearts, who cries out, "My Father!" So you are no longer a servant but a son; and if you are a son, you are heirs through God!

At that time, since you did not know God, you served beings of nature, which are not gods. Now that you know God, or rather, have become known by God, how can you turn back to those weak and miserable elementary principles—do you want to be enslaved again? You carefully observe days, months, seasons, and years; I am afraid that the work I did for you was for nothing.

Become like me because I am like you, brothers. I beg you—do not hurt me. You know that I preached to you the first time through bodily weakness. You did not hate or disdain the difficulty that my body caused you; on the contrary, you received me as if I were an angel of God or Jesus the Messiah. So where is your blessing? I testify to you that if possible, you would have torn out your eyes and given them to me. Have I become your enemy because I am speaking the truth to you? They are not interested in you with good intentions; they want to shut you out so that you may be interested in them. It is good always to be interested in good things, not only when I am present with you. My children, about whom I am again in pain until the Messiah takes shape in you: I wish I could be present with you now and change my tone—I am at a loss because of you!

Tell me—you who want to live under the Law—do you not listen to the Law? It is written that Abraham had two sons: one from the servant girl and one from the free woman. Now the one who was born of the servant girl was born naturally, and the one born of the free woman was born through a promise! These two are used as allegories: they are two covenants. One was from Mount Sinai and gave birth to children into slavery (this is Hagar). Now Hagar is Mount Sinai, which is in Arabia, but this corresponds to the current Jerusalem because it serves with her children. But the Jerusalem from above is the free woman, who is our mother, because it is written:

> Rejoice, infertile lady who does not bear children!
> Fall down and shout, lady who feels no labor pains
> Because the children of the desolate woman far outnumber the children of the one who had a husband!

Now, brothers, you are children of promise in the same way that Isaac was. But in the same way that the one born naturally persecuted the one born spiritually, the same thing is happening even today. Yet what does the Scripture say? "Throw out the servant girl and her son because the servant girl's son will never share an inheritance with the free woman's son." So, brothers, we are not children of the servant girl, but of the free woman!

The Messiah has set us completely free, so stand firm and do not get loaded down with the yoke of slavery again!

Look, I, Paul, am telling you that if you become circumcised, the Messiah will not benefit you in any way. I testify again to every man who has been circumcised that he is obligated to obey the whole Law. You who would try to be made righteous by the Law have been let go from the Messiah! You have fallen from grace! Through the Spirit, we ourselves are waiting for this expectation of righteousness by faith. You see, in Jesus the Messiah, neither circumcision nor uncircumcision amounts to anything. The important thing is faith working through love.

You were running well—who prevented you from being convinced by the truth? That persuasion did not come from the one who called you. A small amount of yeast will leaven the whole batch of dough. I have become convinced in the Master about you—you will not think anything different! The one who is causing trouble with you will bear their condemnation, whoever they may be. Brothers, if I myself still preach circumcision, why am I still being persecuted? If that were true, the cross has ceased to be an obstacle. I wish those who are upsetting you would keep going and castrate themselves!

You were called to freedom, brothers! Just do not use that freedom as an opportunity for your body—instead, serve one another with love. You see, every law is summed up in one statement: "You must love your neighbor as yourself." But if you bite and devour one another, watch out that you are not swallowed up by one another!

I am telling you—live spiritually and do not carry out the desires of the body. You see, the body wants what is against the Spirit, and the Spirit wants what is against the body. These things are set against one another so that you wind up doing what you do not want to do. But you are led by the Spirit and not by the Law. The body's actions are obvious: they are prohibited sexual practices, moral corruption, inappropriate behavior, idolatry, sorcery, hostility, strife, jealousy, a hot temper, rivalry, rebellion, an opinionated attitude, envy, drunkenness, wild partying, and things like these. I am telling you just as I told you about them earlier: those who do things like these will not inherit God's kingdom!

On the other hand, the Spirit's fruit is love, joy, peace, patience, kindness, goodness, faithfulness, restraint, and self-control—there is no law against things like these! Now those who belong to Jesus the Messiah have crucified the body with its passions and desires. If we live by the Spirit, we also will follow the Spirit. May we never become conceited, provoke one another, or be envious of one another!

Brothers, even if someone is overtaken by a certain sin, you who are spiritual need to restore them with a gentle spirit. Each of you must watch out for yourself so that you are not tempted as well. Carry one another's load, and by doing so you will accomplish the Messiah's Law! Now if someone claims to be something when they are nothing, they deceive themselves. But each person must examine their own work—then they will have a reason to take pride in themselves rather than in someone else because each person must bear their own burden. The one who is taught the Word needs to share all their goods with the one who taught them. Do not be deceived—God cannot be outsmarted. One will reap whatever they sow. Whoever sows in their body will reap corruption from their body, and whoever sows in the Spirit will reap eternal life from the Spirit. Let us not become discouraged about doing good things because we will reap in due time if we do not give out. So let us do good things for all men as we have opportunity to do so—especially to those who belong to the household of faith.

Look at how large the letters are that I am writing to you by my hand!

Everyone who wants to impress others with their bodies—these are the ones who are forcing you to be circumcised just to prevent them from being persecuted because of the Messiah's cross. And those who are circumcised—they do not even keep the Law, yet they want you to be circumcised so that they can take pride in your body. May it never be the case that I take pride in anything except for the cross of our Master, Jesus the Messiah, through whom the world is crucified to me and I am to the world. Neither circumcision nor uncircumcision amounts to anything—it is the new creation! As for everyone who lives by that rule, may peace and mercy be on them and on the Israel of God.

From now on let no one cause me any trouble because I carry the branding marks of Jesus in my body.

May the grace of our Master, Jesus the Messiah, be with your spirit, brothers. Amen!

TO THE
EPHESIANS

From Paul, an apostle of Jesus the Messiah through God's will,

To those who are in Ephesus who are holy and faithful in Jesus the Messiah: may grace and peace be yours from God our Father and the Master, Jesus the Messiah.

MAY GOD—THE FATHER OF OUR MASTER, JESUS THE MESSIAH—be praised! In the Messiah, he has blessed us with every spiritual blessing of heaven since he called us in him (before the creation of the world) to be holy and spotless before him in love. He has already determined to adopt us for himself through Jesus the Messiah (as he wished to do) so that his grace that he has given to us in the Beloved may be praised. In Jesus, we have redemption through his blood—the forgiveness of sins—because of the wealth of his grace that he has abundantly given us with all wisdom and understanding. He made known to us the secret of his will, based on the desire that he set forth in Jesus, as a plan of salvation for all time to bring everything together in the Messiah—everything in heaven and on earth is in him! In Jesus, we have obtained an inheritance (since we have already been determined for adoption according to the purpose of the one who does everything as his will decides) so that we who had already set our hope in the Messiah could exist for the praise of his glory. In Jesus, you also heard the Word of Truth: the Good Message about our salvation. In Jesus, you also believed and were sealed by the promised Holy Spirit, who is the down payment of our inheritance and is intended to redeem a possession for the praise of his glory.

Because of this, since I heard about the faith that each of you has in Jesus the Master and the love that you have for all the saints, I also have not ceased to give thanks for you. I mention you in my prayers so that the God of our Master, Jesus the Messiah, the Father of glory, may give you a spirit of wisdom and revelation by knowing him. And when your mind's eye is enlightened, I pray that you may know what each of these are: the hope of God's calling, the wealth of his glorious inheritance among the saints, and the surpassing greatness of his power that is directed toward those of us who believe because of the demonstration of his mighty power. He demonstrated this with the Messiah by raising him from the dead and sitting him down at his right hand in heaven. He is above all rule, authority, power, and dominion and over every reputation that has been held—not only in this world but also in the one that is coming. He has subjected everything under the Messiah's feet and has granted him the right to be the head over all things for the congregation (which is his body, the entirety of the one who fills everything in every way).

Furthermore, you were dead in your infringements and sins. At one time, you lived in them according to the trend of this world, in company with the prince who has authority over air, whose spirit is now at work among the sons of disobedience. Yes, all of us conducted ourselves with these infringements and sins at one time, according to the desires of our bodies, because we did what the mind and body wanted. In that condition, we were children destined for wrath, just like all the rest. But God has had plenty of mercy because of the abundant love with which he has loved us. While we were dead in our infringements, he brought us back to life together with the Messiah—you are saved by grace! Then he raised us and seated us in heaven with Jesus the Messiah so that in the coming age he could demonstrate the overflowing wealth of his grace by showing us kindness in Jesus the Messiah. You are saved by grace through faith, and this does not come from you—it is God's gift! It is not based on actions, so no one can boast about it—we are his handiwork! You see, we have been created in Jesus the Messiah so that we may do good things, which God has already prepared, and live in them instead.

So remember that when you were physically Gentiles (called the "uncircumcision" by the members of the circumcision that is performed in the body by hands), at that time you were without the Messiah. You were alienated from the citizenship of Israel and strangers to the promised covenant. You did not have hope, and you were atheists in the world. However—now that you are in Jesus the Messiah—although you were once far away, you have become close in the Messiah's blood.

You see, he is our peace! He is the one who combined both groups into one, and with his body he destroyed the hostile barrier formed by the wall that was between us. He nullified the Law of commands given in regulations so that he could take the two groups, create one person within himself (creating peace), and reconcile both to God in a single body through the cross (putting the hostility to death in himself). He came and proclaimed peace to you (who were far away) and peace to us (who were near) because we both have access to the Father in one spirit through him. So you are no longer strangers and aliens; instead, you are fellow citizens with the saints and members of God's household! You are built upon the foundation of the apostles and prophets, and Jesus the Messiah is the cornerstone! In him, the whole building that has been put together grows into a holy sanctuary in the Master. In him, you are also being built up into a spiritual dwelling for God in the Spirit.

It is for this reason that I, Paul, am the prisoner of Jesus the Messiah for the benefit of you Gentiles. If you have really heard about the responsibility for God's grace that has been given to me and is intended for you, you know that it was by revelation that the secret was made known to me (I have already written about this briefly). When you read it, you will be able to understand my insight into the secret of the Messiah. This was not made known to mankind at other times in the way that it has now been revealed to his holy apostles and prophets by the Spirit. Here is the secret: the Gentiles may share in the inheritance, body, and partnership that is promised in Jesus the Messiah because of the Good Message! I have become a servant of this Good Message because of the gift of God's grace that was given to me because of his powerful action.

This grace was given to me—the least worthy of all the saints—so that I may preach the immeasurable wealth of the Messiah to the Gentiles and enlighten everyone about the secret plan that has been hidden from the ages in God, who created everything. It was given to me so that God's multifaceted wisdom could be made known by the congregation to the rulers and authorities that are in heaven. This goes right along with the eternal purpose that he accomplished in our Master, Jesus the Messiah. In him, we confidently have boldness and access because of faith in him. So I request that you do not get discouraged by the afflictions I suffer for your sake—this is for your glory!

For that reason, I bow my knees before the Father (from whom every family in heaven and on earth gets its name), that according to the abundance of his glory he would grant you to be strengthened firmly in your inner self through his Spirit, that the Messiah would live in your hearts through faith, and that you may be rooted and established in love. I pray that you, along with all the saints, may have enough strength to grasp the width, length, height, and depth of the Messiah's overflowing love and that you may know it so that you may be filled with everything God has.

Now as for the one who in every respect can do infinitely more than what we ask or think because of the power that is at work in us, to him be glory—in the congregation and in Jesus the Messiah—for all generations, forever and ever, amen!

So as a prisoner in the Master, I beg you to live worthy of the calling that has called you. Live with all humility and restraint, with patience, and put up with one another lovingly. Be diligent to keep the Spirit's unity in the bond of peace:

> One body and one spirit
> Just as you were called in one hope of your calling.
> One Master, one faith, one immersion,
> One God and Father of all,
> Who exists above all things, through all things, and in all things.

But grace has been given to each one of us based on the measure of the Messiah's gift. So it says:

> He ascended to the highest place,
> Has captured prisoners of war,
> And has given gifts to men.

Now what is meant by "he ascended," except that he also came down to the lower region (earth)? The one who came down is the same one who ascended above all the heavens so that he could fulfill all things. He himself has granted that some should be apostles; others, prophets; others, evangelists; others, shepherds; and others, teachers. This was for the purpose of equipping the saints for productive service and building up the Messiah's body until all of us attain unity of the faith and knowledge of God's Son and until we grow into a mature man—a measure of the full maturity of the Messiah. Otherwise, we would be infants who are tossed around and blown around by every doctrinal wind—by human frauds and the trickery of deceitful schemes. On the contrary, by speaking the truth with love, we ought to lead all things to grow up into him. He is the head—the Messiah. From him, the whole body has been put together, and it is held together by each ligament that is supplied, so each part of the body does its part to build itself up with love.

So I am saying this and testifying by the Master: you do not need to live as the Gentiles live anymore—following the worthlessness of their minds. As for their understanding, they are in the dark. They are alienated from God's life because of the ignorance that is among them because of their calloused hearts. Since they have lost feeling, they have given themselves over to sexual self-indulgence and to practice all kinds of filthy things out of greed. But this is not the way that you have learned about the Messiah's Message! If you really listened to it and were taught by it as it exists (the truth in Jesus), then you were taught to rid yourself of that previous conduct—that old man who is ruined by deceptive desires. You were taught to be renewed in your mind's spirit and to put on the new man who has been created in God's image—in true righteousness and holiness.

So when you have rid yourself of lying, "each of you must speak the truth with your neighbor" because we are members of one another's body. "Be angry, but do not sin"; the sun must not set over your angry mood. Do not give the devil any room. The thief must no longer steal. On the contrary, they must work hard, doing good things with their hands so that they can have something to share with someone who is in need. No bad word should come out of your mouth. On the other hand, you should speak if it is something good—something that will build up where it is needed so that it could give grace to those who hear it. Do not annoy God's Holy Spirit, in whom you have been sealed for the day of redemption. Take all bitterness, rage, anger, shouting, and slander away from you, as well as all wickedness. Be kind to each other; be compassionate. Forgive each other in the same way that God has forgiven you in the Messiah. Become imitators of God like dear children: live with love in the same way that the Messiah also loved us and gave himself up as a fragrant offering to God—as an offering and sacrifice for us. Prohibited sexual practices, dirty behavior, and greed must not even be mentioned among you (this is fitting for saints). Shameful behavior, foolish talking, and crude humor are not appropriate; on the other hand, thankfulness is! You see, since you know this, you also know that every person who engages in prohibited sexual practices, dirty behavior, and greediness (which is the same as idol worship) does not have an inheritance in the kingdom of the Messiah and God.

Do not let anyone deceive you with empty statements; God's wrath is coming over those disobedient children because of these practices, so do not share in them with these people. At one time you were darkness, but now you are light in the Master—so live like children of light. The fruit of that light consists of all goodness, righteousness, and truth. Try to learn what is pleasing to the Master, and do not take part in the fruitless actions of the darkness. On the contrary, expose them! It is shameful even to mention the things that they do secretly, but everything that is exposed by the light becomes visible because everything that is visible is light. So it says:

> Get up, sleeper, and rise from the dead,
> And the Messiah will shine on you.

So watch carefully how you live—do not live like foolish people but like wise people! Make the most of your time because these are evil days. Because of this, do not be foolish; understand what the Master's will is. Do not get drunk on wine—which is reckless to do; be full of the Spirit by speaking to one another in psalms, hymns, and spiritual songs. Sing and make music in your heart to the Master. Always give thanks to God the Father for everything in the name of our Master, Jesus the Messiah.

Submit to one another in the fear of the Messiah. Wives, submit to your own husbands as you do to the Master because man is the head of the woman just as the Messiah is the head of the congregation and is the body's savior. Wives are to be submissive to their husbands in everything, in the same way that the congregation submits to the Messiah. Husbands, love your wives just as the Messiah loved the congregation. He gave himself up for it so that he could sanctify it, cleansing it by washing it in water with the Word. He gave himself that he could present the congregation to himself gloriously—without stain, wrinkle, or anything like these—so that it would be holy and without fault. In this way, husbands ought to love their own wives like their own bodies. Whoever loves his wife loves himself. You see, no one has ever hated his own body—on the contrary, he nourishes and cherishes it just as the Messiah does the congregation. We are members of his body. For this reason, a man will leave his father and mother and be joined to his wife. Then the two of them will become one body. This is a great secret! (I'm talking about the Messiah and the congregation.) In any case, each one of you should also do this: each man must love his own wife as himself, and the wife should respect her husband.

Children, obey your parents because of the Master, because this is the right thing to do. "Honor your father and mother," which is the first command issued with a promise: "so that it will go well with you and you will live on the earth for a long time." Fathers, do not anger your children. On the contrary, nourish them with the Master's discipline and warning.

Servants, obey your human masters with fear and trembling and with your whole heart, as you obey the Messiah. Do not do this only to make an impression as though you are trying to please men but like servants of the Messiah, who do God's will from their souls. Serve with a good attitude since you serve the Master and not men. You know that whatever good anyone does, they will receive a reward from the Master, whether they are a servant or free person. Masters, do the same things for your servants and stop threatening because you know that their Master and yours is in heaven, and he shows no favoritism!

Finally, be empowered in the Master with the strength of his might. Put on God's complete armor so that you can be able to withstand the schemes of the devil. You see, our war is not with flesh and blood, but with the authorities, powers, and earthly rulers of this darkness and the evil spiritual forces that are in heaven. Because of this, take God's complete armor; then you can be able to stand your ground on the evil day and remain standing after you have done all of this. So stand your ground with the truth wrapped around your waist like a belt and wearing righteousness like a breastplate. Like shoes on your feet, wear preparation for the Good News of peace. Above everything, take faith as a shield with which you can extinguish all the evil one's flaming arrows. Use your salvation as a helmet and the Spirit (which is God's Word) for a sword. Always pray with the Spirit, using every kind of prayer and pleading. Be careful in this with all your persistence, pleading also for all the saints and for me so that the message may be given to me when I open my mouth and that I may boldly make known the Good Message's secret. It is for this Good Message that I am an ambassador in chains, so pray that I may have the courage to talk about it as I need to do.

Our dear brother Tychicus, a faithful servant in the Master, will explain to you everything so that you may also know how things are going with me. I sent him to you for this very reason so you can know of our experiences and he can encourage your hearts.

May peace—and love coupled with faith—be with the brothers, from God the Father and the Master, Jesus the Messiah. May grace be with all those who eternally love our Master, Jesus the Messiah.

TO THE
PHILIPPIANS

From Paul and Timothy, servants of Jesus the Messiah,

To all the saints in Jesus the Messiah who live in Philippi, as well as the overseers and deacons: grace and peace to you from God our Father and our Master, Jesus the Messiah.

I THANK MY GOD EVERY TIME I REMEMBER YOU, AND I ALWAYS ASK in each of my prayers about all of you. I offer that prayer joyfully because of your close relationship with the Message from the first day until now. I am convinced of this: the one who began that good work in you will complete it by the day of Jesus the Messiah. It is right for me to think about all of you like this. You see, I hold you in my heart, both in my imprisonment and in my defense and confirmation of the Message, since all of you are fellow partakers of grace. God is my witness, as I long for you with the compassion of Jesus the Messiah. I pray this also: that your love may continue to overflow more and more in knowledge and all understanding so that you may discover what is essential—that you may be pure and guiltless in the day of the Messiah and full of the fruit of righteousness that comes through Jesus the Messiah for God's glory and praise.

However, brothers, I want you to know that the things that have happened to me have actually served to advance the Message so that my imprisonment because of the Messiah is visible to the whole Praetorian Guard and to all the rest. Consequently, many of the brothers in the Master have been convinced by my imprisonment to have such abundant courage that they speak the Word fearlessly.

Granted, there are some who preach the Messiah because of envy and strife, and others who do so because of good intentions. These latter ones do it out of love because they know that I have been appointed to give a defense of the Message. But those who proclaim the Messiah because of selfishness do so insincerely because they expect to arouse affliction for my imprisonment. What does it matter? In either case, whether it is done for appearances' sake or for the truth, the Messiah is proclaimed! I rejoice in this now, but I will continue to rejoice because I know that this will lead to my salvation through your prayers and the assistance of the Spirit of Jesus the Messiah. I know this because of my eager expectation and hope, because I will not be disgraced by anything. On the contrary, with all boldness I know, even now (as I always have), the Messiah will be glorified in my body, whether by life or death. As far as I am concerned, living is for the Messiah and dying is for my profit. You see, as far as I am concerned, living in the body would result in productive work, and I do not know which I would choose! I am distressed about choosing between the two. I have the desire to return and be with the Messiah because it would be much better by far. But it would be more necessary to remain in the body because of you. So since I have become convinced of this, I know that I will remain and continue with all of you for the sake of your progress, joy, and faith. Then what you are proud of concerning me would overflow in Jesus the Messiah because of my return to you.

Just live a life that is worthy of the Messiah's Message. That way, whether I come and see you or I am absent and hear of your experiences, you may stand firm in one spirit by striving together with one soul for faithfulness to the Message. Do not be intimidated by your opponents about anything. This is a sign of destruction for them but one of salvation for you. This sign is from God, because you have been granted to do two things on behalf of the Messiah—not only to believe in him but also to suffer for him, engaging in the same struggle that you saw going on with me earlier, which you hear is with me even now.

So if there is any comfort in the Messiah, any consolation offered by love, any partnership in the Spirit, or any affection or sympathy, complete my joy by having the same focus—the same love and unity in spirit, focusing on a single goal. Do nothing because of strife or worthless conceit. On the contrary, each person should humbly consider one another to be a higher priority than themselves. No one should focus on only their own ambitions but also on one another's. Share this mindset among you that was held by Jesus the Messiah:

> Although he was in the form of God,
> He decided that his equality with God was not something to claim.
> Instead, he emptied himself and took on the form of a servant.
> He came in the likeness of humanity.
> When he had appeared in the shape of man,
> He humbled himself by becoming obedient to the point of death—
> even death on a cross.
> So God has also lifted him up
> And has given him the name that is above every name
> So that every knee should bow at the name of Jesus—
> Whether they are in heaven, on earth, or under the earth—
> And that every tongue should confess that Jesus the Messiah is Master
> To the glory of God the Father.

So, my dearly loved ones, just as you have always obeyed (not only as you did when I came but much more now that I am absent), work out your own salvation with fear and trembling. You see, God is the one who operates in you so that you may want—and work—to please him!

Do everything without complaining or arguing so that you may be faultless and innocent—God's guiltless children in the middle of a crooked and corrupt generation! Among them you shine like lights in the world. Hold tightly to the Living Word so that I may have something to be proud of on the day of the Messiah—that I have not run or labored for nothing. Yes! Even if I am offered like a drink offering for a sacrificial service to your faith, I am glad to do it! I also congratulate all of you! So you also need to rejoice in this same thing and congratulate me.

Now I hope in Jesus the Master to send Timothy to you quickly so that I may be encouraged by knowing how you are doing. I have no one else like him who would be so sincerely interested in how you are doing. Everyone seeks their own welfare and not necessarily the welfare of Jesus the Messiah. But you are aware of his character—that he has served with me in the Message like a child with his father. So I hope to send him as soon as I see how things will turn out for me, but I am convinced in the Master that I will also come soon!

Now I considered it necessary to send you Epaphroditus. He is my brother, fellow worker, and fellow soldier, and he is your messenger and assistant to care for my needs. I considered it necessary to send him because he was longing for all of you and has been stressed because you heard that he has been sick. He was really sick—he nearly died! Yet God showed mercy to him (and not to him only—to me also so that I would not have grief upon grief). So I sent him to you with even more urgency so that when you see him, you may rejoice, and I may be free of that anxiety. So receive him in the Master with all joy, and hold all who are like him in high honor, because he came close to dying because of the Messiah's work and risked his life so that he could fully accomplish the assistance you were unable to give me.

Finally, my brothers, rejoice in the Master. Writing the same things to you is not something I hesitate to do—it is safer for you!

Watch out for dogs. Watch out for those who do evil things. Watch out for those who mutilate because we are the true circumcision—the ones who worship with God's Spirit and who take pride in Jesus the Messiah, rather than trusting in bodily circumcision. As a matter of fact, I also have reason to trust in bodily circumcision. If anyone thinks that someone else has a reason to trust in bodily circumcision, I have more reasons! I was circumcised on the eighth day. I was from the nation of Israel—the tribe of Benjamin. I was a Hebrew of Hebrews. As far as the Law is concerned, I was a Pharisee. As far as zeal is concerned, I persecuted the congregation. As far as the righteousness that is in the Law is concerned, I was faultless. But I have considered these things that were profitable for me to be worth losing because of the Messiah. As a matter of fact, I consider everything to be worth losing because of the more important knowledge of Jesus the Messiah, my Master. Because of him, I have cut my losses on all these things. I consider them to be garbage so that I can gain the Messiah and appear in him without having the "righteousness" that is based on the Law. Instead, I want the righteousness that comes through faith in the Messiah—the righteousness that is from God based on faith. I want to know him and the power of his resurrection. I want to take part in his suffering and be like him in his death so that I can somehow attain that resurrection from the dead!

It is not the case that I have already received it or that I have been made perfect. On the contrary, I pursue the resurrection so that I can make it mine (after all, it was because of the resurrection that Jesus the Messiah made me his). Brothers, I do not consider myself to have made it mine yet, but I do one thing: I forget those things that are behind me and reach forward to the things that are in front of me. Like a target, I pursue the prize of God's call to ascend in Jesus the Messiah. Whoever is mature among us needs to have this mindset. And if one of you thinks otherwise, God will reveal this same thing to you also. Nevertheless, we need to follow the rule that we have already reached.

Brothers, be imitators of me, and notice those who conduct themselves like the example that you have from us. As I have told you many times—I even weep now as I tell you again—many are conducting themselves as enemies of the Messiah's cross! As for those who think only of worldly things: their goal is destruction, their god is their belly, and their glory is in their shame! You see, our government is in heaven, from which also we wait for a savior—the Master, Jesus the Messiah. He will transform our humble bodies into the same form as his own glorious body by the strength that empowers him to subject everything to himself.

So, my dear brothers for whom I have a deep longing, my joy and crown: stand your ground in the Master like this, dear loved ones.

I beg Euodia and I beg Syntyche to have the same mindset in the Master. Yes, I ask you also, true friend, to help them because they (as well as Clement and the rest of my fellow workers whose names are in the Book of Life) have struggled together with me in the Message.

Always rejoice in the Master. I tell you again: rejoice. Let your tolerance be known to all men because the Master is near. Do not be worried about anything. On the contrary, make your requests known to God in every situation by prayer and pleading with thankfulness. Then God's peace, which surpasses all understanding, will guard your hearts and minds in Jesus the Messiah.

Finally, brothers, whatever is true, honorable, right, pure, delightful, or commendable—if there is any virtue or praise in it—think about these things. Practice what you have learned, received, heard, and seen in me, and the God of peace will be with you.

I rejoiced greatly in the Master that now you have finally revived your concern for me. Granted, you were concerned about me before, but you had no opportunity to help—not that I am saying this because I need something, because I have learned to be self-sufficient in any circumstance I am in. I know both how to deal with having little and with having an overflow. In any and all circumstances, I have learned the secret of living with being full or hungry—having an overflow or a need. I can endure all things because of the one who empowers me. Nevertheless, you have done well in sharing with me in my affliction.

Now, Philippians, you also know for yourselves that in my early dealings with the Message, when I went out from Macedonia, not a single congregation took part in the matter of give-and-take assistance except for you alone, because even in Thessalonica, time and again you sent to meet my need. It is not that I seek a gift—I seek the fruit that would increase to your account. I have everything and plenty of it—I have been made complete because of what I received from Epaphroditus that you sent—it was a fragrant offering and an acceptable sacrifice to God. My God will meet every one of your needs through Jesus the Messiah because of his glorious wealth. May the glory be to God our Father forever and ever, amen!

Greet all the saints in Jesus the Messiah. Those who are with me greet you. All the saints greet you, especially those who are in Caesar's household.

May the grace of the Master, Jesus the Messiah, be with your spirit!

TO THE COLOSSIANS

From Paul (an apostle of Jesus the Messiah through God's will) and my brother Timothy,
To the saints and faithful brothers in the Messiah who are in Colossae: may grace and peace be yours from God our Father!

WE ALWAYS THANK GOD—THE FATHER OF OUR MASTER, JESUS the Messiah—when we pray for you because we have heard of your faith in Jesus the Messiah. We have also heard of the love that you have for all the saints because of the hope that lies ahead for you in heaven. You heard about this earlier in the Word of truth—the Message that has come to you! Just as it bore fruit and grew throughout the world, it has done the same with you ever since the day you heard it and truly came to know God's grace. Just as you were taught this Message by Epaphras, our dear fellow servant (who is a faithful minister of the Messiah for your sake), he has also shown us your love in the Spirit.

Because of this, ever since we heard about your love, we also have not ceased to pray and ask for you, that you would be filled with the knowledge of his will in complete wisdom and spiritual understanding. We pray this so that you will live in a way that is worthy of the Master and that pleases him in every way because you are bearing fruit and growing in the knowledge of God with every good action. We pray that you will be empowered with complete strength through his glorious power so that you will be completely persistent and patient. We pray that with joy you will thank the Father, who has made you qualified for your part in the saints' inheritance in the light. He has rescued us from the power of darkness and has transferred us into the kingdom of his dear Son (in whom we have redemption: the forgiveness of our sins). The Son is the representation of the invisible God and the firstborn over all of creation because all the things that are in heaven and on earth were created in him, both visible and invisible things. Whether they are kingdoms, dominions, rulers, or authorities—all things have been created by him and for him. He has been in existence since before everything, and everything is held together in him. He is the head of the body (the congregation). He is the beginning—the firstborn from the dead—so that he will have first place in everything. You see, it pleased God that all his nature would dwell in him and that he would reconcile everything (whether on earth or in heaven) to himself through the Son. He made peace through the blood of his cross.

Also, to you who at one time were alienated and hostile in attitude, with evil actions: he has now reconciled you in his fleshly body by his death so that he could present you as being holy, guiltless, and blameless in his presence! This will happen only if you really continue to be founded and firm in the faith, without shifting from the hope offered by the Message that you heard, which has been preached to every creature under heaven and of which I, Paul, am a minister.

Now I rejoice in what I suffer for your sake, and I do my part to complete in my body what is left of the Messiah's affliction for the sake of his body (which is the congregation). I have become a minister of this congregation by an administration of God that was given to me for your benefit so that I could accomplish God's Word—the secret that was hidden from the ages and generations but has now been revealed to his saints. God wanted to make them aware of the glorious wealth of this secret among the nations. Here is the secret: the Messiah in us—the glorious hope! We proclaim him—warning everyone and teaching everyone with all wisdom so that we could present everyone as being complete in the Messiah. For this reason, I labor and struggle, depending on his power that is mightily at work in me.

You see, I want you to know how much of a struggle I have for your sake, for those who are in Laodicea, and for everyone who has not seen my face in person. I struggle so that by being united in love, their hearts will be encouraged to reach a wealth of assurance (which comes from understanding) and the knowledge of God's secret (the Messiah). In the Messiah, all the treasures of wisdom and knowledge are hidden. I am telling you this so that no one can deceive you with persuasive arguments. You see, even if I am absent in body, I am still with you in spirit—rejoicing and seeing your discipline and the firmness of your faith in the Messiah.

So since you have received Jesus the Messiah, our Master, conduct yourself in him by being rooted and built upon him by being strengthened in faith as you were taught to be, and by abounding in thanksgiving. Watch out that no one captures you with the philosophy and empty deceptions that are based on traditions of men—they are consistent with worldly principles, not the Messiah's. You see, all deity dwells in him—in his body—and you are completed in him. He is the head over all rule and authority. You have also been circumcised in him with a circumcision not performed by hand—by removing the body of the flesh by the Messiah's circumcision. This happened when you were buried with him in immersion, and in him you have also been raised through faith in the power of God, who raised him from the dead. As for you who were dead in your sins and your uncircumcised bodies, he has brought you back to life with the Messiah by forgiving us of all our sins and taking away the written record that was against us with its commands. He took it out of the way by nailing it to the cross. When he deposed the rulers and authorities, he displayed them confidently after he triumphed over them by the Messiah.

So do not let anyone condemn you in matters of food and drink or regarding a festival, new month, or Sabbath. These are shadows of what was to come—the Messiah's body. Do not let anyone pass judgment on you, insisting on false humility, worship of angels, and dwelling on visions. That person is pointlessly conceited by their physical mind and does not hold on to the head—from whom the whole body grows with God's growth by the joints and ligaments with which it is supplied and held together.

If you have died with the Messiah from the worldly principles, why do you submit to them as though you were still alive in the world? "Do not have contact." "Do not taste." "Do not touch." All these things are meant for destruction by being consumed, based on the commands and teachings of men. Such things have an appearance of wisdom, with self-made religion, false humility, and severe treatment of the body, but are of no value for satisfying the body's appetite.

So since you have been raised with the Messiah, seek those things that are above (where the Messiah is—seated at God's right hand). Think about those things that are above, not the things that are on the earth. You see, you have died, and your life is buried in God with the Messiah. When the Messiah appears (who is your life), then you also gloriously will be revealed with him!

So put to death whatever is worldly in your body: prohibited sexual practices, filthy behavior, passionate desire, evil lust, and greed (which is idolatry). Because of these, God's wrath is coming upon the sons of disobedience. You also lived with these actions at one time, when you were alive with them, but now you must put all of them away: wrath, rage, malice, slander, and ugly talk must be removed from your mouth. Do not lie to one another because you have taken off the old self with its practices and you have put on the new self, which is renewed in knowledge in the image of the one who created it. There is no Greek or Jew, circumcision or uncircumcision, foreigner, Scythian, slave, or free person. On the contrary, the Messiah is everything in every way!

So like God's holy and dear chosen ones, put on compassion, mercy, goodness, humility, gentleness, and patience. Put up with each other and forgive one another if anyone has a complaint against someone else. You must forgive to the same extent that the Master has forgiven you. On top of all these things, put on love, which is what holds these things together completely. Let the Messiah's peace be in control of your hearts (you were called into this peace in one body). Be thankful. Let the Messiah's Word richly dwell in you by teaching and warning one another with all wisdom and by singing psalms, hymns, and spiritual songs with thankfulness to God in your hearts. Whatever you do (in speech or action), do everything in the name of Jesus the Master, and give thanks to God the Father through him.

Wives, submit to your husbands as it is appropriate to do in the Master. Husbands, love your wives and do not be bitter toward them. Children, obey your parents in everything because this is pleasing to the Master. Fathers, do not provoke your children, or else they might get discouraged.

Slaves, obey your earthly masters in everything. Do not work just to impress them, like people-pleasers; instead, work with a sincere heart because you fear the Master. Whatever you do, work from your soul as though it is for the Master and not for men. You know that you will receive the reward—an inheritance—from the Master. Serve the Master—the Messiah—because the one who causes harm will receive the harm they have done as a repayment, and there is no favoritism! Masters, show fairness and equality with your slaves because you know that you also have a Master in heaven.

Devote yourselves constantly to prayer—be alert in it with thanksgiving. At the same time, pray for us, too, so that God would open the Word's door for us that we will speak the secret about the Messiah. Because of this secret, I am imprisoned, so pray that I will reveal it in the way I ought to speak. Live with wisdom toward those who are outside the congregation, and make the most of your time. Your speech must always be with grace and seasoned with salt so that you may know how you ought to answer everyone.

Tychicus, who is a dear brother, a faithful minister, and a fellow servant in the Master, will explain to you how everything is going with me. For that very reason (so that you would know of our affairs and that he could encourage your hearts), I have sent him to you with Onesimus, the faithful and dear brother. (He is one of you!) They will explain to you everything that is happening here.

Aristarchus (my fellow prisoner) greets you, and so do Mark (the cousin of Barnabas—you received a command about him: if he comes to you, receive him) and Jesus (who is called Justus). These are the only ones from the circumcision who are my fellow workers in God's kingdom. They have become a source of encouragement to me. Epaphras greets you (he is one of you—a servant of Jesus the Messiah). He always struggles for you in his prayers so that you will stand mature and complete in the whole will of God. You see, I can vouch for him, that he feels a lot of stress for your sake, those who are in Laodicea, and those who are in Hierapolis. Luke (the dear physician) and Demas greet you.

Greet the brothers who are in Laodicea, as well as Nympha and the congregation that meets in her house. When this letter has been read by you, make sure that it is read by the congregation in Laodicea and that you also read the letter from Laodicea. Also, tell Archippus, "See to it that you complete the ministry that you have received in the Master."

This greeting is by my hand: Paul. Remember my imprisonment. May grace be with you!

TO THE
THESSALONIANS (I)

From Paul, Silas, and Timothy,

To the congregation of Thessalonica that is in God the Father and the Master, Jesus the Messiah: grace and peace to you.

WE ALWAYS THANK GOD FOR ALL OF YOU AND MENTION YOU IN our prayers. We do not cease to remember your faithful work, your loving labor, and your hopeful persistence in our Master, Jesus the Messiah, in the presence of our God and Father. Brothers loved by God, we know your selection because our Message did not come to you by word alone, but by power, by the Holy Spirit, and with full assurance—you know what kind of people we were among you for your benefit!

You became imitators of us and of the Master because you received the Word with the joy of the Holy Spirit despite affliction. For this reason, you have become an example to all the believers who are in Macedonia and Achaia. The Word of the Master has rung out from you not just in Macedonia and Achaia—your faith toward God has gone out everywhere so that we do not even have to say anything about you. You see, they proclaim to us the kind of welcome we received from you—that you have turned to God from idols so that you could serve the living and true God and wait for his Son to return from heaven, whom God raised from the dead: Jesus, who is rescuing us from the wrath that is coming!

Brothers, you yourselves are aware of the welcome we received from you and that we did not come to you for no reason. But after we had already suffered and were mistreated—as you heard—because of our God, we had the courage in Philippi to speak God's Message to you despite great opposition. You see, our encouragement does not come from delusion, impure motives, or deception. On the contrary, since we were approved by God to be entrusted with the Message, we speak boldly like this to please God, who approves our hearts—not to please people! You see, we never came with flattering words—as you heard—or with greedy, underhanded motives. God is witness to this! We never sought glory from people—from you or anyone else—although we could have thrown our weight around as the Messiah's apostles. But we became like infants among you or like a nursing mother who cherishes her own children. Since we longed for you like this, we were happy to share not only God's Message with you but also our own lives because you have become dear to us. Now, brothers, you remember our labor and hardship—we worked night and day so that we could preach God's Message to you without being a burden to any of you. You are witnesses—and God is too—of how we behaved devoutly, fairly, and blamelessly with you who are faithful. You know just as well that we treated you as a father treats his children—we encouraged, comforted, and testified to you so that you would live worthy of the God who has called you into his own kingdom and glory.

So we also give thanks to God for this without ceasing because when you received God's Word (which you heard from us), you did not accept it as the message of men. On the contrary, you accepted it as it really is: God's Word—which is at work in you who are faithful. You see, brothers, in the Messiah you have become imitators of God's congregations that are in Judea because you have also suffered the very same things at the hands of your own countrymen as they have at the hands of the Jews. They also killed Jesus the Master and the prophets, and they persecuted us severely. They do not please God, and they are opposed to all people. They prevent us from speaking to the Gentiles so that they would be saved—to the extent that their sins are always full to the brim. So wrath will completely engulf them.

Now, brothers, we were made orphans by being separated from you for a short time—by face, not in heart. We have become especially eager with great desire to see your faces because we have wanted to come to you. I (Paul) tried once and again, but Satan has prevented us. Who is our hope, joy, or crown of glory in the presence of Jesus our Master when he comes? Is it not you? You see, you are our glory and joy!

So when we could not stand it anymore, we thought it would be good to remain in Athens alone. So we sent Timothy (our brother and fellow worker of God in the Message of the Messiah) so that he would strengthen and comfort you for the sake of your faith—so that no one would be deceived by these afflictions. You know for yourselves that we were appointed for this affliction because even when we were with you, we told you ahead of time that we were about to be afflicted. It has happened just like that, and you know it! Because of this, when I could not stand it anymore, I sent to know about your faith for fear that the Tempter had tempted you and that our labor was done for nothing.

But now Timothy has come from you to us and has announced to us your faith and love—that you always have mentioned something good about us. You long to see us as much as we long to see you! Brothers, because of this, we are encouraged about you despite every one of our needs and afflictions, because of your faith. Now we can live without worry as long you stand firm in the Master. You see, how could we give enough thanks to God for you? We rejoice with all kinds of joy in the presence of our God because of you! Night and day, we pray as earnestly as possible that we can see your faces and restore what is lacking in your faith.

Our Father God himself and Jesus our Master prepared our way to you. Now may the Master cause you to increase and overflow in love for one another and for everyone just as we also have this kind of love for you! May your hearts be strengthened with holiness so that you may be blameless in the presence of our God and Father when Jesus our Master comes with all his holy ones—amen!

Finally, brothers, you received from us how you should live and please God—which you are doing. We ask and encourage you in Jesus the Master to increase in this even more because you know the kind of charge we gave you by Jesus the Master. You see, this is God's will: your holiness—you need to stay away from prohibited sexual practices! Each of you needs to know how to take control of your own body with holiness and honor—not with lustful passion as the Gentiles (who do not know God) behave. You need to refrain from wronging and cheating your brother in matters because the Master is the avenger of these things, just as we already told you and testified to you. You see, God has not called us for filthy behavior, but instead with holiness. So if someone disregards this, they do not disregard man. On the contrary, they disregard God, who gave his Holy Spirit to you.

Now you do not need anyone to write to you about brotherly love because you have been taught by God to love one another. You even do this toward all your brothers in the whole region of Macedonia. So, brothers, we encourage you to increase in this even more. We encourage you to consider it an honor to be agreeable, mind your own business, and work with your own hands, as we directed you to do. Do this so that you may behave decently toward those who are outside the faith and that you may have no need of anything.

Now, brothers, we do not want you to be uninformed about those who have fallen asleep so that you do not grieve like the rest of the world, which does not have hope. Since we believe that Jesus died and was raised from the dead, in the same way (through Jesus) God will also bring with him those who have fallen asleep. You see, we are telling you this by the Master's Word: those of us who live and remain until the Master comes will not by any means precede those who have fallen asleep. You see, the Master himself will come down from heaven with a cry of command—with the voice of an archangel and God's trumpet—and those who are dead in the Messiah will rise first. Then those of us who are alive and remain will be taken up together with them in the clouds to meet the Master in the air. In this way, we will always be with the Master! So encourage one another with these words.

Now, brothers, you do not need anyone to write to you about the times and seasons when this will happen. You know very well that the day of the Master is coming like a thief in the night. Whenever they say, "Peace and safety," sudden destruction will engulf them as birth pangs engulf a pregnant woman, and they will not escape! However, brothers, you are not in darkness so that the day would surprise you like a thief. You are all sons of light and sons of the day. We are not sons of night or darkness. So we must not sleep like the rest of the world. On the contrary, let us watch and take control of ourselves. Those who sleep do so at night, and those who are drunk get drunk at night. Yet since we are of the day, let us take control of ourselves by being empowered with the breastplate of faith and love and the helmet of salvation's hope. You see, God has not set us aside for wrath, but to obtain salvation through our Master, Jesus the Messiah. He died for us so that, whether we are watching or have fallen asleep, we will live with him together. So encourage one another and edify one another just as you are doing.

Now, brothers, we are asking you to honor those who labor among you, direct you in the Master, and admonish you. Respect them with as much love as possible because of their work. Keep the peace among yourselves. Brothers, we encourage you to admonish those who are disorderly, cheer up those who are discouraged, take interest in those who are weak, and be patient with everyone. See to it that no one repays an evil action for another evil action. On the contrary, always pursue what is good for one another and for everyone.

Always rejoice. Do not cease to pray. Give thanks in every circumstance. This is God's will for you in Jesus the Messiah. Do not put out the Spirit's fire. Do not reject prophecies as unimportant; on the contrary, test everything. Hold tightly to what is good, and stay away from every kind of evil.

May the God of peace himself make you completely holy in every way. May he keep your spirit and life intact, and may he keep your body blameless in the coming of our Master, Jesus the Messiah. The one who calls you is faithful, and he will do this!

Brothers, pray for us too.

Greet all the brothers with a holy kiss. I put you under oath by the Master to read this letter to all the brothers.

May the grace of our Master, Jesus the Messiah, be with you.

TO THE
THESSALONIANS (II)

From Paul, Silas, and Timothy,
To the congregation of Thessalonians that is in God the Father and the Master, Jesus the Messiah: grace and peace to you from God our Father and the Master, Jesus the Messiah.

WE ALWAYS OUGHT TO GIVE THANKS TO GOD FOR YOU, brothers. It is right to do this because your faith has grown explosively, and the love of each and every one of you for one another has abundantly increased. So we ourselves express our pride in you to God's congregations because of your persistence in all the persecutions and afflictions that you endure. This is proof of God's fair judgment. (This is so that you will be worthy of God's kingdom, for which you are suffering!) Indeed, it is right for God to repay those who afflict you by afflicting them and to grant relief with us to you who are being afflicted. This will happen when Jesus the Master is revealed from heaven with his mighty angels. He will execute vengeance with blazing fire on those who do not know God and do not obey the Good Message of our Master Jesus. They will pay the penalty (eternal destruction from the presence of the Master and from his glorious power) when he comes on that day with his holy ones to be glorified and held in awe by those who believe—because our testimony was believed by you. We are also praying for you for this reason: so that our God may make you worthy of the calling and powerfully fill you with every good blessing and faithful work so that the name of Jesus our Master may be glorified among you, and that you may be glorified in him according to the grace of our God and the Master, Jesus the Messiah.

Now, brothers, in reference to the coming of our Master, Jesus the Messiah, and our assembling with him, we beg you not to be shaken too easily from your composure. Do not become frightened by anything—whether it is a spirit, a message, or a letter claiming to be from us—that seems to say that the day of the Master has already come. Do not let anyone deceive you in any way! This will not happen unless the falling away happens first and the wicked man is revealed. He is the son of destruction, who opposes and lifts himself above everything that is called a god or is worshiped. He even takes his seat in God's temple to display himself to be a god. Do you not remember that I said this when I was still with you? Even now, you know who is restraining him until he is to be revealed at his own time. You see, the wicked secret is already at work, but he is restraining him until he gets out of the way. Then the wicked one will be revealed, and the Master will kill him with the breath from his mouth and destroy him when it is revealed that he has come. His coming is fueled by Satan's power with every miracle, sign, and lying wonder and with every unrighteous deception shown to those who are going to be destroyed. They did not accept the love of the truth in place of these deceptions, or else they would have been saved. Because of this, God is sending them this deceptive power that leads them to believe a lie so that everyone who does not believe the truth and is happy with unrighteousness may be condemned.

But we always ought to give thanks to God for you, our brothers loved by the Master, because God has selected you to be among the first to be saved by the Holy Spirit and true faith. He called you into this salvation by our Message so that you may obtain the glory of our Master, Jesus the Messiah. So, brothers, stand firm and hold on to the traditions that you have been taught whether you were taught them by a message or by our letter.

Now may the Master himself—Jesus the Messiah—and God our Father—who loved us and gave us eternal comfort and a good hope by his grace—may they comfort and strengthen your hearts with every good action and word.

Finally, brothers, pray for us so that the Master's Word may run and be glorified in the same way as it was with you. Also, pray that we will be rescued from insubordinate and evil men because not everyone has faith. But the Master is faithful, and he will strengthen you and protect you from the evil one. Also, we are convinced in the Master about you that you will both do and accomplish what we are telling you to do. Now may the Master direct your hearts to have love for God and endurance for the Messiah.

We are directing you now in the name our Master, Jesus the Messiah, to stay away from every brother who behaves inappropriately and does not follow the tradition that he received from us. You know for yourselves that you must imitate us because we did not behave inappropriately among you. We did not eat bread from anyone for free, either. On the contrary, we worked night and day with toil and trouble so that we would not be a burden to any of you. Not that we do not have the right—but we did this so that we may give ourselves to you as an example. Even when we were with you, we gave you this command: whoever does not want to work must not eat. You see, we hear that some are behaving inappropriately—not working, but instead getting into other people's business. Now we command and encourage these people in the Master, Jesus the Messiah, that they work silently and eat their own bread. And as for you, brothers, do not get discouraged from doing what is good. Yet if someone does not listen to the message delivered by letter, take note of them so that you do not associate with them so that they may be ashamed. But do not think of them as an enemy; on the contrary, admonish them like a brother.

May the Master of Peace himself give you peace everywhere through everything. May the Master be with all of you! This is the greeting by my own hand (Paul). It is a sign in every letter—I write like this. May the grace of our Master, Jesus the Messiah, be with all of you!

TO
TIMOTHY (I)

From Paul, an apostle of Jesus the Messiah by the command of God our Savior and Jesus the Messiah, our blessed hope,

To Timothy, my true child in the faith: grace, mercy, and peace from God our Father and our Master, Jesus the Messiah.

AS I ENCOURAGED YOU WHEN I WENT TO MACEDONIA, REMAIN IN Ephesus so that you may command people not to teach a different doctrine. Also, teach them not to pay attention to myths or endless genealogies, which cause meaningless speculations rather than accomplishing God's plan, which comes by faith. Now the target of our command is love—which comes from a pure heart, a good conscience, and a sincere faith. By missing the point of these, some people have turned instead to worthless talking. They want to become teachers of the Law, but they do not understand what they are saying or anything that they confidently claim.

Now we know that the Law is good if someone uses it correctly. Yet we know that the Law does not exist for a righteous person's sake, but for those who are wicked, inappropriate, irreverent, sinners, unholy, profane; it is for those who are murderers of their fathers, mothers, and others—those who participate in prohibited sexual practices, homosexuality, slave trading, lying, oath-breaking, and in anything else that is against the healthy teaching that is based on the glorious Message of our blessed God, with which I have been entrusted.

I am thankful to Jesus the Messiah, our Master, who has empowered me because he considered me trustworthy and placed me into the ministry. Earlier I was a blasphemer, a persecutor, and a violent person, but I have received mercy because I unknowingly acted faithlessly. The grace of our Master overflowed with the faith and love that is in the Messiah. This statement is faithful and is worth being completely accepted: Jesus the Messiah came into the world to save sinners—I am a prime example of this! But this is why I was shown mercy: so that by using me, Jesus the Messiah could demonstrate the fullest extent of patience as a prototype of those who would come to believe in him, resulting in eternal life for them. Now to the eternal King—who is the immortal, invisible, and only God—may there be honor and glory forever and ever, amen!

My son Timothy, I have set this command before you according to the prophecies that were spoken before you came along. I did this so that you may use them to fight the good fight and to have faith and a good conscience. Some have rejected a good conscience and have suffered shipwreck regarding that faith (including Hymenaeus and Alexander, whom I have delivered to Satan so that they would learn not to blaspheme).

So first of all, I encourage petitions, prayers, intercessions, and thanks to be offered for all people. Offer them for kings and all of those who are in places of authority so that we can live our lives in peace and quiet with complete godliness and reverence. This is good and pleasing in the eyes of God our Savior—He wants all people to be saved and come to know the truth. You see, there is one God, and one mediator between God and people—the man Jesus, the Messiah! He gave himself to be the ransom for everyone so that he could be their testimony when their time comes. For this reason, I have been appointed as a preacher and an apostle. I am telling you the truth—I am not lying! I am a teacher of the nations in faith and truth!

So I want men everywhere to pray, lifting up hands that are holy, without anger or arguing. Likewise, women must dress themselves in respectable clothing, with modesty and decency rather than in braids, gold, pearls, or expensive clothing. They need to wear what is proper for women who claim to have reverence for God by doing what is good. A woman must learn silently with total obedience. Now I do not allow a woman to teach or have authority over a man. On the contrary, she is to be silent. You see, Adam was formed first, and Eve was next. Also, Adam was not deceived, but the woman was deceived and went into sin. Yet she will be saved through her bearing of children if she remains in faith, love, and holiness, with self-control.

This statement is faithful: if anyone aspires to be an overseer, he wants to do a good thing. So an overseer must be guiltless, the husband of one wife, levelheaded, sensible, respectable, hospitable, able to teach. He must not be addicted to wine or intimidating. Instead, he should be kind and not argumentative or greedy. He must manage his own household well and have children who are obedient, and he must manage his household with complete reverence. If he does not know how to manage his own household, how can he possibly take care of God's congregation? He must not be a recent convert, or else he may become conceited and fall into condemnation by the devil. Now he must be held in good reputation by those who are outside the congregation, or else he may fall into disgrace and the devil's trap.

Deacons must also be respectable, not two-faced, addicted to excessive wine, or shamelessly greedy. They must hold on to the secret of the faith with a pure conscience. They should be examined first, and then they should serve as deacons if they are blameless. Their wives must also be respectable, not slanderous; they must be levelheaded and faithful in everything. Deacons must each be the husband of one wife and must manage their children and household well because those who serve well as deacons gain a good rank for themselves and a lot of confidence by the faith that is in Jesus the Messiah.

Although I am hoping to come to you soon, I have written these things to you in case I am delayed so that you may know how you must conduct yourself in God's household—which is the living God's congregation, a column and foundation of the truth. Without a doubt, the secret of godliness is great!

> He was revealed in the body,
> Justified by the Spirit,
> Seen by angels,
> Preached among the nations,
> Believed in by the world,
> Received with majesty!

Now the Spirit specifically says that in later times some will fall away from the faith by holding on to deceiving spirits and demonic teachings. They will tell lies hypocritically, and their consciences will be seared. They will forbid others to marry and force them to stay away from certain foods—foods that God created for those who are faithful and know the truth so that they could receive it with thanksgiving. You see, everything God created is good, and it is not to be rejected if it is received with thanksgiving; it is purified by God's Word and prayer!

Lay these things out before the brothers so that you may be a good minister of Jesus the Messiah, because you are trained by the words of faith and good teaching that you follow. Reject profanity and the myths that are shared by the older women, and train yourself for godliness. You see, physical training has some benefit, but godliness is beneficial for everything because it contains promise for this life and the one to come! The statement is faithful and worthy to be accepted in full: it is for this purpose that we labor and struggle because we've set our hope in the living God who is the Savior of all men—especially those who are faithful!

Command and teach these things. Do not let anyone look down on you because of your youthfulness. Instead, be an example of those who are faithful by your speech, conduct, love, faith, and purity. Devote yourself to reading, encouragement, and teaching until I come. Do not neglect the gift that is in you, which was given to you through prophecy and was accompanied by the elders laying their hands on you. Put these things to practice and devote yourself to them so that your progress will be evident to everyone. Be very observant of yourself and your teaching, and stay with these things; by doing this, you will save both yourself and those who will listen to you.

Do not rebuke an older man; instead, encourage him like a father, and encourage younger men like brothers. With complete purity, encourage older women like mothers and younger women like sisters.

Honor widows who are genuine widows. But if any widow has children or grandchildren, those children need to learn to show respect for their own household first by repaying their parents. This is pleasing in God's sight. Now a genuine widow who has been left alone has set her hope in God and continues in her petitions and prayers night and day; but one who lives luxuriously is dead even while she is alive. Command these things so that they will be guiltless. Yet if someone does not provide for their own relatives—especially those of their household—they have denied the faith and are worse than a nonbeliever. A widow is to be selected for assistance if she is at least sixty years old and was the wife of one husband. She must be approved based on the good things she has done—whether she has cared for children, shown hospitality, washed the feet of saints, helped those who were afflicted, or devoted herself to do every good thing she could do. Refuse assistance for younger widows because when they run wild and leave the Messiah, they want to marry and they obtain condemnation because they have disregarded their former faith. Meanwhile, they learn to be lazy, wandering from house to house. Not only do they become lazy, but also they gossip and become nosy—talking about inappropriate things. So I want younger women to marry, raise children, manage their houses, and not give a single opportunity for an adversary to insult them. You see, some have already turned away to follow Satan. If any faithful women have relatives who are widows, these need to take care of them so that the congregation is not burdened—then it can take care of those who are really widows.

Elders who preside well as elders deserve twice as much honor, especially those who labor in the Word and teaching. You see, the Scripture says, "Do not muzzle an ox that is threshing grain," and "the one who works deserves their wages." Do not accept an accusation against an elder unless it is based on the testimony of two or three witnesses. Reprimand sinners in front of everyone so that the rest of them may be afraid. I am begging you before God, Jesus the Messiah, and the chosen angels that you keep these things without discriminating—do nothing out of partiality. Do not hurry to lay your hands on anyone, and do not participate in the sins of others—keep yourself pure. Do not drink only water anymore. Instead, take a little wine because of your stomach and your chronic sickness.

Some people's sins are obvious and precede them all the way to their condemnations, but other sins appear later. In the same way, good actions are obvious, and even if they are not, they will not remain hidden.

All who are slaves under a burden need to consider their masters to be deserving of complete honor so that God's name and the teaching are not blasphemed. Those who have faithful masters must not despise them because they are their brothers. On the contrary, they must serve even more because the ones who receive the benefit of their service are faithful and dear.

Teach and encourage these things. If anyone teaches something different and does not continue to be healthy in the words of our Master, Jesus the Messiah, and in the teaching that is based on godliness, they are conceited and know nothing. No, they have a sickness—arguments and fighting about semantics. These are the source of envy, strife, slander, evil suspicions, and constant friction among people whose minds are corrupted and are without the truth. These people think godliness is a way to make a profit! But godliness is a great profit if it is coupled with satisfaction. You see, we have brought nothing into the world, and we cannot bring anything out of it either. So when we have food and something with which we may cover ourselves, we should be satisfied. But these people who want to become rich fall into temptation, a trap, and many foolish and hurtful desires that plunge people into death and destruction. You see, greed is a root of all kinds of evil, and when some people stretch themselves thin for it, they wander from the faith and impale themselves with many painful things.

But man of God, you need to run away from these things. Instead, pursue righteousness, godliness, faith, love, persistence, and gentleness. Fight faith's good fight; take hold of the eternal life into which you were called when you made the good confession in front of many witnesses. I command you in the presence of God (who gives life to everything) and Jesus the Messiah (who testified to the good confession in front of Pontius Pilate) to keep this command faultlessly and guiltlessly until our Master, Jesus the Messiah, appears. The Blessed One, the only Master, will display him at the proper time. He is the King of Kings and the Master of Masters and is the only one who has immortality. He dwells in unapproachable light that no one has ever seen—no one can even see it! To him be honor and power forever, amen!

I command those who are wealthy in this present age not to think too highly of themselves or to set their hope in uncertain wealth. On the contrary, they must set their hope in God (who richly grants us everything for our enjoyment), do what is good, be rich in good actions, and be generous and sharing so that they will store up for themselves a good foundation for the age that is to come so that they will receive eternal life.

Timothy, guard the deposit by turning away from the worthless chatter and contradictions that are based on what is falsely called knowledge. Some who have claimed to be experts in knowledge have missed the point as far as the faith is concerned.

May grace be with you!

TO TIMOTHY (II)

From Paul, an apostle of Jesus the Messiah through God's will, because of the promise of life that is in Jesus the Messiah,

To Timothy, my dear child: grace, mercy, and peace from God our Father and Jesus the Messiah, our Master.

I GIVE THANKS TO GOD (WHOM I HAVE SERVED WITH A PURE conscience since before I was born) as I mention you unceasingly in my prayers—night and day. I long to see you because I remember the tears you shed so that my joy could be complete. I remember the faith that is in you, which first dwelled in your grandmother Lois and your mother, Eunice. I am convinced that it is in you too. For this reason, I am reminding you to rekindle God's gift that is in you from when I laid my hands on you. You see, God has not given us a cowardly spirit, but rather, a Spirit of power, love, and sensibility. So do not be ashamed of our Master's testimony or of me, his prisoner. On the contrary, share in suffering for the Good Message through God's power. He saved us and called us with a holy calling—not because of our actions, but because of his own purpose and grace, which he gave us in Jesus the Messiah before the world began. This purpose has now been revealed through the unveiling of our Savior, Jesus the Messiah, who not only destroyed the power of death but also brought life and immortality to light through the Message. Because of this Message, I have been appointed as a preacher, apostle, and teacher. It is also for this Message that I suffer, but I am not ashamed. You see, I know the one I have believed, and I am convinced that he can guard my deposit until that day. Hold on to the pattern of healthy words that you heard from me, with the faith and love that are in Jesus the Messiah. Guard that good deposit through the Holy Spirit who dwells in us.

You know this, but everyone in Asia has rejected me, including Phygelus and Hermogenes. May the Master grant grace to the household of Onesiphorus; he has often refreshed me, and he has not been ashamed of my chains. On the contrary, he diligently looked for me—and found me—when he came to Rome. May the Master grant that he finds mercy from the Master on that day! He has been of service to everyone in Ephesus, as you very well know.

So, my child, you need to be empowered by the grace that is in Jesus the Messiah. Set what you have heard from me through many witnesses before faithful men who will be capable of teaching others. Share in suffering as a good soldier of Jesus the Messiah. No one who has become a soldier becomes wrapped up in matters of civilian life, so that he can please his enlisting officer. Also, anyone who competes in athletics does not win unless he competes by the rules. It is necessary for the one who works the ground to have a share of the first produce from it. Pay attention to what I am saying because the Master will give you understanding in everything.

Remember Jesus the Messiah, who, according to the Good Message I have, was raised from the dead and was from the lineage of David. Because of the Good Message, I suffer—even to the point of being tied up like a criminal. But God's Word is not tied up! Because of this, I endure everything for the benefit of the chosen ones so that with eternal glory they can obtain the salvation that is in Jesus the Messiah. This statement is faithful:

> If we have died with him, we will also live with him.
> If we endure, we will also reign with him.
> If we deny him, he will also deny us.
> If we are faithless, he remains faithful because he cannot deny himself.

Remind them of these things, and solemnly urge them before God not to argue over semantics. These arguments have no benefit and cause the ruin of those who hear them. Be diligent to present yourself to God acceptably—as a worker with no reason to be ashamed, who does not waver when it comes to the Word of Truth. But avoid pointless and worthless chatter because it will develop into more irreverence. Its message will spread like cancer. Hymenaeus and Philetus are examples of this. They have missed the point of the truth by saying that the resurrection has already taken place—they are destroying some people's faith! Yet God's firm foundation remains standing. It contains this seal: "The Master knows those who belong to him," as well as "Everyone who calls on the Master's name must keep away from unrighteousness." In a large house, there are not only gold and silver containers but also wooden and earthenware containers. Also, some containers are for honorable purposes, and some are for ordinary purposes. So whoever thoroughly cleanses themselves from these sins will be a container for honorable use—one that is purified and pleasing to the Master—and they will be ready to do everything that is good. Run away from the desires typical of young people, and—with those who call on the Master's name from a pure heart—pursue righteousness, faith, love, and peace. Avoid foolish and uneducated speculations because you know that they breed arguments. It is necessary for a servant of the Master not to be argumentative. Instead, he must be gentle with everyone, able to teach, and tolerant, and he must courteously instruct those who disagree with him. Perhaps God will grant them repentance so that they will come to understand the truth. Then those who have been captured by the devil to do his bidding would come to their senses and escape his trap.

Know this: in later days, difficult times will come. You see, men will become selfish, greedy, boastful, arrogant, slanderous, disobedient to their parents, ungrateful, unholy, heartless, unwilling to compromise, condemning, uncontrolled, savage, unconcerned about the common good, traitors, reckless, and conceited. They will love pleasure instead of God. They have a form of godliness, but they deny its power. Avoid these kinds of people, because from them come those who slip into houses and deceive foolish women who are overwhelmed with sins and led by various kinds of desire. They are always learning, but they can never come to an understanding of the truth. In the same way that Jannes and Jambres opposed Moses, these people also oppose the truth. They are people whose minds are corrupt—they have failed as far as faith is concerned. But they will not progress any further because their foolishness will be obvious to everyone, just as the foolishness of Jannes and Jambres became obvious.

But you have faithfully followed my teaching, conduct, purpose, faith, patience, love, persistence, persecutions, and suffering, such as what happened to me at Antioch, Iconium, and Lystra—what persecutions I have endured! Yet the Master has rescued me from all of them. Indeed, all who want to live godly lives in Jesus the Messiah will be persecuted, and evil men and swindlers will go from bad to worse—deceiving and being deceived. But you must continue in the things you have learned, which have been entrusted to you. Do this because you know the people from whom you learned them and because from the time you were a baby you have known the Holy Scriptures. They can make you wise so that you may be saved through the faith that is in Jesus the Messiah. Every scripture is inspired by God and is useful for teaching, rebuke, correction, and education in righteousness so that God's man may be competent and equipped to do everything that is good.

In the presence of God and Jesus the Messiah, who is going to judge the living and the dead, I solemnly urge you—based on his appearance and his kingdom—to preach the Word. Be ready, whether it is convenient or inconvenient. Reprimand, warn, and encourage with complete patience and teaching. You see, the time will come when they will not put up with healthy teaching. On the contrary, they will accumulate many teachers because of their own desires—they have itching ears. Then they will turn away from the truth—they will turn aside to myths. But you need to control yourself in every way, bear hardship, do the work of an evangelist, and complete your ministry.

You see, I am already being poured out as an offering, and the time of my departure is about to come. I have fought the good fight; I have finished the race; I have kept the faith. Beyond that, the crown of righteousness is reserved for me. The Master (the righteous judge) will give it to me on that day—and not only to me. He will also give it to everyone who has loved his appearance.

Do your best to come to me in a hurry. You see, Demas has abandoned me and has gone to Thessalonica because he loved the present world. Crescens has gone to Galatia, and Titus has gone to Dalmatia. Luke is the only one with me. Bring Mark along with you because he seems to be useful to me for ministry. I have sent Tychicus to Ephesus. When you come, bring the cloak and the scrolls—especially the parchments—that I left with Carpus in Troas. Alexander the metalworker did a lot of harm to me. The Master will repay him based on his actions. You also should avoid him because he was very opposed to our words.

At my first defense hearing, no one stood by me. On the contrary, everyone abandoned me. May it not be counted against them! But the Master was with me and empowered me so that my preaching could be finished, that all the nations could hear, and that I could be rescued from the lion's mouth. The Master will rescue me from every evil action, and he will preserve me for his heavenly kingdom. To him be the glory forever and ever, amen!

Greet Priscilla, Aquila, and the household of Onesiphorus. Erastus stayed in Corinth, and I left Trophimus in Miletus because he was sick. Eubulus, Pudens, Linus, Claudia, and all the

brothers greet you.
May the Master be with your spirit! May grace be with you all!

TO
TITUS

From Paul, God's servant, an apostle of Jesus the Messiah for the benefit of the faith of God's chosen ones and the knowledge of the truth that is based on godliness, because of the hope of eternal life, which God (who cannot lie) promised before the world began. He revealed his message at the proper time using preaching, and I was entrusted with this word by the command of God our Savior.

To Titus, my true child because of our common faith: grace and peace from God our Father and Jesus the Messiah, our Savior.

I LEFT YOU IN CRETE FOR THIS REASON: THAT YOU COULD SET right what is out of order and appoint elders in every city as I directed you to do. An elder must be blameless; he must have one wife, as well as faithful children who are not guilty of being reckless or rebellious. You see, it is necessary that an overseer should be blameless as one of God's administrators—not stubborn, hot-tempered, or addicted to wine, not intimidating or shamelessly greedy. On the contrary, he must be hospitable, love what is good, and be sensible, fair, pure, and self-controlled. He must hold tightly to the Message in accordance with the doctrine of faith so that he can be able to encourage with healthy teaching and reprimand those who oppose it.

You see, there are many—especially those who are from the circumcision party—who are disobedient, who talk idly and mislead. It is necessary to silence them because such people destroy entire houses by teaching things that they should not teach just for the sake of shameful profit. One of their own prophets said, "Cretans are always liars, evil beasts, and lazy gluttons." This testimony is true. Because of this, reprimand them severely so that they may be correct with regard to the faith and not hold on to Jewish myths and human commands by rejecting the truth. Everything is clean to those who are clean. But nothing is clean to those who are filthy and unfaithful. On the contrary, even their minds and consciences are filthy! They claim to know God, but they deny him by what they do. They have become disgusting and disobedient—unfit for any good work.

On the other hand, you need to say what is fitting for healthy teaching. Tell the older men to be levelheaded, respectable, sensible, and healthy with regard to faith, love, and patience.

Likewise, tell the older women to be reverent in their behavior—not gossipers or enslaved to excessive wine, but instead teachers of what is good so that they can mentor the younger women to be affectionate toward their husbands and children, to be sensible and pure, carry out household responsibilities, be good, and submit to their husbands, so that God's Word is not blasphemed. Likewise, encourage younger men to be sensible. Present yourself as an example of good actions in everything. Be pure in your teaching, be respectful, and use healthy speech that cannot be condemned so that whoever opposes us will be put to shame because they have nothing bad to say about us. Tell servants to be submissive to their masters in everything, to do satisfactory work without opposition, and not to embezzle their property. On the contrary, they should demonstrate perfectly good faith so that in everything they may do justice to the teaching of God our Savior.

You see, God's saving grace has appeared to all men. It teaches us to live in a way that is sensible, fair, and godly in this current world by saying no to irreverence and worldly desires. It teaches us to look forward to the blessed fulfillment of our hope—the glorious appearance of our great God and Savior, Jesus the Messiah! He gave himself for us so that he could redeem us from all our offenses and purify a chosen nation for himself that is zealous for good things to do. Say these things to them. Encourage and reprimand them with all authority. Let no one look down on you.

Remind them to be submissive to rulers and authorities, to obey them, and to be ready for every good work. Remind them not to slander anyone or be argumentative, to be tolerant, and to display total humility toward all men. You see, at one time, we also were foolish, disobedient, and deceived, and we served various kinds of desires and pleasures. We spent our lives in wickedness and jealousy; we were despicable and hated one another. But when that goodness and love of mankind appeared from God our Savior, it was not based on actions that we had done with righteousness. On the contrary, he saved us because of his mercy by the cleansing ritual that brought about the rebirth and renewal of the Holy Spirit. He richly poured out this Spirit over us through our Savior, Jesus the Messiah, so that after we had been justified by that grace, we could become heirs with reference to the hope of eternal life.

The saying is trustworthy, and I want you to insist on these things so that those who have set their hope in God may pay attention and show concern for doing good things. This is good and beneficial to other people. But you must avoid foolish controversies, genealogies, strife, and arguments about the Law, because these are useless and worthless. Dismiss a divisive person after the first and second warnings, understanding that this kind of person is twisted. They are sinning and condemning themselves.

When I send Artemus or Tychicus to you, hurry to come to me in Nicopolis, because I have decided to spend the winter there. Send Zenas the lawyer and Apollos on their way in a hurry so that they may lack nothing. May our people learn to show concern for doing good things—to meet urgent needs so that they are not unproductive!

All who are with me greet you. Greet those who consider us friends in the faith.

May grace be with all of you!

TO PHILEMON

From Paul—a prisoner of Jesus the Messiah—and Brother Timothy,

To Philemon, our dear friend and fellow worker; Apphia, our sister; Archippus, our fellow soldier; and the congregation that meets in your house: grace and peace to you from God our Father and the Master, Jesus the Messiah.

I ALWAYS THANK MY GOD WHEN I MENTION YOU IN MY PRAYERS AS I hear of the love and faith that you have toward Jesus the Master and for all the saints. I pray that your faithful fellowship may become powerful by a recognition of everything that is good among us, for the benefit of the Messiah. You see, I have had a lot of joy and encouragement on account of your love because the emotions of the saints have been given rest by you, brother!

So although I had enough confidence to command you to do what is right, I am instead begging you out of love, since I, Paul, am an old man and now also a prisoner of Jesus the Messiah. I am begging you about my child, whom I fathered in my imprisonment: Onesimus. At one time, he was useless to you, but now he is useful both to you and me. I sent him—that is, my own heart—back to you. I wanted to keep him with me so that, on your behalf, he could take care of me in my imprisonment because of the Message. But I did not want to do anything without your knowledge so that your good behavior could be done willingly rather than because of pressure. Perhaps this is why he left you for a short time—so you could have him back eternally. Do not consider him to be a servant anymore but more than a servant—as a dear brother! He is especially dear to me, but how much more he must be to you, both physically and in the Master!

So if you consider me to be a partner, receive him as you would me. If he has hurt you or owes you anything, charge it to my account. I, Paul, wrote this with my own hand—I will pay you whatever he owes, not to mention that you still owe yourself to me. Yes, brother, do me a favor in the Master—give my emotions rest in the Messiah!

Convinced that you will obey, I have written to you because I know that you will do even beyond what I tell you to do. Meanwhile, prepare me a place to stay because I hope that through your prayers I will be released to you!

Epaphras (my fellow prisoner in Jesus the Messiah) greets you, as do Mark, Aristarchus, Demas, and Luke (my fellow workers).

May the grace of the Master, Jesus the Messiah, be with your spirit!

THE
WORD

*THE GENERAL
LETTERS*

TO THE
HEBREWS

LONG AGO, IN VARIOUS PIECES AND BY VARIOUS MEANS, GOD spoke to our fathers by the prophets. At the end of those days, he spoke to us by the Son, whom he appointed as heir of all things, and through whom he also made the world:

> He is a shining source of glory
> And a stamped impression of God's nature,
> And he sustains all things by his powerful word.
> After accomplishing the cleansing of sins,
> He sat at the right hand of majesty in the highest heaven,
> Having become better than the angels to the same extent
> that he inherited a name that was far more excellent than theirs.

For example, to which of the angels did God ever say, "You are my son; I have become your Father today"? And also, "I will be 'Father' to him, and he will be 'Son' to me"?

And when the Firstborn entered the world, God said, "Let all of God's angels worship him!"

Again he says, regarding the angels, "He is the one who makes his angels spirits and his servants flaming fire."

Yet regarding the Son:

> Your throne, God, is forever and ever,
> And the scepter of your kingdom is the scepter of righteousness.
> You have loved righteousness and hated wickedness.
> Because of this, God—your God—has anointed you
> with an oil of gladness instead of your companions.

Also:

> In the beginning, Master, you laid the earth's foundation,
> And the heavens are the work of your hands.
> They will be destroyed, but you will remain,
> And all will age like clothing,
> And you will roll them up like a cloak.
> They will even be changed like clothing;

But you—you are the same, and your years do not cease.

But has he ever said to any of the angels, "Sit at my right hand until I put your enemies under your feet like a footrest"? Are they not all spirits given a service to perform, sent for ministry on account of those who are going to inherit salvation?

Because of this, it's abundantly necessary for us to take care to do the things we have heard—else we drift away. For if the word that was spoken by the angels was confirmed, and every breach of law and disobedience received a just repayment, how shall we escape if we are careless about such a great salvation, which was first spoken by the Master and has been confirmed to us by those who heard him while at the same time God was testifying, both with signs, wonders, and various miracles and with distributions of the Holy Spirit, according to his will?

You see, he did not subject it to the angels (the coming world that we are talking about). However, someone testified in one place:

> What is man so that you are concerned about him?
> What is the son of man so that you look after him?
> You have demoted him for a little while below the angels.
> You have crowned him with glory and honor;
> You have subjected all things under his feet.

Now in the act of subjecting all things under him, he did not leave out anything from being subject to him. However, we do not yet see all things subjected to him; but we do see Jesus demoted for a little while below the angels because of the sufferings of his death and crowned with glory and honor—so that by God's favor he might taste death in behalf of all men.

For it seemed fitting to God (because of whom all things exist and through whom all things exist) for the founder of their salvation to be perfected through suffering so that he may lead many sons to glory. Since the one who sanctifies and those who are being sanctified are all from one, for this reason he is not ashamed to call them brothers. He said, "I will proclaim your name to my brothers; I will sing your praises amid the assembly." And again he said, "I will be confident about him," and "Look at me and the children God gave me!"

Therefore, because the children had flesh and blood in common, he likewise took part in them so that through his death he might bring to nothing the power held by death (which is the devil) and release these children, who by fear of death were held in slavery for their whole lifetime. Obviously, he did not help the angels; on the contrary, he helped Abraham's descendants. Therefore he must in all ways be made like his brothers so that he may become a high priest who is merciful and faithful in all that pertains to the service of God so that he might make atonement for the people's sins. In doing so, he himself has suffered with temptation, and so he is able to come to the rescue for those who are tempted.

Therefore, holy brothers who share in the heavenly calling, think about the apostle and high priest of our confession—Jesus, who was faithful to the one who appointed him as Moses was also faithful with all of God's house. For Jesus has become worthy of more glory than Moses, just as the one who builds the house has more honor than the house itself. For every house is built by someone, but God is the one who built all things! And Moses was indeed faithful in managing all of God's house as a servant for a testimony of the things that were going to be said, but the Messiah was faithful as a son over God's house—and we are his house if we hold tightly to the confidence and hope that we can take pride in. Therefore, just as the Holy Spirit says:

> Today if you would hear his voice,
> Do not harden your hearts as it happened in the rebellion,
> As it happened in the trial in the wilderness,
> Where your fathers put me to the test
> And saw my works for forty years;
> Therefore I was upset with this generation.
> And said, "Their hearts are always going astray,
> But they have not known my ways."
> As I swore in my anger:
> They shall absolutely not enter into my rest!

Watch out, brothers, so that there will not be an evil heart of faithlessness in some of you, by which you fall away from the living God! In contrast, encourage one another every day, while it is still called "today," so that none of you are hardened by the deception of sin—because we have become partners of the Messiah if we truly hold tightly to the source of our original confirmation until the end! Therefore it was said:

> Today if you would hear his voice,
> Do not harden your hearts as it happened in the rebellion.

Who rebelled after they heard his voice? Surely not everyone who came out of Egypt by the direction of Moses! With whom was God angry for forty years? Wasn't it those who sinned, whose corpses fell in the wilderness? About whom did he take an oath that they would not enter into his rest, if it were not those who were faithless? And we see that they were not able to enter because of their faithlessness!

Let us then be afraid so that, while that promise to enter his rest is still available, none of you seems to have fallen short of entering it! Indeed, we ourselves have been given news of salvation just as they were, but the message that they heard did not do them any good because they were not unified by faith with those who obeyed it. For we who are faithful enter into that rest just as he has said, "As I swore in my anger, they shall absolutely not enter into my rest!" And yet his work was finished when the world was created. For he has said somewhere about the seventh day like this, "And God rested on the seventh day from all of his work," and in this passage again, "They will absolutely not enter into my rest."

Therefore since some remained who had yet to enter into it, and those who had earlier been given news of salvation did not enter it because of faithlessness, he has again appointed a day—"today," saying in David's writings a long time afterward just as it was quoted earlier, "Today if you will hear his voice, do not harden your hearts." For if Joshua had given them rest, the psalmist would not have spoken of another day after those days. So then—a Sabbath rest remains for God's people, because the one who enters into his rest will also rest from their work just as God rested from his own work. Therefore let us be diligent to enter into that rest so that no one may fall because of similar disobedience.

God's word is alive and powerful, and it is sharper than any two-edged sword, even cutting through the middle of the soul and spirit and the joints and marrow. It can judge the heart's reflections and thoughts. And no creature is invisible in his presence; on the contrary, all things are exposed and laid open before his eyes, and it is before him that we must give account! Therefore, since we have a great high priest who has gone through the heavens—Jesus, God's son—let us hold tightly to our confession! For we do not have a high priest who cannot sympathize with our weaknesses. No, he has been tempted in every way—in the same way we are—but without sin! Therefore let us come with boldness to the throne of his favor that we might receive mercy and find favor to help us exactly when we need it.

Therefore every high priest who was chosen from among men was appointed to represent men in rituals before God so that he might offer gifts to God, offer sacrifices for sins, and be able to be gentle with those who sinned unknowingly or were deceived (since he, too, was in a position with the same kinds of weaknesses). And because of this, he had to offer sacrifices for his own sins just as he had to do for the people's sins. Furthermore, no one could choose this honor for himself, but each was called by God as Aaron was.

In the same way, the Messiah also did not glorify himself so as to become a high priest, but it was said to him, "You are my son; today I have fathered you," just as it was said in another place, "You are a priest forever in the same way as Melchizedek."

The Messiah, in the days he was in the flesh, offered both prayers and pleas, with loud crying and tears, to the one who was able to save him from death—and gained audience because of his reverence. But although he was "Son," he learned obedience because of what he suffered. And when he had reached perfection, he became the source of eternal salvation for all who obey him because he had been designated by God as a high priest "in the same way as Melchizedek."

As for Melchizedek, we have much to say about him, and it is difficult to explain because you have become too lazy to hear. Although you also should be teachers by this time, you need someone to reteach you the basic fundamentals of God's teachings—you need milk and not solid food. Anyone whose diet consists of milk is not ready for the word of righteousness because this person is an infant; however, the solid food is for those who are mature, who have trained their senses to distinguish between good and evil because they constantly use those senses.

Therefore let's leave the basic part of the Christian message and move on to that maturity—not laying another foundation of repentance from dead works, faith in God, or teaching about washings, laying hands on people, resurrection from the dead, and eternal judgment (and we will get there if God allows).

Now—as for those who were once enlightened, have tasted the heavenly gift, have become partners of the Holy Spirit, and have tasted God's good message and the powers of the coming world—if they fall away, it is impossible to restore them to repentance. As far as they are concerned, they have again crucified the Son of God and made a public example of him. If the ground drinks the rain that often falls on it and sprouts vegetation that is useful for the one who cultivates it, it receives a blessing from God. However, if it produces thorns and thistles, it is worthless and in danger of being cursed (the result of which is burning).

However, we are convinced of better things (things that bring salvation) about you, dear loved ones, even though we are speaking this way, because God is not unfair so as to forget your work and love, which you have shown because of him when you served the needs of the saints—as you continue to do. And we desire of each of you that same demonstration of diligence in attaining the full assurance of hope until the goal of maturity is met, so that you do not become lazy but rather imitators of those who inherit the promise through faith and perseverance. You see, God made a promise to Abraham, and since he had no one greater by which he could swear an oath, "He swore by himself," saying, "I will surely bless you and multiply you." And by persevering as we have said, Abraham obtained the promise. Men swear oaths by someone greater than themselves, and the oath is there as a confirmation to put an end to all arguing. In doing this, God wanted to make it abundantly clear to those who would inherit the promise that his will is unchangeable, so he guaranteed it with an oath. So through two unchangeable things—in which it is impossible for God to lie—we who have fled for refuge have a mighty comfort to take hold of the hope that has been set before us, which we have as a firm and secure anchor for our soul that has entered the inner sanctuary behind the curtain. There Jesus entered as a forerunner on our behalf and has become a high priest forever "in the same way as Melchizedek."

For this "Melchizedek, King of Salem, Priest of the Highest God," is the one who "met with Abraham after Abraham had returned from defeating the kings" and blessed him, after which Abraham divided out a tenth of everything. First of all, his name is translated as "King of Righteousness," and then he is afterward called "King of Salem," which means "King of Peace." He is without father or mother, without genealogy, and having neither a beginning of days nor an end of life, yet he is made like the Son of God because he remains a high priest all the time.

Do you see how great he is? Abraham (our chief ancestor) gave this man a tenth of the best spoils! And even those who are among the sons of Levi—those who received the priesthood—had the legal right according to the Law to collect a tithe from the people; these were their brothers, who had come from Abraham's loins just as the Levites had. However, the one who did not trace his descent from them received a tithe from Abraham and blessed the one who had the promise—and without exception, the lesser is always blessed by the greater! In this case, mortal men receive the tithe, but in that example, it is testified that he lives. Someone might even say that through Abraham, Levi (who received the tithe) also paid a tithe, for while he was still in his father's loins, Melchizedek met with him!

Therefore, if completion of the promise was attained through the Levitical priesthood (because the people received the Law on the basis of the Levitical priesthood), why would there be a need for another priest to rise up "in the same way as Melchizedek" rather than one spoken of in the same way as Aaron? For when the priesthood needs to be changed over, the law must change too! The one about whom this was spoken belonged to another tribe, and no one from that tribe ever tended to the altar. It is clear that our Master was a descendant of Judah, and Moses never said anything about that tribe regarding the priesthood. And it is more abundantly clear that if another priest rose up in the likeness of Melchizedek, he would not have come according to a law met by physical qualifications, but according to the power of an endless life. It is testified that "You are a high priest forever in the same way as Melchizedek." Annulment comes for a former commandment because of its weakness and worthlessness—for the law brought nothing to completion—and a better hope has been introduced, by which we draw near to God.

Indeed, there are those who have become priests without an oath, but God spoke to him with an oath, "The Master swore an oath and will not change his mind; you are a priest forever." To the very same extent that this was not said without an oath, Jesus has become the guarantee of a better covenant. Yes, there have been many who have become priests who have been hindered by death from continuing in that capacity. However, he holds the priesthood continually because he remains forever. Because of this, he is able to save absolutely everyone who comes through him to God; he is always alive to appeal for them.

In this way also he is a fitting candidate for our high priest: he is holy, without deceit, without defilement, and separated from sinners, and he has become higher than the heavens. Unlike the other high priests, he does not need to offer a sacrifice for his own sins first and then one for the people's sins. He offered a sacrifice only once, when he offered himself. For the law appoints a high priest who is weak, but what was spoken with an oath (after the law) appointed the Son, who has been perfected forever!

The main point of what has been said is this: we have the kind of high priest who has sat down at the right hand of the throne of majesty in the heavens. He is a minister in the Holy Place and in the true Tent of Meeting, which the Master—not a man—has set up. Every high priest is appointed to offer both gifts and sacrifices; therefore this one also must have something to offer. Now, if he were on the earth, he would not have been a priest since there are others who offer gifts as prescribed by the Law. Yet they perform their rituals in a copy and shadow of heaven's Tent of Meeting. Just as Moses was warned as he was about to erect the Tent of Meeting—for God said, "See that you make everything as prescribed by the pattern that was shown to you on the mountain"—even now Jesus has obtained an incomparable ritual to perform to the same extent that he is the mediator of a better covenant, which has been enacted based on better promises.

Now if that first covenant were faultless, it would have been out of place for him to seek a second one. Yet he finds fault with it when he says to them:

> "Look! The days are coming," says the Master,
> "When I will establish a new covenant with the house of Israel
> And with the house of Judah.
> It will not be like the covenant I made with their fathers
> on the day I took them by the hand
> to lead them out of the land of Egypt,
> Because they did not continue in my covenant,
> And I have no more concern for them," says the Master.
> "This is the covenant that I will make with the house of Israel
> After those days," says the Master:
> "I will write it on them by putting my law into their minds and into their hearts.
> I will be their God, and they will be my people.
> No one will teach their own neighbor
> Or their own brother by saying, 'Know the Master,'
> Because all will know me,
> from the smallest to the greatest of them.
> I will be merciful for their wrongdoing,
> And I will no longer keep a record of their sins."

By saying "new," he has made the old covenant obsolete, and whatever ages and becomes obsolete is close to being destroyed!

So the first covenant contained regulations concerning the duties of the earthly sanctuary. The first section of the Tent of Meeting was furnished with a lampstand, table, and display of bread—this was the Holy Place. Also behind the second curtain, there was a section called the "Holy of Holies." It contained a gold altar of incense and the Ark of the Covenant (which was covered on all sides with gold and contained a gold jar of manna, Aaron's staff that sprouted buds, and the stone tablets of the covenant). On top of the Ark of the Covenant, there were glorious cherubim overshadowing the place of atonement. However, we cannot talk in detail about all of these right now.

Anyway, when these furnishings were prepared as listed, the priests continually went into the first section of the Tent of Meeting to fulfill their ceremonial ritual. As for the second section: only once per year the high priest alone could enter it, but never without blood, which he offered for himself and for the unintentional sins of the people. This is the Holy Spirit's way of showing that the way to the actual sanctuary was not yet known while the first Tent of Meeting still stood; that Tent of Meeting was merely a symbol for the present time. Because of this, gifts and sacrifices are being offered, but they are unable to perfect the consciences of those performing the ceremonial rituals; they are concerned only with food, drinks, and various washings, which are regulations for the body that are imposed until the time comes to set things right!

Now the Messiah has appeared as a high priest of the good things to come, and he has gone into the better and more perfect Tent of Meeting, which was not made with hands (that is, it is not part of this world!), and entered the Holy of Holies once and for all—and not with the blood of goats or calves, but with his own blood—and thus he obtained eternal redemption. The blood of goats and bulls and the ashes of young cows can be sprinkled on those who are defiled and sanctify them (so that their bodies are clean). The Messiah presented himself by the eternal Spirit as an offering without blemish to God; how much more will his blood cleanse our consciences from lifeless actions so that we may serve the living God!

Because of this, he is the mediator of the new covenant so that by his act of dying for the redemption of sins that were committed under the first covenant, those who are called may receive the promise of the eternal inheritance. Now, a covenant is confirmed by death, since it never has authority while the one who decreed it is alive. Therefore, the first covenant could not be put into effect without blood. When every command had been spoken to all the people by Moses as it was in the Law, he took the blood of calves and goats, with water, hyssop, and a red wool cloth, and sprinkled them on the scroll and all of the people. He said, "This is the blood of the covenant which God has ordained for you." Then he sprinkled it also on the Tent of Meeting and on all of the ceremonial furnishings. So by the Law's prescription, almost everything is sanctified by blood, and there is no forgiveness without shedding blood.

Therefore, it was necessary that the copies of the heavenly utensils be sanctified by these animals. On the other hand, the heavenly utensils are sanctified by better sacrifices than these, because the Messiah did not enter the sanctuary that was made with hands, which is only a copy of the true one—he entered heaven itself and now appears before God's face on our behalf. Furthermore, he did not enter it so that he may offer himself many times (as the high priests enter the sanctuary every year with the blood of something else); otherwise, he would have had to suffer many times since the world was created. In fact, he appeared once, at the end of the ages, to remove sin by sacrificing himself. And just as it is appointed for men to die once, followed by judgment, in the same way the Messiah was also offered once to take up the sins of many. And he will appear a second time to those who have eagerly waited for him—not to deal with sin, but for salvation!

Now, since the Law contains merely a shadow of the good things to come (and not the actual embodiment of these things), it has never been able to perfect those who approach the altar with these same sacrifices, which they offer every year on a regular basis. Otherwise, would they not have stopped offering them, since none of those who worshiped would have any more awareness of sins once they were cleansed? On the contrary, with these sacrifices, there is a reminder of sins every year because the blood of bulls and goats cannot take away sin. Therefore when he enters the world, he says:

> You have not wanted sacrifice or offering,
> But you have prepared a body for me;
> You are not pleased with whole burnt offerings
> or with sin offerings.
> Then I said, "Look: I have come to do your will, God,
> Because this was written about me in the scroll of a book."

In the previous statement, he said "you have not wanted" or been "pleased with" sacrifices and offerings or whole burnt offerings and sin offerings, which are offered as the Law has prescribed. Then he said, "Look: I have come to do your will." He takes away the first will so that he might establish the second, and in that will we are sanctified once and for all by the offering of the body of Jesus!

Indeed, every high priest stood daily, performing ceremonious rituals and frequently offering sacrifices that have never been able to remove sin. Yet this high priest sat down at God's right hand after offering a single sacrifice for sins that is enough for all time. So from now on, he is waiting until his enemies have been put under his feet like a footrest because with a single offering, enough for all time, he perfected those who have been sanctified.

Even the Holy Spirit testifies to us, because after that he said:

> "This is the covenant I will make with them after those days," says the Master.
> "I will write it on them by putting my law into their hearts and into their minds,
> And I will no longer keep a record of their sins and offenses."

Now where there is forgiveness, there is no longer a sin offering! Therefore, brothers, since we have confidence to enter the sanctuary by the blood of Jesus, which he has dedicated for us as a new and living way through the veil (that is, his body), let us approach it with a true heart and full assurance of faith, since our hearts have been sprinkled to cleanse them from an evil conscience, and our bodies have been washed in pure water. Let us hold tightly to the unwavering confession of our hope because the one who made the promise is faithful. Let us consider one another so that we might stir up one another's love and good actions. We must not abandon the practice of assembling ourselves together (as some have); on the other hand, we must encourage more as we see the day drawing near!

When we deliberately sin after we have received knowledge of the truth, there no longer remains a sacrifice for a sin offering, but to the contrary, there is a terrible expectation of judgment and burning anger that is going to consume the enemies of God. Whoever disregarded the Law of Moses died without mercy on the basis of two or three witnesses. How much worse do you think will be the punishment that will be deserved for the one who has treated the Son of God with contempt, has considered the blood of the covenant (by which they were sanctified) as though it were profane, and has insulted the Spirit of grace? We know what he said, "Vengeance is mine, and I will repay," as well as this, "The Master will judge his people." It is a terrible thing to fall into the hands of the living God!

So remember your earlier days, during which you had to endure a hard struggle with suffering after you were enlightened. Sometimes you were put to public shame with disgrace and affliction, and sometimes you shared the burden with those who had also been treated this way. You also sympathized with those who were in prison and joyfully endured the seizure of your possessions, knowing that you have a better and longer-lasting possession. So do not throw away your confidence, which has a great reward. You need endurance so that you may do the will of God and receive the promise because:

> In a very short time, the one who is coming will come
> and no longer delay;
> However, my righteous one will live by faith,
> And if he cowers down, my soul will not be pleased with him.

But we are not of those who cower so that they are destroyed; on the contrary, we have faith so that we preserve our souls! Yes, faith is the confirmation of what we hope for and proof of things that we do not see. With this faith, our ancestors received recognition.

By faith, we understand that the world was created by God's word so that what we see did not come from things that are visible.

By faith, Abel offered a better sacrifice to God than Cain, because of which he was recognized for being righteous because God recognized the gifts he offered; by faith, he still speaks even though he is dead!

By faith, Enoch was taken so that he did not see death, and "he was nowhere to be found because God took him." Before he was taken, he received recognition because "he walked with God." Yet without faith, it is impossible to please him because whoever would approach God must believe that he exists and that he rewards those who search for him.

By faith, when Noah was warned about something that had never been seen before, he was careful to build an ark in order to save his family. In doing this, he condemned the world and became an heir of the righteousness that comes by faith.

By faith, Abraham obeyed when he was called to go out to a place that he would later receive as an inheritance—and he went out, not knowing where he was going. By faith, he lived in the Promised Land like a stranger—he lived in tents with Isaac and Jacob (who were to share in that same promise) because he waited for the structurally reinforced city that God had designed and built. By faith, Sarah, who was infertile, also received the ability to produce offspring, although she was beyond the age of bearing children since she considered that the one who made the promise was faithful. Therefore a countless quantity of people (like the stars of heaven and the sand on the seashore) were born from one man, and he was as good as dead!

All of these died in faith without receiving the promises, but they saw them from a distance and welcomed them; they acknowledged that they were strangers and refugees on the earth. Those who say such things reveal that they are searching for another country, but if they were referring to the country from which they came, they would have had an opportunity to return. On the contrary, they were longing for a better home—a heavenly one. Because of this, God was not ashamed to be called their God—he even prepared a city for them.

By faith, when Abraham was tested, he resolved to offer up Isaac. And the one who was supposed to receive the promise began to offer his uniquely born son, about whom it was said, "Your descendants shall be called through Isaac." Yet he considered that God was able even to raise him from the dead. Therefore he did receive him back in a figurative sense. By faith, Isaac also blessed Jacob and Esau based on these things to come. By faith, Jacob blessed each of his sons when he was dying and then bowed upon the top of his staff. By faith, when he was about to die, Joseph thought of the exodus of the sons of Israel and instructed them about his bones.

By faith, when Moses was born, he was hidden for three months by his parents; because they saw that he was a handsome child, they did not fear the edict of the pharaoh. By faith, when Moses grew up, he refused to be called the son of the pharaoh's daughter and chose to be mistreated with God's people instead of enjoying sin temporarily. He considered the disgrace of the Messiah to be worth more than the treasures of Egypt because he focused on the reward. By faith, he left Egypt behind and did not fear the pharaoh's wrath—he persevered as though he could see what was unseen! By faith, he instituted the Passover and the blood sprinkling so that the destroying angel would not harm their firstborn sons. By faith, he passed through the Red Sea as though he were on dry ground, and when the Egyptians tried to do it, they were drowned.

By faith, the walls of Jericho fell after the Israelites marched around it over a period of seven days. By faith, Rahab the prostitute was not destroyed with those who were disobedient because she welcomed the spies peacefully.

And what else can I say? Time would run out before I could describe the faith of Gideon, Barak, Samson, Jephthah, and David, and also Samuel and the prophets! Through their faith, these men conquered kingdoms, brought about righteousness, obtained promises, shut the mouths of lions, extinguished the power of fire, escaped the edge of the sword, were empowered when they had no strength, became mighty in war, and caused battle lines of others to flee. Women received their dead again through resurrection. Others were tortured, refusing deliverance so that they might obtain a better resurrection. Others experienced mocking and scourging, and still others experienced chains and imprisonment. They were stoned to death, sawn in two, murdered by the sword, wandered around in sheepskin and goatskin, went without necessities, were oppressed, and were tormented. The world did not deserve them—they wandered in deserts, mountains, caves, and holes in the ground.

These were all recognized for their faith, but they have not yet received the promise, because God had provided something better for us so that they would not accomplish it without us.

We even have this large host of witnesses surrounding us! For that very reason, we must lay aside every weight, as well as sin, which so easily gets in our way, and run with persistence the race that is set before us! We must focus on Jesus, who is the founder and finisher of our faith. He persisted, focusing on the joy that was set before him instead of the disgraceful cross, of which he was not afraid. Then he sat down at the right hand of God's throne. Consider him, who endured such great hostility brought against him by sinners, so that you do not become tired and spiritually exhausted. You have not yet resisted to the point of death in your struggle against sin. Yet you have forgotten the comfort that instructs you like sons:

> My son, do not make light of the Master's discipline,
> And do not become tired of being corrected by him,
> Because the Master disciplines the one he loves
> And reprimands every son he accepts.

Endure discipline, because God is treating you like sons! What father has a son whom he does not discipline? On the other hand, if you are not disciplined like all of those who have a part in the family, then you are an illegitimate child and not a son! Since we have had our earthly fathers who disciplined us (and we treated them with respect), shall we not submit ourselves even more to our spiritual Father so we may live? Earthly fathers disciplined us for a few days as they saw fit, but God disciplines us for our benefit so that we might have a part in his holiness! No discipline seems to be enjoyable while it is happening—rather, it is painful! However, afterward it yields a peaceful result (righteousness) for those who were trained with it!

Strengthen your drooping hands and weak knees, and make your path straight for your feet so that the lame leg may not be injured, but quite the opposite—that it may be healed.

Strive for peace with all people and for holiness, without which no one will see the Master. See to it that no one misses out on God's favor and that no root of bitterness springs up to cause trouble, or many will be defiled by it. See to it that no one is sexually immoral or materialistic as Esau was. He traded his rights as the firstborn for one meal. You know that afterwards he wanted to inherit a blessing, but he was rejected because he did not find an opportunity to repent, even though he searched for it tearfully.

You have not approached the mountain that could be touched and that burned with fire and was dark, gloomy, and stormy. There is no sound of a trumpet and no voice whose words led those who heard it to beg that no more messages be given to them. They could not endure the command, "And if an animal touches the mountain, it must be stoned to death." Its appearance was so terrifying, Moses said, "I am afraid and terrified." No, you have approached Zion: the mountain and city of the living God—the heavenly Jerusalem! You have approached tens of thousands of angels and a special gathering and assembly of the firstborn, who are registered in heaven! You have approached God (the judge of all people), the perfected spirits of the righteous, Jesus (the mediator of the new covenant), and the sprinkled blood that speaks better things than Abel's blood does!

Be careful that you do not reject that speaking blood! If those who rejected the earthly warning did not escape, what more can we expect if we turn away from the heavenly one? His voice shook the earth then, but now it has been promised that "One more time, I will shake not only the earth but also the sky!" By saying "one more time," he indicates the removal of the things that will be shaken, just as they were created! Then only what is unshakeable will remain. So, since we are receiving an unshakeable kingdom, we are thankful. Because of this, we worship God in a way that pleases him—with reverence and fear—for our God is a consuming fire.

Brotherly love must continue. Do not neglect hospitality, because by being hospitable, some have welcomed angels as guests without knowing it. Remember to think about those who are in chains as though you were chained with them and those who are mistreated as though you were also a part of their bodies. Keep marriage precious among all of you so that the bed may remain undefiled, because God will judge the sexually immoral and adulterers. Life should be without greed. Help meet whatever need is present, because he has said, "I will never abandon you; I will not leave you behind." Therefore we are confident enough to say,

> The Lord is my helper, and I will not be afraid;
> What can man do to me?

Remember your leaders, who spoke God's word to you; observe the outcome of their conduct and imitate their faith. Jesus the Messiah is the same—yesterday, today, and forever. Do not get carried away with deceitful or foreign teachings. It is good for you to strengthen your heart with God's kindness—not with food regulations, which do no good for those who live by them. We have an altar from which those who perform religious rituals in the earthly Tent of Meeting do not have the right to eat. When the blood of animals was brought into the sanctuary by the high priest for a sin offering, the bodies of these animals were burned outside the camp. Likewise, Jesus suffered outside the gates of Jerusalem so that he might sanctify the people by his own blood. So let us go to him outside the camp that brought disgrace upon him. We do not have a city here that will remain—we are searching for one that is coming! Let us bring up through him a sacrifice of praise to God all the time, which is the fruit of our lips praising his name. Do not neglect to do what is good—or fellowship—because God is very pleased with sacrifices such as these.

Have confidence in your leaders and submit to them, because they lose sleep caring for your souls as those who will have to give an account. Then they can do this with joy instead of groaning because that would not be any good for you.

Pray for us, because we are sure that we have a good conscience and want to conduct ourselves well in all circumstances. Even more so, I encourage you to do this so that I may quickly be restored to you.

May the God of peace (who brought up the Great Shepherd of the sheep, our Master Jesus, with the blood of his eternal covenant) prepare you for every good work so that you may do his will and do with us what is pleasing in his sight through Jesus the Messiah. May the glory be his forever and ever, amen!

Brothers, I encourage you to listen patiently to this word of exhortation, because I have written to you briefly. You know that our brother Timothy has been released, and if he comes soon, I will go with him to see you.

Greet all of your leaders and all of the saints. Those who are from Italy greet you.

May God's favor be with all of you.

FROM
JAMES

From James (a servant of God and the Master, Jesus the Messiah),
To the twelve tribes who are dispersed abroad: hello!

CONSIDER IT A COMPLETE JOY, MY BROTHERS, WHEN YOU FALL victim to various temptations because you know that the tempting of your faith produces persistence. Let that persistence do its complete work so that you may be complete and whole, not lacking in any way. Yet if any of you lacks wisdom, they must ask God who gives generously to all people without mocking them, and it will be given to them. However, they must ask with faith, not wavering in any way. You see, whoever wavers has become like a wave of the sea that is blown by the wind and tossed back and forth. You see, that person must not expect to receive anything from the Master because they are fickle—unstable in all of their ways.

Now the brother or sister who is of humble circumstances must take pride in their high estate, and the wealthy must take pride in their humble circumstances because their wealth will pass away like a flower of the field. You see, the sun has risen with its heat; it has dried up the field. Its flower has fallen off, and its beauty has faded. In the same way, the wealthy person will wither away in their pursuits.

Blessed is the man who endures temptation, because when he has been approved he will receive the crown of life that has been promised to those who love God. No one who is tempted is to say, "I am being tempted by God." You see, God is not tempted by evil, and he does not tempt anyone. However, each person is tempted when they are reeled in and baited by their own desires. Then after desire conceives, it gives birth to sin, and when sin has matured, it gives birth to death.

Do not be deceived, my dear brothers. Every good gift and every perfect present are from above—it descends from the Father of Lights, with whom there is no change of celestial position or any shadow caused by such change. By his will, he gave birth to us through the Word of Truth so that we might be some sort of a "first produce" among his creation.

Know this, my dear brothers: everyone must be quick to hear, slow to speak, and slow to become angry. You see, human anger does not bring about God's righteousness! Therefore, after you put away all of your greediness and rampant wickedness by being humble, receive the implanted Word that is able to save your souls. Now, you must be doers of what the Word says and not just hearers who deceive themselves. You see, whoever is a hearer of the Word and not a doer has become like a man staring at his natural face in a mirror. He stared at himself, went away, and immediately forgot what kind of person he was. But whoever caught a glimpse into the perfect law of freedom and remained in it (that is, they are not just a forgetful hearer, but rather an active doer), they will be blessed in what they do.

If anyone thinks themselves to be religious but does not bridle their tongue, they are instead deceiving themselves—this person's religion is worthless! Pure and undefiled religion before our God and Father is this: to look after orphans and widows in their affliction and to keep oneself spotless from the world.

My brothers, do not hold the faith of our glorious Master, Jesus the Messiah, with favoritism. For example, suppose a man comes into your assembly with gold rings and wearing dignified clothing, and then a poor man also comes in wearing filthy clothing. If you show regard to the one wearing dignified clothing and say, "You should sit here in a good place," while you say to the poor man, "You stand over there," or, "Sit under my footrest," have you not passed judgment among yourselves and become judges because of your evil thoughts?

Listen, my dear brothers: has God not chosen the poor people of the world to be wealthy in faith—as well as heirs of the kingdom that he has promised to those who love him? Yet you dishonor the poor! Are not the wealthy people the ones who enslave you and drag you into lawsuits? If you really keep the royal law as the Scripture says ("You must love your neighbor as yourself"), you are doing well. However, if you show favoritism, you are sinning—convicted as lawbreakers by the Law. You see, whoever keeps the whole law but stumbles in one area of it has become guilty of all of it, because the one who said, "Do not commit adultery," also said, "Do not murder." Now if you do not commit adultery, but you murder, you have still become a lawbreaker. Speak and act as though you are going to be judged by the law of freedom. You see, judgment falls without mercy on the one who does not act mercifully—mercy has the advantage over judgment.

What good is it, my brothers, if someone claims to have faith but does not have actions? Can that faith save them? If a brother or sister is poorly clothed and without food for the day and one of you tells them, "Go in peace, warm up, and be full," and yet you do not give them the things that their body needs, what good is it? In the same way, if faith does not include action, it is dead because it is by itself.

However, someone will say, "You have faith, but I have actions." Show me your faith without actions, and I will show you my faith by my actions. You believe that God "is the only one." Good job—but the demons believe too, and they tremble with fear. Do you want to know, you foolish person, that this kind of faith without action is useless? Abraham our ancestor—was he not justified based on his actions when he offered his son Isaac on the altar? You can see that his faith worked together with his actions, and his faith was made complete by his actions. Thus the Scripture was fulfilled that said, "Abraham had faith in God, and this was credited to him as righteousness," and he was God's friend. You can see that man is justified based on actions and not on faith alone. Likewise Rahab the prostitute—was she not justified by her actions when she welcomed the messengers and sent them out by another way? You see, in the same way that the body is dead without the spirit, faith is also dead when it is without action.

Not many of you should become teachers, my brothers, because you know that we will receive a stricter judgment. You see, we all stumble in many ways. If a man does not stumble in what he says, he is perfect—able to bridle his whole body. Now, if we put bits into the mouths of horses to persuade them to follow us, we can also guide their whole bodies. Observe ships also. Even though they are so large and are driven by harsh winds, a ship is guided by the smallest thing—a rudder—wherever the pilot desires to steer it. In the same way, the tongue is a small part of the body, but it asserts great power! Observe how large of a fire is kindled by such a small spark. The tongue is a fire too. The tongue is a world of unrighteousness set among our body parts. It defiles the whole body and sets nature's cycle on fire—and it is set on fire by hell! You see, among beasts and birds and among reptiles and marine life, every creature is controlled (and has been controlled) by human beings. However, no one can control the tongue. It is a volatile evil full of lethal poison. With it, we bless the Master and Father, and with it, we curse people—who are made in God's likeness! Out of the same opening come blessing and cursing. This should not be the case, my brothers! Can it be that a spring could pour both fresh and saltwater from the same opening? It is impossible, my brothers, for a fig tree to bear olives, for a vine to bear figs, or for a salty spring to produce fresh water.

Who is wise and understanding among you? They must demonstrate their actions by good conduct with the humility of wisdom. On the other hand, if you have bitter jealousy and strife in your hearts, do not be proud of it or lie against the truth. That is not the kind of wisdom that has come down from above. Instead, it is worldly, materialistic, and demonic. You see, where jealousy and strife exist, there is instability and every bad practice. However, the wisdom that is from above is pure, first of all. Then it is peaceable, courteous, obedient, full of mercy and good produce, impartial, and without hypocrisy—and the produce of righteousness is sown in peace by those who make peace. Where do wars come from? Where do fights among you come from? Do they not come from your desires that wage war within the parts of your body? You desire something, and you do not have it. You kill and strive for something, and you cannot obtain it. You fight and go to war, but you do not have it because you do not ask! You ask, but you do not receive because you are asking with evil intent—that you might waste it on your desires. You adulterers! Do you not know that friendship with the world is hostility toward God? Do you think that it is for no reason that the Scripture says that the Spirit he has caused to dwell in us is opposed to jealousy, but that he gives more grace? So it says:

> God opposes the arrogant, but he gives grace to the humble.

So submit to God. Oppose the Devil, and he will flee from you. Draw near to God, and he will draw near to you. Cleanse your hands, sinners! Purify your hearts, fickle people! Be miserable, grieve, and weep! May your laughter be turned to grief and your joy to sadness! Bow down before the Master, and he will raise you up!

Do not slander one another, brothers. Whoever badmouths their brother or judges their brother badmouths the Law and judges the Law. If you are judging the law, you are not a doer of the law—you are a judge. There is only one lawgiver and judge—he can both save and destroy! Who are you to judge your neighbor?

Come on! Some of you are saying, "Today or tomorrow we will go to that city. We will work there a year, and we will do business and make a profit." You do not know what will happen tomorrow. What is your life? You see, you are like steam—which appears for a little while, but then it disappears. Instead of this, you should say, "If the Master wants it to happen, we will live and do this or that." However, at this time you are proud of your arrogance. All of this boasting is evil. So if someone knows to do something good and does not do it, it is a sin for them!

Come on, wealthy people! Weep and cry out because of your misery that is coming! Your wealth has corroded, and your clothing has been eaten by moths. Your gold and silver have rusted, and their rust will be a testimony to you—they will consume your flesh like fire. You have stored up treasure in recent days. Look! The wages that belong to the workers who have harvested your fields—wages that you have withheld from them—are crying out, and the cries of the harvesters have come to the ears of the Master of Armies. You have lived selfishly and luxuriously on the earth and have fattened yourselves in a day of slaughter. You have hurt and murdered the righteous, and they do not fight back against you.

Therefore, brothers, be patient until our Master comes. Look—the farmer receives the earth's precious produce by waiting patiently for it until it receives both the early and late rains. You also must be patient. Strengthen your hearts because the Master's coming is near. Do not complain about one another, brothers, so that you will not be condemned. Look—the judge is standing at the door. Take the prophets who spoke in the Master's name as an example of suffering and patience. Look—we consider those who persisted to be blessed. You have heard of Job's persistence, and you know the end that the Master brought about, because "The Master is very compassionate and merciful."

Above all, my brothers, do not swear an oath by heaven, earth, or by any other oath. Instead, let your yes mean "yes." and your no mean "no" so that you do not fall into condemnation.

If one of you is suffering, they need to pray. If someone is in a good mood, they need to sing praise. If one of you is sick, they need to call the elders of the congregation, and they need to pray for them and anoint them with olive oil in the Master's name. The prayer of faith will save the one who is ill, the Master will raise them up, and if they have committed sins, they will be forgiven of them! So confess your sins to one another and pray for one another so that you may be healed. A righteous person's prayer has great power as it works. Elijah was a person with the same nature as ours, and he prayed a prayer that it would not rain—and it did not rain on the land for three years and six months. Then he prayed again; then the sky sent rain, and the earth sprouted its produce.

My brothers, if one of you wanders away from the truth and someone turns them back, that person ought to know that whoever turns a sinner from the error of their way will save their soul from death and cover a large number of sins.

FROM
PETER (I)

From Peter (an apostle of Jesus the Messiah),

To the pilgrims who are scattered throughout Pontus, Galatia, Cappadocia, Asia, and Bithynia, who are chosen based on Father God's foreknowledge by sanctification from the Spirit so they might be obedient to Jesus the Messiah and be sprinkled with his blood: may grace and peace be multiplied to you!

MAY THE GOD AND FATHER OF OUR MASTER, JESUS THE MESSIAH, be praised! Based on his abundant mercy, he has caused us to be reborn into a living hope through the resurrection of Jesus the Messiah from the dead. He has caused us to be reborn into an immortal, undefiled, and unfading inheritance that has been kept in heaven for us (we are guarded by God's power through faith for the salvation that is ready to be revealed at the end of time). You rejoice because of this, even though you must now be grieved (for a little while) with various kinds of trials. This is so that the testing of your faith (it is much more valuable than gold, which ruins even when it has been tested by fire!) might be found genuine, resulting in praise, glory, and honor when Jesus the Messiah is revealed. You love him even though you have not seen him. You believe in him now, even though you do not see him. Furthermore, you rejoice with a joy that is inexpressible and filled with glory, and you are obtaining the goal of your faith: the salvation of your souls!

The prophets searched and tried to find out about this salvation when they prophesied about the grace that would come to you. They tried to find out what person or what time the Spirit of the Messiah (who was in them) was talking about when he testified beforehand of the sufferings to come for the Messiah and the glory to come after this. It was revealed to them that they performed these services for you—not for themselves. Now these things have been proclaimed to you by those who have preached the Good Message to you by the Holy Spirit, who was sent from heaven. Even angels long to catch a glimpse of these things!

Therefore, by preparing your mind to run the race and taking control of yourselves, put your hope completely in the grace that is being brought to you when Jesus the Messiah is revealed. Act like obedient children—do not become shaped by your desires as you did earlier when you did not know better. On the contrary, just as the one who called you is holy, you also must be holy in all your conduct because it is written, "You will be holy because I am holy."

Since you call on the Father (who judges without favoritism, based on each person's actions), pass the time of your stay here with fear. You know that you were not ransomed from the worthless conduct you inherited from your ancestors with perishable things (like silver or gold). On the contrary, you were ransomed with the precious blood of the Messiah—as if from a guiltless and spotless lamb—who was chosen even before the creation of the world and revealed in this recent time for your sakes. You see, through him you believe in God, who raised him from the dead and gave him glory so that your faith and hope might be in God.

Now that you have purified your lives by obedience to the truth for genuine brotherly love, love one another enthusiastically with a pure heart. You have been born again but not from a decaying seed. On the contrary, you have been born again from an immortal seed—by the Word of God, who lives and remains! See:

> All flesh is like a field,
> And all its glory is like a flower of the field;
> The field has dried up, and the flower has fallen,
> But the Master's Word remains forever!

This Word is what was preached to you! So put away all wickedness, all deceit, hypocrisy, jealousy, and all slander. Like newborn infants, you need to long for the pure spiritual milk so that with it you may grow into salvation. After all, you have tasted that the Master is good! Come to him like living stones that indeed have been rejected by men but are chosen and precious to God. You are being built up like living stones into a spiritual house so that you can be a holy priesthood and offer up spiritual sacrifices through Jesus the Messiah that are very pleasing to God. So the Scripture contains:

> Look! In Zion I am setting a stone—
> A cornerstone that is chosen and precious—
> And whoever puts faith in him will not be ashamed!

Therefore the honor belongs to you who are faithful! However, concerning those who are unfaithful, it says:

> The stone that the builders have rejected—
> That very one has become the cornerstone.

Also:

> It is a stone for tripping and a rock causing offense.

Those who trip by being disobedient to the Word are designated for this purpose. On the other hand, you are a chosen family, a royal priesthood, a holy country, and a nation created to become God's possession so that you would proclaim the praises of the one who has called you out of darkness into his marvelous light!

> You who were not a nation at one time: now you are God's nation.
> You who were not shown mercy: now you have received mercy.

Dear loved ones, I beg you as strangers and pilgrims: stay away from the desires of the body that wage war against the soul. Behave yourselves well among the nations so that even when they slander you as evildoers, after they see your good actions, they might glorify God on the day he intervenes.

Be submissive to every human institution for the Master's sake—whether it is to the emperor as the one who has power or to governors as those who are sent by him to execute justice on evildoers and to praise those who do what is good. You see, this is God's will—that you might silence the ignorance of foolish people by doing what is good. Do what is good since it is your free will; do not use your free will as a cover for your evil actions—behave like God's servants! Honor everyone—love the brotherhood, fear God, and honor the emperor!

Household servants: be submissive to your masters with complete reverence—not only to those who are good and gentle but also to those who are crooked. You see, this results in grace when someone, because of their consciousness of God, endures suffering grief unfairly. What glory is there if you sin and endure rough treatment? On the other hand, if you are doing what is good and you endure suffering, this amounts to grace with God. You see, you were called for this purpose, because the Messiah also suffered for your sakes, thus leaving you an example so that you could follow in his footprints.

> He committed no sin, and no deceit was found in his mouth.
> When he was insulted, he did not insult in return.
> When he suffered, he did not threaten.
> Instead, he committed his cause to the one who judges fairly.
> He himself carried our sins in his body onto the cross
> So that once we were free from sin,
> We might live for righteousness.
> Also, you are healed by his wounds.
> You were like wandering sheep, but now you have
> returned to the flock and the shepherd of your souls!

Also, wives need to be submissive to their own husbands so that if any are disobedient to the Word, they might be won over without a word by the conduct of their wives when they see your reverently holy conduct. Wives' beautification must not be focused on outward things (braided hair, wearing gold, and dressing up), but rather on the hidden person of the heart (with considerate and quiet spiritual beautification that does not wear off). This is worth a lot in God's sight. You see, at one time the holy women who put their hope in God beautified themselves by being submissive to their husbands. For example, Sarah obeyed Abraham and called him "Sir." You have become her children so that you will do what is good and not be frightened by what is terrifying.

Likewise, husbands need to dwell understandingly with their wives as delicate vessels and show honor, as they are fellow heirs of the gift of life, so that your prayers will not be hindered.

Now, the goal is for everyone to have unity, sympathy, brotherly love, compassion, and humility. Do not repay evil with evil or insult with insult. On the contrary, repay with blessing. You see, you were called for this reason so that you could inherit a blessing.

> Whoever wants to love life and see good days
> Must keep their tongue from speaking evil
> And their lips from speaking deceit.
> They must turn from evil and do what is good.
> They must seek peace and pursue it
> Because the eyes of the Master are watching over the righteous,
> And his ears are open to their requests,
> But the Master's face is against those who do what is evil.

Furthermore, who will do harm to you if you are enthusiastic for what is good? Even if you were to suffer because of righteousness, you would be blessed! Do not be afraid of their intimidation or be troubled by it. On the contrary, set apart the Messiah as Master in your hearts, and always be ready to give a defense to everyone who asks you for a reason for the hope that is in you. However, you must do this with courtesy and respect, holding on to a good conscience. Then they will be put to shame because of the badmouthing that has been spoken against you by those who threaten the good conduct that you do in the Messiah. You see, it is better to suffer for doing what is good (if that happens to be God's will) than to suffer for doing what is evil. For example, at one time the Messiah also suffered for our sins—the righteous for the unrighteous—so that he could lead you to God as people who have died to the body but are raised to live for the Spirit. By the Spirit, he also went and preached to the spirits that were imprisoned (those who were disobedient at the time when God's patience waited in the days that Noah was preparing the ark). Only a few were saved on it by water (that is, eight lives). Correspondingly, immersion now saves you—not by removing filth from the body, but by a request for a good conscience that is made to God through the resurrection of Jesus the Messiah. He has gone to the right hand of God—to heaven—and angels, authorities, and power have been placed under his authority.

Therefore since the Messiah also suffered in the body, you also should equip yourselves with the same mindset. You see, whoever suffers in the body has stopped sinning so that they will no longer live out the time they have left based on the desires of men but rather on the will of God. Enough time has been spent fulfilling the intentions of the Gentiles who go around taking part in inappropriate behavior, desires, drinking, gluttonous feasting, partying, and disgusting idolatry. In this respect, those who slander you are amazed that you do not rush with them into the same flood of recklessness as they do. They will give an account to the one who is ready to judge the living and the dead. For this reason, it was preached to the dead also so that although they are judged in the body as men are, they might also live in the Spirit as God does!

The end of everything is near, so be sensible and self-controlled in prayer. More than anything, hold on to an enthusiastic love for one another because love covers a large number of sins. Be hospitable toward one another without complaining. Just as everyone has received a gift, everyone should use it to serve one another like good managers of God's different kinds of grace. Anyone who speaks should speak as they are God's messages. Anyone who serves should serve as God has supplied the strength so that in every way God will be glorified through Jesus the Messiah. To him be the glory and power forever and ever, amen!

Dear loved ones, do not be surprised by the fiery trial that is coming among you to test you (as though something strange is happening to you). However, rejoice to the extent that you take part in the Messiah's sufferings so that when his glory appears, you might also rejoice with excitement! If you are mistreated because of the name of the Messiah, you are blessed because the glorious Spirit of God rests on you. You see, none of you should suffer as a murderer, a thief, an evildoer, or someone who gets in another person's business. However, if any of you suffers as a Christian, you should not be ashamed of it; on the contrary, glorify God with that name. You see, the time has come for judgment to begin, starting with God's household. If it starts with us, what will the outcome be for those who disobey God's Message? "If the righteous is barely saved, where will the ungodly and sinner appear?" Therefore those who suffer on account of God's will should also commit their lives to the faithful Creator by doing what is good.

So as a fellow elder, a witness of the Messiah's sufferings, and a partner in the glory that is about to appear, I encourage the elders who are among you: shepherd God's flock that is among you. Take care of them—not out of compulsion, but voluntarily, as God does. Do not take care of them out of greed; instead do so out of eagerness. Do not be an authoritarian over those allotted to you; instead, be examples to the flock. Then when the Chief Shepherd appears, you will receive the unfading crown of glory!

Likewise, young men, be submissive to your elders. You all should clothe yourselves with humility toward one another because:

> God resists the arrogant, but he gives grace to the humble.

Therefore humble yourselves under God's mighty hand so that he might lift you up when it is time! Cast your concerns on him because he cares about you.

Control yourselves and watch out because your adversary—the devil—is walking around, roaring like a lion seeking what he might devour. Resist him by being firm in faith, because you know that the same sufferings are being experienced by your brotherhood in the world. However, after you have suffered for a little while, the God of all grace (who called you into his eternal glory that is in Jesus the Messiah) will restore you, support you, strengthen you, and establish you. To him belongs the power forever, amen!

It is through Silas (the faithful brother, as I consider him) that I have written to you about a few things so that I might encourage you and affirm that this grace of God (in which you stand) is true. Your fellow chosen congregation that is in "Babylon" and my son Mark greet you. Greet one another with a loving kiss.

Peace to all of you who are in the Messiah!

FROM
PETER (II)

From Simon Peter (a servant and apostle of Jesus the Messiah),

To those who have obtained a faith equal in value to ours because of the righteousness of our God and Savior, Jesus the Messiah: may grace and peace be multiplied to you in the knowledge of God and Jesus our Master!

HIS DIVINE POWER HAS GIVEN US EVERYTHING THAT RELATES TO life and godliness through our knowledge of the one who called us into his own glory and virtue. By his glory and virtue, precious and great promises have been given to us so that through them you could become partners in the divine nature once you have fled from the corruption that is in the world because of selfish desire. For this same reason, be very diligent to:

> Supplement your faith with virtue,
> Your virtue with knowledge,
> Your knowledge with self-control,
> Your self-control with persistence,
> Your persistence with godliness,
> Your godliness with affection for your brothers,
> And affection for your brothers with love.

You see, if you possess these qualities and are growing in them, they will keep you from being useless or unproductive in the knowledge of our Master, Jesus the Messiah. But whoever does not possess these qualities is near-sighted to the point of blindness since they have forgotten that they have been cleansed from their former sins. So, brothers, be all the more diligent to keep your calling and election valid, because if you do these things, you will never fall! You see, in this way the entrance into the eternal kingdom of our Master and Savior, Jesus the Messiah, will be richly supplied to you!

Therefore I am always going to remind you of these things, even though you know them and have been strengthened by the truth that you have. I think that it is right to remind you, as long as I am in this body, to stir you up with this reminder because I know that the time for me to put aside this body is swiftly approaching (just as our Master, Jesus the Messiah, has shown me).

So I will always be diligent to remind you so that you will be able to retain these things in your memory after my departure.

You see, we did not explain to you the power and coming of our Master, Jesus the Messiah, by following clever myths. On the contrary, we did so as eyewitnesses of his majesty! He received honor and glory from Father God when a voice spoke these things by the Magnificent Glory, "This is my dear Son. I am very pleased with him!" Now we heard this voice speak from heaven when we were with him on the holy mountain! We also have the word of prophecy, which is even more convincing! You would do well to pay attention to it as though it were a lamp that shines in a dark place until day breaks and the Morning Star rises in your hearts. Know this first: no prophecy of Scripture comes from anyone's own interpretation. You see, prophecy has never been spoken by the will of man. On the contrary, men who were carried along by the Holy Spirit spoke messages from God!

But false prophets arose among the people just as there will also be false teachers among you. They will introduce destructive opinions and deny the Master who redeemed them. They will bring swift destruction upon themselves, and many will follow after their inappropriate behavior. Because of them, the true way is slandered. They will greedily exploit you with false words. For a long time, their condemnation has not been at rest, and their destruction is not about to fall asleep.

You see, God did not spare the angels who sinned; on the contrary, he has handed them over to be reserved for condemnation by holding them in hell with chains of darkness. Nor did he spare the ancient world; yet he protected a preacher of righteousness, Noah (and seven other people), when he brought the Flood upon the wicked world. Then he reduced the cities of Sodom and Gomorrah to ashes—he condemned them with a catastrophe, giving them as an example of what will come upon the wicked. However, he rescued Lot (a righteous man), who was worn out by the wicked behavior of those disgraceful people. You see, he felt his righteous life tormented by the actions of evil people because of what he saw and heard while he lived among them day after day. Based on these examples, the Master knows how to rescue godly people from temptation and reserve unrighteous people for torment on Judgment Day (especially those who go after the flesh with corrupting desire and despise the Master's ruling power). They are overconfident and arrogant—they are not afraid to blaspheme glorious angels, while angels (although they are greater in strength and power) will not pronounce against them a slanderous condemnation.

These people are like animals—without the ability to think logically and born to be captured and killed. They slander things that they do not even understand. They will be killed in the way that those animals are killed. They will be hurt in compensation for the hurt they caused. They take pleasure in a self-indulgent lifestyle and enjoy the filth and faults that go with their pleasures while they feast together with you. Their eyes are full of adultery and never-ending sins! They reel in the souls of the weak. Their hearts are trained for greed. They are cursed children! They have abandoned the straight way and have wandered off. They are following in the way of Balaam, the son of Beor, who loved the compensation he received for the hurt he caused. (He was rebuked for his evil behavior—a donkey, which does not speak, spoke up with the voice of a man and put an end to the prophet's insanity.) These people are like fountains without water and fog that is driven along by fierce winds—and the shadow of darkness is reserved for them! You see, they speak arrogant things, and with their inappropriate bodily desires they reel in people who have just escaped those who live in error. They promise these people freedom, but they themselves are slaves of corruption. You see, a person is enslaved by whatever has overcome them. Say that they have escaped the world's shameful behavior by coming to know our Master and Savior, Jesus the Messiah—if they become tangled in these things again and are overcome, the last situation has become worse for them than the first. You see, it would have been better for them not to have come to know the way of righteousness than for them to turn away from the holy command that has been given to them once they have come to know it. This has happened to them like in the true allegory:

> A dog has returned to its own vomit;
> A washed pig has returned to roll in the mud.

Dear loved ones, this is already the second letter I have written to you. In them, I am stirring up your sincere mind with a reminder: remember the messages that were spoken by the holy prophets and the command that was sent from your Master and Savior by the apostles. Know this first of all: in the last days, mockers will come with their mockery, and they will go about based on their own desires. They will say, "Where is the promise of his coming? Ever since our ancestors passed away, everything has continued just as it has from the beginning!" They would like to forget this: a long time ago, the heavens and earth came to exist by water, and they have continued to exist by water with God's word. It was by these that the world that existed then was destroyed with water by the Flood. Even now, the heavens and the earth are reserved for fire—they are being kept for the day of the judgment and destruction of wicked men!

Dear loved ones, this is one thing that you must not forget: as far as the Master is concerned, one day is like a thousand years, and a thousand years is like one day. The Master is not late with the promise as some consider it to be late. On the contrary, he is being patient with you! He does not want anyone to be lost—instead, he wants everyone to come to repentance!

The Master's day will come like a thief. On that day, the heavens will disappear with a roar, and the elements of the earth will be consumed by extreme heat. The earth will also be destroyed, and what has been done on it will be laid bare. Since all of these things will be destroyed like this, what kind of people should you be? With holy conduct and godliness, you should expect this and hurry your efforts for the coming of God's day! Because of that day, the heavens will be destroyed by being burned, and the elements of the earth will melt with extreme heat. However, we are expecting "new heavens and a new earth" because of his promise, and righteousness will dwell in them.

Therefore, dear loved ones, since you expect these things, be very diligent so that you can be found by him to be spotless, guiltless, and at peace. Consider our Master's patience to mean salvation just as our dear brother Paul also has written to you by the wisdom that was given to him—just as he has said in all his letters when he speaks in them about these things. In those letters, there are some things that are difficult to understand, and people who are incompetent and unstable distort them as they do the rest of the Scriptures, leading to their own destruction.

Therefore, dear loved ones, since you know this beforehand, you need to guard yourselves, or else you might be carried away into error with these disgraceful people and lose your solid footing. Now grow in grace and knowledge of our Master and Savior, Jesus the Messiah.

To him be the glory, both now and until that eternal day, amen!

FROM
JOHN (I)

IT WAS FROM THE BEGINNING. WE HAVE HEARD ABOUT IT, WE HAVE seen it with our eyes, we have watched it, and our hands have touched it. It pertains to the Word of Life.

That life was revealed, and we have seen and testify of it. So we announce to you that eternal life that was with the Father and was revealed to us. We announce to you what we have seen and heard so that you will have fellowship with us. Our fellowship is also with the Father and with his Son, Jesus the Messiah. We are writing this ourselves so that our joy will be complete.

This is the message that we have heard from him and are proclaiming to you: God is light, and there is no darkness in him at all. If we claim to have fellowship with him but live in darkness, we are lying and not practicing the truth. However, if we live in the light (as he is in the light), we have fellowship with one another, and the blood of Jesus, his Son, cleanses us from all sin. If we claim that we do not have sin, we deceive ourselves, and the truth is not in us. If we confess our sins, he is faithful and fair so as to forgive us of those sins and cleanse us from all wrongdoing. If we claim that we have not sinned, we make him out to be a liar, and his Word is not in us.

My little children, I am writing this to you so that you will not sin. Even if someone sins, we have a representative with the Father: Jesus the Messiah, who is fair! He is the atonement for our sins—and not only for ours but also for the whole world's sins.

By this we know that we have come to know him: we keep his commands. Whoever claims "I know him" but does not keep his commands is a liar, and the truth is not in them. But the Word of God has truly been made complete in anyone who keeps his Word, and by this we know that we are in him. Whoever claims to remain in him needs to live in the same way he did.

Dear loved ones, I am not writing you a new command—no, I am writing an old command that you have had since the beginning (the old command is the Word that you have heard). Then again, I am writing you a new command, which is true in him and in you: the darkness is passing away, and the true light is shining already.

Whoever claims to be in the light but hates their brother is in the darkness to this day. Whoever loves their brother remains in the light, and there is no fault in them. On the other hand, whoever hates their brother is in darkness—they live in darkness and do not know where they are going because the darkness has blinded their eyes.

I am writing to you, little children,
Because your sins have been forgiven because of his name.
I am writing to you, fathers,
Because you have come to know the one who is from the beginning.
I am writing to you, young men, because you have conquered the evil one.

I have written to you, young children,
Because you have come to know the Father.
I have written to you, fathers,
Because you have come to know the one who is from the beginning.
I have written to you, young men, because you are strong,
God's Word remains in you, and you have conquered the evil one.

Do not love the world or what is in the world. If anyone loves the world, the Father's love is not in them. You see, everything that is in the world (the desires of the body, the desires of the eyes, and pride in one's possessions) is not from the Father. No, it is from the world. Furthermore, the world is passing away (as well as its desires), but the one who does God's will remains forever.

Young children, it is the final hour, and just as you heard that an adversary of the Messiah is coming, even now many adversaries to the Messiah have come. Therefore we know that it is the final hour. They went out from among us, but they were not from us. You see, if they were from us, they would have remained with us. However, they went out so that they might be exposed, because not everyone is from us. You have an anointing from the Holy One, and you all know it. I have not written to you because you have not known the truth, but rather because you have known the truth and that no lie comes from the truth.

Who is a liar, if it's not the one who denies him (that is, "Jesus is not the Messiah")? This person is the adversary to the Messiah, who denies both the Father and the Son. Everyone who denies the Son does not have the Father either. Whoever confesses the Son also has the Father. As for you, what you have heard from the beginning must remain in you. If what you heard from the beginning remains in you, then you will also remain in the Son and the Father. This is the promise that he himself promised to us: eternal life!

I have written this to you in reference to those who would deceive you. As for you, the anointing that you have received from him remains on you, and you do not need anyone to teach you. On the contrary, just as his anointing teaches you about everything (and it is true—it is not a lie) and just as it has taught you, remain in him!

Even now, little children, remain in him so that when he appears, we might have confidence and not be ashamed of him when he comes. Since you know that he is righteous, you also know that everyone who does what is right has been born of him.

Look at the type of love that the Father has given us that we might be called God's children—and we are! Because of this, the world does not know us—because it did not know him. Dear loved ones, we are now God's children, and it has not yet been revealed what we will be like. We know that when he appears, we will be like him because we will see him as he really is. Everyone who has this hope in the Messiah purifies themselves just as he is pure.

Everyone who practices sin also practices wickedness; sin is also wickedness. You know that he was revealed so that he would take away sin and that there is no sin in him. Everyone who remains in him does not sin. No one who sins has seen him or come to know him. Little children, do not let anyone deceive you! Whoever does what is right is righteous just as he is righteous. Whoever practices sin belongs to the devil because he has sinned since the beginning. Because of this, the Son of God was revealed so that he might destroy the devil's actions. No one who has been born of God sins, because God's seed remains in them; they cannot sin, because they have been born of God. By this it is clear who the children of God and the children of the devil are: everyone who does not do what is right does not belong to God (including the one who does not love their brother).

You see, this is the message that we have heard since the beginning, that we should love one another. We must not be like Cain, who belonged to the evil one and slaughtered his brother. Why did he slaughter him? His actions were evil, and his brother's were right. Do not be amazed, brothers, if the world hates you. We know that we have gone from death to life because we love the brothers. Whoever does not love remains in death. Everyone who hates their brother is a murderer, and you know that no murderer has eternal life remaining in them. By this we know love: he laid down his life for us. We also ought to lay down our lives for the brothers. However, if anyone who has worldly possessions sees their brother in need and shuts out their compassion for him, how could God's love remain in them? Little children, may we love not only in word or speech but also in action and truth!

By this we will know that we belong to the truth and convince our hearts in his presence. You see, if our hearts condemn us, God is greater than our hearts, and he knows everything. Dear loved ones, if our hearts do not condemn us, we have confidence in God's presence, and we receive from him whatever we ask because we keep his commands and do what is pleasing in his sight. This is his command, that we believe in the name of his Son, Jesus the Messiah, and that we love one another in the way that he commanded us. Whoever keeps his commands remains in him, and God remains in that person. By this we know that we remain in him, by the Spirit whom he has given us.

Dear loved ones, do not believe every spirit. Instead, test the spirits to see whether they are from God. You see, many false prophets have gone out into the world. By this you know God's Spirit: every spirit who confesses that Jesus the Messiah has come in the flesh is from God. Every spirit who does not confess Jesus is not from God—this is the spirit of the Messiah's adversary, who you have heard is coming (even now he is already in the world). However, you belong to God, little children. You have conquered them because the one who is in you is greater than the one who is in the world. They belong to the world. Because of this, they speak out from the world, and the world hears them. We belong to God. Whoever knows God hears us. Whoever does not belong to God does not hear us. From this we know the true Spirit and the deceptive spirit.

Dear loved ones, let us love one another, because love is from God; everyone who loves has been born of God and knows God. Everyone who does not love does not know God, because God is love. By this God's love was revealed in us: God sent his uniquely born Son into the world so that we might live through him. This is love—not that we loved God, but that he loved us and sent his Son to be the atonement for our sins. Dear loved ones, if this is how God loved us, we also must love one another. No one has ever seen God, but if we love one another, God remains in us, and his love is made complete in us.

We know that we remain in him and he remains in us because of his Spirit whom he has given to us. We have seen this, and we testify that the Father sent his Son to be the world's Savior. God remains in anyone who confesses that Jesus is God's Son, and that person remains in God. We ourselves have come to know and believe the love that God has in us.

God is love, and whoever remains in that love also remains in God, and God remains in them. By this his love is made complete with us so that we might have confidence on Judgment Day, because we are just like him in this world. There is no fear in love. No, perfect love throws fear out because fear involves torture. Whoever is afraid has not been made complete in love. We love because he loved us first. Anyone who says, "I love God," but hates their brother, is a liar. You see, whoever does not love their brother (whom they have seen) cannot love God (whom they have not seen). This is the command that we have from him: whoever loves God must love their brother too.

Everyone who believes that Jesus is the Messiah has been born of God, and everyone who loves the Father loves whoever is born of him. By this we know that we love God's children: we love God and do what he commands. You see, this is love for God, that we keep his commands (and his commands are not burdensome). You see, everyone who is born of God conquers the world. This is the victory that has conquered the world: our faith! Who is the one who conquers the world if it is not the one who believes that Jesus is God's Son?

He is the one who came through water and blood, Jesus the Messiah. He did not come with water only, but with water and blood—and the Spirit is the one who testifies of this because the Spirit is the truth. You see, there are three who testify: the Spirit, the water, and the blood—and these three are one! If we accept the testimony of men, God's testimony is greater. You see, this is God's testimony that he bore concerning his Son. (Whoever believes in the Son has the testimony within themselves. Whoever does not believe God makes him out to be a liar because they have not believed in the testimony that God bore concerning his Son.) This is the testimony: God gave us eternal life, and this life is in his Son. Whoever has the Son has this life; whoever does not have God's Son does not have this life.

I have written this to you who believe in the name of God's Son so that you may know that you have eternal life. This is the confidence that we have before him: if we ask anything based on his will, he hears us. If we know that he hears us—whatever we ask—we know that we have the requests that we have asked of him. If anyone sees their brother committing a sin that does not lead to death, they will ask and God will give him life (referring to those who sin not leading to death). There is a sin that leads to death. I am not saying that they should ask about it. All wickedness is sin, and there is a sin that does not lead to death.

We know that everyone who has been born of God does not sin. On the contrary, the One who was born of God keeps them, and the evil one does not touch them. We know that we belong to God and the whole world lies in evil. We know that God's Son has come, and he has given us understanding so that we might know the truth. We are in the True One—in his Son, Jesus the Messiah. He is the true God and eternal life. Little children, guard yourselves from idols!

FROM
JOHN (II)

The elder,

To the chosen lady and her children, whom I truly love (and not I alone, but also everyone who knows the truth) because of the truth that remains in us and will be with us forever: may grace, mercy, and peace be with us in truth and love, from God our Father and Jesus the Messiah, the Father's Son.

I WAS VERY GLAD TO FIND SOME OF YOUR CHILDREN LIVING BY THE truth just as we have received the command from the Father. Even now I ask you, lady—yet not as though I am writing you a new command; on the contrary, it is what we have had since the beginning—that we love one another. This is that love, that we walk in a manner consistent with his commands. This is the command just as you have heard since the beginning so that you might walk in it.

You see, many deceivers have gone out into the world. They do not acknowledge that Jesus the Messiah has come in the flesh. This kind of person is the deceiver and the adversary of the Messiah. Pay attention so that you do not lose what we have worked for. Be careful to receive your full reward. Everyone who goes too far and does not remain in the teaching about the Messiah does not have God. Whoever remains in the teaching has both the Father and the Son. If anyone comes to you and does not bring this teaching, do not receive them into your house and do not greet them. You see, whoever greets them takes part in their evil actions.

Since I had many things to write to you, I did not want to do so with paper and ink. Instead, I hope to come to you and speak face to face so that our joy might be made complete. The children of your chosen sister greet you.

FROM
JOHN (III)

The elder,

To my dear Gaius, whom I truly love:

DEAR LOVED ONE, I PRAY FOR YOU TO FLOURISH AND BE HEALTHY in every way just as your soul has flourished. You see, I was glad when some brothers came and testified to your truth even as you live by the truth. I have no greater joy than this, to hear that my children live by the truth.

Dear loved one, you have acted faithfully in everything you have done for the brothers (and in this case, to strangers!). In front of the congregation, these men testified of your love, and you will do well to send them out in a way worthy of God. You see, they have gone out on behalf of the Name and have received no support from the nations. Therefore we ought to support such people so that we might truly be fellow workers.

I have written to the congregation, but Diotrephes (who tries to control them) refuses to accept us. Because of this, when I come, I will bring up what he is doing. He is ridiculing us with evil words, and not satisfied by doing this, he refuses to receive our brothers. He forbids whoever wants to receive them and throws these people out of the congregation!

Dear loved one, do not imitate evil. Rather, imitate what is good. Whoever does what is good is from God. Whoever does what is evil has not seen God. Everyone has testified well of Demetrius—as has the truth itself! We testify too, and you know that our testimony is true!

I had a lot to write to you, but I do not want to write to you with paper and pen. Instead, I hope to see you soon, and we will talk face to face. Peace to you. Our friends greet you. Greet our friends by name!

FROM
JUDE

From Jude (a servant of Jesus the Messiah and the brother of James),

To those who are called, who are loved in God the Father and preserved in Jesus the Messiah: may grace, peace, and love be multiplied to you!

DEAR LOVED ONES, ALTHOUGH I WAS FULLY EAGER TO WRITE TO you about our shared salvation, I felt it necessary to write to you to encourage you to contend for the faith that once and for all was turned over to the saints. You see, some people have snuck in—since a long time ago, they have been designated for this condemnation. They are irreverent—perverting our God's grace into inappropriate behavior and denying our only Lord and Master, Jesus the Messiah.

I want to remind you (although you know all of this) that even though the Master once saved the people from the land of Egypt, he later destroyed those who were unfaithful. Also, as for the angels who did not keep their office, but rather abandoned their dwelling place, he has kept them in darkness (in invisible chains) for judgment on that great day. They are exhibited as an example of undergoing the punishment of eternal fire—like Sodom, Gomorrah, and the cities around them who indulged (just as they did) in the same kind of prohibited sexual behavior and went after unnatural desire.

However, when these people "see visions," they defile the body in the same way, reject the Master's authority, and insult his glorious ones. When Michael the archangel was arguing with the devil about the body of Moses, he did not dare pronounce an insulting condemnation. On the contrary, he said, "May the Master rebuke you!" On the other hand, these people insult what they do not know, and then, like animals that have no sense of reason, they are destroyed by the physical things that they know. They are in trouble! You see, they have gone the way of Cain, given themselves up to the deception of Balaam, and have been ruined by the rebellion of Korah. These are the hidden reefs who brazenly take part in your fellowship meals and shepherd themselves. They are waterless clouds, carried off by the wind, and trees at harvest time with no fruit, which die twice and are uprooted. They are fierce waves of the sea, foaming up their shameful actions, and wandering stars for whom the shadow of darkness is kept forever.

Even Enoch (the seventh descendant from Adam) prophesied about these things. He said, "Look! The Master came with ten thousand of his holy ones to execute judgment against everyone and to reprimand every living thing for all their irreverent actions that they have committed and for all the harsh words that the irreverent sinners have spoken against him." These people are complainers, unhappy with their circumstances while they go after their own desires. Their mouths speak arrogant things, and they show partiality to gain an advantage.

However, dear loved ones, you need to remember the words that were said by the apostles of our Master, Jesus the Messiah, because they told you, "Later in time, people will be mockers, following after their own irreverent desires." These people are divisive and worldly, and they do not have the Spirit. However, dear loved ones, you need to build one another up with your holy faith, praying by the Holy Spirit. Keep yourselves in the love of God, waiting for the mercy of our Master, Jesus the Messiah, which leads to eternal life. Show mercy on some who are doubtful, but save others by snatching them from the fire. However, show mercy, and fearfully hate even the clothes that are stained by the flesh.

Now to the one who is able to keep you from stumbling and make you stand with celebration in the presence of his spotless glory—to the only God, our Savior through Jesus the Messiah, our Master—be glory, majesty, power, and authority over everything—in the present age and throughout all the ages, amen!

From Jude

THE
WORD

*JOHN'S
REVELATION*

JOHN'S
REVELATION

The revelation from Jesus the Messiah that God granted him so that he can show his servants what must quickly take place. God communicated this when he delivered it by his angel to his servant John. This John bore witness to everything he had seen that related to the Word of God and the Testimony of Jesus the Messiah. Blessed are the one who recites and those who hear the words of this prophecy and who also do what is written in them because the time is near.

John, to the seven congregations that are in Asia:

MAY FAVOR AND PEACE COME TO YOU FROM THE ONE WHO IS, Was, and Is Coming; from the seven spirits that are before his throne; and from Jesus the Messiah. He is Faithful Martyr, Firstborn from the Dead, and Ruler of the Kings of the Earth.

To the one who loved us, who released us from our sins with his blood, and made us a kingdom—priests to God (who is also his Father)—to him be the glory and power forever and ever, amen!

> Look! He is coming with the clouds,
> And every eye will see him—
> Even those who pierced him.
> All the tribes of the earth will mourn because of him.

Yes! Amen!

"I am the Alpha and the Omega," says God our Master, "The one who is, was, and is coming—the Almighty!"

I, John (your brother and partner in the affliction, kingdom, and persistence in Jesus), was on the island called Patmos because of the Word of God and the Testimony of Jesus. I was in the Spirit on the Lord's day, and I heard a loud voice behind me, like a trumpet, that said, "Write what you see into a letter, and send it to these seven congregations: Ephesus, Smyrna, Pergamos, Thyatira, Sardis, Philadelphia, and Laodicea."

So I turned around to see whose voice was speaking to me, and when I turned around, I saw seven gold lampstands. Among the seven lampstands was one like a son of man clothed in a long robe and wearing a gold sash across his chest. His head and his hair were white, like white wool or like snow, and his eyes were like blazing fire. His feet were like bronze glowing in a furnace, and his voice was like the roar of a waterfall. He had seven stars in his right hand, and a sharp, two-edged broadsword was coming out of his mouth. His appearance was like the sun shining at its brightest.

When I saw him, I fell down at his feet like a dead man. He put his hand on me and said, "Do not be afraid; I am the First and the Last, the One who Lives. I was dead, and look! I am alive forevermore, and I have the keys of death and the grave. So write what you see: the things that are happening now and the things that are going to happen after this. This is the secret of the seven stars that you saw in my right hand and of the seven gold lampstands: the seven stars are the angels of the seven congregations, and the seven lampstands are the seven congregations.

"Write this to the angel of the congregation in Ephesus:

> *This is spoken by the one who holds the seven stars in his right hand, who walks among the seven gold lampstands: I know your actions, toil, and persistence and that you cannot stand evil people. You have tested those who claim to be apostles (and are not), and you have found them to be liars. You have persistence, and you have put up with a lot because of my name without becoming tired. But I have something against you: you have abandoned the love you had at first. Therefore consider how far you have fallen, and repent. Do the things you did at first, or else I am coming for you—I will remove your lampstand from its place unless you repent. However, you do have this: you hate the Nicolaitans' actions that I also hate. Whoever has an ear needs to listen to what the Spirit says to the seven congregations. As for the one who conquers, I will grant them the right to eat from the tree of life that is in God's paradise.*

"Write also to the angel of the congregation in Smyrna:

> *This is spoken by the First and the Last, who died and came back to life: I know your affliction and poverty (but you are rich) and the slander of those who claim to be Jews. They are not Jews; they are Satan's synagogue! Do not be afraid of what you are about to suffer. Look! the devil is about to throw some of you into prison so that you may be tested, and you will have affliction for ten days. Be faithful until death, and I will give you the crown of life. Whoever has an ear needs to hear what the Spirit says to the congregations. As for the one who conquers, they will not be hurt by the second death.*

"Write also to the angel of the congregation in Pergamos:

> *This is spoken by the one who has the sharp, two-edged broadsword: I know where you live (where Satan's throne is), and you have held on to my name and have not denied my faith even in the days of Antipas, my martyr and my faithful one who was killed before your eyes where Satan*

lives. However, I have a little something against you. You have there some who are holding on to the teaching of Balaam, who taught Balak to put an obstacle in front of the sons of Israel so that they ate food sacrificed to idols and engaged in prohibited sexual behavior. You have people like this among you, and you hold on to the teaching of the Nicolaitans also. Therefore repent, or else I am coming for you quickly, and I will wage war against them with the broadsword of my mouth. Whoever has an ear needs to hear what the Spirit says to the congregations. As for the one who conquers, I will give them the hidden manna and a white stone, and a new name will be written on the stone that no one knows except for the one who receives it.

"Write also to the angel of the congregation in Thyatira:

This is spoken by the Son of God, whose eyes are like blazing fire and whose feet are like bronze: I know your actions, love, faith, and service and your perseverance, and your most recent actions outnumber the earliest! However, I have something against you: you tolerate that Jezebel of a woman who calls herself a prophet. She teaches and deceives my servants into engaging in prohibited sexual behavior and eating food sacrificed to idols. I have given her time to repent, and she has refused to repent of her sexual behavior. Look! I am throwing her onto a sickbed, and I will throw all of those who have committed adultery with her into great affliction unless they repent of her actions. I will strike her children dead, and all the congregations will know that I am the one who examines minds and hearts and that I will give to each of you as your actions deserve. Yet I say to the rest of you who are in Thyatira, who have not held on to this teaching, who have not, as they say, 'known the depths of Satan,' that I am not putting any other burden on you except that you hold on until I come. As for the one who conquers and keeps my actions until the end, I will give them authority over the nations just as I received it from my Father, and they will shepherd them with an iron staff like ceramic vessels that have been broken into pieces. I will give them the morning star. Whoever has an ear needs to hear what the Spirit says to the congregations.

"Write also to the angel of the congregation in Sardis:

This is spoken by the one who has the seven spirits of God and the seven stars: I know your actions—that you have a reputation of being alive, but you are dead! Be watchful, and strengthen what is still alive, which is about to die, because I have not found your actions to be enough in the presence of my God. Therefore consider what you have received and heard; keep it and repent. So if you are not watchful, I will come like a thief, and you will not know what time I will come to you. However, you have some people in Sardis who have not stained their garments; they will walk with me in white clothes because they are worthy. The one who conquers will be clothed like this, in white garments, and I will not erase their name from the Book of Life. I will acknowledge their name before my Father and before his angels. Whoever has an ear needs to hear what the Spirit says to the congregations.

"Write also to the angel of the congregation in Philadelphia:

This is spoken by the Holy One, the True One, who has the key of David, who opens and no one can shut, and who closes and no one can open: I know your actions. Look: I have set before you an opened door that no one can shut because although you have had little strength, you have kept my word and have not denied my name. Look: I will repay those who are from Satan's synagogue who claim to be Jews and are not (they are liars). I will cause them to come and bow down before your feet, and they will know that I have loved you. Because you have kept my word with persistence, I also will keep you from the hour of trial that is about to come over the entire world to try those who live on the earth. I am coming quickly. Hold on to what you have so that no one takes your crown. As for the one who conquers, I will make them a column in the sanctuary of my God, and they will not go out from it anymore. I will write on them the name of my God, the name of my God's city (New Jerusalem, which comes from God and descends from the heavens), and my new name. Whoever has an ear needs to hear what the Spirit says to the congregations.

"Write also to the angel of the congregation in Laodicea:

This is spoken by the Amen, the Martyr, the Faithful and True, the Ruler of God's creation: I know your actions, that you are neither cold nor hot. It would be better if you were cold or hot. Therefore since you are lukewarm and neither hot nor cold, I am about to vomit you out of my mouth. Because you say, 'I am rich, I have plenty, and I need nothing,' and you do not know that you are miserable, pitiful, poor, blind, and naked, I advise you to buy from me! Buy gold refined by fire so that you will be rich. Buy white garments so that you will be clothed, that the shame of your nakedness will not be revealed. Buy eye ointment to smear on your eyes so that you will see. I reprimand and discipline the ones I love, so be devoted and repent! Look: I am standing at the door and knocking. If anyone hears my voice and opens the door, I will come inside to them; I will eat with them and they with me. As for the one who conquers, I will grant them the right to sit with me on my throne as I also conquered and sat with my Father on his throne. Whoever has an ear needs to hear what the Spirit says to the congregations."

AFTER THIS, I SAW—LOOK AT THIS—A DOOR OPENED IN HEAVEN, and the trumpet-like voice that I heard at first spoke to me. It said, "Come up here, and I will show you what must happen after this."

Immediately I was in the spirit, and imagine! A throne was set in heaven, and someone was seated on the throne! The one who sat on the throne had an appearance like jasper and carnelian stone. There was an emerald-looking halo surrounding the throne. Around the throne were twenty-four thrones, and twenty-four elders were sitting on the thrones. They wore white garments and had gold crowns on their heads. Lightning, noises, and thunder were coming out from the throne, and seven blazing torches were burning before the throne. (These are the seven spirits of God.) Before the throne, there was a pool of crystal-like glass.

Among the throne and encircling the throne were four living creatures that were full of eyes on their fronts and backs. The first living creature looked like a lion, the second living creature like an ox, the third living creature like a man, and the fourth living creature like an eagle in flight. The four living creatures each had six wings full of eyes on the inside and outside. They did not rest day or night but said, "Holy, holy, holy! Lord God Almighty, who was, is, and is coming." And whenever the living creatures give glory, honor, and thanksgiving to the one who sits on the throne and lives forever and ever, then the twenty-four elders fall before the one who sits on the throne and worship the one who lives forever and ever, and they throw their crowns down before the throne. Then the elders say, "You are worthy, our Master and God, to receive the glory, honor, and power because you created all things and by your will they came to be and were created."

I also saw a scroll in the hand of the one who sits on the throne. It was written on the inside and outside and sealed with seven seals. I saw a mighty angel proclaim with a loud voice, "Who is worthy to open the scroll and break its seals?" And no one in heaven, on earth, or under the earth was able to open the scroll or look in it. And I wept deeply because no one was found worthy to open the scroll or look in it. One of the elders said to me, "Stop weeping. Look: the Lion from the tribe of Judah, the Root of David, has conquered so that he may open the scroll and its seven seals."

And in the middle of the throne, the four living creatures, and the elders, I saw a Lamb, standing like it had been slaughtered. It had seven horns and seven eyes, which are the seven spirits of God who are sent to all parts of the earth. He came and took the scroll from the hand of the one who sits on the throne. When he had taken the scroll, the four living creatures and the twenty-four elders fell down before the Lamb. Each one of them had a harp and gold bowls full of incense (which are the prayers of the saints), and they sang a new song:

> You are worthy to take the book and open its seals
> Because you were slaughtered.
> And with your blood you redeemed people for God
> From every tribe, tongue, people, and nation,
> And you made them a kingdom and priests to our God,
> And they will reign over the earth.

And I saw and heard the sound of many angels encircling the throne, the living creatures, and the elders. The number of them was ten thousands of ten thousands and thousands of thousands. They said with a loud voice:

> The Lamb who was slaughtered is worthy to receive
> Power, wealth, wisdom, strength,
> Honor, glory, and blessing.

Then every creature that was in heaven, on earth, under the earth, and in the sea—I heard everything in them say,

> To the one who sits on the throne and to the Lamb
> Be blessing, honor, glory, and power forever and ever.

Then the four living creatures said, "Amen!" The elders fell down and worshiped.

I saw when the Lamb opened one of the seven seals, and I heard one of the four living creatures say with a thunderous voice, "Come!" And I saw a white horse! The one who was riding it had a bow, and a crown was given to him. He came out like a conqueror intent to conquer.

When he opened the second seal, I heard the second living creature say, "Come!" And another horse the color of fire came out. The one who was riding it was granted the right to take peace from the earth so that they would kill one another. He was given a large sword.

When he opened the third seal, I heard the third living creature say, "Come!" And I saw a black horse! The one who was riding it had scales in his hand. I heard what sounded like a voice, in the middle of the four living creatures, that said, "A quart of wheat for a day's wages, three quarts of barley for a day's wages, and do not waste the oil or wine!"

When he opened the fourth seal, I heard the voice of the fourth living creature say, "Come!" And I saw a pale green horse! The one who was riding it was named Death, and the grave followed behind him. Authority was given to them over one-fourth of the earth so that they could kill it with the sword, with famine, with plague, and with wild beasts of the earth.

When he opened the fifth seal, below the altar I saw the souls of those who had been slain because of the Word of God and the Testimony they held. They cried out with a loud voice, "How long, holy and true Master, will you withhold justice and not avenge our blood on those who live on the earth?" A white robe was given to each of them, and they were told to rest for a little while longer until the number of their fellow servants and brothers (who were about to be killed just as they were) was reached.

And I saw when he opened the sixth seal. There was an earthquake, the sun became black like sackcloth, and the moon became like blood. The stars fell from heaven to the earth as a fig tree drops its unripe figs when it is shaken by a strong wind. The sky disappeared like a scroll being rolled up, and every mountain and island was moved from its place. The kings of the earth, the governors, the commanders, the wealthy, and the strong—both slave and free—hid themselves in caves and the rocks of the mountains. They said to the mountains and rocks, "Fall on us and hide us from the face of the one who sits on the throne and from the wrath of the Lamb because the great day of their wrath has come, and who can endure it?"

After this, I saw four angels standing at the four corners of the earth and holding back the four winds of the earth so that they could not blow wind upon the earth, the sea, or any tree. And I saw another angel ascending from the direction of the sunrise, who had the seal of the living God. He cried out with a loud voice to the four angels who were given authority to harm the earth and the sea, "Do not harm the earth, the sea, or any tree until we put a seal on the foreheads of the servants of our God!" And I heard the number of those who were sealed—144,000—who were from every tribe of the sons of Israel:

> 12,000 were sealed from the tribe of Judah.
> 12,000 from the tribe of Reuben.
> 12,000 from the tribe of Gad.
> 12,000 from the tribe of Asher.
> 12,000 from the tribe of Naphtali.
> 12,000 from the tribe of Manasseh.
> 12,000 from the tribe of Simeon.
> 12,000 from the tribe of Levi.
> 12,000 from the tribe of Issachar.
> 12,000 from the tribe of Zebulun.
> 12,000 from the tribe of Joseph.
> 12,000 were sealed from the tribe of Benjamin.

AFTER THIS, I SAW—GET THIS—A LARGE CROWD THAT NO ONE could number, from every nation, tribe, people, and language, standing before the throne and before the Lamb. They were clothed in white robes and had palm branches in their hands, and they cried out with a loud voice, "Salvation belongs to our God who sits upon the throne and to the Lamb." And all the angels who stood around the throne, as well as the elders and the four living creatures, fell down on their faces before the throne and worshiped God. They said, "Amen! Blessing, glory, wisdom, thanksgiving, honor, power, and strength be to our God forever and ever! Amen!"

One of the elders asked me, "These who are wearing white robes—who are they, and where have they come from?"

I said to him, "Sir, you know as well as I do."

So he said to me, "These are the ones who come from the great affliction:

> They have washed their robes
> And have made them white with the Lamb's blood.
> Because of this, they are standing before God's throne
> And they worship him day and night in his sanctuary.

> The one who sits on the throne will prepare a dwelling for them.
> They will not hunger anymore or thirst anymore,
> Nor will the sun's glare or any heat fall upon them
> Because the Lamb who is in the middle of the throne shepherds them
> And he will lead them by streams of living water.
> And God will wipe every tear from their eyes."

And when he opened the seventh seal, there was silence in heaven for about half an hour. I saw the seven angels who were standing before God, and seven trumpets were given to them. Another angel also came and stood by the altar. He had a gold censer, and he was given a lot of incense so that he could offer the prayers of all the saints upon the golden altar that was before the throne. The smoke rose out of the incense, with the prayers of the saints, from the hand of the angel who was standing before God. Then the angel took the censer and filled it with wood from the fire of the altar; he threw it to the earth, and it began to thunder, rumble, lightning, and quake. Then the seven angels who had the seven trumpets prepared to sound them.

The first sounded his trumpet! Then hail and fire, mixed with blood, were thrown down to the earth, and a third of the earth was consumed. A third of the trees were consumed, and all green grass was consumed.

The second angel sounded his trumpet! Then something like a huge, burning mountain was thrown down into the sea, and a third of the sea became blood. A third of the creatures that lived in the sea died, and a third of the ships were destroyed.

The third angel sounded his trumpet! Then a large, burning star fell from heaven like a torch. It fell upon a third of the rivers and upon the streams of water. The name of the star was Wormwood, and a third of the waters became wormwood, and everyone who drank from the water died because it had become poisoned.

The fourth angel sounded his trumpet! Then a third of the sun was struck, as well as a third of the moon and a third of the stars, so that a third of each of them was darkened. And so a third of the day there was no light, and night was the same way.

Then I saw an eagle flying in the middle of the heavens and heard it speak with a loud voice, "Trouble! Trouble! Those who live on the earth are in trouble because of the three blasts of the trumpet from the three angels who are about to sound them!

Then the fifth angel sounded his trumpet! Then I saw a star that had fallen from heaven to earth. The key to the shaft to the underworld was given to him. Then he opened the shaft to the underworld, and smoke rose up from the shaft like the smoke of a large furnace, and the sun and air were darkened by the smoke from the shaft. Then out of the smoke came locusts upon the earth. They were given authority similar to what the scorpions of the earth have: they were told not to harm the grass of the earth, any green plant, or any tree—only the people who did not have God's seal on their foreheads. They were not granted the right to kill them—the people were only to be tormented by them for five months. The agony they caused was like the agony of a scorpion whenever it stings a person. In those days, men sought death, but they could not find it anywhere; they desired to die, but death fled from them.

Now the appearance of the locusts was like horses prepared for war. Upon their heads were things like golden crowns, and their faces were like human faces. Their hair was like women's hair, and their teeth were like the teeth of lions. They had chests like iron breastplates, and the sound of their wings was like many horse-drawn chariots running into battle. They had tails and stings like scorpions, and in their tails they had the power to harm people for five months. They had a king—the angel of the underworld, whose name in Hebrew is Abaddon. In Greek, his name means "Destroyer."

> The first trouble has passed. Look!
> There are still two troubles coming after this!

Then the sixth angel sounded his trumpet! I heard the voice of one of the four horns of the golden altar that was before God's throne say to the sixth angel (the one who had the trumpet), "Release the four angels that are bound by the great Euphrates River." Then the four angels that were prepared for that hour, day, month, and year were released so that they could kill a third of the people. The number of cavalry troops was twenty thousands of ten thousands—I heard the number of them. This is how I saw the horses and their riders in the vision: they had breastplates the color of fire, blue, and sulfur. The horses' heads were like lions' heads, and fire, smoke, and sulfur came out of their mouths. A third of the people were killed by these three plagues—from the fire, the smoke, and the sulfur that came out of their mouths. The power of the horses is in their mouths and in their tails, for their tails are like snakes, and the tails have heads, and they hurt people with them.

And the rest of the people (those who were not killed by these plagues) did not repent of the things they made with their hands. Otherwise, they would have stopped worshiping demons and idols made of gold, silver, bronze, stone, and wood, which cannot see, hear, or walk. They also did not repent of their murder, sorcery, prohibited sexual behavior, or theft.

And I saw another mighty angel descend from heaven, wrapped in a cloud. There was a halo on his head, and his face was like the sun. His feet were like columns of fire. In his hand, he held a small, open scroll. He placed his right foot upon the sea and his left on the earth. Then he cried out with a loud voice like the roar of a lion. When he cried out, the seven thunders spoke with their own voices. When the seven thunders spoke, I was about to write it down, but I heard a voice from heaven say, "Seal up the things that the seven thunders have spoken, and do not write them."

Then the angel whom I saw standing on the sea and earth raised his right hand to heaven and swore an oath by the one who lives forever and ever, who created heaven and what is in it, earth and what is in it, and the sea and what is in it. He said, "There will not be any more delay, but in the days of the seventh angel's sounding—since he is about to sound his trumpet—then the secret of God will be completed as he announced to his servants the prophets!"

Then the voice I had heard from heaven spoke to me another time and told me, "Go and take the opened scroll that is in the hand of the angel who is standing on the sea and the earth." So I went to the angel and said to him, "Give me the little scroll." Then he said to me, "Take it and eat it. It will make your stomach bitter, but it will be as sweet as honey in your mouth."

So I took the little scroll from the angel's hand and ate it, and it was as sweet as honey in my mouth, but when I swallowed it, my stomach became bitter. Then I was told, "You must prophesy again to many people, nations, languages, and kingdoms!"

I was given a reed like a shepherd's staff, and I was told, "Rise and measure God's temple, the altar, and those who worship in the temple. Disregard the outer court of the temple, and do not measure it because it has been granted to the nations—they will trample the holy city for forty-two months.

"I will give charge to my two witnesses, and they will prophesy 1260 days clothed in sackcloth. These are the two olive trees and the two lampstands that are standing before the Master. If someone wishes to harm them, fire comes out of their mouths and consumes their enemies. If someone wanted to harm them, that person must be killed in this way. These two witnesses have the authority to shut the heavens so that no rain may fall during the days of their prophecy, and they have the authority over the waters so they can turn them to blood and strike the earth with whatever plagues they wish to use.

"And when they have completed their testimony, the beast that rises from the underworld will wage war with them, and it will conquer and kill them. Then their corpses will lie in the street in that great city that is spiritually called Sodom and Egypt, where their Master was also crucified. Then some of the people, tribes, languages, and nations will see their corpses for three and a half days, and they will not be allowed to bury them in a tomb. Then those who live on the earth will rejoice because of them and celebrate—they will exchange gifts with one another—because these two prophets tortured those who live on the earth."

And after those three and a half days, the breath of life from God entered them, and they stood on their feet. Then great fear fell on those who watched them. Then they heard a loud voice from heaven tell them, "Come up here!" Then they rose into heaven in the cloud, and their enemies watched them rise! Then at that hour, there was a great earthquake, and a tenth of the city fell. Seven thousand individuals were killed in the earthquake, and the rest of the men became afraid and glorified God in heaven.

> The second trouble has passed. Look!
> The third trouble is coming soon!

Then the seventh angel sounded his trumpet! Loud voices coming from heaven said, "The kingdom of the world that belongs to our Master and his Messiah has come, and he will reign forever and ever!"

Then the twenty-four elders, who were sitting on their thrones before God, fell down on their faces and worshiped God. They said:

> We thank you, Master—almighty God, who is and who was—
> Because you have received your majestic power
> And have begun to reign!
> The nations were outraged,
> And your wrath has come,
> As well as the time for the dead to be judged
> And for you to give wages to your servants the prophets,
> To the saints, and to those who fear your name—
> Both small and great—
> And for you to ruin those who have ruined the earth.

Then the sanctuary of God that is in heaven was opened, his Ark of the Covenant appeared in his sanctuary, and there were lightning, rumbles, thunders, an earthquake, and large hail.

Then a great sign appeared in the sky: a woman clothed with the sun. She had the moon under her feet and a twelve-starred crown on her head. She was pregnant, and she cried out, suffering with the pain and agony of childbirth. Another sign appeared in the sky. Get this—it was a huge, fiery dragon that had seven heads, ten horns, and seven crowns on its heads. His tail swiped a third of the stars from the sky and threw them to the earth. Then the dragon stood before the woman who was about to give birth so he could devour her child.

She gave birth to a male child who is going to shepherd all the nations with an iron staff. Her child was snatched up to God and to his throne, and the woman fled into the wilderness, where she had a place that was prepared by God so that they could provide for her for 1260 days.

Then there was a war in heaven: Michael and his angels drew up for battle against the dragon. The dragon and his angels also drew up for battle, but he did not prevail, and there was no longer any place for them in heaven. Then the great dragon fell—that old serpent that is called the devil and Satan, who deceives the whole world—he was thrown down to the earth, and his angels were thrown down with him. And I heard a loud voice in heaven say:

> Now the salvation, power, and kingdom of our God has come,
> As well as the authority of his Messiah,
> Because the one who accused our brothers has been thrown down—
> The one who accused them before our God day and night!
> They have conquered him because of the Lamb's blood
> And the Word of their Testimony!
> They have not loved their lives even in the face of death!
> Because of this, rejoice, heavens, and all who live in them!
> You are in trouble, earth and the sea,
> Because the devil has come down to you.
> He has great wrath because he knows he has only a short time."

When the dragon saw that he had been thrown down to earth, he pursued the woman who had given birth to the male child. Then the woman was given two large eagles' wings so she could fly away from the serpent into the wilderness to her place (where she received provision for three and a half years). The serpent spewed water out of his mouth like a river, following the woman so he could sweep her away by the river. However, the earth helped the woman; the earth opened its mouth and swallowed the river that the dragon had spewed out of his mouth. The dragon was outraged at the woman and went away to wage war against the rest of her children who kept God's commands and had the Testimony of Jesus.

I was standing on the seashore, and I saw a beast rising from the sea. It had ten horns and seven heads. There were ten crowns on its horns, and blasphemous names were on its heads. Now the beast that I saw was like a leopard; its feet were like those of a bear, and its mouth was like a lion's mouth. The dragon gave it his power, his throne, and majestic authority. One of the beast's heads looked like it was fatally wounded, but its fatal wound was healed.

Then the whole earth was amazed at the beast and worshiped the dragon because he gave authority to the beast. They also worshiped the beast, saying, "Who is like this beast, and who can go to war against it?"

A mouth was given to it so that it spoke presumptuous and blasphemous things. Authority was given to it to work for forty-two months. It opened its mouth with blasphemies directed toward God to blaspheme his name, his dwelling place, and those whose dwelling is in heaven. It was granted ability to wage war with the saints and conquer them. It was granted authority over every tribe, people, language, and nation. It was worshiped by all those who live on the earth whose names are not written in the Book of Life, which belongs to the Lamb who was slain from the beginning of the world.

> Whoever has an ear needs to listen!
> Whoever is appointed for captivity will go away into captivity.
> Whoever is appointed to be killed by the sword
> will be killed by the sword.
> Here is the persistence and faith of the saints.

I saw another beast ascend from the earth. It had two horns like a lamb's, and it spoke like the dragon. It worked in the presence of the first beast with all of that beast's authority, and it caused the earth and those who live on it to worship the first beast, whose fatal wound was healed. It performed great signs. For instance, in front of men it made fire come down from heaven to the earth. It deceived those who live on the earth with the signs that it was granted to perform in the presence of the beast, and it told those who live on the earth to make idols for the beast that was wounded by the sword and survived.

It was given authority to give life to the beast's idol so that the beast's idol would also speak and act and that whoever refused to worship the beast's idol would be killed. It caused everyone, both small and great, both rich and poor, both free and slave, to receive an imprint on their right hands or on their foreheads. It also made it so that no one could buy or sell unless they had the imprint of the beast's name or the number of its name. Here is wisdom: whoever has understanding needs to interpret the number of the beast, because it is the number of a human. Its number is 666.

Then I saw—get this—the Lamb standing on Mount Zion, and there were 144,000 with him. They had his name and his Father's name written on their foreheads. I heard a voice from heaven that sounded like a waterfall and like the sound of loud thunder. The voice I heard was similar to harpists playing music on their harps. They sang what seemed to be a new song before the throne and before the four living creatures and the elders, and no one could learn the song except the 144,000 who were redeemed from the earth. These are those who have not defiled themselves with women, because they are virgins. These are the ones who followed the Lamb wherever he went. They were redeemed from among men to be a possession of God and the Lamb, and there was no lie in their mouths—they are blameless.

I also saw another angel, flying in the middle of heaven, that had an eternal message to preach against those who live on the earth—and against every nation, tribe, language, and people. He said with a loud voice, "Fear God and give him glory because the hour of his judgment has come! Worship the one who made heaven, earth, the sea, and the streams of water!"

Then another one, a second angel, followed him and said, "Great Babylon has fallen—it has fallen—the city from which all the nations have drunk the wine of her prohibited sexual practices."

Then another one, a third angel, followed them and said with a loud voice, "If anyone worships the beast and its idol and receives the imprint on their forehead or on their hand, they will drink from the wine of God's wrath, which was poured out into the cup of his wrath without watering it down. They will be tortured with fire and sulfur before the holy angels and before the Lamb, and the smoke of their torture will rise forever and ever. Those who worship the beast and its idol, and whoever receives the imprint of its name, will have no rest, day or night. Here is the persistence of the saints—those who keep God's commands and the faith of Jesus."

Then I heard a voice from heaven say, "Write: 'Blessed are the dead who die in the Master from now on. Yes!' says the Spirit, 'So that they may rest from their works because their actions follow them.'"

Then I saw—get this—a white cloud. Someone who looked like a son of man was sitting on the cloud, and he had a gold crown on his head and a sharp sickle in his hand. Another angel went out from the sanctuary and cried out with a loud voice to the one who sat on the cloud, "Send your sickle and reap because the hour to harvest has come. The earth's harvest is ripe." So the one who sat on the cloud swung his sickle toward the earth, and the earth was harvested.

Then another angel went out from the heavenly sanctuary, he himself having a sharp sickle. Another angel also went out from the altar who was in charge of the altar fire. He spoke with a loud voice to the one who had the sharp sickle, "Send your sharp sickle and gather in the grape cluster from the earth's vine because its bunches of grapes are in their prime." So the angel swung his sickle to the earth, gathered the earth's vine, and threw it into the large vat of God's wrath. Then the vat was trampled outside the city, and blood went out from the vat until it reached the height of a horse's bridle two hundred miles away.

Then I saw another great and marvelous sign in heaven: seven angels who had seven plagues related to the end. With these plagues, God's wrath was completed. Then I saw what looked like a sea of glass mixed with fire. Those who prevailed over the beast, over its idol, and over the number of its name were standing on the sea of glass, and they had the harps of God. Then they sang the song of God's servant Moses and the song of the Lamb:

> Your actions are great and marvelous, Master God Almighty;
> Your ways are righteous and true, King of the Nations;
> Who has not feared you, Master, and glorified your name?
> Because you are worthy!
> All the nations have come and worshiped before you;
> They have seen your righteous deeds.

AFTER THIS, I SAW THE SANCTUARY OF THE TENT OF MEETING opened in heaven. The seven angels who had the seven plagues went out from the sanctuary, clothed in pure, bright linen, with gold sashes wrapped around their chests. Then one of the four living creatures gave seven gold bowls to the seven angels. These bowls were full of the wrath of God, who lives forever and ever. Then the sanctuary was filled with smoke because of the glory of God and his power, and no one could enter the sanctuary until the seven angels' seven plagues were completed.

Then I heard a loud voice from the sanctuary say to the seven angels, "Go and pour out the bowls of God's wrath onto the earth."

So the first went and poured out his bowl onto the earth; it became an evil and wicked ulcer on the men who had the beast's imprint and on those who worshiped its idol.

Then the second poured his bowl into the sea, and it became like a dead man's blood, and every living thing that was in the sea died.

Then the third poured out his bowl into the rivers and streams of water, and they became blood. And I heard the angel of the waters say:

> You are righteous, one who is and was, the Holy One,
> Because you have judged these things.
> For they poured out the blood of the saints and prophets,
> And you have given them blood to drink—they deserve it!

Then I heard the altar say, "Yes, Master—Almighty God—your judgments are true and righteous!"

Then the fourth poured out his bowl upon the sun. He was given authority to scorch men with fire. Then those men were scorched with great fire, and they blasphemed God's name—who had authority over these plagues—and they did not repent so as to give him glory.

Then the fifth poured out his bowl upon the beast's throne, and its kingdom became darkened. They bit their tongues in pain and blasphemed the God of heaven because of their pain and the ulcers, and they did not repent of their actions.

Then the sixth poured out his bowl into the great Euphrates River, and its water was dried up, thus preparing the way for the kings from the direction of the sunrise. Then I saw three unclean spirits, like frogs, come from the dragon's mouth, the beast's mouth, and the false prophet's mouth. These are the spirits of demons who do wonders, and they go to the kings of the whole world to gather them to war on God Almighty's great day. "Look! I am coming like a thief. Blessed are the ones who watch and keep their clothing so they do not walk around naked, and people see their disgrace." He gathered them at the place called Armageddon in Hebrew.

Then the seventh angel poured out his bowl into the air, and a loud voice came out of the sanctuary from the throne, which said, "It is done!" It began to lightning, rumble, thunder, and quake greatly in a way that had never happened since man existed on the earth—it was that big of an earthquake! Then the great city became three parts, and the cities of the nations fell. And Babylon the Great was mentioned before God in a request that he would give it the wine cup of his angry wrath. Every island fled away, and the mountains were nowhere to be seen. One-hundred-pound hailstones came down from the sky upon the men. Then the men blasphemed God because of the hail plague, because this plague was very intense.

Then one of the seven angels who had the seven bowls came and spoke to me, "Come, and I will show you the judgment of the great prostitute that sits on many waters. The kings of the earth have committed prostitution with her, and those who live on the earth have become drunk from the wine of her prostitution." Then he brought me in the spirit into the wilderness, and I saw a woman sitting on a scarlet beast that was covered in blasphemous names and had seven heads and ten horns. The woman was clothed in purple and scarlet and was wearing gold, precious stones, and pearls. She had a gold cup in her hand full of disgusting things—filth from her prostitution. A secret name was written on her forehead: Babylon the Great, the Mother of Prostitutes and the Disgusting Things of the Earth. Then I saw the woman drinking the blood of the saints—the blood of the witnesses of Jesus!

I was bewildered with astonishment when I saw her. Then the angel said to me, "Why are you astonished? I will tell you the secret of the woman and the beast that carries her, which has seven heads and ten horns. The beast that you saw was present once, but it is not today. However, it is about to rise from the underworld and will go away into destruction. Then those who live on the earth will be astonished—those whose names are not written Book of Life from the creation of the world—when they see the beast. You see, it was present, and it is not today, but it will be present. Here is the mind that has wisdom: the seven heads are seven mountains on which the woman sits—they are seven kings. Five have fallen, one lives today, and another has not come yet. Whenever he comes, he must remain for a little while. And the beast that was present but is not now, it is the eighth. It is from among the seven, and it will go away into destruction. The ten horns that you saw are ten kings who have not yet received a kingdom. However, with the beast, they will receive kingly authority for an hour. These men have a single purpose, and they give their power and authority to the beast. They will wage war with the Lamb, and the Lamb will conquer them because he is Master of Masters and King of Kings. Those who are with him are called, chosen, and faithful."

Then he said to me, "The waters that you saw (where the woman sits), they are people, crowds, nations, and languages. The ten horns that you saw, as well as the beast, will hate the woman and leave her deserted and naked—they will eat her flesh and destroy her with fire because God has given this into their hearts so that he may accomplish his purpose through their single purpose and give their kingdom to the beast until God's words are finished. And the woman whom you saw is the great city that has a kingdom that is over the kings of the earth."

AFTER THIS, I SAW ANOTHER ANGEL DESCENDING FROM HEAVEN possessing great authority, and the earth was illuminated by his glory. He cried out with a loud voice, saying:

> It has fallen! Babylon the Great has fallen!
> It has become the dwelling place for demons
> And a prison for every unclean spirit.
> It is a prison for every unclean and hated bird,
> Because all the nations have drunk from the wine of wrath
> Because of her prostitution.
> The kings of the earth have committed prostitution with her,
> And the merchants of the earth have become wealthy
> Because of her luxurious power.

Then I heard another voice say from heaven:

> My people: come out of her so that you do not share in her sins
> And so that you do not receive her plagues,
> Because her sins have piled up as high as heaven,
> And God has remembered her unrighteous behavior.
> Repay her as she herself has paid; double what she doubled,
> According to her actions.
> Give her a drink that is twice as strong
> As the one she mixed in that cup.
> To the extent that she glorified herself and lived in luxury,
> To the same degree, give her torture and mourning.
> Because she has said in her heart,
> "I sit like a queen; I am not a widow,
> And I have not experienced mourning,"
> All her plagues will come upon her in one day:
> Death, mourning, and famine.
> She will be destroyed by fire,
> Because the God who judges her is a strong Master!

"Then the kings of the earth, who committed prostitution with her and lived in luxury with her, will weep and beat themselves up when they see the smoke of her inferno. Because of their fear of her torture, they will stand at a distance and say:

> Trouble! You are in trouble, great city—Babylon, the strong city—
> In a single hour your judgment has come!

"Then the merchants of earth will weep and mourn for her because no one will buy their merchandise anymore. This merchandise consisted of gold, silver, precious stones, pearls, fine linen, purple fabric, silk, and scarlet. It included every scented tree, every ivory container, and every container made of valuable wood, bronze, iron, and marble. There was merchandise of cinnamon, Indian spice, incense, ointment, and frankincense, as well as wine, olive oil, flour, wheat, beasts of burden, sheep, horses, carts, and the bodies and lives of slaves. They cried out:

> The fruit that you desired in life has left you.
> All the expensive and delightful things
> Have been destroyed in front of you,
> And not a single one of them will be found again.

"These merchants who became wealthy because of her will stand at a distance because of their fear of her torture, and they will weep, mourn, and say:

> Trouble! The great city is in trouble—
> The one that was clothed in fine linen, purple, and scarlet
> And wore gold, precious stones, and pearls—
> Because this wealth was wasted in a single hour.

"Then everyone who pilots a ship and everyone who sails anywhere—both sailors and those who work in the sea for a living—stood at a distance and cried out when they saw the smoke of her inferno. They said, 'Who is like the great city?' Then they threw dust over their heads and cried out, weeping and mourning. They said:

> Trouble! The great city is in trouble—
> In which everyone who has ships in the sea
> Has become wealthy because of its prosperity—
> Because it was wasted in a single hour.
> Rejoice over her, heaven, saints, apostles, and prophets!
> God has condemned her
> With the condemnation that she intended for you.

Then one mighty angel picked up a stone that was like a large millstone, and he threw it into the sea and said:

> Just like this, the great city of Babylon will be thrown down violently,
> And it will not be seen again.
> The sound of people playing harps, music, flutes, and trumpets
> Will not be heard in you anymore.
> No artist of any kind will be found in you anymore.
> The sound of the mill will not be heard in you anymore.
> Lamplight will not be seen in you anymore.
> The voice of the groom and bride will not be heard in you anymore.
> You will be thrown down
> Because your merchants were the important people of the world
> And all the nations were deceived by your sorcery.
> Also, blood was found in you from the prophets and the saints
> And from all those who have been slaughtered on the earth.

AFTER THIS, I HEARD WHAT SOUNDED LIKE THE ROAR OF MANY people in heaven who said:

> Hallelujah!
> Salvation, glory, and power belong to our God
> Because his judgments are true and righteous!
> For he has condemned the great prostitute,
> Who destroyed the earth with her prostitution,
> And he avenged the blood of his servants from her hands.

A second said:

> Hallelujah! Even her smoke rises forever and ever!

Then the twenty-four elders and the four living creatures fell down and worshiped God, who sits on the throne. They said,

Amen! Hallelujah!

Also, a voice that came out of the throne spoke:

Praise our God, all who serve him and those who fear him, both small and great!

Then I heard what sounded like the roar of a large crowd—like the sound of a waterfall and like loud thunder—that said:

Hallelujah!
For the Master reigns—our Almighty God!
We rejoice and celebrate and give him glory
Because the Lamb's wedding celebration has come
And his bride has prepared herself!
She has been given a bright, clean linen gown to wear.

(The linen gown represents the righteous actions of the saints.)

Then he said to me, "Write this: Blessed are those who are invited to the Lamb's wedding reception!" Then he said to me, "These are true words of God." Then I fell down before his feet to worship him, but he said to me, "Do not do that! I am a fellow servant with you and your brothers who have the Testimony of Jesus—worship God!" (Now the Testimony of Jesus is the Spirit of prophecy.)

Then I saw heaven opened, and look! There was a white horse, and the one who rode it was called Faithful and True. He judges and wages war righteously. Now his eyes were like blazing fire, and there were many crowns on his head. He had a name written down, which no one knew except for him. He wore a garment dipped in blood, and he was called by the name Word of God. The army of heaven followed him on white horses, clothed in clean, white linen. A sharp broadsword went out from his mouth so that he could strike down the nations. He will shepherd them with an iron staff, and he will trample the wine vat of God Almighty's angry wrath. He has a name written on his garment and on his thigh: King of Kings and Master of Masters.

Then I saw one angel standing on the sun. He cried out with a loud voice to all the birds that were flying in the middle of the heavens, "Come and gather for God's great feast so that you may eat the flesh of kings, commanders, mighty men, horses and riders, and everyone else, both free men and slaves, small and great!" I also saw the beast, with the kings of the earth and their armies gathered to wage war against the one who sat on the horse and his army. Then the beast was captured, as well as the false prophet who performed signs before it that were used to deceive those who received the beast's imprint and worshiped its idol. The two of them were thrown alive into the fiery lake that burns with sulfur. Then the rest of the armies were killed with the broadsword belonging to the one who sat on the throne. It went out of his mouth, and thus all of the birds had their fill of their flesh.

Then I saw an angel descend from heaven, holding the key to the underworld, and a large chain was in his hand. He seized the dragon, that ancient serpent who is the devil and Satan, and he tied him up for a thousand years. Then he threw him into the underworld, locked it, and put a seal over it so that the dragon would not deceive the nations until the thousand years were completed. After that, he must be released for a little while.

Then I saw thrones, and people were sitting on them who were given authority to judge. I also saw the souls who had been executed because of the Testimony of Jesus and the Word of God, as well as those who did not worship the beast or its idol and did not receive its imprint on their foreheads and hands. They were alive and reigned with the Messiah for a thousand years. The rest of the dead did not live again until the thousand years were completed. This is the first resurrection. Whoever has a part in the first resurrection is blessed and holy because the second death has no power over them. They will be priests of God and the Messiah and will reign with him for a thousand years.

When the thousand years were completed, Satan was released from his prison and went out to deceive the nations that are in all directions on the earth—Gog and Magog—so that he could assemble them for war. The number of them was like the sand of the sea. They went up to earth's battlefield and circled the camp of the saints and the dearly loved city, but fire came from heaven and devoured them. Then the devil, who deceived them, was thrown into the lake of fire and sulfur, where both the beast and false prophet were, and they will be tortured day and night, forever and ever.

Then I saw a large, white throne and someone sitting on it. The earth and heaven fled from his presence, and there was no place for them. I also saw the dead, both great and small, standing before the throne. Books were opened, as well as another book (which is the Book of Life), and the dead were judged by what was written in the books, based on their actions. The sea gave up the dead who were in it, and death and the grave gave up the dead who were in them, and each one was judged based on their actions. Then death and the grave were thrown into the lake of fire (this lake of fire is the second death), and whoever was not found written in the Book of Life was thrown into the lake of fire.

Then I saw a new heaven and a new earth because the first heaven and earth were gone, and there was no more sea. I also saw the holy city—New Jerusalem—coming down out of heaven from God, prepared like a bride dolled up for her husband. Then I heard a loud voice in heaven say, "Look! God's dwelling place is with mankind, and they will live with him—they will be his people, and God himself will be with them as their God! He will wipe every tear from their eyes, and there will be no more death, mourning, weeping, or pain because the first things are gone."

Then the one who sat on the throne said, "Look! I make all things new!" Then he said, "Write this, because these words are faithful and true." He said to me, "It has happened. I am the Alpha and the Omega, the Beginning and the End. I will grant that those who are thirsty may drink freely from the spring of living water! Whoever conquers will inherit these things; I will be their God, and they will be my sons and daughters. But as for those who are cowardly, unfaithful, disgusting, and murderers, those who are participants in illicit sexual activity, sorcery, and idolatry, as well as all liars—their part is in the lake that burns with fire and sulfur (which is the second death)."

Then one of the seven angels who had the seven bowls full of the seven final plagues came to me and spoke to me, "Come, and I will show you the bride, the wife of the Lamb." So he led me in the spirit to a large, high mountain and showed me the holy city, Jerusalem, which came down out of heaven from God. It had God's glory; its radiance was like precious stones—like crystal-clear jasper. It had a large, high wall that had twelve gateways. There were twelve angels at the gateways. Names were written on the gateways—the names of the twelve tribes, Israel's sons. There were three gateways on the east, three gateways on the north, three gateways on the south, and three gateways on the west. The wall of the city had a twelve-layered foundation, with twelve names on them—the names of the Lamb's apostles.

Then the one who spoke to me had a gold measuring reed so he could measure the city, its gateways, and its wall. The city was set out as a square, and its length was the same as its width. Using the reed, he measured the city to be 1,500 miles, with its length, width, and height measuring the same. He measured the wall to be seventy-two yards in human measurement, which is the same as an angel's measurement. The wall was made out of jasper, and the whole city was built from crystal-clear, pure gold. The city wall's foundations were decorated with every kind of precious stone. The first layer of the foundation was jasper; the second, sapphire; the third, chalcedony; and the fourth, emerald. The fifth layer was sardonyx; the sixth, carnelian; the seventh, chrysolite; and the eighth, beryl. The ninth layer was topaz; the tenth, chrysoprase; the eleventh, jacinth; and the twelfth, amethyst. The twelve gateways were composed of twelve pearls, with each one of the gateways being made from a single pearl. The city's street was made of pure gold, as transparent as crystal.

I did not see a sanctuary in it because the Master, Almighty God, is its sanctuary—and the Lamb is too. The city does not need the sun or moon to shine on it because God's glory illuminates it and the Lamb is its lamp. All the nations will live off of its light, and the kings of earth bring their glory into it. Its gateways are not shut during the day (because there is no night there), and the glory and honor of the nations will be brought into it. No one who is profane or who makes disgusting or deceiving idols will ever enter into it—none will enter it unless they are written in the Lamb's Book of Life.

Then he showed me a river of living water that was as bright as a crystal. It was flowing out from God's throne and the Lamb. In between the street and the river, with one on each side, was the tree of life, which bore twelve kinds of fruit. Every month it yielded its fruit, and the tree's leaves were used for healing the nations. No cursed thing will exist again. The throne of God and the Lamb will be in it, and his servants will serve him. They will see his face, and his name will be on their foreheads. Night will no longer exist, and they will not need lamplight or sunlight because the Master, God, gives them light, and they will reign forever and ever.

Then he said to me, "These words are faithful and true, and the Master, the God of the prophets' spirits, sent his angel to show his servants what must quickly take place. Look! I am coming quickly! Blessed is the one who keeps the words of this book's prophecy!"

I, John, am the one who heard and saw these things, and when I heard and saw them, I fell down to worship before the feet of the angel who showed me these things.

Then he said to me, "Do not do that! I am a fellow servant with you, your brothers the prophets, and those who keep the words of this book. Worship God!" Then he said to me, "Do not seal up the words of this book's prophecy because the time is near. Let the one who behaves wickedly continue to behave wickedly, and let the one who is filthy continue to be filthy. Let the righteous continue to do what is righteous, and let the holy one continue to be holy."

Look! I am coming quickly, and my reward is with me, so I can repay everyone as their actions deserve. I am the Alpha and the Omega, the First and the Last, and the Beginning and End.

REVELATION

Blessed are those who wash their robes so that they can have a right to the tree of life and to enter the city through the gateways. Those who are outside the city are dogs, sorcerers, the sexually immoral, murderers, idolaters, and everyone who loves and carries out lies.

I, Jesus, have sent my angel to testify these things to you in all of the congregations. I am the root and the successor of David, the bright and morning Star. The Spirit and the bride say, 'Come.' Let whoever hears say, 'Come.' Let the thirsty come—whoever wants—let them drink the living water freely.

I myself testify to everyone who hears the words of this book's prophecy: if anyone adds to them, God will add to them the plagues that are written in this book. If anyone takes away from the words of this prophetic book, God will take away their share from the tree of life and the holy city, which are written in this book."

The one who testifies to these things says, "Yes, I am coming quickly!"

Amen! Come, Master Jesus!
May the grace of Jesus our Master be with all of you!

www.ingramcontent.com/pod-product-compliance
Lightning Source LLC
Chambersburg PA
CBHW071804080526
44589CB00012B/679